Edexcel IGCSE
Accounting

Student Book

Sheila Robinson with Frank Wood

A PEARSON COMPANY

Published by Pearson Education Limited, a company incorporated in England and Wales, having its registered office at Edinburgh Gate, Harlow, Essex, CM20 2JE. Registered company number: 872828.

www.pearsonschoolsandfecolleges.co.uk

Edexcel is a registered trademark of Edexcel Limited

Text © Pearson Education Ltd 2010

This edition first published 2010

20 19 18 17 16 15 14 13 12 11

IMP 10 9 8 7 6 5 4 3 2

British Library Cataloguing in Publication Data
A catalogue record for this book is available from the British Library.

ISBN 978 0 435991 29 6

Copyright notice
All rights reserved. No part of this publication may be reproduced in any form or by any means (including photocopying or storing it in any medium by electronic means and whether or not transiently or incidentally to some other use of this publication) without the written permission of the copyright owner, except in accordance with the provisions of the Copyright, Designs and Patents Act 1988 or under the terms of a licence issued by the Copyright Licensing Agency, Saffron House, 6–10 Kirby Street, London EC1N 8TS (www.cla.co.uk). Applications for the copyright owner's written permission should be addressed to the publisher.

Designed by Richard Ponsford

Typeset by Gantec Publishing Solutions, LLC

Cover design by Creative Monkey

Cover photo/illustration © Digital Vision

Printed in Italy by Rotolito Lombarda

Acknowledgements
The author acknowledges with gratitude the contributions made in the writing of this book from earlier publications in Book-keeping and Accounts on which she collaborated with the late Frank Wood.

The author also wishes to thank Malcolm Robinson for his support and contribution in the production of this book. Also thanks to Stephen Clark, my information technology advisor, for his help and assistance.

The publishers and author would also like to thank Edexcel for permission to reproduce questions from their examination papers.

Picture Credits
The publisher would like to thank the following for their kind permission to reproduce their photographs:

(Key: b-bottom; c-centre; l-left; r-right; t-top)

Alamy Images: Jeffrey Blackler 184c, Kevin Britland 221l, Capture + 95cr, Corbis Super RF 245bl, Carolyn Jenkins 98cr, Keith Morris 57c, Olaf Kowalzik - editorial collection 160tl, Neil Overy 68cr, Chris Potter 224bl, studiomode 43cl, Lana Sundman 195tr, Nick Turner 209cl, Vario Images GmbH & Co.KG 44tl, 176tr, Vario Images GmbH & Co.KG 44tl, 176tr; **Getty Images:** Jeremy Liebman 172br, Peter MacDiarmid 235l, Per-Anders Pettersson 232t, The Bridgeman Art Library 11cl, Time & Life Pictures 164c; **iStockphoto:** 1bl, 8tr, 25tr, 92tl, 169tr, 280tr; **Photolibrary.com:** 63tr, Michael Blann 197tr, Janis Christie 111cr, Tetra Images 15cl; **Press Association Images:** PA Archive 242t; **Rex Features:** Kristy-Anne Glubish / Design Pics Inc. 179r; **Thinkstock:** 142c

All other images © Pearson Education Ltd 2010

Every effort has been made to trace the copyright holders and we apologise in advance for any unintentional omissions. We would be pleased to insert the appropriate acknowledgement in any subsequent edition of this publication.

Websites
The websites used in this book were correct and up to date at the time of publication. It is essential for tutors to preview each website before using it in class so as to ensure that the URL is still accurate, relevant and appropriate. We suggest that tutors bookmark useful websites and consider enabling students to access them through the school/college intranet.

Disclaimer
This Edexcel publication offers high-quality support for the delivery of Edexcel qualifications.

Edexcel endorsement does not mean that this material is essential to achieve any Edexcel qualification, not does it mean that this is the only suitable material available to support any Edexcel qualification. No endorsed material will be used verbatim in setting any Edexcel examination/assessment and any resource lists produced by Edexcel shall include this and other appropriate texts.

Copies of official specifications for all Edexcel qualifications may be found on the Edexcel website, www.edexcel.com.

Contents

About this book ... v

Section A: Books of original entry

Chapter 1: Introduction to accounting principles ... 1

Chapter 2: Double entry for cash transactions ... 11

Chapter 3: Double entry for credit transactions ... 22

Chapter 4: Balancing of accounts and preparation of a Trial Balance ... 32

Chapter 5: Value Added Tax ... 43

Section B: The ledger

Chapter 6: Business documentation ... 51

Chapter 7: Capital and revenue expenditure ... 57

Chapter 8: Books of original entry and ledgers – Sales day book and sales ledger including VAT ... 62

Chapter 9: Purchases day book and purchase ledger including VAT ... 71

Chapter 10: Sales returns day book and purchase returns day book ... 77

Chapter 11: Cash books ... 86

Chapter 12: Petty cash and the imprest system ... 98

Chapter 13: Bank reconciliation statements ... 106

Chapter 14: The journal ... 116

Chapter 15: Sales ledger and purchase ledger control accounts ... 132

Section C: Final accounts

Chapter 16: Trading account and profit and loss account of a sole trader ... 142

Chapter 17: The Balance sheet ... 152

Chapter 18: Financial statements: other considerations ... 158

Section D: Adjustments

Chapter 19: The concept of depreciation of fixed assets ... 168

Chapter 20: Double entry for depreciation and disposal of a fixed asset ... 176

Chapter 21: Bad debts and provision for doubtful debts ... 184

Chapter 22: Accruals, prepayments and other adjustments for financial statements ... 194

Section E: Incomplete records

Chapter 23: Incomplete records ... 209

Section F: Non-profit organisations

Chapter 24: Accounting for non-profit making organisations ... 221

Section G: Manufacturing accounts

Chapter 25: Manufacturing accounts ... 231

Section H: Partnerships

Chapter 26: Partnership accounts ... 241

Section I: Limited companies

Chapter 27: Limited company accounts ... 255

Section J: Analysis of accounts

Chapter 28: Analysis and interpretation of financial statements ... 266

Chapter 29: Computers and accounting systems ... 280

Glossary

Glossary of accounting terms ... 287

Index

Index ... 294

About this book

This book has several features to help you with IGCSE Accounting.

Introduction
Each chapter has a short Getting started introduction to help you start thinking about the topic and let you know what is in the chapter.

End of Chapter Checklists
These lists summarise the material in the chapter. They could also help you to make revision notes because they form a list of things that you need to revise.

Margin boxes
The boxes in the margin give you extra help or information. They might explain something in a little more detail or guide you to linked topics in other parts of the book.

Questions
There are short questions contained in each chapter. These help to develop your understanding as you go along. There is also an exam style question at the end of each chapter. These are designed to help you develop the skills needed when answering exam questions, such as analysis and evaluation. The questions:
– with X: for teachers' answers, follow the link
  www.pearsonschoolsandfecolleges.co.uk
– without an X: Answers are provided on CD at the back of the book.

Preface

The book is written for students following the Edexcel specification for the IGCSE in Accounting whose programme assumes a 30 week teaching year being taught over two years. The book contains learning material to cover these two years and closely follows the Edexcel suggested course order, but centres can decide to deliver the topics in any order. The Activebook CD which accompanies the book is an integral part of the course material.

The sequence of topics in the book provides the students with knowledge, understanding and skill enabling them to consolidate these key features as they progress through the book.

The structure of each chapter follows a similar layout for easier learning as follows:

- Edexcel specification – for example in Chapter 2 'The Ledger 2.1, 2.2, 2.3, 2.6'. This provides a cross-reference of the Edexcel specification to the chapter content.
- Getting started, the aims of the chapter.
- Introduction to the chapter topic.
- Explanation of the topic and worked examples.
- Summary, a reminder of the topic and useful for later reference when revising.
- Questions to practice and assess ones competence. Note answers will be found on the Activebook CD except for those marked with 'X' which are available to teachers only.
- Glossary follows Chapter 29 giving the definition of the accountancy terms used in the book.

In the margin throughout the book there are definitions, reminders, hints and tips which are intended to reinforce your knowledge and understanding of the unique terms in Accountancy.

The Activebook CD provides further course material in the form of model layouts and self-assessment questions:

- Model layouts for financial statements and worksheets.
- Worked example of the final accounts of a sole trader and a step-by-step guide.
- Multiple choice questions.
- Answers to multiple choice questions.
- Answers to questions except for those marked 'X'.

Sheila Robinson

May 2010

Section A: Books of original entry

Chapter 1: Introduction to accounting principles

1.1 Aims of a business

The aim of any business is to make a profit and to ensure it remains in operation for the long term. To achieve these aims the owners of the business must practise sound management techniques. These can include the ability to sell the product/service, to purchase materials and products wisely, to manage and motivate staff, but crucially, to manage the finances of the business.

In setting up the business the owners would have invested money in what they felt was a worthwhile venture. This would normally be referred to as 'introducing capital' in accountancy terms. The capital introduced would be used to enable the business to start trading. In the simplest of terms, this would involve purchasing goods and then selling them at a higher price. The owners would have worked hard to establish good trading relationships with their customers but there can be difficulties if some customers are late paying for the goods or default altogether.

To ensure that capital is not put at risk and the trading effort has not been wasted, good financial control is vital. A good control system would inform the owners of the financial status of the business at all times and enable them to make appropriate decisions.

Getting started

**Edexcel specification:
Adjustments 4.1**

After you have studied this chapter you should be able to:

- appreciate the aims of a business
- understand the importance and need for accounting and sound financial control
- identify the main users of accounting information
- appreciate and define an accounting concept
- understand the fundamental accounting concepts
- understand what is meant by the 'accounting equation'
- distinguish between the different types of business organisations
- understand basic accounting terminology.

AIMS OF A BUSINESS – to make a profit and remain a viable enterprise.

It is essential to have good financial control.

1.2 Basic concept of financial control

All businesses whether small, i.e. sole traders, through to very large organisations use the same concept of financial control as shown in Exhibit 1.1:

Exhibit 1.1 The basis of financial control

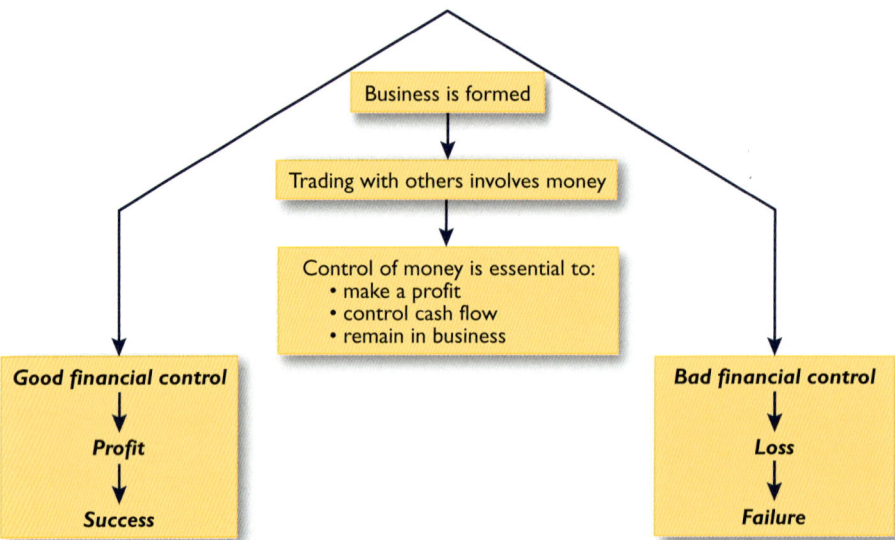

This can be further illustrated using the following example:

Thomas recently won some money on the lottery and decided that he would like to use some of his winnings to start his own business selling leather goods. He rents a shop, purchases a stock of leather goods and commences trading on 1 July.

The cost of the initial stock of leather goods was £14,000 which Thomas sold for £20,000 during the first three months of trading. His expenses for the same period, including the rent for the shop, amounted to £2,800. How successful has Thomas been in his first months of trading?

	£
Thomas sells his goods for	20,000
Less Cost Price	14,000
Profit (before expenses)	6,000
Less Expenses	2,800
Profit (after expenses)	3,200

As can be seen from the above example, Thomas has bought his stock of goods wisely and been able to sell them for more than he paid for them, producing a profit before expenses of £6,000. After paying his rent and other expenses, his profit is £3,200. His venture for his first three months of trading is certainly successful.

Financial control is a major function of a business but there are other aspects that are equally important if a business is to be successful:

- a competitive product and/or service
- a good business strategy
- a competent workforce.

None of these would be of any use unless there is a market (people or businesses willing to buy the product and/or service). It is, however, a fact that businesses which practise good recording of financial data will have the information to make sound management decisions with a far better chance of success.

1.3 Importance and need for accounting

As stated earlier, businesses must operate profitably otherwise they will cease to exist. The **financial statements** produced by a business's accounting department aim to show clearly the profit or loss that has been made and the financial position of the business. The two most important statements are:

1. the trading and profit and loss account – shows whether the business has made a profit/loss

2. the balance sheet – shows the financial position.

Both these statements have to be checked and verified by a firm of auditors as part of the legal requirements for correct financial reporting. It is essential that accurate financial information is available to the auditors to enable them to fulfil their functions properly.

> Financial statements consist of a Trading and Profit and Loss Account and Balance Sheet.

Financial statements provide management with the means to measure the financial performance of the business. They will have the information to enable them to make rational decisions and to formulate revised plans as necessary. Financial plans are usually known as **budgets**.

There are, however, other groups who are keenly interested in the activities of the business. The main interested parties are shown in Exhibit 1.2.

Exhibit 1.2

Interested party	Reason
HM Revenue and Customs (HMRC)	Legally required to collect tax such as employees' tax, national insurance contributions, business tax, VAT, etc.
Investors	Could be private individuals, companies, banks, etc. who will want to monitor the performance of the business to ensure it is profitable.
Suppliers	They will need to be assured of the viability of the business before accepting orders.
Customers	Before placing orders with a business they will need to know that it is financially stable.
Employees	They need to know of a business's financial status, usually via unions or professional bodies.

1.4 Accounting concepts

At the end of a financial year organisations prepare their financial statements, i.e. Trading and Profit and Loss Account and Balance Sheet. There are, however, other issues to consider with the preparation of the financial statements which are known as 'accounting concepts' or 'rules of accounting'. These concepts or rules have evolved over the years for practical as much as theoretical reasons. As a

> ACCOUNTING CONCEPT – the rules which lay down the way the activities of a business are recorded.

consequence, this has made the preparation of the financial statements more standardised enabling the information to be more easily understood and reliable, and to enable clearer comparisons between different businesses.

Definition

A concept may be defined as an idea. Thus, an **accounting concept** is an assumption that underlies the preparation of the financial statements of the organisation. These are accounting procedures that have developed over the years to form the 'basic rules of accounting'.

Fundamental accounting concepts

The **going concern concept** implies that the business will continue to operate for the foreseeable future. In other words, it is assumed that the business will continue to trade for a long period of time and there are no plans to cease trading and/or liquidate the business.

The **consistency concept** requires that the same treatment be applied when dealing with similar items not only in one period but in all subsequent periods. The concept states that when a business had adopted a method for the accounting treatment of an item, it should treat all similar items that follow in the same way when preparing the financial statements. Examples of when the consistency concept is used include:

- methods of depreciation (see Chapter 19)
- stock valuation (see Chapters 16 and 17).

This concept is important since it assists in analysis of financial information and decision-making, and it is vital that the organisation uses the same accounting principles each year. If the organisation was constantly changing its methods then this would result in misleading profits being calculated and inaccurate analyses, hence the reason why the convention of consistency is used. However, this does not mean that the business must always use a particular method; it may make changes provided it has good reason to do so and each change is declared in the notes to the financial statements.

The **prudence concept**. When preparing financial statements, accountants often have to use their judgement in determining the valuation of a particular asset, i.e. premises, machinery etc., or perhaps deciding whether an outstanding debt will ever be paid. It is the accountant's duty and responsibility to ensure that the financial statements are prepared as accurately as possible in disclosing the appropriate facts about a business. Therefore, the accountant should ensure that assets are not overvalued and similarly all liabilities should be identified. In other words, the accountant should display a certain amount of caution when forecasting a business's net profit or when valuing assets for balance sheet purposes.

The prudence concept means that accountants will take the figure that will understate rather than overstate the profit. They must also ensure that all losses are recorded in the books but equally so ensure that profits are not anticipated by recording them before they have been gained.

The **accrual concept** (or **matching concept**) says that net profit is the difference between revenues and expenses rather than the difference between cash received and cash paid.

$$\text{Revenues} - \text{Expenses} = \text{Net Profit}$$

Sales are **revenues** when the goods or services are sold and *not* when the money is received, which can be later in the accounting period. Purchases are **expenses** when goods are bought, *not* when they are paid for. In Chapter 22 you will see items such as rent, insurance and motor expenses are treated as expenses when they are incurred, not when they are actually paid. Adjustments are made when preparing financial statements for expenses owing and those paid in advance (prepayments). Other adjustments that are also made include adjusting for depreciation of fixed assets and for probable bad debts, both of which will be discussed later.

Identifying the expenses used up to obtain the revenues is referred to as *matching* expenses against revenues, which is why this concept is also called the **matching concept**.

By showing the actual expenses *incurred* in a period matched against revenues *earned* in the same period, a correct figure of net profit will be shown in the profit and loss account.

The **materiality concept** applies when the value of an item is relatively insignificant and as such does not warrant separate recording, for example, the purchase of a box of paper clips, calculator or small clock for the office. Such small expenditures are regarded as 'not material' and their purchase would not be recorded in separate expense accounts but grouped together in a sundry or general expense account.

The **money measurement concept** states that only transactions and activities that can be measured in terms of money and whose monetary value can be assessed with reasonable objectivity will be entered into the accounting records.

The **business entity concept** implies that the affairs of a business are to be treated as being quite separate from the personal activities of the owner(s) of the business. In other words, only the activities of the business are recorded and reported in the business's financial statements. Any transactions involving the owner(s) are kept separate and are excluded.

The only time that the personal resources of the owner(s) affect the business's accounting records is when they introduce new capital into the business or take drawings.

1.5 Accounting standards and the legal framework

At one time there were quite wide differences in the ways that accountants calculated profits, until the late 1960s when a number of high-profile cases in the United Kingdom led to a widespread outcry against the lack of uniformity in financial reporting.

In response, in 1971, the UK accounting bodies formed the Accounting Standards Committee (ASC) who issued many accounting standards known as Statements of Standard Accounting Practice (SSAPs). In 1990 the accountancy bodies replaced the ASC with the Accounting Standards Board (ASB) who issued further accounting standards known as Financial Reporting Standards (FRSs). Both the SSAPs and FRSs are compulsory and enforceable by Company Law.

Since SSAPs and FRSs were generally developed for larger companies, the ASB issued a third category of accounting standards in 1997 called Financial Reporting Standard for Smaller Entities (FRSSE). These were issued to make it easier for the small companies to adhere to more manageable standards.

Accounting standards are drafted so that they comply with the laws of the United Kingdom and the Republic of Ireland and anyone preparing financial statements for publication must observe the rules laid down in the accounting standards.

1.6 International accounting standards

In addition to the accounting standards issued by the ASB for the United Kingdom and Republic of Ireland there is also an international organisation that issues accounting standards. The International Accounting Standards Committee (IASC) was established in 1973 and in 2000 this committee changed its name to the International Accounting Standards Board (IASB). The IASB is an independent body and has 15 full-time members who are responsible for setting accounting standards.

The need for such a body is said to have been necessary due to:

a) the rapid expansion of global investment, trade and production;

b) many companies operating in a number of countries and needing to produce financial statements which are acceptable to all;

c) some smaller countries being unable to establish an accounting standards system of their own and adopting the IASB standards.

It should be noted that the details provided in Sections 1.5 and 1.6 are a brief explanation of the standards that the accountancy profession is required to operate within. You will not be assessed in this topic at this stage in your studies.

1.7 The accounting equation

Accounting is based upon a concept known as the **accounting equation**, which is simply that, at any point in time, the total amount of resources supplied by the owner equals the resources in the business. Assuming that the owner of the new business supplies all the resources then this can be shown as follows:

> Resources supplied by the owner = Resources in the business

CAPITAL – the total resources supplied to a business by its owner.

In accounting, the various terms have special meanings. The amount of resources supplied by the owner is called **capital**. As mentioned above, the actual resources that are in the business are called **assets**. If the owner of the business has supplied all of the resources, the accounting equation can be shown as:

$$\text{Capital} = \text{Assets}$$

> ASSETS – resources owned by a business.

In many cases, other people besides the owner of the business will have supplied some of the assets, i.e. money in the form of a loan, or perhaps equipment purchased on credit. The amounts owing to these people are called **liabilities** (see below). When this is the case the accounting equation changes to:

$$\text{Capital} = \text{Assets} - \text{Liabilities}$$

> LIABILITIES – money owed for assets supplied to the business.

This is the most common way in which the accounting equation is presented since the two sides of the equation will have the same totals because we are dealing with the same thing but from two different points of view. First, the value of the owners' investment in the business and secondly, the value of what is owned by the business, which is ultimately owned by the owners.

Unfortunately, with this form of the accounting equation, it is no longer possible to see at a glance what value is represented by the resources in the business. This can be seen more clearly if you change assets and capital around to give an alternative form of the accounting equation:

$$\text{Assets} = \text{Capital} + \text{Liabilities}$$

This can then be replaced with words describing the resources of the business:

$$\text{Resources: what they are} = \text{Resources: who supplied them}$$
$$(\text{Assets}) \qquad (\text{Capital} + \text{Liabilities})$$

It is a fact that no matter how you present the accounting equation, the totals of both sides will *always* equal each other, and this will *always* be true irrespective of the number of transactions. The actual assets, capital and liabilities may change, but the total of the assets will always equal the total of capital + liabilities. Or, reverting to the more common form of the accounting equation, the capital will always equal the assets of the business minus the liabilities.

Assets consist of property of all kinds, such as buildings, machinery, equipment, stocks of goods and motor vehicles. Other assets include debts owed by customers and the amount of money in the bank account.

Liabilities include amounts owed by the business for goods and services supplied to the business, and expenses incurred by the business but still outstanding. Funds borrowed by the business are also included.

Capital is often called the owner's **equity** or **net worth**. This comprises the funds invested in the business by the owner plus any **profits** retained for use in the business less any share of the profits paid out to the owner by the business.

This topic is covered more fully in Chapter 17.

1.8 Types of organisations

Organisations are classified according to their structure and financial make-up and are mainly classified as follows. The classification will determine an organisation's legal status and what financial reporting is required of it:

- A **sole trader** is an individual trading alone in his or her own name, or under a recognised trading name. He or she is solely liable for all business debts, but when the business is successful can take all the profits.

- A **partnership** is a group of a minimum of two people up to a maximum of 20 who together carry on a particular business with a view to making a profit. This topic will be covered in Chapter 26.

- **Limited companies**, both private and public:
  - A **private limited company** is a legal entity with at least two shareholders. The liability of the shareholders is limited to the amount that they have agreed to invest.
  - A **public limited company** is also a legal entity with limited shareholder liability, but unlike a private company it can ask the public to subscribe for shares in its business. See Chapter 27.

SOLE TRADER – a business owned by one person.

PARTNERSHIP – a business owned by two or more people.

LIMITED COMPANY – an organisation owned by its shareholders.

- **Non-trading organisations** include clubs, associations and other non-profit-making organisations which are normally run for the benefit of their members to engage in a particular activity rather than to make a profit. Their financial statements will take the form of income and expenditure accounts, to be covered in Chapter 24.

1.9 Accounting definitions

Accounting is the skill of maintaining accounts and preparing financial statements and reports for use by the management and owners of a business to aid financial control, management and budget forecasts.

Assets are resources owned by the business, i.e. premises, machinery, motor vehicles etc.

Auditors are a specialist firm of accountants appointed by an organisation to examine and verify that its financial statements have been presented fairly, comply with accounting practice and meet legal requirements.

Book-keeping is the process of recording, in the book accounts or on computer, the financial effect of business transactions and managing such records. The process of recording the financial information is the initial stage in the preparation of financial statements.

Budgets are financial plans produced by an organisation.

Capital is the total resources supplied to a business by its owner(s), i.e. money.

Financial statements are formal documents prepared by an organisation to show the financial position of the business at a specific date. They include a Trading and Profit and Loss Account and a Balance Sheet. See later chapters for more details.

Liabilities are amounts owed for assets supplied to the business.

Owner's equity is another name for the capital supplied by the owner of the business, also referred to as 'net worth'.

End of Chapter Checklist

Summary

- The basis of any business is trading with others and providing good products and/ or services to meet customer requirements; to manage the business well, ensuring costs are controlled and cash flow maintained, resulting in a successful and profitable business.
- Financial statements are prepared by a business to show the profit/loss made and the financial position; these are known as the 'Trading and Profit and Loss Account' and the 'Balance Sheet'. These financial statements enable management to measure the performance of the business and make appropriate decisions and financial plans known as 'budgets'.
- Various groups/organisations are interested in the financial performance of a business, i.e HMRC, investors, suppliers, customers, employees.
- An 'accounting concept' is an accounting procedure developed over the years to form the 'basic rules of accounting'.
- The fundamental accounting concepts are: going concern, consistency, prudence, accruals (or matching concept), materiality, money measurement and business entity.
- The whole of accounting is based on the accounting equation, namely, that the resources supplied by the owner (the capital) will always equal the resources in the business (the assets).
- There are various types of business organisations, including: sole traders, partnerships and limited companies, which may be either a private limited company or a public limited company, plus non-trading organisations.
- There are many terms which are used when dealing with accounting and financial matters. Some of these are: accounting, assets, auditors, book-keeping, budgets, capital, financial statements, liabilities, owner's equity.

Reminder: A glossary of accounting terms can be found in Appendix A at the end of the book.

Questions

1.1 *Explain briefly why good financial control is important to any business.*

1.2X *Profit is the aim of all businesses. Explain in simple terms how this can be attained.*

1.3 *State the two most important financial statements that are required to be produced by a company.*

1.4X *A sole trader is an individual trading alone. State one drawback and one positive aspect of trading in this way.*

1.5 *Explain what you understand by an 'accounting concept'.*

1.6 *Accounting concepts are used in preparing the financial statements of a business. Briefly explain the following concepts:*

  a) Going concern concept
  b) Accrual concept
  c) Consistency concept
  d) Prudence concept

1.7X *In the following circumstances which accounting concept would be used.*

  a) The purchase of a waste-paper basket for use in the office.
  b) Tom has just purchased a set of golf clubs for his own personal use but wonders if he could charge them to his business.
  c) Alice, who runs her own hairdressing business, considers her staff to be worth several hundred pounds to her business yet nothing is entered in her books of account.
  d) A debt has been written off as a bad debt even though there is still a chance that the debtor may eventually be able to pay it.

1.8 *Explain why employees would have a keen interest in the financial performance of their employer's business.*

Section A: Books of original entry

Chapter 2: Double entry for cash transactions

2.1 Introduction and history of the 'double entry system of accounting'

Since early times, various forms of record-keeping existed to record such things as rents, taxes and fines due, although at this time no formal or standard system of book-keeping was present. It wasn't until the fifteenth century, when Father Luca Pacioli first invented the 'double entry system of accounting', that the process of formalised book-keeping and accounting began. Since that time the principle of 'double entry' has progressed to the world-wide system we see today.

It is important for anyone in business today to keep accounting records for the following reasons:

- to record business transactions
- to know how much the business owes and is owed at any point of time
- to know how much cash the business has
- whether or not the business is making a profit.

In Chapter 1 the concept of the 'accounting equation' was introduced whereby the resources supplied by the owner of the business, i.e. the capital, will always equal the resources owned by the business, i.e. the assets. In other words, the transaction has affected **two** items, i.e. the capital and the assets. Double entry book-keeping is thus based upon the accounting equation in that every transaction affects two aspects.

Getting started

Edexcel specification
The ledger, 2.1, 2.2, 2.3 and 2.6

After you have studied this chapter you should be able to:

- understand what is meant by the double entry system
- explain how the double entry system follows the rules of the accounting equation
- understand the rules for double entry book-keeping
- be able to draw up 'T accounts' and understand the terms 'debit' and 'credit'
- be able to record transactions in the T accounts.

2.2 The double entry system

The system of double entry book-keeping is a method of recording transactions in the books of account of a business and, as mentioned above, every transaction

DOUBLE ENTRY BOOK-KEEPING – a system where each transaction is entered twice, once on the debit side and once on the credit side.

affects two items. The information for every item that is entered into the books of account is obtained from a source document, i.e. an invoice, credit note, cheque book stub, paying in book, etc. (see Chapter 6). The next important stage is to understand the double entry system of book-keeping.

Business transactions deal with money or money's worth and each transaction always affects two things. For example, if a business buys stationery valued at £40 and pays for it by cash then two aspects have occurred:

- the money in the business's cash account will have decreased by £40
- the business has acquired stationery to the value of £40.

Here is another example: if a business buys some equipment costing £2,000 and pays for it by cheque, then again two things have been affected:

- the money in the business's bank account will have decreased by £2,000
- the business will have acquired equipment valued £2,000.

ACCOUNT – contains details of transactions relating to a specific asset, liability or capital.

Each transaction is entered into an **account** which shows the 'history of' the particular business item. It is the place in the records where all the information referring to a particular item, for example, the bank account or motor vehicle account, is recorded. If manual records are kept, then each account is usually shown on a separate page; if a computerised system is used, then each account is given a separate code number and the information is stored on the accounting package and back-up systems.

The accounts for double entry

Each account should be shown on a separate page. The double entry system divides each page into two halves. The left-hand side of each page is called the **debit** side, while the the right-hand side is called the **credit** side. The title of each account is written across the top of the account at the centre – see Exhibit 2.1. Note that the word 'Debit' is often shown in a short form as *Dr*, while 'Credit' is often shown as *Cr*.

Exhibit 2.1

Dr	Title of account written here				Cr
Date	Details	£	Date	Details	£

Left-hand side of the page. This is the **'debit'** side.

Right-hand side of the page. This is the **'credit'** side.

The words 'debit' and 'credit' in book-keeping terms do not mean the same as in normal language and should be viewed differently from the start to avoid confusion. Students new to studying double entry may find it useful to think of 'IN' when looking at the entry of a debit item, and to think of 'OUT' when looking at the entry of a credit item. We will consider this later in Section 2.4.

2.3 Rules for double entry

RULES FOR DOUBLE ENTRY – it is important to learn these rules.

Double entry is relatively easy to learn and understand if these four rules are followed:

1. Double entry means that every transaction affects two things and should, therefore, be entered twice: once on the *Debit* side and once on the *Credit* side. Later on in your studies you may have more than two accounts in which to record a transaction, for example, when an item is purchased and part of it is paid for in cash and part paid by cheque.

2. The order in which the items are entered does not matter – although students may find it easier to deal with any cash or bank transaction first using the 'IN' and 'OUT' principle.

3. A **debit** entry is always an asset or an expense. A **credit** entry is a liability, capital or income.

4. To increase or decrease assets, liabilities or capital, the double entry rules are as shown in Exhibit 2.2.

Exhibit 2.2

Accounts	To record	Entry in the account
Assets	↑ an increase	Debit
	↓ a decrease	Credit
Liabilities	↑ an increase	Credit
	↓ a decrease	Debit
Capital	↑ an increase	Credit
	↓ a decrease	Debit

Let's look once again at the accounting equation:

In the previous chapter we saw how the money invested by the owner(s) of the business, i.e. their 'capital', was invested in the business in the form of an 'asset', i.e. cash. At that point, remember that:

Capital (the owner's/owners' money) = Assets (cash in hand)

Capital = Assets

Let us assume that business then buys stock of goods and pays for them by cash. Following on from the above, the accounting equation would look like this:

Capital (the owner's/owners' money) = Assets (cash in hand less amount spent on the stock of goods) + stock of goods

Again, the accounting equation is the same except that we now have two assets, cash in hand and stock of goods.

Capital = Assets

If the business incurred a liability, i.e. obtained a loan from the bank, then the accounting equation would be represented as follows:

$$\text{Assets} = \text{Capital} + \text{Liabilities}$$

An alternative way of using the accounting equation is:

$$\text{Capital} = \text{Assets} - \text{Liabilities}$$

In other words, the capital will always equal the assets less the liabilities. Using the example above, let us assume that the capital is £10,000 which is deposited in the business's bank account. In addition, the business also obtains a loan from the bank for £5,000. The accounting equation would be:

Capital £10,000 = Assets − Liabilities = £10,000

Calculated as (Bank £10,000 + Loan £5,000) − Bank Loan = £10,000

The double entry rules for assets, liabilities and capital are as follows:

Capital account		Any asset account		Any liability account	
Decreases	Increases	Increases	Decreases	Decreases	Increases
−	+	+	−	−	+

> **'IN' AND 'OUT' APPROACH** – money goes INTO the bank and cash accounts on the debit side of the account and comes OUT of the accounts on the credit side.

2.4 The 'IN' and 'OUT' approach

A useful hint in deciding on which side of each account the items should be entered is to think of the debit side being 'IN' to the account, and the credit side being 'OUT' of the account.

Two examples using this approach are shown below:

Example 1: Paid cash £3,000 to buy second hand van.

The double entry for this transaction would be as follows:

Effect	Action
(a) Van comes 'IN'	A *debit* entry in the Van account
(b) Cash goes 'OUT'	A *credit* entry in the Cash account

Example 2: Took £500 out of the cash in hand of the business and paid it into the business's bank account.

The double entry for this transaction would be as follows:

Effect	Action
Money comes 'IN' to the bank	A *debit* entry in the Bank account
Cash goes 'OUT' of the cash till	A *credit* entry in the Cash account

2.5 'T accounts'

Business transactions are entered into accounts known as **'T accounts'**. This is because the accounts are in the shape of a 'T' as shown below:

Account title here: the top stroke of the T	
Debit side	Credit side

The line divides the two sides and is the downstroke of the T.

2.6 Worked examples for cash transactions

In this chapter we are going to deal with double entry for cash transactions, whilst in Chapter 3 we will consider double entry for credit transactions. For the purpose of accounting, the word 'cash' means not only items being paid for or money received being in cash but also items paid for by cheque and cheques received. The transfer of money is also increasingly carried out electronically.

The entry of a few transactions can now be attempted:

Example 3: The proprietor starts the business with £50,000 in cash on 1 January 2011.

Effect	Action
a) Increases the asset of cash	Debit the cash account – cash goes 'IN'
b) Increases the capital	Credit the capital account – cash comes 'OUT' of the owner's money

These are entered as follows:

Dr		Cash Account			Cr
	'IN'			'OUT'	
2011		£			
Jan 1	Capital	50,000			

Dr		Capital Account			Cr
	'IN'			'OUT'	
			2011		£
			Jan 1	Cash	50,000

The date of the transaction is entered on both accounts, i.e. 1 Jan 2011. A description is also shown on each account to cross-reference them. The 'Cash Account' shows the entry 'Capital' whilst the 'Capital Account' shows the entry 'Cash'. The double entry rules are now met as shown in Section 2.3.

Further examples now follow:

Example 4: Equipment is bought for £4,200 cash on 2 January 2011.

Effect	Action
Decreases the asset of cash	Credit the cash account – cash goes 'OUT'
Increases the asset of equipment	Debit the equipment account – equipment comes 'IN'

Dr		Cash Account			Cr
	'IN'			'OUT'	
			2011		£
			Jan 2	Equipment	4,200

Dr		Equipment Account			Cr
	'IN'			'OUT'	
2011		£			
Jan 2	Cash	4,200			

Example 5: Bought goods for resale, paying by cash £5,000 on 4 January 2011.
Note: goods bought for resale are recorded in a 'Purchases Account' but are often referred to as 'stock'.

Effect	Action
(a) Increases the asset of purchases	Debit the purchases account – purchases come 'IN'
(b) Decreases the asset of cash	Credit the cash account – cash goes 'OUT'

Dr		Purchases Account			Cr
	'IN'			'OUT'	
2011		£			
Jan 4	Cash	5,000			

Dr		Cash Account			Cr
	'IN'			'OUT'	£
			2011		
			Jan 4	Purchases	5,000

Example 6: Bought a motor van paying by cash £10,000 on 5 January 2011.

Effect	Action
(a) Decreases the asset of cash	Credit the cash account – cash goes 'OUT'
(b) Increases the asset of motor van	Debit the motor van account – motor van comes 'IN'

Dr		Cash Account			Cr
	'IN'			'OUT'	
			2011		£
			Jan 5	Motor van	10,000

Dr		Motor Van Account			Cr
	'IN'			'OUT'	
2011		£			
Jan 5	Cash	10,000			

Example 7: Transactions to date.

Taking the transactions numbered 3 to 6 above, the records will now appear thus:

Dr		Cash Account			Cr
	'IN'			'OUT'	
2011		£	2011		£
Jan 1	Capital	50,000	Jan 2	Equipment	4,200
			Jan 4	Purchases	5,000
			Jan 5	Motor van	10,000

Dr		Capital Account			Cr
	'IN'			'OUT'	
			2011		£
			Jan 1	Cash	50,000

Dr		Equipment Account			Cr
	'IN'			'OUT'	
2011		£			
Jan 2	Cash	4,200			

Dr		Purchases Account			Cr
	'IN'			'OUT'	
2011		£			
Jan 4	Cash	5,000			

Dr		Motor Van Account			Cr
	'IN'			'OUT'	
2011		£			£
Jan 5	Cash	10,000			

Example 8: A further example introduces both cash and bank transactions. Remember that each item has to be entered twice:

- once on the debit side of the account, and
- once on the credit side of the account.

Whilst it does not matter which order the transaction is entered, it is often easier to deal with the monetary aspect of the transaction first, i.e. enter the item into either the cash account or bank account after deciding if the money is coming 'IN' or going 'OUT'. The second entry will need to be entered into the other account on the opposite side.

2011
1 July   Started business with £20,000 cash.
1 July   Opened a bank account and deposited £19,000 of the cash into the account.
7 July   Paid rent for premises, £500 by cheque.
7 July   Bought goods for resale and paid £3,000 by cheque.
12 July   Paid £2,000 by cheque for a second-hand van.
14 July   Sold some goods for cash, £600.
24 July   Bought fixtures and paid £800 by cheque.
28 July   Paid for motor expenses, £65 by cash.
30 July   Sold goods £2,000 and received a cheque which was paid into the bank.

The accounts for July are now shown below:

Dr		Cash Account				Cr
	'IN'				'OUT'	
2011			£	2011		£
July 1	Capital		20,000	July 1	Bank	19,000
July 14	Sales		600	July 28	Motor expenses	65

Dr		Capital Account				Cr
	'IN'				'OUT'	
			£	2011		£
				July 1	Cash	20,000

Dr		Bank Account				Cr
	'IN'				'OUT'	
2011			£	2011		£
July 1	Cash		19,000	July 7	Rent	500
July 30	Sales		2,000	July 7	Purchases	3,000
				July 12	Van	2,000
				July 24	Fixtures	800

Dr		Rent Account				Cr
	'IN'				'OUT'	
2011			£			
July 7	Bank		500			

Dr		Purchases Account				Cr
	'IN'				'OUT'	
2011			£			£
July 7	Bank		3,000			

Dr		Van Account				Cr
	'IN'				'OUT'	
2011			£			£
July 12	Bank		2,000			

> EXPENSES are costs incurred in running the business, i.e. rent, motor expenses.

Dr		Sales Account			Cr
	'IN'			'OUT'	
			2011		£
			July 14	Cash	600
			July 30	Bank	2,000

Dr		Fixtures Account			Cr
	'IN'			'OUT'	
2011		£			
July 24	Bank	800			

Dr		Motor Expenses Account			Cr
	'IN'			'OUT'	
2011		£			£
July 28	Cash	65			

NB: Value Added Tax (VAT)

Students studying accountancy will be aware that in the UK many goods and services are subject to Value Added Tax (VAT). This has been ignored in this chapter to avoid confusing students at this early stage.

End of Chapter Checklist

Summary

- The chapter covers the concept of double entry book-keeping whereby every transaction affects two things. Each item has to be entered twice in the book-keeping records, once on the debit side of an account and once on the credit side of an account.
- Double entry follows the rules of the accounting equation.
- The use of 'T' accounts to record information is illustrated.
- A fully worked example using the double entry system of accounting is illustrated.

Questions

2.1 State which are assets and which are liabilities from the following list:

a) Stock of goods
b) Office equipment
c) Bank loan
d) Cash in hand
e) Motor vehicles
f) Loan from finance company

2.2X State which of the following are shown under the wrong heading for J Chan's business:

Assets	Liabilities
Money owing to bank	Motor van
Cash at bank	Stock of goods
Computer equipment	Loan from finance company
Premises	
Furniture and fittings	

2.3 Complete the following table showing which accounts are to be credited and which are to be debited:

a) Introduced capital in cash
b) Deposited cash into the bank account
c) Bought stock of goods for cash
d) Bought office machinery paying by cheque
e) Bought stationery paying by cash.

Account to be debited	Account to be credited

2.4X Complete the following table showing which accounts are to be debited and which accounts are to be credited:

a) Started business by depositing capital into a business bank account
b) Bought stock of goods paying by cash
c) Bought a motor car paying by cheque
d) Borrowed cash from Uncle Joe
e) Paid cash for petrol for the motor car
f) Paid cash for computer equipment
g) Bought office desk and chair and paid cash.

Account to be debited	Account to be credited

End of Chapter Checklist

Questions

2.5 You are required to enter the following transactions in double entry records of Max Morgan for the month of January 2011.

2011	
Jan 1	Started business with £30,000 in the bank
Jan 5	Bought stock of goods paying by cheque £2,770
Jan 7	Bought second-hand van £4,800 paid by cheque
Jan 9	Sold goods for cash £680
Jan 10	Bought office desk and chair and paid £110 by cash
Jan 15	Sold goods £500 received a cheque
Jan 22	Paid cash for motor expenses £92
Jan 27	Bought computer for the office and paid by cheque £2,100
Jan 29	Sold goods for cash £325
Jan 30	Bought more goods paying by cheque £1,090.

2.6X You are required to enter the following transactions in the double entry records of Jane Mellor for the month of May 2011.

2011	
May 1	Started in business with £22,000 in cash
May 3	Paid £20,000 of the cash into the bank
May 7	Paid rent for premises £500 by cheque
May 10	Bought goods for resale £1,700 paid by cheque
May 15	Bought display units for £400 paid by cheque
May 20	Sold goods for cash £328
May 22	Paid £72 cash for stationery
May 23	Bought goods for resale £400 paid by cheque
May 25	Sold goods £560 and received payment by cheque
May 31	Bought second-hand van £3,000 paid by cheque.

Section A: Books of original entry

Chapter 3: Double entry for credit transactions

Getting started

Edexcel specification
The ledger, 2.1, 2.2, 2.3, 2.5 and 2.6

After you have studied this chapter you should be able to:

- understand what is meant by 'credit transactions'
- record the purchase of goods on credit using the double entry system
- record the sale of goods on credit using the double entry system
- record the return of goods in the sales returns account using the double entry system when customers return goods to the business
- record the return of goods in the purchases returns account using the double entry system when the business returns goods to the supplier
- record transactions involving expenses and services provided on credit
- explain the meanings of the terms 'purchases' and 'sales' as used in accounting
- understand the differences in recording sales for cash compared with sales made on credit.

3.1 Introduction to credit transactions

In the last chapter double entry transactions involving items that had been bought and paid for by cash or cheque were dealt with, together with cash and cheques received. In addition to cash and cheque transactions, many businesses deal with items that are bought but paid for at a later date and these are known as 'credit transactions'.

When an item is bought on credit the customer obtains the goods without paying for them initially. They then have to adhere to the supplier's 'terms and conditions' which usually requires the customer to pay for the goods within 30 days. This credit facility assists the customer by providing short-term cash facilities which helps the business's cash flow. As an incentive to encourage the customer to pay within the 30 days, often a 'cash discount' is offered whereby the customer is able to deduct a small percentage, e.g. 2.5%, from their invoice provided they pay promptly. Buying and selling on credit is widely used in most businesses today.
Note: Cash discount is dealt with fully in Chapter 11.

Once the goods have been received 'on credit' by the customer they incur a liability, i.e. they owe the supplier for the cost of the goods supplied. At a later date, usually at the end of the month, the customer then pays the supplier for those goods. We will now consider the double entry requirements for the purchase and sale of stock.

3.2 Purchase of stock on credit

PURCHASES – goods bought by the business for the purpose of resale.

On 1 May 2011 D Ahmed buys goods costing £2,300 on credit from B Carter.

First, the twofold effect of the transaction must be considered so that the book-keeping entries can be worked out. This is shown in the following:

The asset of stock is increased. An increase in an asset needs a debit entry in an account. Here, the account is a stock account showing the particular movement of stock; in this case it is the 'purchases' movement, so the account must be the purchases account.

There is an increase in a liability. This is a liability to B Carter's business because the goods supplied have not yet been paid for. An increase in a liability needs a credit entry, therefore a credit entry is made in B Carter's account.

Here again, we can use the idea of the debit side being 'IN' to the account, and the credit side being 'OUT' of the account. In this example, purchases have come 'IN', thus creating a debit in the Purchases Account; and the goods have come 'OUT' of B Carter, needing a credit in the account of B Carter:

D Ahmed's Books

Dr	Purchases Account			Cr
	'IN'		'OUT'	
2011		£		
May 1	B Carter	2,300		

Dr	B Carter Account			Cr
	'IN'		'OUT'	
		2011		£
		May 1	Purchases	2,300

On 30 May 2011 D Ahmed pays B Carter a cheque for £2,300 in full settlement of the goods supplied. The double entry to record the payment of the cheque to B Carter can now be shown:

- Credit the Bank account – the money goes 'OUT' of the bank
- Debit B Carter's account – the money goes 'IN' to Carter's account.

Dr	Bank Account			Cr
	'IN'		'OUT'	
		2011		£
		May 30	B Carter	2,300

Dr	B Carter Account			Cr
	'IN'		'OUT'	
2011		£	2011	£
May 30	Bank	2,300	May 1 Purchases	2,300

In B Carter's account shown above you will see that it records the purchase of the goods on 1 May and the payment of those goods on 30 May and the account is now clear.

> SALES – goods sold by the business which were bought with the intention of resale.

3.3 Sales of stock on credit

On 16 June 2011, Paine & Co sold goods on credit to M Chan for £1,000. In this example:

a) *An asset account is increased.* This is the account showing that M Chan is a debtor, a person who owes money to Paine & Co for goods supplied. The increase in the asset of debtors requires a debit and the debtor is M Chan, so the account concerned is that of M Chan. (Goods have gone 'IN' to M Chan – debit M Chan's account.)

b) *The asset of stock is decreased.* For this, a credit entry to reduce an asset is needed. The movement of stock is that of 'Sales' and so the account credited is the Sales Account. (Sales have gone 'OUT' – credit the Sales Account.)

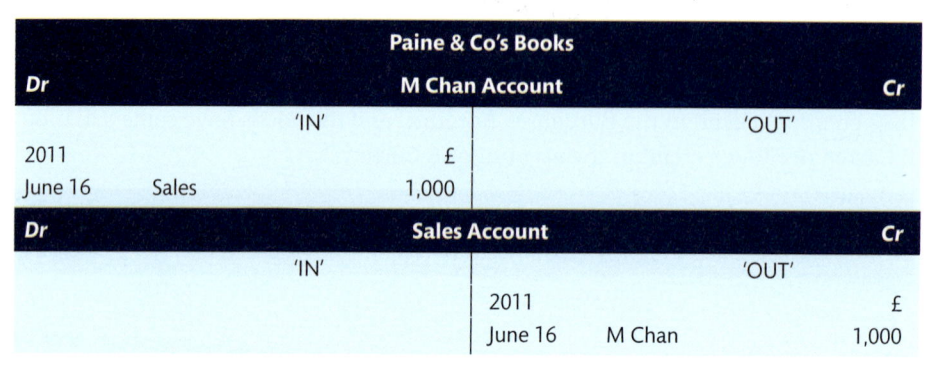

Paine & Co's Books

Dr		M Chan Account			Cr
	'IN'			'OUT'	
2011		£			
June 16	Sales	1,000			

Dr		Sales Account			Cr
	'IN'			'OUT'	
			2011		£
			June 16	M Chan	1,000

On 12 July M Chan sends Paine & Co a cheque for £1,000 in full settlement of the amount due. This is recorded in the books of Paine & Co as follows:

- Debit the Bank account – the money goes 'IN' to the Bank account
- Credit M Chan's account – the money comes 'OUT' of M Chan's account.

Dr		Bank Account			Cr
	'IN'			'OUT'	
2011		£			
July 12	M Chan	1,000			

Dr		M Chan Account			Cr
	'IN'			'OUT'	
2011		£	2011		£
June 16	Sales	1,000	July 12	Bank	1,000

3.4 Returns

Purchases and sales returns occur when goods that have been previously bought are returned to the supplier. This could be for various reasons, such as:

- the goods sent to the customer are of the incorrect specification
- the goods have been damaged in transit
- the goods are of poor quality.

Since the original purchase or sale was entered in the double entry system, so the return of those goods must also be entered. It is therefore appropriate to consider the double entry required in dealing with both 'Purchase Returns' and 'Sales Returns'.

Purchase returns represent goods which were purchased, and are now being returned to the supplier for one of the reasons stated above. Let us consider the following example:

On 14 April 2011, goods previously bought for £540 are returned by the business to F Baker. Thus:

a) *The liability of the business to F Baker is decreased by the value of the goods returned to him.* The decrease in a liability needs a debit, this time in the F Baker's Account. (The goods have gone 'IN' to F Baker – debit the F Baker Account.)

b) *The asset of stock is decreased by the goods sent out.* A credit representing a reduction in an asset is needed, and the movement of stock is that of 'Purchase Returns', so the entry will be a credit in the purchase returns account. (The returns have gone 'OUT' – credit the Purchase Returns Account.)

> PURCHASE RETURNS – goods returned by the business to its suppliers.

Dr	F Baker Account			Cr
	'IN'		'OUT'	
2011		£		
April 14	Purchase returns	540		

Dr	Purchase Returns Account			Cr
	'IN'		'OUT'	
		2011		£
		April 14	F Baker	540

An alternative name for a purchase returns account is a returns outwards account.

> **SALES RETURNS** – goods returned to the business by its customers.

Sales returns represent goods sold which have subsequently been returned by a customer for one of the reasons stated above. The double entry for sales returns is shown below in the following example.

On 19 March 2011, goods which had previously been sold to Lucy Chang for £178 have been returned by her. As a result:

a) *The asset of stock was increased by the goods returned.* A debit representing an increase of an asset is needed, and this time the movement of stock is that of 'Sales Returns'. The entry required therefore is a debit in the Sales Returns Account. (The goods have come 'IN' – debit the Sales Returns Account.)

b) *An asset is decreased.* The debt of Lucy Chang to the business is now reduced, and to record this a credit is required in Lucy Chang's account. (The goods have come 'OUT' of Lucy Chang's – credit the Lucy Chang Account.)

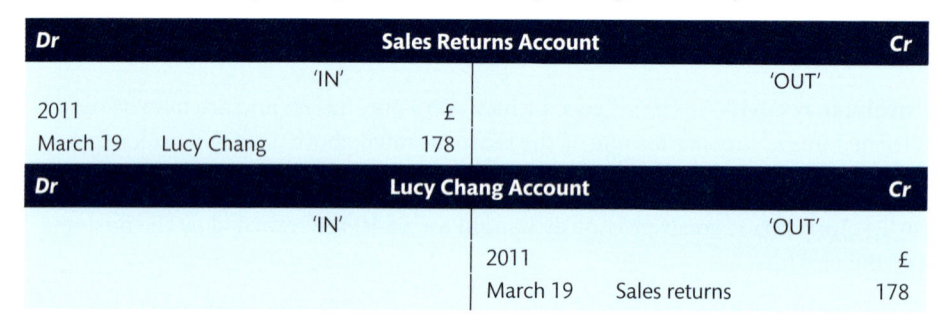

Dr	Sales Returns Account			Cr
	'IN'		'OUT'	
2011		£		
March 19	Lucy Chang	178		

Dr	Lucy Chang Account			Cr
	'IN'		'OUT'	
		2011		£
		March 19	Sales returns	178

An alternative name for a sales returns account is a returns inwards account.

3.5 Expenses on credit

In addition to businesses purchasing and selling goods on credit, they may also incur business expenses and services which initially are provided to them on credit with the business agreeing to pay at a later date.

On 24 February 2011 a business asks Smithy Garage to service the business's van and later receives an invoice for £246, the invoice being due for payment within 30 days. The initial double entry entries are as follows:

- Debit the Motor expenses account – services are received by the business; the benefit goes 'IN'

- Credit Smithy Garage account – the business owes Smithy Garage for the servicing of the van, therefore a liability is incurred; a liability is always a credit entry.

Dr	Motor Expenses Account			Cr
	'IN'		'OUT'	
2011		£		
Feb 24	Smithy Garage	246		

Dr	Smithy Garage Account			Cr
	'IN'		'OUT'	
		2011		£
		Feb 24	Motor expenses	246

On 20 March 2011 the business sends a cheque for £246 to Smithy Garage in payment of the outstanding account. The double entry for the payment of the account is as follows:

- Credit the Bank account – the cheque is paid 'OUT' of the bank account, hence a credit entry
- Debit Smithy Garage account – the cheque is paid to the Smithy Garage, it goes 'IN' to their account, hence a debit entry and the debt is now paid.

Dr		Bank Account			Cr
	'IN'			'OUT'	
			2011		£
			Mar 20	Smithy Garage	246

Dr		Smithy Garage Account			Cr
	'IN'			'OUT'	
2011		£	2011		£
March 20	Bank	246	Feb 24	Motor expenses	246

3.6 A worked example

Enter the following transactions in suitable double entry accounts:

2011
July 1   Bought goods on credit, £1,350 from Richards & Co
July 5   Bought goods on credit, £3,400 from Shah & Sons
July 8   Bought stationery £83, for office use, on credit from PG Supplies
July 12   Sold goods on credit, £632 to G Walker
July 14   Returned goods to Richards & Co. £190
July 16   Bought goods on credit, £2,960 from Jogia Ltd
July 20   Van serviced by Ash Tree Garage for £210 on credit
July 22   Sold goods for cash, £900
July 25   G Walker returned goods to us, £76
July 30   Paid PG Supplies £83 by cash

The double entry can now be shown:

Dr		Purchases Account			Cr
2011	'IN'	£		'OUT'	
July 1	Richards & Co	1,350			
July 5	Shah & Sons	3,400			
July 16	Jogia Ltd	2,960			

Dr		Richards & Co Account			Cr
	'IN'			'OUT'	
2011		£	2011		£
July 14	Purchase Returns	190	July 1	Purchases	1,350

Dr		Shah & Son Account			Cr
	'IN'			'OUT'	
			2011		£
			July 5	Purchases	3,400

Dr		Stationery Account			Cr
	'IN'			'OUT'	
2011		£			
July 8	PG Supplies	83			

Dr		PG Supplies Account			Cr
	'IN'			'OUT'	
2011		£	2011		£
July 30	Cash	83	July 30	Stationery	83

Dr		Sales Account			Cr
	'IN'			'OUT'	
			2011		£
			July 12	G Walker	632
			July 22	Cash	900

Dr		G Walker Account			Cr
	'IN'			'OUT'	
2011		£	2011		£
July 12	Sales	632	July 25	Sales Returns	76

Dr		Purchase Returns Account			Cr
	'IN'			'OUT'	
			2011		£
			July 14	Richards & Co	190

Dr		Jogia Ltd Account			Cr
	'IN'			'OUT'	
			2011		£
			July 16	Purchases	2,960

Dr		Motor Expenses Account			Cr
	'IN'			'OUT'	
2011		£			
July 20	Ash Tree Garage	210			

Dr		Ash Tree Garage Account			Cr
	'IN'			'OUT'	
			2011		£
			July 20	Motor Expenses	210

Dr		Cash Account			Cr
	'IN'			'OUT'	
2011		£	2011		£
July 22	Sales	900	July 30	PG Supplies	83

Dr		Sales Returns Account			Cr
	'IN'			'OUT'	
2011		£			
July 25	G Walker	76			

3.7 Special meaning of 'sales' and 'purchases'

It must be emphasised that 'sales' and 'purchases' have a special meaning in accounting language.

Purchases in accounting means *the purchase of those goods which the business buys with the prime intention of selling*. Sometimes the goods may be altered, added to or used in the manufacture of something else, but it is the element of *resale* that is important. To a business that trades in computers, for instance, computers are purchases. Buying a motor van for use by the business cannot be called a purchase in accountancy terms since it is not intended for resale.

Similarly, **sales** means *the sale of those goods in which the business normally deals and that were bought with the prime intention of resale*. The description 'sales' must never be given to the disposal of other items.

3.8 Comparison of cash and credit transactions for purchases and sales

The difference between the records for cash and credit transactions can now be seen.

The complete set of entries for purchases of goods where they are paid for immediately by cash would be:

a) **debit the purchases account**

b) **credit the cash account.**

On the other hand, the complete set of entries for the purchase of goods on credit can be broken down into two stages. First, the purchase of the goods, and second, the payment for them. The first part is:

a) **debit the purchases account**

b) **credit the supplier's account.**

The second part is:

a) **debit the supplier's account**

b) **credit the cash account.**

The difference can now be seen. With the cash purchase, no record is kept of the supplier's account. This is because cash passes immediately and therefore there is no need to keep a check of indebtedness (money owing) to a supplier. On the other hand, in the credit purchase the records should show to whom money is owed until payment is made. A comparison of cash sales and credit sales can be seen below:

Cash Sales	Credit Sales
Complete entry: • debit cash account • credit sales account	First part: • debit customer's account • credit sales account Second part: • debit cash account • credit customer's account

End of Chapter Checklist

Summary

- Recording the purchase and sale of goods on credit is shown using the double entry system of book-keeping.
- Recording transactions involving expenses and services which are supplied on credit is shown using the double entry system.
- Various accounts are used to record the movement of stock because stock is normally sold at a higher price than its cost.
- The accounts used to record the movement of stock are:
  - **purchases account** to record the purchases of stock as debit entries in the account since the goods come 'IN' to the business
  - **sales account** for the sale of the goods as credit entries in the account because the goods go 'OUT' of the business
  - **sales returns account** to record goods that a customer returns to the business as debit entries since the goods are returned 'IN' to the business
  - **purchase returns account** to record goods that the business returns to its suppliers as the goods go 'OUT' of the business.
- The special meaning in accounting terms of 'purchases' and 'sales', namely that purchases refer to goods bought for resale. Purchases of assets, such as a motor van to be used in the business, are recorded separately in the asset account, motor van. Sales refer to goods sold in the normal course of business. The disposal of an asset such as equipment should never be recorded in the sales account but recorded separately in a disposal account to be discussed later.
- Purchases for cash are *never* entered in the supplier's account while purchases on credit are *always* entered in the supplier's (creditor's) account.
- Sales for cash are *never* entered in the customer's account while sales on credit are *always* entered in the customer's (debtor's) account.

Questions

3.1 *For each of the following, state which account is to be debited and which is to be credited:*

a) Goods bought on credit from P Hart
b) Goods sold for cash
c) Bought motor car from Morgan Motors on credit
d) Bought goods on credit from Cohens Ltd
e) Returned some of the goods, which were faulty, to P Hart
f) Sold goods on credit to H Perkins
g) Goods sold, a cheque being received on the sale
h) Sold some of the office furniture for cash.

3.2X *For each of the following, state which account is to be debited and which is to be credited:*

a) Bought computer for use in the business on credit from J Kershaw
b) Paid cash for stationery
c) Bought goods for resale on credit from J Leung
d) Sold goods on credit to Daswani & Co
e) Purchased goods paying by cheque
f) Daswani & Co returned goods as unsuitable
g) Sold goods for cash
h) We return faulty goods to J Leung.

End of Chapter Checklist

Questions

3.3 You are required to enter the following transactions in the double entry records of Kendrick Products for the month of January 2011:

2011	
Jan 1	Started business with £20,000 in cash
Jan 2	Bought goods on credit from T Peters, £2,543
Jan 5	Put £18,000 cash into a bank account
Jan 7	Bought goods on credit from J Leigh, £349
Jan 9	Bought goods, £592, and paid cheque
Jan 16	Sold goods on credit to P Lamond, £210
Jan 18	Returned faulty goods to T Peters, £160
Jan 24	Bought stationery and paid by cash, £45
Jan 26	Paid cheque to T Peters, £2,383
Jan 26	Sold goods on credit to D Gurkan, £1,008
Jan 30	P Lamond returned goods to us, £60
Jan 31	Bought second-hand van on credit from Harper Motors Ltd, £5,250.

3.4X Enter the following transactions using double entry for Marks & Co for the month of April 2005:

2005	
April 1	Started business with £40,000 in the bank
April 3	Bought goods on credit, £845 from E Shah
April 5	Bought goods on credit, £950 from C Chang
April 9	Bought motor van on credit from Ash Car Sales, £10,400
April 12	Sold goods on credit to Naik Bros., £147
April 14	Bought goods, £2,300, paid by cheque
April 16	Returned faulty goods to E Shah, £72
April 20	Bought goods on credit from E Shah, £920
April 23	Sold goods for cash, £369
April 26	Paid for petrol, £40 in cash
April 28	Paid C Chang cheque, £950
April 29	Sold goods on credit to Curtis & Co for £420
April 30	Paid cheque to Ash Car Sales, £5,400 on account.

Section A: Books of original entry

Chapter 4: Balancing of accounts and preparation of a Trial Balance

Getting started

Edexcel specification
The ledger, 2.1, 2.4, 2.8, 2.9, 2.15–2.20

After you have studied this chapter you should be able to:

- understand what is meant by 'balancing off' accounts
- balance off accounts at the end of a period and bring down the opening balance to the next period
- distinguish between a debit balance and a credit balance
- prepare accounts in a three-column format, as used in computerised accounts
- understand the purpose of a trial balance
- understand why the trial balance totals should equal one another
- appreciate that some kinds of errors can be made but the trial balance totals will still equal one another
- understand what steps to take if the trial balance doesn't balance.

BALANCING ACCOUNTS – finding the difference between the two sides of an account (balance) and entering this on the lesser side to ensure both sides agree.

CREDITOR – a person whom money is used for goods or services.

DEBTOR – a person who owes money to the business for goods or services.

4.1 Introduction

In the last two chapters entries into the various accounts have been shown. In this chapter we will now look at what is known as 'balancing off' accounts, a procedure which is usually carried out at the end of each month prior to the preparation of the trial balance.

'Balancing off' simply means finding the difference between the two sides of an account, i.e. the difference between the total debit entries and the total credit entries in a particular account. The 'difference' between the two sides is known as the 'balance' and this figure is inserted on the side of the account that shows the least amount of money. If both sides of the account are then totalled up, they should agree, having inserted the 'balance'; if they do not add up correctly, then an error may have been made in the calculation of the balance or perhaps in adding up the account. The calculation will then need to be rechecked.

Sometimes an account simply requires closing off; this is when both the debit and credit sides total up to exactly the same amount and thus there is no balance.

4.2 Balancing the accounts

Balancing off the accounts is a procedure carried out by most businesses on a monthly basis so that they can keep a check on various accounting issues such as knowing:

- how much money they have in their cash account
- the balance in the bank account
- how much money they owe to other people, i.e. creditors
- how much money other people owe the business, i.e. debtors
- the value of the business's assets
- the amount incurred on various expenses
- how much their stock has cost, i.e. purchases
- what the sales figures are to date
- the capital invested in the business by the owner(s) and any drawings taken.

In the following example the bank account has been balanced off at the end of the period and the balance brought down to the next accounting period:

Dr			Bank Account			Cr
2010		£	2010			£
Oct 1	Capital	20,000	Oct 4	Purchases		2,400
Oct 11	Sales	550	Oct 7	Rent		500
			Oct 31	Balance c/d		17,650
		20,550				20,550
Nov 1	Balance b/d	17,650				

The procedure for 'balancing off' the bank account is now shown in the following step-by-step guide:

1. Add up both sides to find out their totals. Do not write anything permanent in the account at this stage, but you could write the figures lightly in pencil or on a piece of paper. In the bank account, the debit side totals £20,550 whilst the credit side totals £2,900.

2. Deduct the smaller total from the larger total to find the balance. In our example above, this is £20,550 − £2,900 = £17,650.

3. Now enter the balance on the side with the smallest total, in the example above this is the credit side. Note that the date entered is usually the last day of the month – in our case, 31 October – followed by 'Balance c/d', which stands for 'carried down', then enter the balance, i.e. £17,650.

4. Enter the totals on a level with each other. Note that totals in accounting are shown with a single line above them and a double line underneath.

5. Now enter the balance on the line below the totals. The balance below the totals should be on the opposite side to the balance shown above the totals. First enter the date, which is the first day of the next period – in the example above, 1 November – followed by 'Balance b/d', which stands for balance brought down.

You will see in the bank account that there is a balance brought down of £17,650 on 1 November. This is a **debit balance** indicating that £17,650 is the money available in the business's bank account. Remember, a debit balance is always an asset.

Sometimes the balances brought down are credit balances as shown in the following example of K Grant, a creditor:

Dr			K Grant Account			Cr
2010		£	2010			£
Jan 30	Bank	120	Jan 1	Purchases		120
Jan 31	Balance c/d	1,910	Jan 15	Purchases		610
			Jan 21	Purchases		1,300
		2,030				2,030
			Feb 1	Balance b/d		1,910

In K Grant's account you will see that during the month purchases totalled £2,030 (120 + 610 + 1,300 = 2,030) and payment was made on 30 January of £120 leaving a balance outstanding of £1,910 (2,030 − 120 = 1,910). This is shown as a **credit balance** brought down showing that £1,910 is owed to K Grant at the end of January. This is a liability and, remember, a liability is always a credit balance.

In the next example of D Araimi, a debtor, you will see that at the end of the month there is no balance outstanding:

Dr				D Araimi Account			Cr
2010			£	2010			£
May 1	Sales		100	May 31	Bank		834
May 15	Sales		734				
			834				834

In this example, goods were sold during May to D Araimi totalling £834 which was paid for in full on 31 May, therefore the account is clear.

Further examples:

An asset account

Dr			Machinery Account		Cr
2010			£		
Sept 1	Bank		6,435		

Sometimes there is only one item in an account, as shown above in the Machinery Account. In these circumstances it is not necessary to balance the account off since it can easily be seen that the amount shown – £6,435 – represents the total machinery the business owns. Machinery is an asset, hence the **debit balance**.

An expense account

Dr			Motor Expenses Account			Cr
2010		£	2010			£
Mar 5	Cash	32	Mar 31	Balance c/d		405
Mar 16	Bank	301				
Mar 21	Bank	72				
		405				405
Apr 1	Balance b/d	405				

The above account shows that, for the month of March, £405 has been incurred in motor expenses. This is a **debit balance** which is always an asset or an expense. In this example it is an expense.

4.3 Three-column accounts

Sometimes accounts may be shown using three columns: a debit column, a credit column and a column showing the balance on the account. This method of presenting accounts is used in computerised accounting packages. Let us look at some examples of three-column accounts:

A debtor's account using a three-column account

			T Baldwin Account		
		Debit	Credit	Balance (and whether debit or credit)	
2010		£	£	£	
May 1	Sales	1,200		1,200	Dr
May 12	Sales	411		1,611	Dr
May 19	Bank		1,200	411	Dr
May 24	Sales	260		671	Dr

A creditor's account using a three-column account

			D Kemel Account		
		Debit	Credit	Balance (and whether debit or credit)	
2010					
May 7	Purchases		510	510	Cr
May 9	Purchases		82	592	Cr
May 26	Bank	510		82	Cr

The capital account using a three-column account

			Capital Account		
		Debit	Credit	Balance (and whether debit or credit)	
2010		£	£	£	
May 1	Bank		30,000	30,000	Cr

An expense account using a three-column account

			Stationery Account		
		Debit	Credit	Balance (and whether debit or credit)	
2010		£	£	£	
May 17	Cash	45		45	Dr
May 20	Bank	231		276	Dr
May 27	Cash	22		298	Dr

4.4 A worked example

The following accounts have been extracted from the books of James Lau who runs a successful retail business. You will see that all the accounts have been balanced off by the book-keeper and a trial balance prepared (see below).

James Lau's books

Dr			Bank Account			Cr
2010		£	2010			£
June 1	Capital	20,000	June 3	Motor car		9,000
June 30	A Cope	1,350	June 3	Rent		1,500
			June 21	Computer		1,650
			June 29	J Wang		2,700
			June 30	G Moore		630
			June 30	Balance c/d		5,870
		21,350				21,350
July 1	Balance b/d	5,870				

Dr			Cash Account		Cr
2010		£	2010		£
June 5	Sales	540	June 14	Stationery	55
June 12	Sales	440	June 30	Balance c/d	925
		980			980
July 1	Balance b/d	925			

Dr			Sales Account		Cr
2010		£	2010		£
June 30	Balance c/d	3,350	June 5	Cash	540
			June 10	A Cope	1,770
			June 12	Cash	440
			June 22	B Singh	600
		3,350			3,350
			July 1	Balance	3,350

Dr			Sales Returns Account		Cr
2010		£	2010		£
June 23	A Cope	420			

Dr			Purchases Account		Cr
2010		£	2010		£
June 3	J Wang	2,700	June 30	Balance c/d	4,800
June 4	G Moore	750			
June 18	G Moore	1,350			
		4,800			4,800
July 1	Balance b/d	4,800			

Dr		Purchase Returns Account		Cr
	£	2010		£
		June 6	G Moore	120

Dr			Computer Account		Cr
2010		£			£
June 21	Bank	1,650			

Dr			Motor Car Account		Cr
2010		£			£
June 3	Bank	9,000			

Dr		Rent Account			Cr
2010			£		£
June 3	Rent		1,500		

Dr		Stationery Account			Cr
2010			£		£
June 14	Cash		55		

Dr		Capital Account			Cr
			£	2010	£
				June 1 Bank	20,000

Dr		B Singh Account			Cr
2010			£		£
June 22	Sales		600		

Dr		A Cope Account			Cr
2010			£	2010	£
June 10	Sales		1,770	June 23 Sales returns	420
				June 30 Bank	1,350
			1,770		1,770

Dr		J Wang Account			Cr
2010			£	2010	£
June 29	Bank		2,700	June 3 Purchases	2,700

Dr		G Moore Account			Cr
2010			£	2010	£
June 6	Purchase Returns		120	June 4 Purchases	750
June 30	Bank		630	June 18 Purchases	1,350
June 30	Balance c/d		1,350		
			2,100		2,100
				July 1 Balance b/d	1,350

James Lau

Trial Balance as at 30 June 2010

	Dr	Cr
	£	£
Bank	5,870	
Cash	925	
Sales		3,350
Sales returns	420	
Purchases	4,800	
Purchase returns		120
Computer	1,650	
Motor Car	9,000	
Rent	1,500	
Stationery	55	
Capital		20,000
B. Singh	600	
G. Moore		1,350
	24,820	24,820

> TRIAL BALANCE – a list of all debit and credit balances in the books at a particular point of time. Provided no errors have occurred, the two columns should agree.

4.5 The trial balance

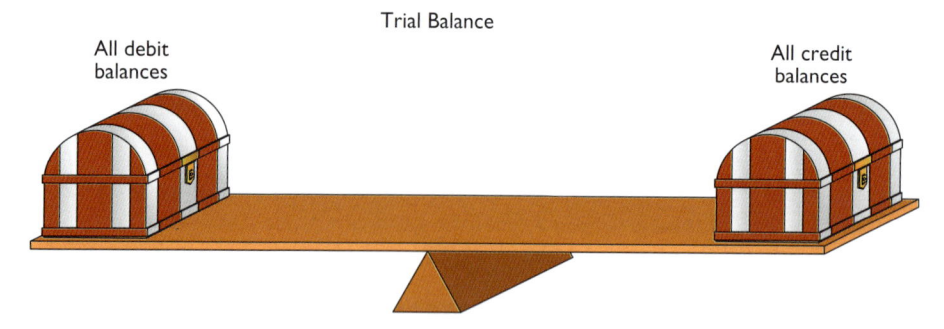

Trial Balance

All debit balances — All credit balances

A trial balance is an essential stage in ensuring the accuracy of the book-keeping entries prior to the preparation of the financial statements. It is a list of account titles and their balances in the ledger on a specific date. The trial balance lists the name of each account together with the balance shown in either the debit or credit columns. Since every entry in double entry book-keeping should have a corresponding credit entry then, provided no errors have occurred, the two columns should agree when totalled.

It is often assumed that when a trial balance 'balances', the entries in the accounts must be correct. *This, however, may not be true.* It means that certain types of error have not been made, but there are several types of error that are not apparent when balancing a trial balance, such as omitting a transaction altogether. Another example might be a credit sale of £87 to a customer that is inadvertently debited to the sales account instead of being credited; the customer's account then being credited instead of being debited. Since both the debit and the credit entries are of the same amount, the error will not affect the agreement of the trial balance.

4.6 Errors not revealed by a trial balance

> ERRORS NOT REVEALED BY TRIAL BALANCE –
> P – Principle
> O – Original entry
> R – Reversal
> C – Compensating
> O – Omission
> W – Wrong account
> 'POR COW'

As stated above, the trial balance would still appear to balance even though certain errors have occurred. These errors are as follows:

- **Errors of principle** – where an item is entered in the wrong type of account. For example, a fixed asset is entered in an expense account.

- **Error of original entry** – where an item is entered using an incorrect amount. For example, an invoice received showing goods purchased to the value of £260.00 is entered in both the purchases account and the supplier's account as £26.00.

- **Complete reversal of entries** – where the correct amounts are entered in the correct accounts but each item is shown on the wrong side of each account.

- **Compensating errors** – where two errors of equal amounts, but on opposite sides of the accounts, cancel out each other.

- **Error of omission** – where a transaction is completely omitted from the books. For example, if a cheque received is lost and therefore never entered in the books of account.

- **Errors of commission (wrong account)** – where a correct amount is entered, but in the wrong person's account. For example, a sale of goods to J Roberts is entered in error, in J Robertson's account.

4.7 Steps to take if the trial balance does not balance

If the trial balance does not balance, i.e. the two totals are different, then this is evidence that one or more errors have been made in either the double entry bookkeeping or in the preparation of the trial balance itself. In this case, the following steps should be taken to locate the error(s):

1. If the trial balance is badly written and contains many alterations, then rewrite it.

2. Again, add each side of the trial balance. If you added the numbers 'upwards' the first time, then start at the top and work 'downwards' the second time, and vice versa.

3. Find the amount of the discrepancy and then check in the accounts for a transaction of this amount and, if located, ensure that the double entry has been carried out correctly.

4. Halve the amount of the discrepancy. Check to see whether there is a transaction for this amount and, if located, ensure the double entry has been carried out correctly. This type of error may have occurred if an item has been entered on the wrong side of the trial balance.

5. If the amount of the discrepancy is divisible by nine, this indicates that when the figure was originally entered it may have had digits transposed. For example, £63 entered in error as £36, or £27 entered as £72.

6. Check that the balance on each account has been correctly calculated and entered onto the trial balance in the right column using the correct amount.

7. Ensure that every outstanding balance from all the ledgers and the cash book have been included in the trial balance and tick each balance after ensuring it is entered correctly.

8. If the error has still not been identified, then the error must be sought in the accounts themselves. It may be necessary to check all the entries from the date of the last trial balance.

End of Chapter Checklist

Summary

- Accounts are 'balanced off' at the end of a period and the opening balances brought down at the beginning of the next period.
- Opening balances brought down on the debit side are referred to as debit balances, whereas those brought down on the credit side are known as credit balances.
- 'Debtors' are people or organisations who owe money to the business. Their accounts in your accounting records show a greater value on the debit side, hence they are your debtors.
- 'Creditors' are people or organisations that the business owes money to. Their accounts in your accounting records show a greater value on the credit side, hence they are your creditors.
- A trial balance is a list of account titles and their balances in the ledger at a specific date which is prepared to check the arithmetical accuracy of the book-keeping entries and locate any error(s).
- A trial balance also assists in the preparation of the financial statements.
- A worked example of a trial balance is shown.
- The balancing of a trial balance does not always indicate that no errors have been made since certain errors can be made and the trial balance will still agree.
- What steps to take if a trial balance totals do not agree.

Questions

4.1 You are required to enter the following transactions for the month of May 2010 for a small electrical retailer. Balance the accounts off and extract a trial balance as at 31 May 2010.

2010	
May 1	Started in business with capital of £2,500, which was paid into the bank
May 2	Bought goods on credit from the following: D Ellis £540; C Mendez £87; K Gibson £76
May 4	Sold goods on credit to: C Bailey £430; B Hughes £62; H Spencer £176
May 6	Sold goods for cash, £500
May 8	Paid rent by cash, £120
May 9	C Bailey paid us £250 by cheque on account
May 10	H Spencer paid us £150 on account by cheque
May 12	We paid the following by cheque: K Gibson £76; D Ellis £370 on account
May 15	Bought stationery for cash, £60
May 18	Bought goods on credit from: D Ellis £145; C Mendez £234
May 19	Paid rent by cash, £120
May 25	Sold goods on credit to: C Bailey £90; B Hughes £110; H Spencer £128
May 31	Paid C Mendez £87 by cheque

4.2X Jenny Moore opened a bookshop on 1 August 2010 and her transactions for the first month's trading are shown below.

2010	
Aug 1	Started in business with £22,000 in the bank
Aug 1	Paid three months rent on premises £1,800 by cheque
Aug 7	Bought shop fittings and shelving, paying by cheque £3,230
Aug 7	Bought books, paying by cheque £5,000
Aug 9	Took £1,000 out of the bank and put it into a cash account
Aug 9	Bought stationery £163, paying by cash
Aug 10	Bought more books, this time on credit from Book Supplies, £4,200
Aug 14	Book sales paid into the bank, £980
Aug 16	Paid sundry expenses, £28 in cash
Aug 20	Book sales paid direct into the bank, £1,300
Aug 25	Purchased further books on credit from Delta Books, £1,500
Aug 28	Book sales paid direct into the bank, £2,000
Aug 30	Paid salaries by cheque, £2,100

End of Chapter Checklist

Questions

Required

a) To enter the transactions for August 2010 and 'balance off' the accounts at the end of the month.

b) Prepare a trial balance as at 31 August 2010.

4.3 You are required to enter the following transactions in the necessary accounts for April 2010 of a home furnishing business. At the end of the month 'balance off' the accounts and prepare a trial balance.

2010	
April 1	Started in business with £15,000 in the bank
April 3	Bought goods on credit from: Bowman Furnishers £320; Howe Homes £460; W Hunt £1,800; J Bond £620
April 7	Cash sales, £480
April 9	Paid rent by cheque, £500
April 11	Paid rates by cheque, £190
April 12	Sold goods on credit to: L Clark £480; K Allen £96; R Gee £1,170
April 14	Paid wages in cash, £400
April 17	We returned faulty goods to: Bowman Furnishers £28; J Bond £60
April 20	Bought goods on credit from: J Bond £220; W Hunt £270; Bowman Furnishers £240
April 23	Goods were returned to us from: K Allen £20; L Clark £40
April 25	Bought motor car on credit from Bates Motors, £5,000
April 26	Cash sales, £175
April 27	We paid the following by cheque: Bowman Furnishers £532; Howe Homes £460; W Hunt £2,070
April 28	Bought second-hand motor van, £3,000 paid by cheque
April 29	Bought stationery and paid in cash, £56
April 30	Received cheques from: L Clark £440; K Allen £76
April 30	Paid Bates Motors by cheque, £5,000

4.4 State whether the following accounts would be either a debit or credit balance.

a) Capital
b) Sales
c) Stationery
d) Cash
e) T Khan (a creditor)
f) Machinery
g) Rent
h) D Allen (debtor)
i) Bank loan
j) Purchases

4.5 The following trial balance has been drawn up incorrectly by a junior member of staff. You are required to rewrite and balance the trial balance after making the necessary corrections.

Trial balance of P Brown as at 31 May 2010	Dr £	Cr £
Capital	20,000	
Drawings	7,000	
General expenses		500
Sales	38,500	
Purchases		29,000
Debtors		6,800
Creditors	9,000	
Bank balance (Dr)	15,100	
Cash		200
Plant and equipment		5,000
Heating and lighting		1,500
Rent	2,400	

4.6 The following trial balance has been drawn up incorrectly. You are required to make any necessary corrections and rewrite the trial balance ensuring that it balances.

Trial balance of S Higton as at 30 June 2010	Dr £	Cr £
Capital	19,956	
Sales		119,439
Stationery	1,200	
General expenses	2,745	
Motor expenses		4,476
Cash at bank	1,950	
Stock 1 July 2009	7,668	
Wages and salaries		9,492
Rent and rates	10,500	
Office equipment	6,000	
Purchases	81,753	
Heating and lighting		2,208
Rent received	2,139	
Debtors	10,353	
Drawings		4,200
Creditors		10,230
Motor vehicle	7,500	
Interest received	1,725	
Insurance		3,444
	153,489	153,489

End of Chapter Checklist

Questions

4.7X From the following list of balances, prepare a trial balance as at 31 December 2010 for Ms Anita Hall:

	£
Plant and machinery	21,450
Motor vehicles	26,000
Premises	80,000
Wages	42,840
Purchases	119,856
Sales	179,744
Rent received	3,360
Telephone, printing and stationery	3,600
Creditors	27,200
Debtors	30,440
Bank overdraft	2,216
Capital	131,250
Drawings	10,680
General expenses	3,584
Lighting and heating	2,960
Motor expenses	2,360

4.8X State what type of error has occurred in the following examples:

a) Purchases account has been debited with the purchase of office furniture.
b) Sale of goods to J Clarkson has been entered in J Clark's account.
c) Sale of goods to N Ward has been completely omitted from the books of account.
d) A sale of goods to K Kirk for £49 has been entered in the books as £94.
e) A payment of cash, £58 to M Dawson, was entered on the receipts side of the cash book in error, and credited to M Dawson's account.
f) A second-hand motor van bought for £4,000 was entered in the motor expenses account.

Section A: Books of original entry

Chapter 5: Value Added Tax

5.1 Value Added Tax

Value Added Tax (VAT) is a tax charged on the supply of most goods and services supplied by businesses within the UK with a certain amount of turnover (sales). Such businesses must be registered for VAT. The turnover threshold usually increases each year as part of the Government's budget. VAT is administered in the UK by HM Revenue and Customs (HMRC) whose website at www.hmrc.gov.uk provides all aspects of VAT.

Once a business has been registered for VAT it is issued with a VAT Registration Number which must be quoted on all its business documentation, for example, order forms, invoices, etc. When the business makes a sale of its goods or supplies a service to a customer VAT is added to the purchase price of the goods, this is known as **output VAT**. Any purchases or services bought by the supplier are also subject to VAT; from the purchaser's point of view, this is known as **input VAT**.

There are exceptions to the goods and services supplied to which VAT is charged and this will be discussed later on in this chapter.

VAT is collected by businesses and paid to HMRC, usually on a quarterly basis. However, some businesses may decide to opt for the payment of VAT on an annual basis. There is also a scheme known as the **flat rate scheme** whereby businesses calculate VAT as a percentage of annual sales, thereby avoiding the necessity to calculate input and output VAT on individual transactions. This scheme was designed to help small businesses and to eliminate the work involved in accounting for VAT.

Payment of VAT

Once a business has been registered for VAT it is required to complete a VAT Return each quarter (or each year if it is using the annual basis of return) in which details of the business's purchases and sales and the VAT elements are listed. The VAT due for payment to HMRC is calculated as follows:

- the amount of VAT charged on sales, i.e. output VAT *less*
- the amount of VAT paid on purchases, i.e. input VAT.

Getting started

Edexcel specification
The ledger, 2.11, 2.12 and 2.13

After you have studied this chapter you should be able to:

- understand how the value added tax (VAT) system operates in the UK
- understand how VAT is collected and paid to HM Revenue and Customs (HMRC)
- distinguish between the various rates of VAT
- calculate VAT on goods and services
- calculate VAT when this is included in the total price of the goods and services
- prepare sales invoices including charges for VAT and where cash discount is offered
- record VAT transactions in the book-keeping system.

VAT – a tax charged on the supply of most goods and services. The tax is borne by the final consumer, not the business selling them to the consumer.

VAT is administered by HMRC.

OUTPUT VAT – VAT charged by a business on its supplies (outputs).

INPUT VAT – VAT charged to a business on its purchases and expenses (inputs).

In most cases, businesses have to pay the difference between output VAT and input VAT to HMRC. However, some businesses have more input VAT than output VAT and in these circumstances the business will receive a refund of VAT from HMRC.

VAT rates

There are three rates of VAT in operation at the time of writing, although these rates may change at any time according to governmental decisions:

- standard rate, currently 17.5%
- reduced rate, currently 5%
- zero rate.

VAT RATES:-
- Standard, currently 17.5%
- Reduced, currently 5%
- Zero rated

Goods and services applicable to VAT

1. Standard rate VAT

Most goods and services are subject to VAT at the standard rate of 17.5%.

2. Reduced rate VAT

This reduced rate of 5% applies to certain goods and services such as:

- domestic fuel or power
- installation of energy-saving materials
- grant-funded installation of heating equipment
- security goods or connection of gas supplies
- renovation and alteration of dwellings and residential conversions
- women's sanitary products
- child car seats.

3. Zero-rated goods and services

Some goods and services are zero-rated which means that VAT on these products is charged at 0%. Some examples are:

- food for human consumption (there are some exceptions such as chocolate biscuits, some confectionery, etc.)
- books and periodicals
- clothing and footwear for young children.

4. Exempt goods and services

There are also goods and services which are exempt from accounting for VAT. Such businesses neither add VAT onto the selling price of their goods or services, nor do they obtain a refund of VAT on the amount they pay on the products they purchase. Examples of **exempt supplies** are:

- financial services
- postal services
- certain types of education.

Business categories

- **Zero-rated businesses** – Businesses that do not have to add VAT to goods and services supplied to others by them, but they can receive a refund of VAT paid on goods and services purchased by them.

- **Exempted businesses** – Businesses that do not have to add VAT to the price of goods and services supplied by them, and that cannot obtain a refund of VAT paid on goods and services purchased by them.

- **Partly exempt businesses** – These will sell some goods that are exempt from VAT and some goods that are either standard-rated or zero-rated. They may reclaim part of the input VAT paid by them.

VAT Records

All VAT Records must be retained by a business for a period of six years.

> VAT RECORDS must be retained by a business for six years.

5.2 How the VAT system works

In Exhibit 5.1 it can be seen that VAT is payable to HMRC whenever a sale is made. This progressive method of tax collection ensures a steady flow of funds for the government.

Example: A toymaker manufactures toys from scraps of material and sells them to a wholesaler for £200 plus VAT. The wholesaler sells these to a retailer for £300 plus VAT, who in turn retails the toys to a number of private customers who are not VAT registered.

Exhibit 5.1 Calculation of VAT at 17.5% payable to HMRC

	Net (£)	Vat (£)	Type of VAT	VAT due to HMRC
Toymaker				
Sale of toys	200.00	35.00	Output	
less cost of materials	–	–		
VAT		35.00		£35.00
Wholesaler				
Sale of toys	300.00	52.50	Output	
less cost of toys	200.00	35.00	Input	
VAT		17.50		£17.50
Retailer				
Sale of toys	400.00	70.00	Output	
less cost of materials	300.00	52.50	Input	
VAT		17.50		£17.50
				£70.00

Exhibit 5.1 shows the total tax of £70 has been paid to HMRC at various stages in the distribution of the toys. It also shows that the retailer has charged its customers a total output VAT of £70. These customers are not VAT registered and have no input VAT to offset against the £70 paid by them.

5.3 VAT calculations

Adding VAT to the basic cost of goods and/or services

Assuming that the VAT rate is 17.5% and the cost of the goods is £50, the calculation is as shown below:

$$£50 \times \frac{17.5}{100} = £8.75$$

Therefore total cost including VAT = £50.00 + £8.75 = £58.75

Calculating VAT when it has already been included in the price

Often, only the gross amount of an item is known. This figure will, in fact, be made up of the net amount plus VAT. To find the amount of VAT that has been added to the net amount, the formula below can be used with any rate of VAT.

$$\text{VAT} (£) = \frac{\text{\% rate of VAT}}{(100 + \text{\% rate of VAT})} \times \text{Gross Amount}$$

If the gross amount was £940 and the rate of VAT was 17.5% it is only necessary to insert these figures in the formula.

$$\text{VAT} (£) = \frac{17.5}{(100 + 17.5\%)} \times 940 = \frac{17.5}{117.5} \times 940 = £140$$

The net amount would then be £940 − £140 = £800. Alternatively, the net amount can be calculated thus:

$$\text{Net Amount} (£) = \frac{100}{(100 + \text{\% rate of VAT})} \times \text{Gross Amount}$$

$$\text{Net Amount} (£) = \frac{100}{(100 + 17.5)} \times 940 = \frac{100}{117.5} \times 940 = £800$$

Preparing a sales invoice

If a business is VAT registered it will need to add VAT onto the value of goods sold to a customer when they are preparing their sales invoice. The following example illustrates the preparation of a sales invoice:

Example: On 16 November 2009, S Shah, who runs a business selling electrical appliances, of Park House, Bankside Road, York YK6 24BD, sold the following goods to Cooper's Ltd, Unit 77, Astley Business Park, York YK6 72PQ. Their order number is N/9721

    10 Deluxe Electric Kettles @ £12.00 each

    6 Slow Cookers @ £28.00 each

    2 Bedside Lamps @ £45.00 each

SALES INVOICE – subject to VAT.

All goods are subject to 17.5% VAT. The sales invoice is numbered 4/58319.

INVOICE

S Shah
Park House, Bankside Road
York YK6 24BD
VAT Reg No. 873 7902 93

To: Cooper's Ltd
Unit 77
Astley Business Park
York YK6 72PQ
Order No. N/9721

Invoice No. 4/58319

Date: 16 November 2009

	£
10 Deluxe Electric Kettles @ £12.00 each	120.00
6 Slow Cookers @ £28.00 each	168.00
2 Bedside Lamps @ £45.00 each	90.00
	378.00
Add VAT 17.5%	66.15
	444.15

Terms: Net monthly

5.4 VAT and cash discounts

Where a cash discount is offered for prompt payment, VAT is calculated on an amount represented by the value of the invoice less such a discount. Even if the cash discount is lost because of late payment, the amount of VAT charged will not change. For example:

> Goods are sold to Hey & Co for £4,000 less trade discount of 20%. The terms of payment state 2.5% cash discount if payment is made within 30 days. Assuming VAT is at the rate of 17.5% the amount to be charged on the invoice is as follows:

	£
Goods	4,000.00
Less 20% trade discount	800.00
	3,200.00
*Add VAT @ 17.5%	546.00
	3,746.00

> **VAT AND CASH DISCOUNT** – calculate VAT on the net price of the goods *after* cash discount has been deducted.

*The VAT has been calculated on the net price of £3,200 *less* 2.5% cash discount (2.5% × £3,200 = £80) thus £3,200 − £80 = £3,120. Therefore, VAT = 17.5% × £3,120 = £546.

5.5 The Value Added Tax Account

VAT registered businesses must keep details of their purchases, sales and expenses to enable them to calculate how much value added tax they owe at the end of a particular period. The following example provides the information for completion of the Value Added Tax Account and VAT Return, however, completion of the VAT Return will be covered later on in your studies.

Example: The following financial data for the quarter ended 30 June 2010 for Radford & Co is shown below:

	Purchases		
	Total	Net	VAT
2010	£	£	£
30 April	11,750	10,000	1,750
31 May	17,625	15,000	2,625
30 June	21,150	18,000	3,150
	50,525	43,000	7,525

	Sales		
	Total	Net	VAT
2010	£	£	£
30 April	23,500	20,000	3,500
31 May	35,250	30,000	5,250
30 June	42,300	36,000	6,300
	101,050	86,000	15,050

The company's expenses for the quarter were as follows:

	Expenses		
	Total	Net	VAT
2010	£	£	£
30 April	470	400	70
31 May	705	600	105
30 June	1,175	1,000	175
	2,350	2,000	350

Note: The details shown above would be entered in the business's day books which are dealt with in Chapters 8, 9 and 10. In this example, they have been listed above to demonstrate the various items that are entered into both the VAT Account and VAT Return.

The above information is now entered into the company's VAT Account as follows:

Dr		VAT Account				Cr
2010				2010		
April 30	Purchases Day Book	1,750		April 30	Sales Day Book	3,500
"	Expenses	70		May 31	Sales Day Book	5,250
May 31	Purchases Day Book	2,625		June 30	Sales Day Book	6,300
"	Expenses	105				
June 30	Purchases Day Book	3,150				
"	Expenses	175				
"	Balance c/d	7,175				
		15,050				15,050
July 19	Bank	7,175		July 1	Balance b/d	7,175

> VAT PAYABLE –
> VAT collected on sales　　　　　　XXX
> Less: VAT on purchases and expenses　XX
> VAT due to HMRC　　　　　　　　XX

In the VAT Account above you will see that the VAT collected by the business on the sale of their goods is shown on the **credit side** of the account since this is a liability and is owed to HMRC. Against this liability the business is able to offset any amount they have paid on their purchases and expenses:

	£
VAT collected on sales	15,050
Less: VAT on purchases and expenses	
(total of the debit side of the account)	7,875
Amount due to HMRC	***7,175**

The amount outstanding is shown as a **credit balance b/d** and is therefore a liability. Assuming the amount due to HMRC was paid by the business on 19 July, the book-keeping entries would be:

- **Debit** – Value Added Tax Account (money goes into Value Added Tax Account)
- **Credit** – Bank Account (money goes 'OUT').

As mentioned earlier in the chapter, there are occasions when a business does not charge VAT on its sales, for example a children's outfitters, where the business is zero-rated. In this case, the business can claim back any VAT incurred on their expenses and would receive a refund from HMRC. At the end of a quarter the balance on the VAT Account in this example would therefore be a **debit balance b/d** prior to receiving a refund from HMRC.

End of Chapter Checklist

Summary

- Value added tax (VAT) is a tax levied on sales by the UK government. It is described as an 'indirect tax' and ultimately the tax is paid by the final consumer of the goods or services.
- VAT is administered in the UK by HM Revenue and Customs (HMRC).
- There are currently three rates of VAT, namely: standard rate, currently 17.5%; reduced rate, currently 5%; and zero rate.
- The way in which the VAT system operates is explained whereby VAT is paid at various stages in the distribution chain.
- Businesses may be classified as standard-rated, zero-rated, exempt or partially exempt.
- A sales invoice which is subject to VAT is prepared.
- Where cash discount is allowed VAT is calculated on the sales value less any cash discount offered. If the cash discount is lost because of late payment the VAT will not change.
- The book-keeping entries for recording VAT are shown in a VAT Account.

Questions

5.1 On 1 March 2011, C Black, Curzon Road, Stockport, sold the following goods on credit to J Booth, 89 Andrew Lane, Stockport, under Order No 1697:

20,000 coils sealing tape	@ £4.70 per 1,000 coils
40,000 sheets A5 paper	@ £4.50 per 1,000 sheets
30,000 sheets A4 paper	@ £4.20 per 1,000 sheets
All goods are subject to VAT at 17.5%.	

Required:

a) Prepare the sales invoice to be sent to J Booth.
b) Show the entries in the personal ledgers of J Booth and C Black.

5.2X Brack's garage is situated in Manchester and sells petrol and accessories in addition to carrying out repairs and maintenance on vehicles. During January 2010 the garage issued the following invoices in respect of sales etc. for the month.

2010	Name of customer	Net Amount £
Jan 2	D Woolham & Co	230.00
Jan 6	C Crawford	348.00
Jan 7	S Brocklehurst	1,980.00
Jan 9	L Price & Partners	520.00
Jan 13	D Woolham & Co	56.00
Jan 18	L Price & Partners	200.00
Jan 21	C Crawford	340.00
Jan 24	C Crawford	44.00
Jan 29	S Brocklehurst	846.00
Jan 31	L Price & Partners	722.00

Required:

a) Calculate the amount of VAT at 17.5% to be added to each invoice.
b) Show the total of each invoice, i.e. the net amount, VAT and total due.
c) Total the invoices for January showing the total net sales, VAT and total sales.

End of Chapter Checklist

Questions

5.3 a) Photoprint Ltd recently purchased 22 reams of special printing paper for Job No. 67 at a cost of £3.75 per ream each plus VAT. When the job was complete Photoprint Ltd charged the customer £235.00 inclusive of VAT. How much VAT is owed to HMRC in respect of Job No. 67?

b) The following amounts include VAT at a rate of 17.5%. For each item calculate both the net and VAT amounts.

£47.00
£2.35
£62.60
£3.76

5.4 At the quarter ending 30 June 2010 the following details of purchases, sales and VAT were extracted from the books of Ivy & Co.

	Purchases		Sales	
	Net	VAT	Net	VAT
2010	£	£	£	£
April	50,000	8,750	52,600	9,205
May	42,000	7,350	48,000	8,400
June	55,000	9,625	60,000	10,500

Required:

a) Write up and balance the VAT account in the books of Ivy & Co for the quarter ended 30 June 2010.
b) Explain the significance of the outstanding balance and how it will be cleared.

5.5X The following information was extracted from the books of Mason Motors Ltd for the quarter ended 31 December 2010.

	Purchases		Sales	
	Net	VAT	Net	VAT
2010	£	£	£	£
October	37,600	6,580	75,000	13,125
November	39,400	6,895	62,000	10,850
December	52,000	9,100	68,000	11,900

Required:

a) From the above details write up the VAT account for the quarter ended 31 December 2010.
b) For what period of time must VAT records be kept?

Section B: The ledger

Chapter 6: Business documentation

6.1 Introduction

All businesses and organisations are involved in trading, i.e. the buying and selling of goods and/or services in order to make a profit. The financial transaction of buying and selling involves some very important documents which are used by both the buyer and the seller. The documents have been in general use for many years and are part of an established procedure. Their proper use enables trading to proceed smoothly and, in the event of a dispute between a buyer and a seller, the matter can normally be settled quickly. Since both parties use the same documents they will be dealt with in the sequence normally found in the trading activity.

Exhibit 6.1 Flow of Source Documents

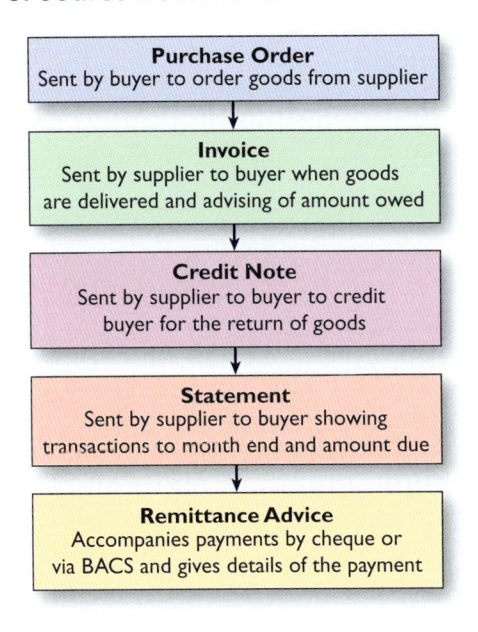

Purchase Order
Sent by buyer to order goods from supplier

↓

Invoice
Sent by supplier to buyer when goods are delivered and advising of amount owed

↓

Credit Note
Sent by supplier to buyer to credit buyer for the return of goods

↓

Statement
Sent by supplier to buyer showing transactions to month end and amount due

↓

Remittance Advice
Accompanies payments by cheque or via BACS and gives details of the payment

Getting started

Edexcel specification
Books of original entry, 1.3, 1.4

After you have studied this chapter you should be able to:

- understand the various documentation used in the buying and selling process
- follow the purchasing process from the purchase order and subsequent invoice
- appreciate the use of a credit note when goods or services are not satisfactory
- understand the need for the supplier to send a statement of account to the purchaser at the end of the month
- appreciate the use of a remittance advice which is usually provided by the purchaser of the goods or services.

6.2 Purchase order

When a business or organisation decides to buy goods or engage the services of another company it usually issues a **purchase order**. This document contains the following information:

- name and address of supplier
- purchase order number
- date of order
- details of the goods or services ordered including part numbers or catalogue references
- quantity required
- delivery date
- authorised signature of a senior member of the company such as the buyer.

PURCHASE ORDER – document prepared by the purchaser and containing details of goods/services required.

It is normally raised by the customer's purchasing office and then sent to the supplier. Once it has been accepted by the supplier a formal contract will exist between the two parties. An example of a purchase order is shown in Exhibit 6.2.

Exhibit 6.2

PURCHASE ORDER

Champion Sports
Fairway,
Leeds, LS2 8BD

Tel: 0131 874428
Ace Sports
High Street
Manchester
MM1 4TC
Please supply

VAT Reg: 811 6571 56
order number: 4355
date: 6 April 2009

quantity	description	unit price £	£
20	Rugby Shirts	12.00	240.00
20	Rugby Shirts	8.00	160.00
			400.00
		VAT at 17.5%	70.00
			470.00

Delivery Required: Early May

T. Smith
Purchasing Manager

> INVOICE – document prepared by the seller and sent to the purchaser giving details of goods/service supplied.

6.3 Invoice

An invoice is a document prepared by the seller whenever it sells goods or provides services on credit. The invoice is usually numbered for easy identification and for filing in a suitable storage system. It contains the following information:

- seller's name and address
- seller's VAT registration number
- purchaser's name and address
- purchaser's order number and date
- date of delivery
- description of goods and services supplied including part number and catalogue reference
- quantity
- price per item
- VAT payable
- total amount due
- terms and conditions of sale.

From a book-keeper's point of view the invoice is one of the most important documents since details of the transaction need to be entered in the books of account of both the seller and the buyer. An example of an invoice is shown in Exhibit 6.3.

Exhibit 6.3

INVOICE

Ace Sports
High Street, Manchester, MM1 4TC
Tel: 0161 229 9229
VAT Reg: 338 9366 72

Champion Sports
Fairway
Leeds
LS2 8BD

invoice number: 3189
date: 4 May 2009

quantity	description	unit price £	£
20	Rugby Shirts	12.00	240.00
20	Rugby Shirts	8.00	160.00
			400.00
		VAT at 17.5%	70.00
			470.00

Terms: 30 days

NB: Chapters 8 and 9 deal with the entry of invoices.

6.4 Credit note

Once the supplier has decided to give credit then a **credit note** will be raised for the value of the returned goods including the applicable amount of VAT. The note will then be sent to the customer.

A credit note is usually printed in red to distinguish it from an invoice and while it contains similar information to that found in an invoice some details will differ. For instance, the customer may only have returned a part of a consignment and this will need to be clearly identified on the credit note.

Again, credit notes are important documents which need to be entered in the books of account as the amount owed by the buyer will be reduced by the amount of the credit note. Chapter 10 deals with the entry of credit notes.

Exhibit 6.4 illustrates a credit note which, as mentioned above, is usually printed in red.

> CREDIT NOTE – document sent to customer showing allowance given by supplier in respect of unsatisfactory goods.

Exhibit 6.4

CREDIT NOTE
Ace Sports
High Street, Manchester, MM1 4TC
Tel: 0161 229 9229
VAT Reg: 338 9366 72

Champion Sports
Fairway
Leeds
LS2 8BD

credit note number: 118
date: 14 May 2009

quantity	description	unit price £	£
2	Rugby Shirts	12.00	24.00
			24.00
		VAT at 17.5%	4.20
			28.20

Reason for credit: Faulty stitching

> **STATEMENT OF ACCOUNT** – document sent to purchasers at month end stating amount outstanding.

6.5 Statement of account

At the end of each month businesses send out a document known as a **statement of account**. This statement contains details of all the customer's transactions during the previous month, starting off with the opening balance outstanding from the previous month plus the amounts owing from the current month's invoices. Any amounts that are paid are deducted together with any credit note allowances. This gives the total amount outstanding which is then due for payment at the end of the month.

On receipt of the statement of account the customer should check the details with their own records to ensure that they agree with the statement. Provided the invoices listed on the statement have been approved for payment, then arrangements will be made to pay the account. An example of a statement is shown in Exhibit 6.5.

Exhibit 6.5

STATEMENT
Ace Sports
High Street, Manchester MM1 4TC
Tel: 0161 229 9229
VAT Reg : 338 9366 72

Champion Sports
Fairway
Leeds
LS2 8BD

Statement date: 31 May 2009
Account No: C 52
Page No: 1

Date	Reference	Debit	Credit	Balance
04/5/09	Invoice No 3189	470.00		470.00
14/5/09	Credit Note No 118		28.20	441.80
	Total outstanding			441.80

Terms: 30 days from date of invoice

6.6 Remittance advice

When payment is made from one business to another it is important that the recipient of the money has details of the payment so that the money may be correctly allocated. Therefore, the business making the payment usually includes a **remittance advice**. This document is rather like a statement, and may in fact be prepared at the same time, in that it shows details of the business's most recent transactions and final balance outstanding which is represented by the accompanying cheque or advice if the payment is made by Bankers' Automated Clearing Service (BACS) – see Chapter 13.

If any invoice has not been paid for any reason it will be left outstanding and can then be queried. A remittance advice is shown in Exhibit 6.6.

> REMITTANCE ADVICE – document which accompanies payment by cheque or via BACS and gives details of the payment.

Exhibit 6.6

REMITTANCE ADVICE

Champion Sports,
Fairway
Leeds, LS2 8BD

Tel: 0131 874428

VAT Reg: 811 6571 56
Remittance Advice: 6/151
Date: 26 June 2009

Ace Sports
High Street
Manchester
MM1 4TC

Account Number: C 52

Date	Invoice or credit note no	Invoice	Credit note	Payment
4/5/2009	3189	470.00		470.00
14/5/2009	118		28.20	(28.20)
			Total Payment	441.80

End of Chapter Checklist

Summary

- Organisations use many documents within their trading activity (see Exhibit 6.1).
- Once the buyer has decided to purchase the goods or services, it issues a 'purchase order' to the supplier. This document details the goods or services required by the purchaser.
- An 'invoice' is then sent by the supplier to the buyer detailing the goods or services supplied and the amount outstanding. The payment details are also included on the invoice.
- When goods are faulty or unsatisfactory they are often returned to the supplier by the buyer who issues a returns note to accompany the goods. The supplier, upon receipt, will then issue the purchaser with a credit note which will give details of the amount to be deducted from the original invoice.
- Usually, at the end of the month, the purchaser receives a statement of account from the supplier detailing the invoices and credit notes issued during the particular period and the total amount outstanding and due for payment. Any payment made should be accompanied by a remittance advice detailing the invoices included in the payment.

Questions

6.1 *Describe the functions of the following documents:*

    a) remittance advice
    b) statement
    c) credit note
    d) invoice

6.2 *You are asked to complete the following sentences:*

    a) Clover Designs Ltd sends a _____ to a supplier to order goods.
    b) An _____ is sent by the seller to the buyer of goods or services to advise them how much is owed for the goods or services supplied.
    c) The supplier sends Clover Designs Ltd a _____ at the end of the month requesting payment of the outstanding invoices.
    d) Clover Designs Ltd sends a _____ with a payment to a supplier to indicate which invoices are being paid.

6.3X *You are employed as an accounts clerk for a printing company. At the end of each month one of your tasks is to prepare statements of account to be sent to customers. Below are details from the account of one of your customers, John Ashley Ltd.*

Invoices sent during the month:

May 2	Invoice No. 7821	£43.75
May 8	Invoice No. 7955	£35.00
May 17	Credit Note No. 304	£10.20
May 23	Invoice No. 8204	£74.50
May 28	Received cheque	£51.50

The amount outstanding on May 1 amounted to £101.50.

You are required to draft a statement of account showing details of how much John Ashley Ltd has outstanding at the end of May.

6.4X *Source documents in accounting are very important.*

    a) Describe the contents of both an invoice and a credit note.
    b) State when each of these would be used.

Section B: The ledger

Chapter 7: Capital and revenue expenditure

7.1 Capital expenditure

Capital expenditure occurs when a business spends money either to:

- buy fixed assets, or
- add to the value of an existing fixed asset.

Included in such amounts should be the costs of:

- acquiring fixed assets
- bringing them into the business
- legal costs of buying premises
- carriage inwards (cost of transport) on machinery/equipment purchased
- any other cost needed to get the fixed asset ready for use, i.e. installation costs.

7.2 Revenue expenditure

Revenue expenditure is expenditure that does not increase the value of fixed assets but is incurred in the day-to-day running expenses of the business.

The difference between capital and revenue expenditure can be seen when considering the cost of purchasing and running a motor vehicle. The expenditure incurred in acquiring the motor vehicle is classed as capital expenditure, whilst the cost of the petrol used to run the vehicle is revenue expenditure. This is because the revenue expenditure is used up in a few days and does not add to the value of the fixed asset.

7.3 Difference between capital and revenue expenditure

The difference between capital and revenue expenditure can be seen more generally in the following table (Exhibit 7.1). Revenue expenditure is the day-to-day running expense of the business and, as such, is chargeable to the trading and profit and loss account. Capital expenditure, in contrast, results in an increase in the fixed assets shown in the balance sheet.

Getting started

Edexcel specification
The ledger 2.7

After you have studied this chapter you should be able to:

- *distinguish between capital expenditure and revenue expenditure*
- *understand that some expenditure is part capital expenditure and part revenue expenditure*
- *understand that if revenue expenditure is incorrectly treated as capital expenditure, or vice versa, then it will affect the profit and the financial statements.*

CAPITAL EXPENDITURE – money spent by a business on buying or adding value to a fixed asset.

REVENUE EXPENDITURE – expenses incurred in the day-to-day running of the business.

Exhibit 7.1

Capital	Revenue
Premises purchased	Rent of premises
Legal charges for conveyancing	Legal charges for debt collection
New machinery	Repairs to machinery
Installations of machinery	Electricity costs of using machinery
Additions to assets	Maintenance of assets
Motor van	Repairs to van
Delivery charges on new assets	Carriage on purchases and sales
Extension costs of new offices	Redecorating existing offices
Cost of adding air-conditioning to room	Interest on loan to purchase air-conditioning

Buying a van is capital expenditure

Repairs to a van is revenue expenditure

7.4 Joint expenditure

In certain cases, an item of expenditure will need dividing between capital and revenue expenditure. Suppose a builder was engaged to carry out some work on your premises, the total bill being £60,000. If two-thirds of this was for improvements and one-third for repair work, then £40,000 should be identified as capital expenditure and added to the value of the business's premises and shown as such in the balance sheet, whilst £20,000 should be charged to profit and loss account as a revenue expense. See Exhibit 7.2.

Exhibit 7.2

Builder's cost for improvements and repairs to premises £60,000

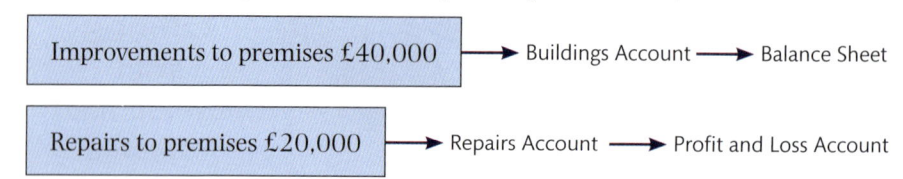

Improvements to premises £40,000 ⟶ Buildings Account ⟶ Balance Sheet

Repairs to premises £20,000 ⟶ Repairs Account ⟶ Profit and Loss Account

7.5 Incorrect treatment of expenditure

If one of the following occurs:

Capital expenditure is incorrectly treated as revenue expenditure, or

Revenue expenditure is incorrectly treated as capital expenditure

Then both the balance sheet figures and trading and profit and loss account figures will be incorrect. This means that the net profit figure will also be incorrect.

If capital expenditure is incorrectly posted to revenue expenditure – for example, if the purchase of a photocopier is posted in error to the stationery account instead of the office equipment account – then:

Net profit would be understated, *and*

Balance sheet values would not include the value of the asset.

If revenue expenditure is incorrectly posted to capital expenditure – for example, if stationery is posted to office equipment instead of the stationery account – then:

Net profit would be overstated, *and*

Balance sheet values would be overvalued.

If the expenditure affects items in the trading account, then the **gross profit** figure will also be incorrect.

7.6 Treatment of loan interest

If money is borrowed to finance the purchase of a fixed asset, then interest will have to be paid on the loan. The **loan interest**, however, is *not* a cost of acquiring the asset but is simply a cost of financing its acquisition. This means that loan interest is revenue expenditure and *not* capital expenditure, and should be charged to the profit and loss account.

7.7 Capital and revenue receipts

When an item of capital expenditure is sold, the receipt is called a capital receipt. Suppose a motor van is bought for £10,000 and sold five years later for £2,000. The £10,000 was treated as capital expenditure; the £2,000 received is treated as a capital receipt.

Revenue receipts are sales or other revenue items, such as rent receivable or commissions receivable.

> CAPITAL RECEIPT – proceeds from the sale of fixed assets.

> REVENUE RECEIPTS – receipts from the sale of goods and services.

End of Chapter Checklist

Summary

- It is important to distinguish between capital and revenue expenditure since this can ultimately affect the recording of profits and balance sheet valuations.
- Expenditure can be either:

Capital expenditure	or	Revenue expenditure
a) Buying fixed assets		a) For daily running expenses of the business
b) Adding value to fixed assets		b) Not adding value to fixed assets

- Some items are both capital and revenue expenditure and the costs involved need to be apportioned carefully.
- If capital expenditure or revenue expenditure is mistaken one for the other, then either gross or net profit (or both) will be incorrectly stated. The value of the assets in the balance sheet will also be affected.
- It is also important to classify capital receipts, i.e. the sale of a fixed asset, from revenue receipts which are accounted for from sales or other revenue items.

Questions

7.1 Newton Data Systems specialises in providing computer services to small commercial businesses. You are required to state whether the following transactions should be classified as capital or revenue expenditure, giving reasons for your choice:

a) Salaries of the computer operators.
b) Purchase of new computer for use in the office.
c) Purchase of computer printout paper.
d) Insurance of all the company's computer hardware.
e) Cost of adding additional storage capacity to main computer to be used by the company.
f) Cost of providing additional security to the company's offices.

7.2 Cairns Engineering Company extracted the following information from their financial records:

	£
a) New stationery and brochures	411
b) Purchase of new pickup truck	18,000
c) Purchase of new lathe	5,200
d) Delivery cost of new lathe	200
e) Electricity (including new wiring £1,800, part of premises improvement)	3,900
f) Wages (including wages of two of Cairns' employees for improvement work on Cairns' premises, amount involved £20,000)	65,000

You are required to:

- State whether each of the items listed above are capital or revenue expenditure and state how much the company has spent on each category for the year.
- Briefly explain the difference between capital and revenue expenditure.

7.3X a) Star Fashions Ltd, which manufactures children's clothing, is planning to purchase a new cutting machine costing £20,000. Would the following items of expenditure be classed as capital or revenue expenditure?

(i) The purchase price of the cutting machine.
(ii) The cost of installing the machine.
(iii) The significant cost of initial training for the staff to operate the new machine.
(iv) The cost of future repairs and maintenance of the machine.

b) If capital expenditure is treated as revenue expenditure, then:

(i) How would the total expenses and the net profit for the period be affected?
(ii) What effect would the error have on the value of the fixed assets in the balance sheet?

End of Chapter Checklist

Questions

7.4 a) For each of the following transactions indicate whether the item is an example of capital expenditure, revenue expenditure, revenue receipt or capital receipt by ticking the correct box in the table below:

Transaction	Capital expenditure	Capital receipt	Revenue expenditure	Revenue receipt
(i) Purchase of computer equipment				
(ii) Cost of new extension to offices				
(iii) Decorating existing offices				
(iv) Sale of old office furniture				
(v) Purchase of goods for resale				
(vi) Rent received for sub-letting building				
(vii) Motor van repairs				

b) Why is it important to distinguish between capital expenditure and revenue expenditure?

7.5X Indicate which of the following would be revenue items and which would be capital items in a wholesale bakery:

a) Purchase of a new motor van.
b) Purchase of replacement engine for existing motor van.
c) Cost of altering interior of new van to increase carrying capacity.
d) Cost of motor taxation licence for new van.
e) Cost of motor taxation licence for existing van.
f) Cost of painting business's name on new van.
g) Repair and maintenance of existing van.

Section B: The ledger

Chapter 8: Books of original entry and ledgers – Sales day book and sales ledger including VAT

Getting started

Edexcel specification
Books of original entry, 1.4, 1.5, 1.6, 1.7 and 1.8
The ledger, 2.11, 2.16

After you have studied this chapter you should be able to:

- appreciate how the books of original entry are used alongside the ledgers
- explain what each book of original entry is used for
- understand the ledgers used in recording financial information
- distinguish between personal and impersonal accounts
- distinguish between a cash sale and a credit sale and the way each are recorded in the books of account
- enter invoices into the sales day book and post transactions to the appropriate accounts in the sales ledger and general ledger
- understand what is meant by trade discount
- understand the importance of internal control
- appreciate the need for credit control over debtors.

BOOKS OF ORIGINAL ENTRY – books where the first entry of a transaction is made.

8.1 Introduction

A small business can satisfactorily maintain the double entry accounts in one account book called the ledger. Larger businesses, however, require a better system due to the amount of financial data that needs recording. Consequently, several books are used to record the many different transactions and these are explained below:

Books of original entry

A **book of original entry** is where a transaction is first recorded. There are separate books for each different kind of transaction, for example sales will be entered in one book, purchases in another book, cash in another book, and so on. All transactions that are entered into the book-keeping system originate from a **source document** such as an invoice, credit note, cheque book stub, paying-in slip, and so on.

In this and the next two chapters we will be looking at invoices and credit notes that are raised when goods or services are sold to customers. Chapter 11 deals with cash books, which illustrates how cash and cheques are recorded in the accounting records.

Types of books of original entry

There are several types of books of original entry these are:

- **Sales Day Book** – for credit sales (this chapter)
- **Purchases Day Book** – for credit purchases (Chapter 9)
- **Sales Returns Day Book** – for sales returns from customers (Chapter 10)
- **Purchase Returns Day Book** – for goods returned to the supplier (Chapter 10)
- **Cash Book** – for receipts and payments of cash (Chapter 11)
- **Petty Cash Book** – for recording small items of expenditure (Chapter 12)
- **Journal** – for other items (Chapter 14).

8.2 The ledgers

Once the details of the transaction have been entered into the books of original entry the information is then entered into the ledgers by means of the double entry system. This procedure is often referred to as **posting**. Sales transactions are posted to the sales ledger, purchase transactions are posted to the purchase ledger and other items are posted to the accounts in the general or nominal ledger (see below).

> LEDGER – a book of account in which all double entry transactions are recorded.

Types of ledgers

The different types of ledgers used are as follows (their alternative names are shown in brackets).

Types of ledger		
Sales ledger (Debtors' ledger)	**Purchase ledger** (Creditors' ledger)	**General ledger** (Nominal ledger)
Shows records of customers' personal accounts.	Shows records of suppliers' personal accounts.	Contains the remaining double entry accounts, such as assets, capital, expenses and income.

Private ledger

Occasionally, a business may keep a private ledger in order to ensure privacy for the proprietor(s) when recording such transactions as their capital and drawings accounts and other similar accounts.

The various books used in accounting are shown linked in Exhibit 8.1

Exhibit 8.1 Diagram of accounting books

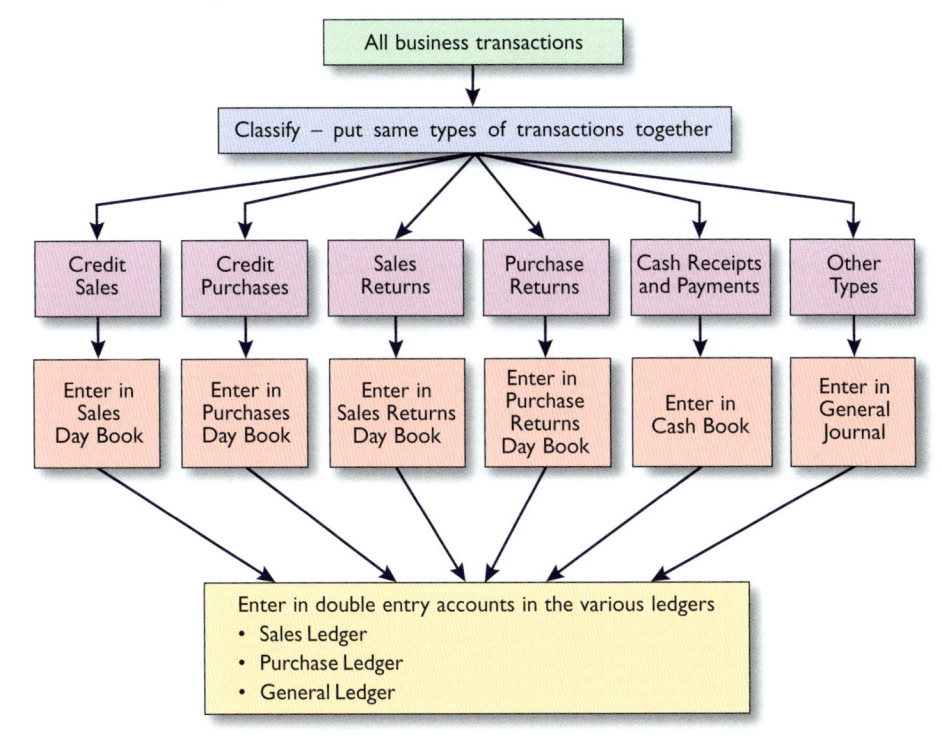

All business transactions
↓
Classify – put same types of transactions together

- Credit Sales → Enter in Sales Day Book
- Credit Purchases → Enter in Purchases Day Book
- Sales Returns → Enter in Sales Returns Day Book
- Purchase Returns → Enter in Purchase Returns Day Book
- Cash Receipts and Payments → Enter in Cash Book
- Other Types → Enter in General Journal

↓

Enter in double entry accounts in the various ledgers
- Sales Ledger
- Purchase Ledger
- General Ledger

PERSONAL ACCOUNTS – accounts for people or businesses, i.e. debtors and creditors.

IMPERSONAL ACCOUNTS – all other accounts except debtors and creditors, i.e. Real and Nominal accounts.

8.3 Classification of accounts

Accounts are divided into **personal accounts** and **impersonal accounts** as follows:

- **Personal Accounts** – these are accounts for people or businesses, i.e. the debtors and creditors.
- **Impersonal Accounts** – these are for all other accounts and are divided into:
  - **Real accounts** are those which deal with possessions of the business, for example, buildings, machinery, computer equipment, fixtures and fittings, stock, etc.
  - **Nominal accounts** are those in which expenses and income are recorded, for example, sales, purchases, wages, electricity, commissions received, etc.

Exhibit 8.2 Classification of accounts

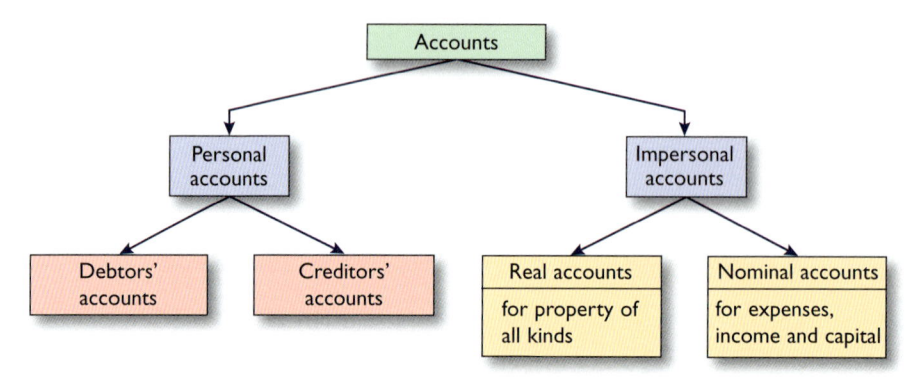

```
                    Accounts
                   /        \
         Personal              Impersonal
         accounts              accounts
         /      \              /        \
   Debtors'   Creditors'   Real accounts   Nominal accounts
   accounts   accounts     for property    for expenses,
                           of all kinds    income and capital
```

8.4 Cash and credit sales

Cash sales

When goods are purchased by a customer who pays for them immediately by cash, then there is no necessity to enter the sale of these goods into the sales day book or the sales ledger since the customer is not in debt to the business. Keeping details of these customers' names and addresses is, therefore, not needed.

Credit sales

In many businesses most of the sales will be made on credit rather than for cash. In fact, the sales of some businesses or organisations will consist entirely of credit sales.

For each credit sale the supplier will send a document to the buyer showing details and prices of the goods sold. This document is known as a sales invoice to the supplier and a purchase invoice to the buyer. An example of an invoice was shown in Exhibit 6.3.

Most businesses have individually designed invoices but inevitably they follow a generally accepted accounting format. All invoices will be numbered and contain the names and addresses of both the supplier and the customer. In Exhibit 6.3 the supplier is Ace Sports and the customer is Champion Sports.

Sales invoices

Once the goods have been despatched to the buyer a **sales invoice** is made out by the supplier. The top copy of the sales invoice is sent to the buyer, further copies are retained by the supplier for use within the organisation. For example, one copy is sent to the accounts department to enable the sale of goods on credit to be recorded in the sales day book and sales ledger, another copy may be passed to the sales department, and so on.

SALES INVOICE – document showing details of goods/services supplied and their cost.

The accounts department then enters all the sales invoices into the Sales Day Book as follows:

- date of the invoice
- customer's name
- goods (net cost)
- VAT charged
- total amount due.

Exhibit 8.3 shows a **sales day book** which illustrates how the invoices are entered, starting with the entry of the invoice shown in Exhibit 6.3. (Assume that the entries are on page 26 of the sales day book.)

SALES DAY BOOK – book of original entry for credit sales.

Exhibit 8.3

	Sales Day Book				(page 26)
Date	Details	Folio	Goods	VAT	Total
2010			£	£	£
May 4	Champion Sports	SL12	400.00	70.00	470.00
May 12	BD Sports Ltd	SL39	84.00	14.70	98.70
May 22	Delta Products	SL125	120.00	21.00	141.00
May 29	Zhang Sports	SL249	178.00	31.15	209.15
			782.00	136.85	918.85
			GL44	GL50	*

Posting credit sales to the sales ledger

Once the invoices have been entered into the sales day book the next step is to post each invoice into the individual customer's account in the sales ledger. At the end of the period, usually each month, the totals in the sales day book are then posted to the 'Sales Account' and 'VAT Account' in the General Ledger. The double entry requirements are now shown below:

- **debit** each customer's account in the sales ledger with the **total** of each individual invoice (the goods go 'IN' to their account)
- **credit** the sales account with total of the 'net sales' (the sales come 'OUT' from the supplier)
- **credit** the VAT account with the total of the 'VAT' charged (this is a liability and is owed to HMRC).

*NB: The 'Total' column in the above sales day book is posted to the 'Sales/Debtors' Control Account' but this will be dealt with in Chapter 15.

An example of posting credit sales

Using the sales day book from Exhibit 8.3 and following the double entry procedures, we will now post each of the invoices to the customers' accounts in the Sales Ledger.

Notice the completion of the folio columns with the sales day book reference in the ledger accounts and the ledger references in the day book.

	Sales Ledger			(page 12)
Dr	Champion Sports Account			Cr
2010		Folio	£	
May 4 Sales		SB 26	470.00	

				(page 39)
Dr	BD Sports Account			Cr
2010		Folio	£	
May 12 Sales		SB 26	98.70	

				(page 125)
Dr	Delta Products Account			Cr
2010		Folio	£	
May 22 Sales		SB 26	141.00	

				(page 249)
Dr	Zhang Sports Account			Cr
2010		Folio	£	
May 29 Sales		SB 26	209.15	

The postings to the General Ledger are shown below:

	General Ledger			(page 44)
Dr	Sales Account			Cr
	2010		Folio	£
	May 31	Credit sales for the month	SB 26	782.00

				(page 50)
Dr	VAT Account			Cr
	2010		Folio	£
	May 31	Sales Day Book: VAT	SB 26	136.85

Exhibit 8.4 Sales invoices – sequence of entries

8.5 Trade discount

Trade discount is an amount deducted by traders from the list price of goods when they are selling to other traders/businesses. Whilst the discount may be allowed to other traders, it is not available to the general public. VAT is always calculated on the net amount of the invoice after deduction of the trade discount, for example:

Using Exhibit 6.3, the invoice from Ace Sports to Champion Sports, let us assume that trade discount is 20%. The cost of the rugby shirts was £400.00 plus VAT; if, however, 20% trade discount is allowed the invoice total would be:

	£
Rugby Shirts	400.00
Less Trade Discount 20%	80.00
	320.00
Add 17.5% VAT (17.5% × £320)	56.00
Invoice total	376.00

It is important to note that trade discount is never shown in the accounts; only the net amount is recorded in the books of account.

NB: Cash Discount is dealt with in Chapter 11.

> TRADE DISCOUNT – a reduction given to a customer when calculating the selling price of goods.

8.6 Credit control

Credit control is a crucial function in any organisation that sells goods and/or provides services on credit. It should follow a strict procedure to monitor that debtors pay in full and on time. A business that does not receive payment when it is due may reach the stage when it can no longer pay its creditors. In these circumstances, it is very likely to fail.

The following procedures will help the business to maintain a positive cash flow situation:

1. Set a credit limit for each debtor which should not be exceeded. The limit should take account of the debtor's payment record and its importance to the business as a customer.

2. As soon as the payment date has been reached, check to see whether payment has been made or not. Failure to pay on time may mean you refuse to supply any more goods unless payment is made quickly.

3. If payment is not made then it may be decided to sue the customer for the debt.

4. Customers should be made aware in the supplier's terms and conditions of the action that may be taken for non-payment by the due date.

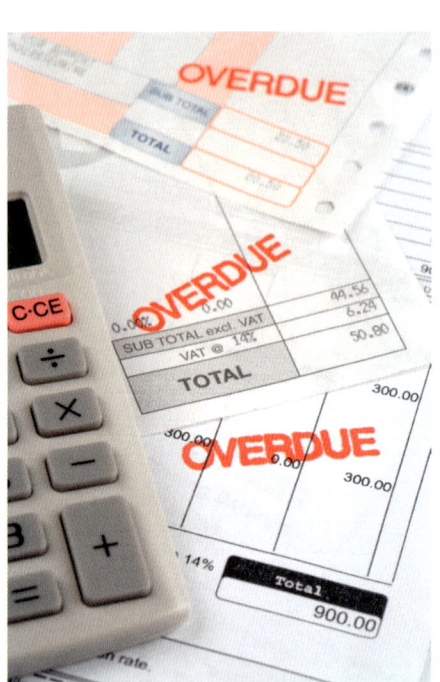

> CREDIT CONTROL – important to ensure customers pay their accounts on time.

Internal checks

- **Sales invoices**

When sales invoices are prepared they should be checked very carefully to ensure that the correct quantity of goods supplied is invoiced at the correct price. This also applies when invoicing services. To avoid the possibility of errors being made, or indeed fraud occurring, it is prudent for one staff member to prepare the invoice, which is then passed to a senior member for checking.

- **Purchase invoices**

Similarly, the purchaser needs to ensure that the goods or services to which the purchase invoice refers have been received and are as the order in terms of price and specification.

> INTERNAL CHECKS – important to check both sales and purchase invoices.

End of Chapter Checklist

Summary

- As the business expands, so does the requirement of additional books to record the accounting transactions.
- Books of original entry are where a transaction is entered first from the source document, i.e. invoice, credit note, etc.
- There are various books of original entry: sales and purchases day books, sales returns and purchase returns day books, cash book, petty cash book and the journal.
- When goods or services are sold for cash it is not necessary to enter the details into the sales day book and sales ledger since the customer is not in debt to the business.
- When goods or services are sold on credit then an invoice will need to be prepared and sent to the buyer. This document is known as a 'sales invoice' to the supplier and a 'purchase invoice' to the buyer. Several copies of the invoice are usually made to enable the accounts staff to record the sale in the books of account and other copies may be required for internal use.
- Sales invoices are a 'source document' and are entered into the sales day book which is a book of original entry. They are then posted to each individual customer's account in the sales ledger (a debit entry). At the end of the period, total net sales will be posted to the sales account (credit entry) and the total VAT to the VAT account (credit entry) in the general ledger.
- Trade discount is a discount or reduction given to a customer when calculating the price of goods. No entry is made of trade discount in the accounting records.
- Credit control within an organisation is important for the business to maintain a healthy cash flow.
- Other areas that are important include the checking of invoices prior to entry in the books of account and before payment is made.

Questions

8.1 For each of the following types of transactions, state the book of original entry, and the ledger and type of account, in which you would enter the transaction:

a) Sales invoice
b) Bank receipt
c) Purchase invoice
d) Bank payment
e) Sales credit note
f) Purchase credit note

8.2X a) State which document(s) would be entered into the following books of original entry:

(i) Purchases day book (iv) Sales day book
(ii) Sales returns day book (v) Purchase returns day book.
(iii) Cash book

b) *Distinguish between personal and impersonal accounts.*

8.3 From the following list of sales invoices you are required to calculate the amount of VAT at 17.5% for each invoice, then enter the invoices in the sales day book using the following columns: 'Goods', 'VAT' and 'Total'.

Post the items to the relevant accounts in the sales ledger and then show the entries in the sales and VAT accounts in the general ledger. Folio references are not required.

2010	Sales Invoices	Net (£)
Nov 2	T Bates	186.00
Nov 3	D Cope	166.00
Nov 9	F Chan	12.00
Nov 11	T Bates	54.00
Nov 13	B Ho	66.00
Nov 18	D Cope	32.00
Nov 23	M Saka & Sons	20.00
Nov 30	F Chan	320.00

End of Chapter Checklist

Questions

8.4X During July 2011 the following credit sales were made by Select Stationery Supplies:

NB: Folio references are not required.

2011	Sales Invoices	Net (£)
July 1	Hall Products	520.00
July 5	Ash & Co	62.00
July 8	K Meakin	18.00
July 14	A Ballearic	110.00
July 19	Hall Products	880.00
July 26	G Huang	126.00
July 28	A Ballearic	42.00
July 31	J Stead	98.00

a) For each of the above invoices calculate the amount of VAT to be charged.

b) Draw up a sales day book and enter the above invoices into the day book for the month of July, using columns for 'Goods', 'VAT' and 'Total'.

c) Open an account for each customer and post the sales invoices from the sales day book to each account in the sales ledger.

d) Post the net sales to the sales account and the total VAT charged to the VAT account in the general ledger.

8.5 *Why is it important to ensure that sales invoices are thoroughly checked before being sent out to customers?*

Section B: The ledger

Chapter 9: Purchases day book and purchase ledger including VAT

9.1 Purchase invoices

When a business purchases goods or services from a supplier on credit they are sent a purchase invoice detailing the goods or services supplied and their price. Just as the sales invoices were entered into the sales day book in the previous chapter, so purchase invoices (source documents) are entered into a purchases day book as follows:

- date of the invoice
- name of the supplier from whom the goods were purchased
- goods (net cost)
- VAT charged
- total amount due.

An invoice is common to both supplier and customer. The invoice shown in Exhibit 6.3 was prepared and sent by Ace Sports to their customer Champion Sports.

- In the accounting records of Ace Sports it is a **sales invoice**.
- In the accounting records of Champion Sports it is a **purchase invoice**.

Another name for the purchases day book is purchases journal.

Exhibit 9.1 shows a **purchases day book** which has several invoices entered for the month of December 2010.

Getting started

Edexcel specification
Books of original entry, 1.4, 1.5, 1.7 and 1.8
The ledger, 2.11

After you have studied this chapter you should be able to:

- appreciate that an invoice is common to both supplier and customer
- enter purchase invoices into the purchases day book
- post the purchases day book to the purchase ledger
- post the purchases day book to the general ledger
- authorise and code invoices for payment.

PURCHASE INVOICE – document received by purchaser showing details of goods/services bought and prices.

PURCHASES DAY BOOK – book of original entry for credit purchases.

Exhibit 9.1

Purchases Day Book						(page 38)
Date	Details	Folio	Goods	VAT	Total
2010			£	£	£
Dec 8	Jarvis & Sons	PL 8	144.00	25.20	169.20
Dec 14	Morton Products	PL 30	280.00	49.00	329.00
Dec 17	K Howard	PL 17	520.00	91.00	611.00
Dec 30	T Joshi	PL 27	72.00	12.60	84.60
			1,016.00	177.80	1,193.80
			GL 43	GL 67	*

***NB:** The 'Total' column' in the above purchases day book is posted to the 'Purchases/Creditors' Control Account' but this will be dealt with in Chapter 15.

PURCHASE LEDGER – a ledger for suppliers' personal accounts.

Posting credit purchases to the purchase ledger

Once the invoices have been entered into the purchases day book the next step is to post each invoice into the individual supplier's account in the purchase ledger. At the end of the period, usually each month, the totals in the purchases day book are then posted to the 'Purchases Account' and 'VAT Account' in the general ledger. The double entry requirements are now shown:

- **credit** each supplier's account in the purchases ledger with the **total** of each individual invoice (the goods have come 'OUT' of each supplier)
- **debit** the purchases account with the total of the 'net purchases' (the purchases have come 'IN' to the purchases account)
- **debit** the VAT account with the total of the 'VAT' column (this is the amount of VAT paid by the business on their purchases which can be offset against the liability incurred on sales).

An example of posting credit purchases

Using the purchases day book from Exhibit 9.1 and following the double entry procedures, we will now post each of the invoices to the suppliers' accounts in the Purchase Ledger.

Again, the folio columns have been completed with the purchases day book page number reference, i.e. P38 in the purchase ledger, whilst the day book shows the ledger references, i.e. PL8.

Purchase Ledger *(page 8)*

Dr			Jarvis & Sons Account			Cr
'IN'					'OUT'	
			2010			£
			Dec 8	Purchases	PB 38	169.20

(page 30)

Dr			Morton Products Account			Cr
'IN'					'OUT'	
			2010			£
			Dec 14	Purchases	PB 38	329.00

(page 17)

Dr			K Howard Account			Cr
'IN'					'OUT'	
			2010			£
			Dec 17	Purchases	PB 38	611.00

(page 27)

Dr			T Joshi Account			Cr
'IN'					'OUT'	
			2010			£
			Dec 30	Purchases	PB 38	84.60

		General Ledger			(page 43)
Dr		Purchases Account			Cr
	'IN'			'OUT'	
2010					
Dec 31	Credit purchases for the month	PB 38	1,016.00		

		VAT Account			(page 67)
Dr					Cr
	'IN'			'OUT'	
2010					
Dec 31	Purchases Day Book: VAT	PB 38	177.80		

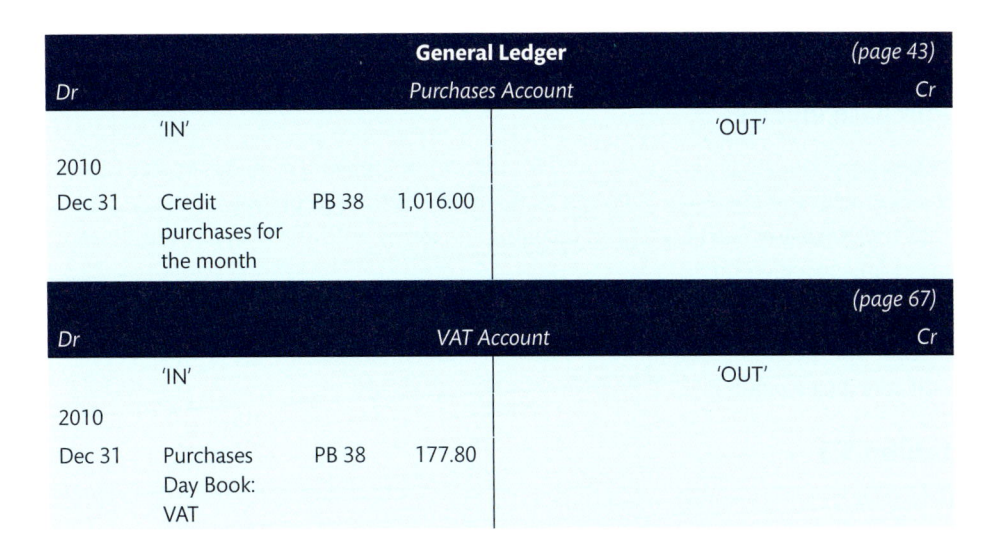

Exhibit 9.2 Purchase invoices – sequence of entries

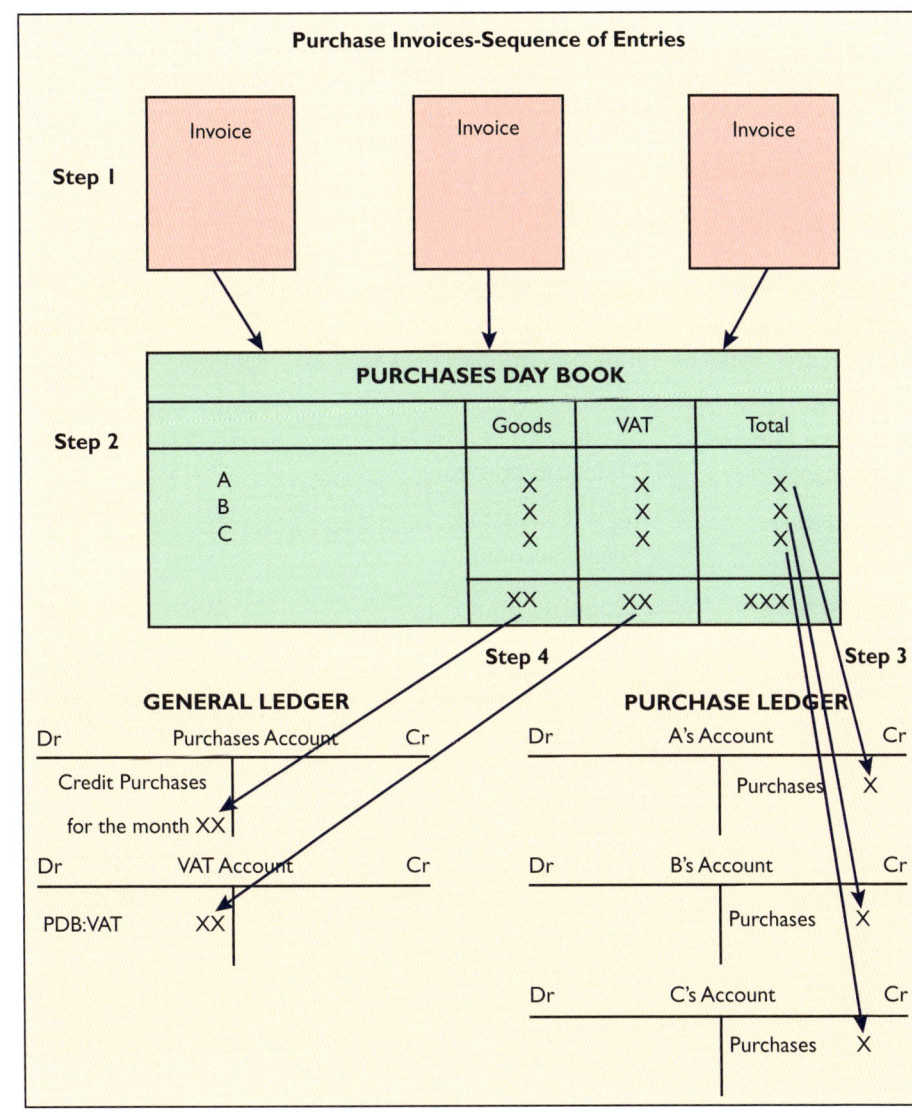

Purchase Invoices-Sequence of Entries

Step 1: Invoice, Invoice, Invoice

Step 2: PURCHASES DAY BOOK

	Goods	VAT	Total
A	X	X	X
B	X	X	X
C	X	X	X
	XX	XX	XXX

Step 4 | Step 3

GENERAL LEDGER

Dr	Purchases Account	Cr
Credit Purchases for the month XX		

Dr	VAT Account	Cr
PDB:VAT XX		

PURCHASE LEDGER

Dr	A's Account	Cr
	Purchases	X

Dr	B's Account	Cr
	Purchases	X

Dr	C's Account	Cr
	Purchases	X

9.2 Authorisation and coding of invoices

Purchase invoices

When purchase invoices are received from various suppliers of goods or services, it is important to check the invoices for accuracy in the calculations and to ensure that the goods invoiced have been received and agree with the relevant purchase order and specifications.

On receipt, each purchase invoice should be numbered, recorded and stamped with an appropriate rubber stamp (see Exhibit 9.3) to enable the invoice to be checked and coded (see below).

Exhibit 9.3

Invoice no.	
Purchase order no.	
Goods received	
Extensions	
Passed for payment	
Code	

Coding of invoices

> CODING OF INVOICES – a process used to code invoices to the supplier or purchaser and relevant account in the general ledger. Mainly used in computerised accounting.

When using a computerised accounting package it is necessary to code invoices prior to entering them in the accounting records. Each invoice will need to be checked as mentioned above and then the appropriate code added to enable the invoice to be charged to the correct account in the general ledger. Examples of code numbers used when operating accountancy packages are as follows:

			Account Number
Purchase Ledger	–	Needhams Ltd account	0211
		Young Bros account	0245
Sales Ledger	–	Biggs & Bentley account	1078
		J Leigh account	1097
General Ledger	–	Capital account	4001
		Purchases account	5001

A register of code numbers allocated to specific accounts must be maintained and updated as necessary. This register may be a manual one or held on the computer system.

End of Chapter Checklist

Summary

- When businesses purchase goods or services from suppliers they are sent a purchase invoice detailing the goods or services and their price. The invoice is used by both buyer and seller: to the buyer it is a purchase invoice and to the seller a sales invoice.
- Only invoices relating to goods bought on credit are entered into the purchases day book which is merely a list showing details of each credit purchase, i.e. the date of purchase, name of supplier, reference number and amount due.
- Each purchase invoice is then posted to the individual customer's account in the purchase ledger (a credit entry).
- At the end of the period, usually a month, the net purchases are posted to the purchases account (debit entry) and the total VAT to the VAT account (debit entry) in the general ledger.
- Many businesses have a system of coding the invoices prior to entry into the books of account. Part of this process involves authorising the invoice for payment.

Questions

NB: *Folio references are not required in the following exercises.*

9.1 As accounts clerk for White Bros one of your tasks is to look after the purchase ledger. During May 2010 the following purchase invoices have been received by the company.

Date	Supplier	Goods	VAT	Total
May 1	Bould & Co	104.00	18.20	122.20
May 7	Harlow & Brown	48.00	8.40	56.40
May 16	T Adams Ltd	234.00	40.95	274.95
May 23	Bould & Co	170.00	29.75	199.75
May 26	JL Products	320.00	56.00	376.00
May 28	Harlow & Brown	62.00	10.85	72.85
May 31	P Yeung Ltd	446.00	78.05	524.05

Required:

a) Draw up a purchases day book, enter the invoices and total up the columns at the end of the month, ensuring that the day book balances.
b) Open accounts for each of the suppliers and post the invoices to the suppliers' accounts in the purchase ledger.
c) Post the totals to the purchases account and VAT account in the general ledger.

9.2 Barkers Electrical Co employs an accounts assistant who is responsible for the purchase ledger. During July 2010 the following purchase invoices were received:

Date	Supplier	Goods	VAT	Total
July 3	Peak Electrical	722.00	126.35	848.35
July 8	Leigh Electrics	84.00	14.70	98.70
July 12	Thomas Motors	274.00	47.95	321.95
July 17	Naik & Sons	160.00	28.00	188.00
July 21	Peak Electrical	158.00	27.65	185.65
July 23	WD Services	46.00	8.05	54.05
July 25	Leigh Electrics	210.00	35.70	245.70
July 30	Naik & Sons	178.00	31.15	209.15

Required:

a) Draw up a purchases day book, enter the invoices and total up the columns at the end of the month, ensuring that the day book balances.
b) Open accounts for each of the suppliers and post the invoices to the suppliers' accounts in the purchase ledger.
c) Post the totals to the purchases account and VAT account in the general ledger.

End of Chapter Checklist

Questions

9.3X You are employed as accounts assistant for a catering company, Tasty Foods, that specialises in providing buffet meals for corporate functions. During August 2010 the following purchase invoices are received:

Date	Supplier	Goods
Aug 1	Barker Foods Ltd	62.00
Aug 6	Fern Bros	48.00
Aug 10	Ash Catering Co	224.00
Aug 14	Barker Foods Ltd	136.00
Aug 22	Farm Produce	98.00
Aug 27	Fern Bros	166.00
Aug 29	Singh & Sons	84.00
Aug 30	Ash Catering Co	366.00

Required:

a) Calculate the amount of VAT and total invoice amount for each of the invoices listed above.
b) Draw up a purchases day book, enter the invoices and total up the columns at the end of the month, ensuring that the day book balances.
c) Open accounts for each of the suppliers and post the invoices to the suppliers' accounts in the purchase ledger.
d) Post the totals to the purchases account and VAT account in the general ledger.

9.4X Why is it important to check invoices prior to payment?

Section B: The ledger

Chapter 10: Sales returns day book and purchase returns day book

10.1 Sales returns (returns inwards) and purchase returns (returns outwards)

When goods are bought and sold it is inevitable that occasionally they are unsuitable for various reasons, such as when the goods are:

- faulty or damaged
- not suitable for the particular requirement, for example, wrong type, size, colour
- part of an incomplete consignment
- subject to an overcharge on the invoice.

When this happens, the supplier will need to make an allowance to the customer to correct the situation.

Note: There are alternative names which are used for sales and purchase returns. Sales returns are often referred to as **returns inwards** while purchase returns are known as **returns outwards.**

10.2 Sales returns (returns inwards) and credit notes

If goods supplied are unsuitable then the supplier will need to rectify the situation. Since the customer (debtor) will have already been sent an invoice at the time the goods were delivered, they will be in debt to the supplier (creditor) for the value of the goods. Therefore, when the supplier makes an allowance for goods that have been returned, or a reduction in price has been agreed, the supplier will issue a **credit note** to the customer (debtor) showing the amount of the agreed reduction. An example of a credit note was shown in Chapter 6, Exhibit 6.4.

Book-keeping entries for sales credit notes

Credit notes are source documents and are listed in a separate day book called the 'Sales Returns Day Book', also called 'Returns Inwards Day Book'. In Chapter 8 we entered various invoices into the Sales Day Book (see Exhibit 8.3). Let us assume that two of our customers had a problem with some of the goods invoiced and were each sent a credit note to rectify the situation. The credit notes have been entered into the Sales Returns Day Book, see below:

Exhibit 10.1

	Sales Returns Day Book				(page 11)
Date	Details	Folio	Goods	VAT	Total
2010			£	£	£
June 11	Champion Sports	SL12	72.00	12.60	84.60
June 24	Zhang Sports	SL249	56.00	9.80	65.80
			128.00	22.40	150.40
			GL45	GL50	*

Getting started

Edexcel specification
Books of original entry, 1.4, 1.5, 1.7 and 1.8
The ledger, 2.11

After you have studied this chapter you should be able to:

- appreciate the need for sales returns and purchase returns to be made when goods or services are unsatisfactory
- enter credit notes in the Sales Returns Day Book and post to the appropriate individual customer's account in the Sales Ledger and the totals to the relevant accounts in the General Ledger at the end of the period
- enter credit notes in the Purchase Returns Day Book and post to the appropriate individual customer's account in the Purchase Ledger and the totals to the relevant accounts in the General Ledger at the end of the period
- appreciate the need for keeping separate returns accounts
- reconcile ledger accounts with suppliers' statements.

SALES RETURNS – goods returned to a business by its customer(s).

77

Posting credit notes to the sales and general ledger

After entering the credit notes into the Sales Returns Day Book, the next step is to post each credit note into the individual customers' accounts. Again, at the end of the month the total 'net goods returned' and 'VAT' are posted to the Sales Returns and VAT accounts in the General Ledger. The book-keeping entries are:

- **credit** each customer's account in the sales ledger with the **total** of each individual credit note
- **debit** the sales returns account with the total of 'net goods returned'
- **debit** the VAT account with the total of the 'VAT' column.

Again, you may find it easier to use 'IN' and 'OUT', i.e. goods returned to us are entered on the 'IN' side of the sales returns account since the goods are coming 'IN' to us, and on the 'OUT' side of the individual customers' accounts as they are sending the goods back to the supplier (OUT).

***NB:** The 'Total' column in the above sales returns day book is posted to the 'Sales/Debtors' Control Account' but this will be dealt with in Chapter 15.

An example of posting sales credit notes

Using the sales returns day book from Exhibit 10.1 and the sales ledger accounts from the example in Chapter 8, we will now post each of the credit notes to the customers' accounts in the Sales Ledger. The folio references have also been completed.

		Sales Ledger				(page 12)
Dr		Champion Sports Account				Cr
2010		Folio	£	2010 Folio		£
May 4 Sales		SB 26	470.00	June 11 Sales returns	SR11	84.60

						(page 249)
Dr		Zhang Sports Account				Cr
2010		Folio	£	2010		£
May 29 Sales		SB 26	209.15	June 24 Sales returns	SR11	65.80

The totals from the Sales Returns Day Book are now posted to the Sales Returns and VAT accounts in the General Ledger.

		General Ledger				(page 44)
Dr		Sales Returns Account				Cr
2010		Folio	£		Folio	£
June 30 Total SRDB		SR11	128.00			

						(page 50)
Dr		VAT Account				Cr
2010		Folio	£	2010	Folio	£
June 30 Total SRDB		SR11	22.40	May 31 Total SDB	SB 26	136.85

10.3 Purchase returns (returns outwards) and purchase credit notes

When a business buys goods for resale but then has to return some of the goods for any of the reasons already discussed they are known as 'purchase returns' or 'returns outwards'. Once the goods have been returned to the supplier they will issue a credit note which is then sent to the customer.

PURCHASE RETURNS – goods returned by the business to its suppliers.

Book-keeping entries for purchase credit notes

The credit notes are listed in a **Purchase returns day book,** also called the 'Returns Outwards Day Book'. In Chapter 9, Exhibit 9.1, various invoices were entered into the Purchases Day Book. Let us assume that some of the goods received from two of the business's suppliers were not to specification ordered and had to be returned. The suppliers then issued credit notes to rectify the situation. The credit notes have been entered below into the Purchase Returns Day Book.

Exhibit 10.2

Purchase Returns Day Book					(page 40)
Date	Details	Folio	Goods	VAT	Total
			£	£	£
2011					
Jan 15	Jarvis & Sons	PL 8	32.00	5.60	37.60
Jan 26	K Howard	PL17	100.00	17.50	117.50
			132.00	23.10	155.10
			GL 45	GL67	*

Posting credit notes to the purchase and general ledger

After entering the credit notes into the Purchase Returns Day Book, the next step is to post each credit note into the individual suppliers' accounts. Again, at the end of the month the total 'net goods returned' and 'VAT' are posted to the Purchase Returns and VAT accounts in the General Ledger. The book-keeping entries are:

- **debit** each individual suppliers' account in the purchase ledger with the **total** of each credit note
- **credit** the purchase returns account with the total of the 'net goods returned'
- **credit** the VAT account with the total of the VAT column.

Using 'IN' and 'OUT', the entries would be as follows: the goods returned by us to the supplier go 'IN' to the suppliers' accounts and come 'OUT' of the purchase returns account.

*NB: The 'Total' column in the purchase returns day book is posted to the 'Purchases/Creditors' Control Account' but this will be dealt with in Chapter 15.

An example of posting purchase credit notes

Using the purchase returns day book from Exhibit 10.2 and the purchase ledger accounts from the example in Chapter 9, we will now post each of the credit notes to the suppliers' accounts in the Purchase Ledger. Again, the folio columns have been completed.

Purchases Ledger (page 8)

Dr — Jarvis & Sons Account — **Cr**

2011		Folio	£	2010		Folio	£
Jan 15	Purchase returns	PR40	37.60	Dec 8	Purchases	PB 38	169.20

(page 17)

Dr — K Howard Account — **Cr**

2011		Folio	£	2010		Folio	£
Jan 26	Purchase returns	PR40	117.50	Dec 17	Purchases	PB 38	611.00

General Ledger (page 45)

Dr — Purchase Returns Account — **Cr**

		Folio	£	2011		Folio	£
				Jan 31	Total PRDB	PR 40	132.00

(page 67)

Dr — VAT Account — **Cr**

2010			£	2011			£
Dec 31	Total PDB	PB 38	177.80	Jan 31	Total PRDB	PR 40	23.10

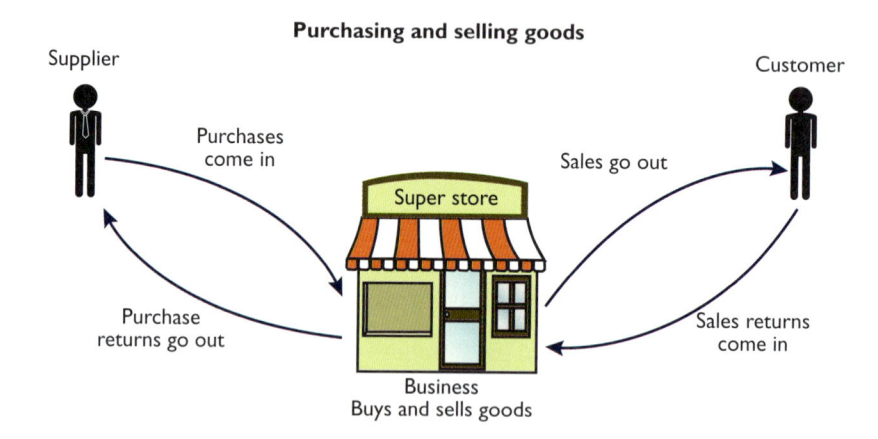

Purchasing and selling goods

Supplier → Purchases come in → Super store (Business Buys and sells goods) → Sales go out → Customer

Purchase returns go out ← Business ← Sales returns come in

10.4 Reasons for keeping separate returns accounts

It is important for businesses to monitor the amount of goods being returned and the reasons why the goods or services were unsuitable. For this reason, separate returns accounts are kept, i.e. 'Sales Returns Account' and 'Purchase Returns Account'. Recording the returns in these accounts would indicate any excessive amounts of sales returns and/or purchase returns which would enable management to investigate the reason.

10.5 Reconciliation of our ledger accounts with suppliers' statements

Statements

At the end of each month a **statement of account** should be sent to each debtor that owes money on the last day of that month. It is really a copy of the debtor's account in the seller's books. It should show:

- the amount owing at start of the month
- the amount of each sales invoice sent to the debtor during the month

- any credit notes sent to the debtor during the month
- cash and cheques received from the debtor during the month
- the amount due from the debtor at the end of the month.

Debtors will use these statements to check that the details shown on the statement agree with their own accounting records. Statements act as a reminder to debtors that money is owed, and will show the date by which payment should be made.

An example of a statement was shown in Chapter 6, Exhibit 6.5.

Reconciliation of suppliers' statements

A supplier's statement of account should be checked against its ledger account in the business's own books and the balance reconciled before making a payment. Sometimes, because of the differences in timing, the balance on a supplier's statement on a certain date can differ from the balance on that supplier's account in the business's purchase ledger. This is similar to a bank statement where the balance may differ from that in the cash book and require the preparation of a **bank reconciliation statement** to reconcile the two balances. This is dealt with in Chapters 11 and 13.

If the balance on the statement of account does differ from the supplier's account in the purchase ledger, then it will be necessary to check the statement against the ledger account and reconcile the difference by preparing a supplier's reconciliation statement. The reasons for the differences in balances may be due to:

- goods returned by the customer but not recorded by the supplier until after the statement of account has been issued
- a supplier sending goods to a customer, together with an invoice, but neither being received by the customer until a later date: the customer is, therefore, unable to enter the invoice in their books of the account until receipt
- payments in transit
- other errors which may be made by either the supplier or buyer when entering data, i.e. transposing figures, or an error in the calculation of a balance where manual accounts are maintained.

Exhibit 10.3 shows the account of C Young Ltd in the purchase ledger of A Hall Ltd and the statement of account received from the supplier, C Young Ltd, together with the reconciliation.

Exhibit 10.3

(a) A Hall Ltd Books

Purchase ledger

C Young Ltd Account

Dr			£				£
2010				2011			
Jan 10	Bank		1,550	Jan 1	Balance b/d		1,550
Jan 29	Returns (1)		116	Jan 6	Purchases		885
Jan 31	Balance c/d		1,679	Jan 18	Purchases		910
			3,345				3,345
				Feb 1	Balance b/d		1,679

(b) Supplier's statement

STATEMENT
C Young Ltd
Market Place, Leeds

Account Name: A Hall Ltd

Date: 31 January 2010
Account Number: H93

		Debit	Credit	Balance
2010		£	£	£
Jan 1	Balance			1,550 Dr
Jan 4	Invoice No 3250	885		2,435 Dr
Jan 13	Payment received		1,550	885 Dr
Jan 18	Invoice No 3731	910		1,795 Dr
Jan 31	Invoice No 3894 (2)	425		2,220 Dr

Comparing the purchase ledger account with the supplier's statement, two differences can be seen:

1 A Hall Ltd returned goods value £116 to C Young Ltd, but it had not received them and recorded them in its books by the end of January.

2 C Young Ltd sent goods to A Hall Ltd, but the latter had not received them and therefore had not entered the £425 in its books by the end of January.

A reconciliation statement can be drawn up by A Hall Ltd as on 31 January 2010.

Reconciliation of Supplier's Statement C Young Ltd as on 31 January 2010

		£	£
Balance per our purchases ledger			1,679
Add Purchases not received by us	(ii)	425	
Returns not received by supplier	(i)	116	
			541
Balance per supplier's statement			2,220

End of Chapter Checklist

Summary

- A credit note is a document issued by a supplier and sent to a purchaser showing details of an allowance made in respect of unsatisfactory goods or services.
- Credit notes are entered into a sales returns day book. The total returns for the month are posted to the debit side of the sales returns account in the general ledger. Each transaction is also posted to the credit side of the individual customers' accounts in the sales ledger.
- A useful hint: goods returned to us are entered on the 'IN' side of the sales returns account and on the 'OUT' side of the individual customers' accounts.
- Purchase credit notes are entered into a purchase returns day book. Each transaction is then posted to the debit side of the individual suppliers' accounts in the purchase ledger. The total returns for the month are posted to the credit side of the purchase returns account in the general ledger.
- A useful hint: the goods returned by us to the supplier go 'IN' to the suppliers' accounts and come 'OUT' of the purchase returns account.
- To monitor the number of returns being made it is important to have separate accounts for sales returns and purchase returns.
- Statements are issued by suppliers and sent to their customers, i.e. their debtors, requesting payment of amounts due. The debtor uses the statement to check the suppliers' records against their own records and if correct will make payment against the statement.
- Statements are also used to reconcile the records of the supplier to those of the customer. Differences are identified and if errors or discrepancies have arisen then amendments can be made.

Questions

10.1 From the list shown below, calculate the amount of VAT, at 17.5%, to be added to the cost of the goods on each of the following invoices and credit notes. Enter up the sales day book and the sales returns day book with columns for 'Goods', 'VAT' and 'Total'. Then post to the customers' accounts in the sales ledger and show the transfers to the general ledger. Folio references are not required.

2010	
June 1	Credit sales to: J Alcock £180; P Twigg £60
June 9	Credit sales to: Bell Products £140; Travis Ltd £330
June 12	Goods returned to us by: J Alcock £12
June 23	Credit sales to: B Seddon £780
June 28	Goods returned to us by: Travis Ltd £50
June 30	Credit sales to: P Twigg £440

10.2 You are to enter up the purchases day book and the purchase returns day book from the details of the invoices and credit notes listed below. Post the items to the creditors' accounts in the purchase ledger and show the transfers to the relevant accounts in the general ledger at the end of the month. Folio references are not required.

2010	
May 1	Credit purchase from J Yau Ltd £120 plus VAT £21
May 5	Credit purchases from the following: S Wager £80 plus VAT £14; Ash Bros £220 plus VAT £38.50
May 9	Goods returned by us to the following: J Yau £30 plus VAT £5.25
May 14	Credit purchase from J Yau Ltd £60 plus VAT £10.50
May 19	Credit purchases from the following: D Wong £300 plus VAT £52.50; Rughani & Co £280 plus VAT £49; Ash Bros £80 plus VAT £14
May 27	Goods returned by us to the following: D Wong £42 plus VAT £7.35
May 31	Credit purchases from: A Davies £56 plus VAT £9.80; Rughani & Co £172 plus VAT £30.10

End of Chapter Checklist

Questions

10.3X Anderson's Ltd is a small company which specialises in fancy goods. At the beginning of the new financial year, 1 January 2010, the following balances appeared in the ledgers:

Sales Ledger	
	£
J Jeynes	1,490 Dr
Marlow (Fancy Gifts)	552 Dr
F & J Shah	780 Dr
Purchase Ledger	
	£
R James & Co	1,600 Cr
Naylor's Ltd	900 Cr
Roberts & Sons	490 Cr

During January 2010 the following transactions took place:

Jan 2	Purchased goods from Naylor's Ltd, £1,300 plus VAT
Jan 5	Purchased goods from Roberts & Sons, £668 plus VAT
Jan 12	Sold goods to Marlow (Fancy Gifts), £656 plus VAT
Jan 13	Received credit note from Naylor's Ltd, £84 plus VAT, in respect unsuitable goods returned by us
Jan 19	Purchased goods from R James & Co, £1,512 plus VAT
Jan 26	Sold goods to J Jeynes, £2,468 plus VAT and Birch Bros £340 plus VAT
Jan 28	Sold goods to F & J Shah, £5,000 plus VAT and Marlow (Fancy Gifts) 380 plus VAT
Jan 30	Received credit note from R James & Co, £400 plus VAT; sent a credit note to Marlow (Fancy Gifts) for £60 plus VAT in respect of faulty goods returned to us

Required:

a) Open personal accounts for the debtors and creditors and enter the outstanding balances at 1 January 2010.
b) Calculate the amount of VAT, at 17.5%, to be charged on the invoices and credit notes shown above and enter them into the day books using columns for 'Goods, 'VAT' and 'Total'.
c) Post the above transactions to the accounts in the sales and purchase ledgers.
d) Post the totals of the day books to the relevant accounts in the general ledger.
e) Balance off all the accounts and explain the significance of the balance on the VAT account.

NB: Folio references are not required.

10.4X As accounts clerk for Perris Design Company one of your tasks is to reconcile the company's suppliers' accounts statements with the purchase ledger accounts prior to payment. Shown below are statements received from two of your suppliers: Bennetts Ltd and Kirkhams Products Ltd.

STATEMENT

BENNETTS LTD
The Green, Brentwood, Essex.
Customer:
    Perris Design Co
    Deansgate
    Ipswich.

Tel: 0277 371832
Date: 31st July 2010
Account No: 47310

Date 2010	Description/reference	Debit £ p	Credit £ p	Balance £ p
30 June	Balance b/f			252.41
2 July	002361 Inv.	84.96		
9 July	003123 Inv.	42.50		379.87
16 July	Cash		252.41	127.46
23 July	003972 Inv.	696.32		823.78
30 July	003989 Inv.	121.50		945.28
AMOUNT NOW DUE				
	Interest will be charged on overdue accounts			

End of Chapter Checklist

Questions

STATEMENT

KIRKHAMS PRODUCTS LTD
Riverside Works, Romford.

Tel: 0708 649685
Date: 31st July 2010

Customer:
Perris Design Co
Deansgate
Ipswich.

Account No: PX/32971

Date	Description/reference	Debit £ p	Credit £ p	Balance £ p
July 1	Balance b/f			1,829.00
July 15	Invoice No. 49606	531.75		
July 13	Invoice No. 822663	54.62		
July 21	Invoice No. 84133	459.23		
July 24	Invoice No. 82624	68.42		2,943.02
July 30	Cash		1,432.30	1,510.72

AMOUNT NOW DUE — N.B. Our Inv. No. 821503 for £396.70 is overdue

Interest will be charged on overdue accounts

The ledger accounts are shown below:

PURCHASE LEDGER

Bennetts Ltd a/c

Dr			£				Cr £
2010				2010			
July 10	Bank		252.41	July 1	Balance b/d		252.41
27	Returns		63.50	2	Purchases		84.96
31	Balance c/d		760.28	9	Purchases		42.50
				23	Purchases		696.32
			1,076.19				1,076.19
				Aug 1	Balance b/d		760.28

Kirkhams Products Ltd

Dr			£				Cr £
2010				2010			
July 30	Bank		1,432.30	July 1	Balance b/d		1,829.00
30	Purchases Returns		54.62	15	Purchases		531.75
31	Balance c/d		1,387.68	13	Purchases		54.62
				21	Purchases		459.23
			2,874.60				2,874.60
				Aug 1	Balance b/d		1,387.68

You are required to prepare reconciliation statements for Bennetts Ltd and Kirkham Products Ltd reconciling the statements with the accounts shown in the purchase ledger.

Section B: The ledger

Chapter 11: Cash books

Getting started

Edexcel specification
Books of original entry, 1.10, 1.11, 1.14, 1.15 and 1.16

After you have studied this chapter you should be able to:

- enter data, including 'contra items' into two- and three-column cash books
- balance off the cash book at the end of a period
- use folio columns for cross-referencing purposes
- understand and complete entries for discounts allowed and discounts received, both in the cash book and at the end of a period, in the discount accounts in the general ledger.

11.1 Cash books

The cash book consists of the cash account and the bank account put together in one book. Initially, these two accounts were shown on different pages of the ledger; now it is easier to put the two sets of account columns together. This means that we can record all money received and paid out on a particular date on the same page.

In the cash book, the debit column for cash is put next to the debit column for bank. The credit column for cash is put next to the credit column for bank.

Drawing up a cash book

In Exhibit 11.1 the cash account and bank account are shown as separate accounts whereas in Exhibit 11.2 the cash and bank accounts are shown together in a cash book. The bank columns contain details of the payments made by cheque and direct transfer from the bank account and the money received and paid into the bank account. The bank will also keep a copy of the customer's account in its own records.

Periodically, or on request, the bank sends a copy of the account in its books to the business. This document is known as a **bank statement**. Upon receipt of the bank statement the business will check the transactions against the bank columns in its own cash book to ensure that there are no errors.

Exhibit 11.1

Dr			Cash Account			Cr
2010		£	2010			£
Aug 2	T Moore	33	Aug 8	Postage		20
Aug 5	K Charles	25	Aug 12	C Potts		19
Aug 15	F Hughes	37	Aug 28	Stationery		25
Aug 30	H Howe	18	Aug 31	Balance c/d		49
		113				113
Sept 1	Balance b/d	49				

Dr			Bank Account			Cr
2010		£	2010			£
Aug 1	Capital	1,000	Aug 7	Rates		105
Aug 3	W P Ltd	244	Aug 12	F Small Ltd		95
Aug 16	K Noone	408	Aug 26	K French		268
Aug 30	H Sanders	20	Aug 31	Balance c/d		1,204
		1,672				1,672
Sept 1	Balance b/d	1,204				

Exhibit 11.2

Dr			Cash	Bank			Cash	Bank
			Cash Book					**Cr**
2010			£	£	2010		£	£
Aug 1	Capital			1,000	Aug 7	Rates		105
Aug 2	T Moore		33		Aug 8	Postage	20	
Aug 3	W P Ltd			244	Aug 12	C Potts	19	
Aug 5	K Charles		25		Aug 12	F Small Ltd		95
Aug 15	F Hughes		37		Aug 26	K French		268
Aug 16	K Noone			408	Aug 28	Stationery	25	
Aug 30	H Sanders			20	Aug 31	Balance c/d	49	1,204
Aug 30	H Howe		18					
			113	1,672			113	1,672
Sept 1	Balances b/d		49	1,204				
'Money in'					'Money out'			

Cash paid into the bank

In Exhibit 11.2 the payments into the bank were cheques received by the business, which were banked on receipt. We must now consider cash being paid into the bank.

1 Let us look at the position when a customer pays his account in cash, and later, a part of this cash is paid into the bank. The receipt of the cash is debited to the cash column on the date received, the credit entry being in the customer's personal account. The cash is subsequently banked as follows:

Effect	Action
a) Asset of cash is decreased	**Credit** the asset account, i.e. the cash account that is represented by the cash column in the cash book.
b) Asset of bank is increased	**Debit** the asset account, i.e. the bank account that is represented by the bank column in the cash book.

Now let us look at an example:

Example 1: On 1 August 2010 cash of £100 is received from M Davies. On 3 August the business banks £80 of the cash, the cash book entries are as follows:

Dr		Cash	Bank			Cash	Bank
		Cash Book					**Cr**
		Cash	Bank			Cash	Bank
2010		£	£	2010		£	£
Aug 1	M Davies	100		Aug 3	Bank	80	
Aug 3	Cash		80				

The details column shows entries against each item, stating the name of the account in which the completion of double entry has taken place. In the above example, on the credit side of the cash book against the cash payment of £80 appears the word 'bank', indicating that the debit entry for £80 is to be found in the bank account. On the debit side of the cash book against the receipt of the £80 appears the word 'cash', indicating that the corresponding entry is in the cash account.

2. Where the whole of the cash received is banked immediately, the receipt can be treated in exactly the same manner as a cheque received, i.e. it can be entered directly in the bank column.

3. If the business requires cash, it may withdraw this from the bank by presenting one of its own cheques to the bank in exchange for cash.

The twofold effect and the action required is:

Effect	Action
a) Asset of bank is decreased	**Credit** the asset account, i.e. the bank column in the cash book.
b) Asset of cash is increased	**Debit** the asset account, i.e. the cash column in the cash book.

This can be shown in the following example:

Example 2: A withdrawal of £75 cash on 1 June 2010 from the bank would appear in the cash book as:

Dr		Cash Book					Cr
		Cash	Bank			Cash	Bank
2010		£	£	2010		£	£
June 1	Bank		75	June 1	Cash	75	

Both the debit and credit entries for this item are in the same book. When this happens it is known as a **contra** item and the letter **'c'** is written in the folio column (see below).

11.2 The use of folio columns

FOLIO COLUMNS – columns used for entering references.

As already illustrated, the 'details column' in an account contains the name of the account in which the other part of the double entry has been entered. Anyone looking through the books should, therefore, be able to locate the other half of the double entry in the ledgers. However, when many books are being used, just to mention the name of the other account may not be enough information to find the other account quickly. More information is needed, and this is given by using **folio columns**.

In each account and in each book being used, a folio column is added, always shown on the left of the money columns. In this column, the name of the other book and the number of the page in the other book where the other part of the double entry was made is stated against each and every entry. The double entry must always be completed before the folio columns are filled in.

An entry for receipt of cash from C Kelly whose account was on page 45 of the sales ledger, and the cash recorded on page 37 of the cash book, would have the following folio column entries:

- in the cash book, the folio column entry would be SL 45
- in the sales ledger, the folio column entry would be CB 37.

Note how each of the titles of the books is abbreviated so that it can fit into the space available in the folio column. Each of any contra items (transfers between bank and cash) being shown on the same page of the cash book would use the letter 'C' (for 'contra') in the folio column. There is no need also to include a page number in this case. The act of using one book as a means of entering transactions into the accounts in order to complete the double entry is known as **posting** the items.

> CONTRA ITEMS – this is where both the debit and credit entries are shown in the cash book.

Advantages of folio columns

The advantages of using folio columns are as follows:

- Folio references are essential to help locate where entries have been posted.
- Entering references in the folio columns confirms the transaction has been posted. Therefore, any item without a reference can easily be identified and subsequently posted.

11.3 Cash discounts

Businesses prefer it if customers pay their accounts quickly since this helps cash flow. A business may accept a smaller sum in full settlement if payment is made within a certain period of time. The amount of the reduction of the sum to be paid is known as a **cash discount**. The term 'cash discount' thus refers to the allowance given for quick payment. It is still called a cash discount even if the account is paid by cheque or by direct transfer into the bank account.

> CASH DISCOUNT – an allowance given for prompt payment of an account owing.

The rate of cash discount is usually stated as a percentage. Full details of the percentage allowed, and the period within which payment is to be made, are quoted on all sales documents by the selling company. A typical period during which a discount may be allowed is one month from the date of the original transaction.

Discounts allowed and discounts received

A business may have two types of cash discounts in its books. These are:

- **Discounts allowed** – cash discounts *allowed* by a business to its customers when they pay their accounts quickly.
- **Discounts received** – cash discounts *received* by a business from its suppliers when they pay their accounts quickly.

We can now see the effect of discounts by looking at two examples.

Example 1: W Clarke owed us £100. On 2 September 2010 he pays by cash within the time limit and the business allows him 5% cash discount.

Therefore, Clarke will pay £100 less £5 cash discount = £95 in full settlement of his account.

Effect	Action
1 Of cash:	
Cash is increased by £95.	**Debit**: Cash Account, i.e. enter £95 in debit column of cash book.
Asset of debtors is decreased by £95.	**Credit**: W Clarke £95.
2 Of discounts:	
Asset of debtors is decreased by £5. (After the cash was paid there remained a balance of £5. As the account has been paid this asset must now be cancelled.)	**Credit**: W Clarke £5.
Expenses of discounts allowed increased by £5.	**Debit**: Discounts allowed account £5.

This means that W Clarke's debt of £100 has now been shown as fully settled, and exactly how the settlement took place has also been shown.

Example 2: A business owed S Small £400 and paid him on 3 September 2010 by cheque within the specified 30 days thus claiming $2\frac{1}{2}$% cash discount. The amount paid to S Small is £400 less £10 cash discount = £390 in full settlement of the account.

Effect	Action
1 Of cheque:	
Asset of bank is reduced by £390.	**Credit:** Bank, i.e. enter in credit bank column, £390.
Liability of creditors is reduced by £390.	**Debit:** S Small's account £390.
2 Of discounts:	
Liability of creditors is reduced by £10. (After the cheque was paid, the balance of £10 remained. As the account has been paid, the liability must now be cancelled.)	**Debit:** S Small's account £10.
Revenue of discounts received increased by £10.	**Credit:** Discounts received account £10.

The accounts in the business's books for both W Clarke and S Small would be as follows:

(page 32)

Dr					Cash Book				Cr
		Folio	Cash	Bank			Folio	Cash	Bank
2010			£	£	2010				£
Sept 2	W Clarke	SL 12	95		Sept 3	S Small	PL 75		390

General Ledger (page 17)

Discounts Allowed Account

Dr								Cr
2010		Folio		£				
Sept 2	W Clarke	SL 12		5				

(page 18)

Discounts Received Account

Dr								Cr
				2010		Folio		£
				Sept 3	S Small	PL 75		10

Sales Ledger (page 12)

W Clarke Account

Dr				£	2010		Folio	£	Cr
2010				100	Sept 2	Cash	CB 32	95	
Sept 1	Balance				Sept 2	Discount	GL 17	5	
				100				100	

Purchase Ledger (page 75)

S Small Account

Dr			Folio	£	2010		Folio	£	Cr
2010									
Sept 3	Bank		CB 32	390	Sept 1	Balance	b/d	400	
Sept 3	Discounts		GL 18	10					
				400				400	

It is an accounting custom to enter the word 'Discount' in the personal accounts, not stating whether it is a discount received or a discount allowed.

Discount columns in the cash book

The discounts allowed account and the discounts received account are in the general ledger, along with all the other revenue and expense accounts. It has already been stated that every effort should be made to avoid too much reference to the general ledger.

In the case of discounts, this is done by adding an extra column on each side of the cash book in which the amounts of discounts are entered. Discounts received are entered in the discounts column on the credit side of the cash book, and discounts allowed in the discounts column on the debit side of the cash book.

The cash book, if completed for the two examples so far dealt with, would appear thus:

Cash Book (page 32)

		Folio	Discount	Cash	Bank			Folio	Discount	Cash	Bank
2010			£	£	£	2010			£	£	£
Sept 2	W Clarke	SL 12	5	95		Sept 3	S Small	PL 75	10		390

To make entries in the discount accounts in the General Ledger

Total of discounts column on receipts side of cash book } Enter on **debit** side of Discounts Allowed Account

Total of discounts column on payments side of cash book } Enter on **credit** side of Discounts Received Account

A worked example

The following is an example of a three-column cash book for the month of May showing the ultimate transfer of the totals of the discounts columns to the discount accounts in the General Ledger.

2010		£
May 1	Balances brought down from April:	
	Cash Balance	29
	Bank Balance	654
	Debtors' accounts:	
	B King	120
	N Campbell	280
	D Shand	40
	Creditors' accounts:	
	U Barrow	60
	A Allen	440
	R Long	100
May 2	B King pays us by cheque, having deducted $2\frac{1}{2}$% cash discount £3	117
May 8	We pay R Long his account by cheque, deducting 5% cash discount £5	95
May 11	We withdrew £100 cash from the bank for business use	100
May 16	N Campbell pays us his account by cheque, deducting $2\frac{1}{2}$% discount £7	273
May 25	We paid expenses in cash	92
May 28	D Shand pays us in cash after having deducted $2\frac{1}{2}$% cash discount	38
May 29	We pay U Barrow by cheque less 5% cash discount £3	57
May 30	We pay A Allen by cheque less $2\frac{1}{2}$% cash discount £11	429

(page 64)

Dr					Cash Book						Cr
		Folio	Discount	Cash	Bank			Folio	Discount	Cash	Bank
2010			£	£	£	2010			£	£	£
May 1	Balances	b/d		29	654	May 8	R Long	PL 58	5		95
May 2	B King	SL 13	3		117	May 11	Cash	C			100
May 11	Bank	C		100		May 25	Expenses	GL 77		92	
May 16	N Campbell	SL 84	7		273	May 29	U Barrow	PL 15	3		57
May 28	D Shand	SL 91	2	38		May 30	A Allen	PL 98	11		429
						May 31	Balances	c/d		75	363
			12	167	1,044				19	167	1,044
Jun 1	Balances	b/d		75	363						

Sales Ledger *(page 13)*

Dr					B King Account				Cr
2010		Folio		£	2010		Folio		£
May 1	Balance	b/d		120	May 2	Bank	CB 64		117
					May 2	Discount	CB 64		3
				120					120

(page 84)

Dr					N Campbell Account				Cr
2010		Folio		£	2010		Folio		£
May 1	Balance	b/d		280	May 16	Bank	CB 64		273
					May 16	Discount	CB 64		7
				280					280

(page 91)

Dr					D Shand Account				Cr
2010		Folio		£	2010		Folio		£
May 1	Balance	b/d		40	May 28	Cash	CB 64		38
					May 28	Discount	CB 64		2
				40					40

Purchases Ledger *(page 15)*

Dr					U Barrow Account				Cr
2010		Folio		£	2010		Folio		£
May 29	Bank	CB 64		57	May 1	Balance	b/d		60
May 29	Discount	CB 64		3					
				60					60

(page 58)

Dr					R Long Account				Cr
2010		Folio		£	2010		Folio		£
May 8	Bank	CB 64		95	May 1	Balance	b/d		100
May 8	Discount	CB 64		5					
				100					100

Dr			A Allen Account				(page 98) Cr
2010		Folio	£	2010		Folio	£
May 30	Bank	CB 64	429	May 1	Balance	b/d	440
May 30	Discount	CB 64	11				
			440				440

General Ledger (page 77)

Dr			Expenses Account				Cr
2010		Folio	£	2010		Folio	£
May 25	Cash	CB 64	92				

General Ledger (page 88)

Dr			Discounts Received Account				Cr
		Folio	£	2010		Folio	£
				May 31	Cash book	CB 64	19

General Ledger (page 88)

Dr			Discounts Allowed Account				Cr
2010		Folio	£			Folio	£
May 31	Cash book	CB 64	12				

Is the above method of entering discounts correct? You can easily check. See the following:

Discounts in Ledger Accounts	Debits		Credits	
		£		£
Discounts received	U Barrow	3	Discounts	
	R Long	5	Received	
	A Allen	11	Account	19
		19		
		£		£
Discounts allowed	Discounts		B King	3
	Allowed		N Campbell	7
	Account	12	D Shand	2
				12

You can see that the double entry has been carried out correctly since equal amounts, in total, have been entered on each side of the account.

VAT and cash discounts

This was dealt with in Chapter 5, Section 5.4.

11.4 Bank overdrafts and the cash book

BANK OVERDRAFT – occurs when more money is drawn out from the bank account than was deposited.

Banks may offer businesses overdraft facilities. This is where the business is allowed to pay more out of their bank account than the money available. When this happens the business takes advantage of the **bank overdraft** which, in effect, is borrowing money on a temporary basis from the bank, provided the bank has agreed to offer this facility. So far, in the examples in this chapter, the bank balances have shown money in the bank, i.e. debit balances brought down, an asset. When the account is overdrawn the balance brought down becomes a credit balance, i.e. a liability.

Taking the cash book shown earlier, suppose that the amount payable to A Allen was £1,429 instead of £429. Thus, the amount in the bank account, £1,044, is exceeded by the amount withdrawn. The cash book would appear as follows:

Dr					Cash Book				Cr
		Discount	Cash	Bank			Discount	Cash	Bank
2010		£	£	£	2010		£	£	£
May 1	Balances b/d		29	654	May 8	R Long	5		95
May 2	B King	3		117	May 11	Cash			100
May 11	Bank		100		May 25	Expenses		92	
May 16	N Campbell	7		273	May 29	U Barrow	3		57
May 28	D Shand	2	38		May 30	A Allen	11		1,429
May 31	Balances c/d			637	May 31	Balances c/d		75	
		12	167	1,681			19	167	1,681
Jun 1	Balance b/d		75		Jun 1	Balance b/d			637

On a balance sheet a bank overdraft will be shown as an item included under the heading Current Liabilities.

11.5 Cash books with columns for VAT

Some businesses use a cash book with columns for VAT received on cash sales and VAT paid on expenses. The following example shows a cash book with columns for VAT and Bank which has been written up for the month of June.

Dr					Cash Book			Cr
		VAT	Bank				VAT	Bank
2010		£	£	2010			£	£
June 1	Balance b/d		4,800.00	June 2	Rates			420.00
June 4	Cash sales	91.00	611.00	June 6	M Lake			1,560.00
June 12	T Hughes		329.40	June 8	Stationery		14.70	98.70
June 18	Cash sales	29.75	199.75	June 18	Rent			500.00
June 23	Belmont Ltd		241.50	June 26	Printing		27.65	185.65
June 30	Cash sales	78.05	524.05	June 30	Balance c/d			3,941.35
		198.80	6,705.70				42.35	6,705.70
July 1	Balance b/d		3,941.55					

At the end of the month the total VAT columns are posted to the VAT account as follows:

Dr				VAT Account			Cr
2010		Folio	£	2010		Folio	£
June 30	Bank (Cash Book)		42.35	June 30	Bank (Cash Book)		198.80

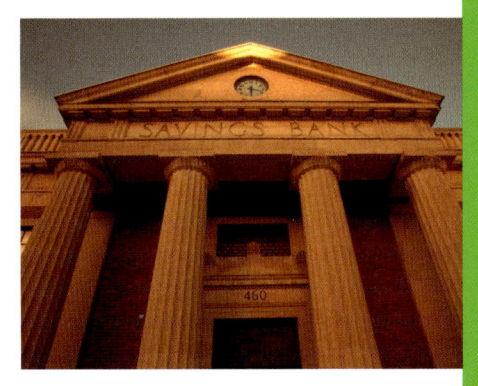

95

End of Chapter Checklist

Summary

- A cash book is made up of a cash account and a bank account put together into one book.
- Entries made on the debit side of the cash book are in respect of monies received via cash, cheque or bank transfer. The money comes 'into' the business and is therefore entered on the debit 'in' side of the cash book.
- Entries made on the credit side of the cash book are in respect of monies paid out via cash, cheque or bank transfer. Money is paid 'out' of the business so entries are made on the 'out' side of the account.
- Folio columns are used in the cash book so that items may easily be traced to other accounts in the ledgers and to provide assurance that the double entries have been completed.
- Cash discounts are given to encourage prompt payment of outstanding accounts.
- Discount allowed is the amount of discount allowed by a business to its customers when their accounts are settled promptly and within the time limit.
- Discount received is when the business's suppliers allow them to deduct discount if they pay the account within the stated terms of trade.
- Discounts allowed and received are entered into the appropriate column in the cash book, totalled at the end of the period, and the amount transferred to the discount accounts in the general ledger.
- Should the balance at the bank go into an overdraft position then the balance brought down will appear on the credit side of the cash book since it is a liability.
- A cash book containing columns for VAT is illustrated.

Questions

11.1 A two-column cash book is to be written up from the following, carrying the balances down to the following month:

2010	
Jan 1	Started business with £4,000 in the bank
Jan 2	Paid for fixtures by cheque, £660
Jan 4	Cash sales £225: Paid rent by cash, £140
Jan 6	T Thomas paid us by cheque, £188
Jan 8	Cash sales paid direct into the bank, £308
Jan 10	J King paid us in cash, £300
Jan 12	Paid wages in cash, £275
Jan 14	J Walters lent us £500 paying by cheque
Jan 15	Withdrew £200 from the bank for business use
Jan 20	Bought stationery paying by cash, £60
Jan 22	We paid J French by cheque, £166
Jan 28	Cash drawings £100
Jan 30	J Scott paid us by cheque, £277
Jan 31	Cash sales £66

11.2X As a trainee accounts clerk at Jepsons & Co you have as one of your tasks the job of entering up the business's cash book at the end of each month.

Required:

From the details listed below, enter up the cash book for February 2010, balance off at the end of the month, and bring the balances down.

2010		£
Feb 1	Balances brought down from January:	
	Cash in hand	76.32
	Cash at bank	2,376.50
Feb 2	Paid electricity bill by cheque	156.00
Feb 4	Paid motor expenses by cash	15.00
Feb 6	Received cheques from the following debtors:	
	D Hill	300.00
	A Jackson	275.00
	H Wardle	93.20
Feb 7	Paid for stationery by cash	3.70

End of Chapter Checklist

Questions

Feb 10	Sold goods for cash	57.10
Feb 12	Paid for purchases from Palmer & Sons by cheque	723.50
Feb 14	Received loan by cheque from D Whitman	500.00
Feb 16	Paid Wright Brothers by cheque for repairs to office machinery	86.20
Feb 17	The proprietor, Stan Jepson, took cash for his own use.	50.00
	He asks you to pay his personal telephone bill by cheque to the post office	140.60
Feb 22	J Smith paid his account by cheque	217.00
Feb 23	Petrol bill paid by cash	21.00
Feb 26	Received cheque for sale of goods	53.00
Feb 27	Bought new photocopier from Bronsons of Manchester and paid by cheque	899.00
Feb 28	Paid monthly salaries by cheque	2,400.00

11.3 *Enter up a three-column cash book from the following details. Balance off at the end of the month, and show the relevant discount accounts as they would appear in the general ledger.*

2010		
May 1	Started business with £6,000 in the bank	
May 1	Bought fixtures paying by cheque, £950	
May 2	Bought goods paying by cheque, £1,240	
May 3	Cash sales £407	
May 4	Paid rent in cash, £200	
May 5	N Morgan paid us his account of £220 by a cheque for £210, we allowed him £10 discount	
May 7	Paid S Thompson & Co £80 owing to them by means of a cheque £76, they allowed us £4 discount	
May 9	S Cooper paid us her account £380 by cheque, we allowed her £20 discount	
May 12	Paid rates by cheque, £410	
May 14	L Curtis pays us a cheque for £115	
May 16	Paid M Monroe his account of £120 by cash £114, having deducted £6 cash discount	
May 20	P Exeter pays us a cheque for £78, having deducted £2 cash discount	
May 31	Cash sales paid direct into the bank, £88	

11.4X *You are to write up a three-column cash book for M Pinero from the details that follow. Then balance off at the end of the month and show the discount accounts in the general ledger.*

2010	
May 1	Balances brought forward:
	Cash in hand £58
	Bank overdraft £1,470
May 2	M Pinero pays further capital into the bank, £1,000
May 3	Bought office fixtures by cheque, £780
May 4	Cash sales, £220
May 5	Banked cash, £200
May 6	We paid the following by cheque, in each case deducting $2\frac{1}{2}$% cash discount: B Barnes £80; T Horton £240; T Jacklin £400
May 8	Cash sales, £500
May 12	Paid motor expenses in cash, £77
May 15	Cash withdrawn from the bank, £400
May 16	Cash drawings, £120
May 18	The following paid us their accounts by cheque, in each case deducting a 5% discount: L Graham £80; B Crenshaw £140; H Green £220
May 20	Wages paid in cash, £210
May 22	T Weiskopf paid us his account in cash, £204
May 26	Paid insurance by cheque, £150
May 28	Banked all the cash in our possession except for £20 in the cash till
May 31	Bought motor van, paying by cheque, £4,920

Section B: The ledger

Chapter 12: Petty cash and the imprest system

Getting started

Edexcel specification
Books of original entry, 1.12, 1.13.

After you have studied this chapter you should be able to:

- understand why businesses use a petty cash book
- make entries in a petty cash book and understand the imprest system
- post the appropriate amounts from the petty cash book to the various accounts in the general ledger at the end of the period.

PETTY CASH VOUCHER – form used for claiming small items of expenditure.

12.1 Petty cash

All businesses frequently incur low-value (petty) items of expenditure for cash by employees. Such expenditure could include train and bus expenses, car mileage expenses, postage, stationery, cleaning materials, hospitality expenses and so on. The petty cash procedure enables staff members who have purchased items or incurred expenditure to readily seek reimbursement provided a receipt is available to verify the expense.

A junior member of the finance department is normally made responsible for making payments to claimants for the cost of purchases or expenditure incurred and for keeping records of the expenses. The float is a sum of money made available for a period, i.e. a month; it is normally held in a lockable box which is additionally held in a lockable safe, desk or cupboard.

To make a claim the staff member must complete a petty cash voucher showing the date and details of the item(s) purchased or expenditure incurred, including VAT if applicable, be signed by the claimant and countersigned by their manager (see Exhibit 12.1). If the claim exceeds the authority of the petty cashier, say £25, then the claim would have to be referred to the senior cashier or accountant.

Exhibit 12.1

Petty Cash Voucher		
	No.	1
	Date	2 May 2009
Description		Amount
	£	p
Stationery (including VAT £ 2.10)	14	10
Signature Ken Boardman		
Authorised Sandra Ashford		

Only items of expenditure approved by the business will be reimbursed unless prior agreement has been received for a particular expense claim.

The petty cash book is a book of original entry since items are first entered, i.e. petty cash vouchers.

12.2 The imprest system

The imprest system simply means topping up a previously established petty cash allowance of, say, £150 by the amount of expenses incurred in a particular period. If the expenses for a period amounted to, say, £145 then the accountant would give the petty cashier £145 to restore the amount back to £150, often called the 'float'. The periods involved can be weekly or, more usually, monthly. Exhibit 12.2 illustrates the above example:

> THE IMPREST SYSTEM – a system for controlling expenditure of small items which are recorded in the petty cash book. Any amount spent in a period is reimbursed to restore the balance to its original amount.

Exhibit 12.2

		£
Period 1	The cashier gives the petty cashier	150
	The petty cashier pays out in the period	145
	Petty cash now in hand	5
	The cashier now gives the petty cashier the amount spent	145
	Petty cash in hand at the end of period	150

The amount of the cash float can be increased if deemed necessary. If it was decided to increase the float to £180 the amount given to the petty cashier would be £145 to reimburse for the expenses incurred + £30 to increase the float = £175. Then with the balance of £5 + £175 = £180 cash float.

> CASH FLOAT – a sum of money (often fixed) held by petty cashier.

12.3 Advantages of imprest system

- The task of maintaining the imprest system is straightforward and can be carried out by a junior member of the finance department.
- The amount of cash can be checked at any time since the cash in the float plus the total of the vouchers should equal the original amount of the float.
- Using the petty cash book means many small value items are eliminated from being entered in the main cash book and ledgers.

12.4 A worked example

A small company offering secretarial services to local businesses incurs the following items of expenditure during May 2010. The items shown in Exhibit 12.3 will initially require entering in the petty cash book.

Exhibit 12.3

2010	
May 1	The petty cashier received a cash float of £200.00 from the cashier
May 2	Stationery £14.10 including VAT £2.10 (see petty cash voucher no. 1)
May 4	Postage stamps, £22.00
May 6	Tea and coffee for office visitors, £8.00
May 9	Travel expenses, £16.00
May 10	Computer disks, £12.80 including VAT £1.91
May 12	Postage on parcel, £3.60
May 15	Office cleaner, £25.00
May 22	Milk for office, £4.20
May 25	Received £6.00 from Anita Kerr, office manager, for personal photocopying*
May 27	Office cleaner, £25.00
May 27	Cleaning materials, £4.40 plus VAT 77p, total spent £5.17
May 31	Travel expenses, £23.00
May 31	The cashier reimbursed the petty cashier with the amount spent during the month

Each of the above items will have had a petty cash voucher completed by the person who had incurred the expenditure on behalf of the business. For illustration purposes just one petty voucher is shown, petty cash voucher no. 1 (see previous Exhibit 12.1).

Receipts

Occasionally, a member of staff may wish to purchase stamps from the petty cashier or perhaps have some photocopying done for their own personal use. In these cases, the petty cashier will issue a receipt to the staff member for the amount received. For example, see Exhibit 12.4.

Exhibit 12.4

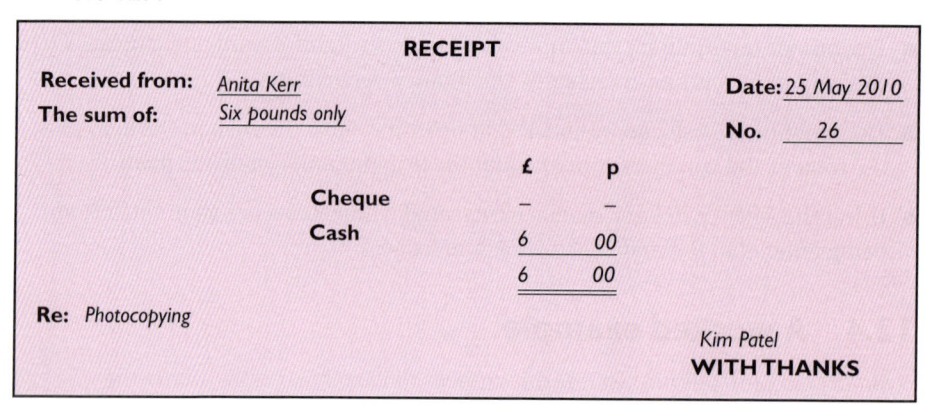

RECEIPT

Received from: Anita Kerr   Date: 25 May 2010
The sum of: Six pounds only   No. 26

	£	p
Cheque	–	–
Cash	6	00
	6	00

Re: Photocopying

Kim Patel
WITH THANKS

PETTY CASH BOOK – a cash book used for recording small items of expenditure.

The above items of expenditure and the receipt are entered in the petty cash book, as illustrated in Exhibit 12.5.

Exhibit 12.5

Petty Cash Book

Receipts £ p	Date	Details	Voucher Number	Total £ p	VAT £ p	Postage £ p	Cleaning £ p	Travel Expenses £ p	Stationery £ p	Sundry Expenses £ p
200.00	2010 May 1	Cash	CB 19							
	May 2	Stationery	1	14.10	2.10				12.00	
	May 4	Postage stamps	2	22.00		22.00				
	May 6	Tea, coffee	3	8.00						8.00
	May 9	Travel expenses	4	16.00				16.00		
	May 10	Computer disks	5	12.80	1.91				10.89	
	May 12	Postage on parcel	6	3.60		3.60				
	May 15	Office cleaner	7	25.00			25.00			
	May 22	Milk	8	4.20						4.20
6.00	May 25	Anita Kerr Photo-copying	26							
	May 27	Office cleaner	9	25.00			25.00			
	May 27	Cleaning materials	10	5.17	0.77		4.40			
	May 31	Travel expenses	11	23.00				23.00		
				158.87	4.78	25.60	54.40	39.00	22.89	12.20
	May 31	Balance	c/d	47.13	GL 17	GL 19	GL 29	GL 44	GL 56	GL 60
206.00				206.00						
47.13	June 1	Balance	b/d							
152.87	June 1	cash	CB 22							

Reimbursement equals the total amount spent in May 2010 (£158.87 − £6.00 Receipt ∴ £152.87 reimbursed)

Total amount spent in May 2010

Entering the petty cash book

On 1 May the petty cashier received £200.00 cash float from the senior cashier for the month.

The cashier would enter this item on the credit side of the cash book, the money comes 'OUT' of the bank. The debit entry is now shown on the 'Receipts' side of the petty cash book, the money comes 'INTO' the petty cash. Note that the folio reference 'CB 19' (Cash Book page 19) is also entered to cross-reference the entry. Each petty cash voucher is then entered in date order as follows:

- Enter the date.
- Enter the details of each payment.
- A voucher number is then given to each petty cash voucher and entered on the voucher itself and in the 'voucher number' column.
- The total amount of the expenditure incurred is then entered in the 'total' column.
- The expenditure is then analysed into an appropriate expense column.
- If VAT has been incurred then the VAT amount is entered in the 'VAT' column and the remaining expense in the appropriate column. For example, the petty cash voucher shown in Exhibit 12.1 is for stationery amounting to £14.10. In the total column £14.10 is entered, £2.10 is then entered in the VAT column and the cost of the stationery £12.00 is then entered in the stationery column.

For any money received from the sale of sundry items to a member of staff, as in the case of Anita Kerr who had some personal photocopying, then the receipt of the cash is entered into the 'receipts' column, in this example £6.00. The date, details and receipt number are also entered in the appropriate columns.

The petty cash book now requires balancing off at the end of the month as follows:

- Add up the 'total' column.

- Add up each of the expense columns. The total of all the expense columns added together should now equal the amount shown in the 'total' column. In Exhibit 12.5 this would be:

	£ p
VAT	4.78
Postage	25.60
Cleaning	54.40
Travel expenses	39.00
Stationery	22.89
Sundry expenses	12.20
Total	158.87

- The petty cashier now needs to calculate the amount of money needed to restore the imprest to £200.00 for the beginning of the next period. This is as follows:

	£ p
Amount of float at beginning of May	200.00
Money received during month, Anita Kerr – Photocopying	6.00
	206.00
Less Amount spent (see above)	158.87
Cash in hand at 31 May 2010	47.13
Amount of float	200.00
Less Cash in hand at 31 May 2010	47.13
Cash required to restore the imprest	152.87

- The balance of cash in hand at 31 May 2010, £47.13, is now entered into the petty cash book and shown as *Balance c/d*, £47.13 (see Exhibit 12.5).

- The *receipts* and *total* columns are now added up and should equal each other, i.e. £206.00. These totals should be shown on the same line and both double underlined.

- The *Balance b/d* on 1 June, £47.13, is now entered in the *receipts* column and underneath that entry the amount received from the cashier to restore the imprest £152.87 is also entered.

The double entry for each of the expense columns is now carried out:

- The total of each expense column is debited to the expense account in the general ledger.

- The folio number of each general ledger account is entered under each of the expense columns in the petty cash book. This enables cross-referencing and also means that the double entry to the ledger account has been completed.

The double entry for all the items in Exhibit 12.5 appears as Exhibit 12.6.

Exhibit 12.6

Cash Book (Bank column only)			(page 19)
Dr			Cr
	2010	Folio	£
	May 1 Petty Cash	PCB 31	200.00
	June 1 Petty Cash	PCB 31	152.87

General Ledger (page 17)

Dr	VAT Account		Cr
2010	Folio	£	
May 31 Petty Cash	PCB 31	4.78	

(page 19)

Dr	Postages Account		Cr
2010	Folio	£	
May 31 Petty Cash	PCB 31	25.60	

(page 29)

Dr	Cleaning Account		Cr
2010	Folio	£	
May 31 Petty Cash	PCB 31	54.40	

(page 44)

Dr	Travel Expenses Account		Cr
2010	Folio	£	
May 31 Petty Cash	PCB 31	39.00	

(page 56)

Dr	Stationery Account		Cr
2010	Folio	£	
May 31 Petty Cash	PCB 31	22.89	

(page 60)

Dr	Sundry Expenses Account		Cr
2010	Folio	£	
May 31 Petty Cash	PCB 31	12.20	

Paying creditors from petty cash

Occasionally a creditor may be paid their account out of the petty cash. If this arises then the book-keeping entries would be to record the payment in the petty cash book, using a column headed 'ledger accounts', then post the item to the debit side of the creditor's account in the purchase ledger. This transaction is very rare and would only occur where the item to be paid was small, or if a refund was made out of petty cash to a customer who may have overpaid their account.

End of Chapter Checklist

Summary

- The petty cash book is used to record transactions involving small items of expenditure incurred by a member of staff on behalf of the business.
- Claims for reimbursement of monies paid out are usually made on a petty cash voucher. The voucher should be completed with all the relevant details, together with receipt (if possible), duly signed and authorised.
- The imprest system is used by many businesses to operate the petty cash system. Here, an amount of money called a 'float' is given to the petty cashier at the start of a period. At the end of the period the amount spent by the petty cashier is reimbursed by the cashier to restore the imprest to its original amount.
- There are several advantages to using the petty cash book and the imprest system, the main one being able to check the float at any point in time since the amount of cash in hand, together with the total of the expenditure to date, should equal the amount of the original float.
- The petty cash book is totalled, balanced off and the double entry completed with postings to the ledger accounts in the general ledger.

Questions

12.1 You are employed as accounts clerk for Kitchen Designs who operate their petty cash using the imprest system. At the beginning of the month there was £18.52 left in the petty cash box from the previous month and the cashier has just given you £131.48 to restore the imprest to £150.

The following are details of the petty cash vouchers that have been authorised for payment by the cashier for June 2010, together with a receipt for cash received.

2010		£
June 1	Window cleaner	10.00
June 3	Postage stamps	7.60
June 4	Petrol (including VAT of £5.60)	37.60
June 6	Stationery (including VAT of £1.45)	9.75
June 10	Sold stamps to Jean Ford £2.00 (receipt no. 8)	
June 14	Office cleaner	20.00
June 16	Parcel postage	1.35
June 19	Magazine for reception (no VAT)	3.00
June 21	Computer disks (including VAT £1.05)	7.95
June 23	Petrol (including VAT £2.10)	14.10
June 27	Refreshments for clients (no VAT)	4.20
June 29	Office cleaner	20.00

Required:

a) Enter the balance brought down and the cash received to restore the imprest in the petty cash book on 1 June 2010. The petty cash book page number to use is 47.
b) Enter the above transactions into the petty cash book using the following analysis columns, VAT, postage, cleaning, motor expenses, stationery and sundry expenses. The next petty cash voucher number is 32.
c) Total and balance the petty cash book on 30 June and bring down the balance on 1 July. Show the amount of cash received from the cashier to restore the imprest to £150.

End of Chapter Checklist

Questions

12.2X Singh's Estate Agents operates their petty cash system on a fortnightly basis using the imprest system with a float of £100. On 15 October 2010 there was an opening balance of £23.40 in the petty cash box. The following transactions took place during the period commencing 15 October 2010.

2010		£
Oct 15	Received amount from cashier to restore the imprest	
Oct 16	Envelopes and files (including VAT of £1.66)	11.66
Oct 17	Tea, coffee and milk (for clients no VAT)	7.40
Oct 18	Special delivery postage charges	8.60
Oct 20	Office cleaner	20.00
Oct 20	Cleaning materials (including VAT 63p)	4.23
Oct 23	Received £3.50 from M Lloyd for sale of stationery (receipt no. 78)	
Oct 23	Postage stamps	7.00
Oct 25	Travel expenses	16.42
Oct 27	Flowers for reception (including VAT 74p)	4.99
Oct 28	Photocopying paper (including VAT £1.40)	9.40
Oct 31	Received cash to restore imprest	

Required:

a) Enter the balance brought down and the cash received to restore the imprest on 15 October 2010 in the petty cash book page 33.
b) Enter the above transactions into the petty cash book using the following analysis columns, VAT, postage, cleaning, travel expenses, stationery and sundry expenses. The next petty cash voucher number is 80.
c) Total and balance the petty cash book on 31 October and bring down the balance on 1 November. Show the amount of cash received from the cashier to restore the imprest to £100.

Section B: The ledger

Chapter 13: Bank reconciliation statements

Getting started

Edexcel specification
Books of original entry, 1.17, 1.18, 1.19, 1.20, 1.21.

After you have studied this chapter you should be able to:

- understand the reason for preparing bank reconciliation statements
- reconcile cash book balances with bank statement balances
- understand how bank overdrafts affect the reconciliation process
- make necessary entries in the account for dishonoured cheques.

TIP – tick items which are the same in both the cash book and on the bank statement prior to preparing the bank statement.

13.1 Introduction

In Chapter 11 we saw how businesses record monies coming into and out of the business in their cash book. Cash items being entered in the 'cash columns' and cheques and other bank items being entered in the 'bank columns'.

The bank will also be recording the business's bank transactions in the business account at the bank. If all the items entered in the cash book were the same as those entered in the business's account with the bank, then obviously the bank balance per the business's books and the bank balance per the bank's books would equal each other. However, this is not usually the case.

There may be items paid into or out of the business bank account which have not been recorded in the cash book. There may also be items entered in the cash book which have not yet been entered in the bank's records of the business's account. To see if any differences have occurred between the two balances the business will need to obtain a bank statement from the bank and use this to compare its own records with those of the bank.

Banks usually issue bank statements to their customers on a regular basis but one can easily be obtained from the bank on request.

An example of a cash book and a bank statement is shown in Exhibit 13.1. The items that are the same in both sets of records have been ticked off.

Exhibit 13.1

Dr		Cash Book (bank columns only)				Cr
2010			£	2010		£
June 1	Balance b/f		80	June 27	I Gordon ✓	35
June 28	D Jones ✓		100	June 29	B Tyrell	40
				June 30	Balance c/d	105
			180			180
July 1	Balance b/d		105			

	Bank Statement	Dr	Cr	Balance
2010			£	£
June 26	Balance b/f	✓		80 Cr
June 28	Banking	✓	100	180 Cr
June 30	I Gordon	✓	35	145 Cr

By comparing the cash book and the bank statement, it can be seen that the only item that was not in both of these was the cheque payment to B Tyrell for £40 in the cash book. The reason why this was entered in the cash book but does not appear on the bank statement is simply one of timing. The cheque had been posted to B Tyrell on 29 June, but there had not been time for it to be banked by Tyrell and passed through the banking system. Such a cheque is called an **unpresented cheque** because it has not yet been presented at the drawer's bank.

To prove that the balances are not different because of errors, even though they show different figures, a bank reconciliation statement is drawn up. This statement compares the cash book balance with the bank statement balance, see Exhibit 13.2 below:

> UNPRESENTED CHEQUE – cheque issued by a business that has not been presented to the bank by the payee (person receiving the cheque).

Exhibit 13.2

Bank Reconciliation Statement as at 30 June 2010	
	£
Balance in hand as per cash book	105
Add unpresented cheque: Tyrell	40
Balance in hand as per bank statement	145

It would have been possible for the bank reconciliation statement to have started with the bank statement balance:

> BANK RECONCILIATION STATEMENT – a statement prepared to explain the difference(s) between the cash book balance and the bank statement balance.

Bank Reconciliation Statement as at 30 June 2010	
	£
Balance in hand as per bank statement	145
Less unpresented cheque: Tyrell	40
Balance in hand as per cash book	105

Note that in the business's cash book the bank account shows a debit balance brought down because, to the business, the balance is an asset since it is money in the bank. In the bank's book, however, the account will show a credit balance because it is a liability, i.e. money owed by the bank to the business.

13.2 Reasons for differences in balances

We can now look at a more complicated example in Exhibit 13.3. Similar items in both cash book and bank statement are shown ticked.

Exhibit 13.3

Dr				Cash Book				Cr
2009			£	2009				£
Dec 27	Total b/f		2,000	Dec 27	Total b/f			1,600
Dec 29	J Potter	✓	60	Dec 28	J Jacobs	✓		105
Dec 31	M Johnson (B)		220	Dec 30	M Chatwood (A)			15
				Dec 31	Balance c/d			560
			2,280					2,280
2010								
Jan 1	Balance b/d		560					

Bank Statement				
2009		Dr £	Cr £	Balance £
Dec 27	Balance b/f			400 Cr
Dec 29	Cheque ✓		60	460 Cr
Dec 30	J Jacobs ✓	105		355 Cr
Dec 30	BGC*: L Shaw (C)		70	425 Cr
Dec 30	Bank charges (D)	20		405 Cr

*BGC = bank giro credit (see below)

BANK GIRO CREDIT (BGC) – method used by businesses to pay creditors, wages etc. Funds are automatically transferred from the business's bank account to each of the respective people or organisations.

The balance brought forward in the bank statement, £400, is the same figure as that in the cash book, i.e. totals b/f £2,000 – £1,600 = £400. However, items (A) and (B) are in the cash book only, and (C) and (D) are on the bank statement only. We can now examine these in detail:

A This is a cheque recently sent by us to Mr Chatwood. It has not yet passed through the banking system nor been presented to our bank, and it is therefore an **unpresented cheque**.

B This is a cheque banked by us on our visit to the bank when we collected the copy of our bank statement and would not appear on the statement.

C A customer, L Shaw, has paid his account by instructing his bank to pay us direct through the banking system, instead of paying by cheque. Such a transaction is usually called a **bank giro credit (BGC)**.

D A charge of £20 for operating our account has been taken by the bank.

Having taken into account the above differences, the bank reconciliation statement can now be prepared. As mentioned earlier, there are two ways in which a bank reconciliation statement can be prepared. You can start with the balance as shown in the cash book (see first example shown below) or, alternatively, you can start with the balance as shown on the bank statement in the second example. Examining bodies may ask for either method of presentation so ensure you know exactly which method is required before attempting the question.

Bank Reconciliation Statement as at 31 December 2009	£	£
Balance in hand as per cash book		560
Add Unpresented cheque – M Chatwood	15	
Bank giro credits	70	
		85
		645
Less Bank charges	20	
Bank lodgement not yet entered on bank statement	220	
		240
Balance in hand as per bank statement		405

A bank reconciliation statement starting with the bank statement balance appears thus:

Bank Reconciliation Statement as at 31 December 2009

	£	£
Balance in hand as per bank statement		405
Add Bank charges	20	
Bank lodgement not yet entered on bank statement	220	
		240
		645
Less Unpresented cheque – M Chatwood	15	
Bank giro credits	70	
		85
Balance in hand as per bank statement		560

13.3 Updating the cash book before attempting a reconciliation

> TIP – it is usually easier to update the cash book before preparing the bank reconciliation statement.

The easiest way to prepare a reconciliation statement is to complete any outstanding entries in the cash book first. All items on the bank statement will then be entered in the cash book. This means that the only differences will be items in the cash book but not on the bank statement. At the same time, any errors found in the cash book by such a check can be corrected.

Although this would be the normal way to proceed before actually drawing up a bank reconciliation statement, it is possible that an examiner will ask you not to do it this way. If, in Exhibit 13.3, the cash book had been written up before the bank reconciliation statement was drawn up, then the cash book and the reconciliation statement would have appeared as follows:

Exhibit 13.4

Dr			Cash Book			Cr
2009		£	2009			£
Dec 27	Total b/fwd	2,000	Dec 27	Total b/fwd		1,600
Dec 29	J Potter	60	Dec 28	J Jacobs		105
Dec 31	M Johnson	220	Dec 30	M Chatwood		15
Dec 31	BGC:		Dec 31	Bank charges*		20
	L Shaw*	70	Dec 31	Balance c/d		610
		2,350				2,350
2010						
Jan 1	Balance b/d	610				

*Adding items that appear in the bank statement but not in the cashbook.

Bank Reconciliation Statement as on 31 December 2009

	£
Balance in hand as per cash book	610
Add Unpresented cheque – M Chatwood	15
	625
Less Bank lodgement not yet entered on bank statement	220
Balance in hand as per bank statement	405

> **BANK OVERDRAFT** – what results when more money has been paid out of the business bank account than was paid in.

13.4 Bank overdrafts

When there is a bank overdraft (shown by a credit balance in the cash book), the adjustments needed for reconciliation work are opposite to those needed for a debit balance.

Exhibit 13.5 shows a cash book, and a bank statement showing an overdraft. Only the cheque for G Cumberbatch (A) £106 and the cheque paid to J Kelly (B) £63 need adjusting. Work through the reconciliation statement in Exhibit 13.5 and then compare it with the reconciliation statement in Exhibit 13.4.

Exhibit 13.5

Dr				Cash Book (bank columns only)			Cr
2009			£	2009			£
Dec 5	I Howe		308	Dec 1	Balance b/f		709
Dec 24	L Mason		120	Dec 9	P Davies		140
Dec 29	K King		124	Dec 27	J Kelly (B)		63
Dec 31	G Cumberbatch (A)		106	Dec 29	United Trust		77
Dec 31	Balance c/f		380	Dec 31	Bank charges		49
			1,038				1,038
				2010			
				Jan 1	Balance b/f		380

Bank Statement				
		Dr	Cr	Balance
2009		£	£	£
Dec 1	Balance b/f			709 O/D
Dec 5	Cheque		308	401 O/D
Dec 14	P Davies	140		541 O/D
Dec 24	Cheque		120	421 O/D
Dec 29	K King: BGC		124	297 O/D
Dec 29	United Trust: Standing order	77		374 O/D
Dec 31	Bank charges	49		423 O/D

Note: On a bank statement an overdraft is often shown with the letters O/D following the amount; or else it is shown as a debit balance, indicated by the letters DR after the amount.

Bank Reconciliation Statement as at 31 December 2009	
	£
Overdraft as per cash book	380
Add Bank lodgements not on bank statement	106
	486
Less Unpresented cheque	63
Overdraft per bank statement	423

Now compare the reconciliation statements in Exhibits 13.4 and 13.5. This comparison reveals the following:

	Exhibit 13.4 Balances	Exhibit 13.5 Overdrafts
Balance/Overdraft per cash book	XXXX	XXXX
Adjustments		
Unpresented cheque	PLUS	LESS
Banking not entered	LESS	PLUS
Balance/Overdraft per bank statement	XXXX	XXXX

Adjustments are, therefore, made in the opposite way when there is an overdraft.

13.5 Dishonoured cheques

When a cheque is received from a customer and paid into the bank, it is recorded on the debit side of the cash book. It is also shown on the bank statement as a deposit to the bank. However, at a later date, it may be found that the customer's bank will not pay us the amount due on the cheque. The cheque is therefore worthless. It is known as a **dishonoured cheque**.

DISHONOURED CHEQUE – a cheque that the bank refuses to honour (pay).

There are several possible reasons for this. As an example, let us suppose that K King gave us a cheque for £5,000 on 20 May 2010. We banked it, but on 25 May 2010 our bank returned the cheque to us. Typical reasons are:

- King had put £5,000 in figures on the cheque, but had written it in words as five thousand five hundred pounds. You will have to give the cheque back to King for amendment or reissue.

- King had put the year 2009 on the cheque instead of 2010. Normally, cheques are considered 'stale' six months after the date on the cheque; in other words, the banks will not pay cheques over six months' old.

- King simply did not have sufficient funds in his bank account. Suppose he had previously only got a £2,000 balance and yet he has given us a cheque for £5,000. His bank has not allowed him to have an overdraft. In such a case, the cheque would be dishonoured. The bank would write on the cheque 'refer to drawer', and we would have to get in touch with King to see what he was going to do to settle his account.

In all of these cases the bank would show the original banking as being cancelled, by showing the cheque paid out of our bank account. As soon as this happens, they will notify us. We will then also show the cheque being cancelled by a credit in the cash book. We will then debit that amount to this account.

When King originally paid his account, our records would appear as:

Dr			K King Account			Cr
2010			£	2010		£
May 1	Balance b/d		5,000	May 20	Bank	5,000

Dr			Bank Account			Cr
2010			£			
May 20	K King		5,000			

After recording the dishonoured cheque, the records will appear as:

Dr			K King Account			Cr
2010		£	2010			£
May 1	Balance b/d	5,000	May 20	Bank		5,000
May 25	Bank: cheque dishonoured	5,000				

Dr			Bank Account			Cr
2010		£	2010			£
May 20	K King	5,000	May 25	K King: cheque dishonoured		5,000

In other words, King is once again shown as owing us £5,000.

13.6 Some other reasons for differences in balances

Another reason why there is a difference between the balance in the business's cash book and the balance on the bank statement is because of standing orders and direct debits, i.e.

- **Direct debits** – where the business gives permission for an organisation to collect amounts owing direct from its bank account. This method is often used to pay mortgages, insurance premiums, etc.
- **Standing order** – instructions given by a business to a bank to pay specified amounts at given dates.

Both these payments are made by the bank on behalf of the business and, until the bank statement is received by the business, the entries into cash book may not have been made.

A more recent method of making payments is by **Bankers' Automated Clearing Service (BACS)** which is a computerised payment transfer system that is a very popular way of paying creditors, wages and salaries. Again, details of such payments will appear on the bank statement and will require entry into the business's cash book.

End of Chapter Checklist

Summary

- The purpose of preparing a bank reconciliation statement is to find the reasons for the differences in the balance as shown in the cash book with that shown on the bank statement.
- By preparing a bank reconciliation statement errors may be identified in either the cash book or the bank statement and be corrected.
- The differences in balances may be caused by quite valid reasons and are usually due to the varying dates that the business and the bank record monies paid into and out of their particular account.
- It is easier to write up the cash book first before preparing a bank reconciliation statement since the only differences will be items in the cash book but not on the bank statement.
- If the account is showing a bank overdraft then preparing a bank reconciliation statement is the opposite to when there is a balance in the account.
- If a business receives a cheque from a customer which ultimately 'bounces', i.e. insufficient funds in the account for the cheque to be paid, then it is known as a 'dishonoured cheque'.

Questions

13.1 The following are extracts from the cash book and the bank statement of J Roche.

You are required to:

a) write the cash book up to date, and state the new balance as on 31 December 2010
b) draw up a bank reconciliation statement as on 31 December 2010.

Dr			Cash Book			Cr
2010		£	2010			£
Dec 1	Balance b/f	1,740	Dec 8	A Dailey		349
Dec 7	T J Masters	88	Dec 15	R Mason		33
Dec 22	J Ellis	73	Dec 28	G Small		115
Dec 31	K Wood	249	Dec 31	Balance c/d		1,831
Dec 31	M Barrett	178				
		2,328				2,328

Bank Statement					
			Dr	Cr	Balance
2010			£	£	£
Dec 1	Balance b/f				1,740
Dec 7	Cheque			88	1,828
Dec 11	A Dailey		349		1,479
Dec 20	R Mason		33		1,446
Dec 22	Cheque			73	1,519
Dec 31	BGC: J Walters			54	1,573
Dec 31	Bank charges		22		1,551

13.2X The following are extracts from the cash book and bank statement of Preston & Co:

Dr			Cash Book		Cr
2010		£	2010		£
Dec 1	Balance b/d	8,700	Dec 6	S Little	1,745
Dec 7	T J Blake	440	Dec 14	L Jones	165
Dec 20	P Dyson	365	Dec 21	E Fraser	575
Dec 30	A Veale	945	Dec 31	Balance c/d	9,155
Dec 31	K Woodburn	300			
Dec 31	N May	890			
		11,640			11,640

Bank Statement					
			Dr	Cr	Balance
2010			£	£	£
Dec 1	Balance b/d				8,700
Dec 9	Cheque			440	9,140
Dec 10	S Little		1,745		7,395
Dec 19	L Jones		165		7,230
Dec 20	Cheque			365	7,595
Dec 26	BGC: P Todd			270	7,865
Dec 31	Bank charges		110		7,755

You are required to:

a) write up the cash book and state the new balance on 31 December 2010
b) prepare a bank reconciliation statement as on 31 December 2010.

End of Chapter Checklist

Questions

13.3 The bank statement for James Baxter for the month of March 2010 is as follows:

Bank Statement		Dr	Cr	Balance
2010		£	£	£
Mar 1	Balance b/d			2,598 O/D
8	L Young	61		2,659 O/D
16	Cheque		122	2,537 O/D
20	A Duffy	104		2,641 O/D
21	Cheque		167	2,474 O/D
31	BGC: A May		929	1,545 O/D
31	Standing Order: Oak plc	100		1,645 O/D
31	Bank charges	28		1,673 O/D

The cash book for March 2010 is shown below:

Dr		Cash Book					Cr
2010			£	2010			£
Mar 16	N Morris		122	Mar 1	Balance b/d		2,598
" 21	P Fraser		167	" 6	L Young		61
" 31	Southern Elect. Co		160	" 30	A Duffy		104
" 31	Balance c/d		2,804	" 30	C Clark		490
			3,253				3,253

You are required to:

a) write the cash book up to date
b) draw up a bank reconciliation statement as at 31 March 2010.

13.4X Following is the cash book (bank columns) of E Flynn for December 2010:

Dr		Cash Book				Cr
2010		£	2010			£
Dec 6	J Hall	155	Dec 1	Balance b/d		3,872
Dec 20	C Walters	189	Dec 10	P Wood		206
Dec 31	P Miller	211	Dec 19	M Roberts		315
Dec 31	Balance c/d	3,922	Dec 29	P Phillips		84
		4,477				4,477

The bank statement for the month is:

		Dr	Cr	Balance
2010		£	£	£
Dec 1	Balance			3,872 O/D
Dec 6	Cheque		155	3,717 O/D
Dec 13	P Wood	206		3,923 O/D
Dec 20	Cheque		189	3,734 O/D
Dec 22	M Roberts	315		4,049 O/D
Dec 30	Mercantile: Standing order	200		4,249 O/D
Dec 31	K Saunders: BGC		180	4,069 O/D
Dec 31	Bank charges	65		4,134 O/D

You are required to:

a) write the cash book up to date to take the necessary items into account
b) draw up a bank reconciliation statement as on 31 December 2010.

End of Chapter Checklist

Questions

13.5 On 2 May 2010 Real Kitchen Suppliers received the following bank statement for the previous month ending 30 April 2010

National Bank plc
31 The Street
Marchtown

Account Name: Real Kitchen Suppliers
Account Number: 3419765
Date: 30 April 2010

STATEMENT OF ACCOUNT

Date	Detail	Payments £	Receipts £	Balance £
2010				
01 April	Balance B/f			8,000Cr
06 April	Cheque 10123	1,200		6,800Cr
08 April	Cash Paid In		800	7,600Cr
12 April	Cheque 10124	1,300		6,300Cr
14 April	Cash Paid In		550	6,850Cr
15 April	Direct Debit: Marchtown Council	250		6,600Cr
20 April	Direct Debit: Premier Insurance	80		6,520Cr
21 April	Cash Paid In		650	7,170Cr
22 April	Credit Transfer from M Bell		1,230	8,400Cr
28 April	Bank Charges	120		8,280Cr
30 April	Dishonoured Cheque	280		8,000Cr

(a) Explain the meaning of the term 'dishonoured cheque' shown in the bank statement.

(b) You are required to update the cash book (below) with the relevant items from the bank statement. and bring down the balance at the end of the month.

TIP – you may find it useful to copy the cash book into your notes before completing the question.

Date	Narration	£	Date	Narration	£
Apr 1	Balance b/d	8,000	Apr 2	F Bashir (10123)	1,200
Apr 7	Sales Banked	800	Apr 8	M Tyler (10124)	1,300
Apr 13	Sales Banked	550	Apr 15	H Joshi (10125)	1,250
Apr 20	Sales Banked	650			
Apr 30	Sales Banked	750			

(c) Prepare a bank reconciliation statement as at 30 April 2010.

IGCSE

Section B: The ledger

Chapter 14: The journal

Getting started

Edexcel specification
Books of original entry, 1.2
The ledger, 2.21, 2.22, 2.23, 2.24.

After you have studied this chapter you should be able to:

- identify the journal as an original book of entry used for entering a range of different transactions which are then posted to the ledger(s)
- distinguish between different types of errors and correct them using the journal
- understand that there are two types of error, those that affect the agreement of the trial balance and those that do not
- understand the reason for using a suspense account
- create a suspense account in order to balance the trial balance
- correct errors using a suspense account
- appreciate the advantages of using a journal
- appreciate how to tackle journal questions in an examination.

THE JOURNAL – a book used to record rare or exceptional transactions that do not appear in other books.

JOURNAL ENTRIES – prepare a 'Workings Sheet' and work out the double-entry entries prior to preparing the journal entry.

14.1 Introduction

In earlier chapters we have seen that transactions are initially entered into a book of original entry. For example, all items involving receipts and payments are recorded in the cash book, while purchase and sales invoices are entered in the respective day books. Occasionally, it is necessary to record a much less common transaction like writing off a bad debt or perhaps when a debtor is unable to pay an outstanding invoice and offers a fixed asset in full settlement of the debt. It is just as important to record these transactions as it is to record the purchase of goods for resale. Such a transaction is therefore recorded in another book of original entry – the **journal**.

The layout of the journal is shown below:

	The Journal			
Date		Folio	Dr	Cr
	The name of the account to be debited.			
	The name of the account to be credited.			
	The narrative.			

The journal is like a diary in which details of less common transactions are recorded prior to them being posted to the ledger accounts. For each transaction the following details are recorded:

- the date
- the name of the accounts to be debited and credited and the amount
- a description and explanation of the transaction, which is known as the **narrative**
- a reference number for the source document as proof of the transaction.

Typical uses of the journal

Some of the less common transactions that the journal may be used for include:

- the purchase and sale of fixed assets on credit
- writing off bad debts
- other items: adjustments to any of the entries in the ledgers
- the correction of errors.

14.2 Writing up journal entries

Since many students have difficulty in preparing journal entries it may be useful to approach journal entries slightly differently, as follows. Initially, the entries are shown as they would appear in the double entry accounts; secondly, the journal entries for the transaction is shown. We will now look at a few examples, including the folio references.

Purchase and sale of fixed assets

Example 1: A drilling machine was bought on credit from Toolmakers Ltd for £5,500 on 1 July 2010 (ignore VAT). This transaction involves the acquisition of a new drilling machine, which is an asset, but the business also incurs a liability since it has purchased the machine on credit from Toolmakers Ltd. The double entry for this transaction is a debit entry in the Machinery Account since the business has acquired an asset and a credit entry in Toolmakers Ltd account to whom the money is owed, a liability.

		General Ledger		
Dr		Machinery Account		(Folio GL 1) Cr
2010		Folio	£	
Jul 1	Toolmakers	PL 55	5,500	

		Purchase Ledger		
Dr		Toolmakers Ltd Account		(Folio PL 55) Cr
		2010	Folio	£
		Jul 1 Machinery	GL 1	5,500

These entries now need recording in the journal. Remember, the journal is simply a kind of diary, not in account form but in ordinary written form. It says which account has to be debited, which account has to be credited, then gives a narrative that simply describes the nature of the transaction. For the transaction above, the journal entry will appear as follows:

	The Journal			
Date	Details	Folio	Dr	Cr
			£	£
2010				
Jul 1	Machinery	GL 1	5,500	
	Toolmakers	PL 55		5,500
	Purchase of milling machine on credit, purchase invoice no. 7/159			

Example 2: A business purchases a laptop for use by one of the managers at a cost of £600 plus VAT at 17.5% on credit from Newdata Systems Ltd on 12 May 2010.

This example includes VAT so initially it is necessary to calculate the VAT payable, i.e. 17.5% of £600 = £105 making the total amount owing to Newdata Systems Ltd £705. Assuming that the business is registered for VAT and can claim a refund of the VAT paid, the double entry required to enter this transaction would be:

		General Ledger		
Dr		Computer Equipment Account		(Folio GL 16) Cr
2010		Folio	£	
May 12	Newdata Systems Ltd	PL 37	600	
Dr		VAT Account		(Folio GL 73) Cr
2010		Folio	£	
May 12	Newdata Systems Ltd	PL 37	105	

Purchase Ledger				
Dr	Newdata Systems Ltd Account		(Folio PL 37)	Cr
		2010	Folio	£
		May 12 Journal	GL 16	705

Note that the cost of purchasing the laptop is £600 since the business will be able to reclaim £105 VAT. If, however, the business had not been registered for VAT, then the cost would be £705.

The journal entries to record the above transaction are as follows:

The Journal				
Date	Details	Folio	Dr	Cr
2010			£	£
May 12	Computer equipment	GL 16	600	
May 12	VAT	GL 73	105	
May 12	Newdata Systems Ltd	PL 37		705
	Purchase of laptop on credit, purchase invoice no. 7890			

Example 3: Some office furniture which is no longer required is sold for £300 on credit to K King on 2 July 2010. Here, again, it is not difficult to work out what entries are needed in the double entry accounts. They are as follows:

Sales Ledger				
Dr	K King Account		(Folio SL 79)	Cr
2010		Folio	£	
Jul 2	Office Furniture	GL 51	300	

General Ledger				
Dr	Office Furniture Account		(Folio GL 51)	Cr
		2010	Folio	£
		Jul 2 K King	SL 79	300

These are shown in journal form as follows:

The Journal				
Date	Details	Folio	Dr	Cr
2010			£	£
Jul 2	K King	SL 79	300	
	Office furniture	GL 51		300
	Sale of some office furniture no longer required – see letter ref: CT 568			

Writing off bad debts

Example 1: A debt of £78 owing to us from H Mander is written off as a bad debt on 31 August 2010. In this example we need to cancel the amount owing by crediting H Mander's account and, since a bad debt is an expense, the bad debts account will need to be debited.

In double entry form this is shown as:

General Ledger

Dr				Bad Debts Account			(Folio GL 16) Cr
2010			Folio	£			
Aug 31	H Mander		SL 99	78			

Sales Ledger

Dr				H Mander Account			(Folio SL 99) Cr
2010		Folio	£	2010		Folio	£
Aug 1	Balance	b/d	78	Aug 31	Bad debts	GL 16	78

The journal entry showing the same transaction would be as follows:

The Journal

Date	Details	Folio	Dr	Cr
2010			£	£
Aug 31	Bad debts	GL 16	78	
	H Mander	SL 99		78
	Debt written off as bad. See letter in file 9/8906			

Correction of errors

Most errors are discovered after a period of time has elapsed. Once identified, they need to be corrected properly via the journal and not by crossing out items or tearing a page out of a ledger or even using correcting fluid. If the latter was permitted then there is more risk of fraudulent transactions taking place.

There are errors that do not affect the agreement of the trial balance and some errors that will lead to the trial balance failing to balance. First of all, we will look at errors that **do not** affect the trial balance agreement.

14.3 Errors not affecting trial balance agreement

The following types of error do not affect the balancing of the trial balance as mentioned previously in Chapter 4, Sections 4.5 and 4.6:

1 **Errors of commission** – arise when a correct amount is entered in the books, but in the wrong person's account.

   Example: D Long paid us £50 by cheque on 18 May 2010. The transaction is correctly entered in the cash book, but it was entered by mistake in the account for D Longman. This means that there had been both a debit of £50 and a credit of £50. It has appeared in the personal account as:

Dr	D Longman Account			Cr
	2010			£
	May 18	Bank		50

119

The error was found on 31 May 2010. This will now have to be corrected and requires two entries:

Accounting entries	Explanation
Debit D Longman's account	To cancel out the error on the credit side of that account
Credit D Long's account	To enter the amount in the correct account

The accounts will now appear thus:

Dr			D Longman Account			Cr
2010			£	2010		£
May 31	D Long: Error corrected		50	May 18	Bank	50

Dr			D Long Account			Cr
2010			£	2010		£
May 1	Balance b/d		50	May 31	Cash entered in error in D Longman's account	50

The journal entry will be thus:

The Journal			
		Dr	Cr
2010		£	£
May 31	D Longman	50	
	D Long		50
	Cheque received . . . entered in wrong personal account, now corrected.		

2 Errors of principle – is where a transaction is entered in the wrong type of account. For instance, the purchase of a fixed asset should be debited to a fixed asset account. If in error it is debited to an expense account, then it has been entered in the wrong type of account.

Example: The purchase of a motor car for £9,500 by cheque on 14 May 2010 has been debited in error to a motor expenses account. In the cash book it is shown correctly. This means that there has been both a debit of £9,500 and a credit of £9,500.

It will have appeared in the expense account as:

Dr		Motor Expenses Account		Cr
2010		£		
May 14	Bank	9,500		

The error is detected on 31 May 2010 and is corrected. To do so, two entries are needed:

Accounting entry	Explanation
Debit Motor Car account	To put the amount in the correct account
Credit Motor Expenses account	To cancel the error previously made in the Motor Expenses account

The accounts then are corrected thus:

Dr		Motor Expenses Account				Cr
2010			£	2010		£
May 14	Bank		9,500	May 31	Motor car error corrected	9,500

Dr		Motor Car Account			Cr
2010			£		
May 31	Bank: entered originally in Motor expenses		9,500		

The journal entries to correct the error will be shown as:

	The Journal		
		Dr	Cr
2010		£	£
May 31	Motor car	9,500	
	Motor expenses		9,500
	Correction of error where by purchase of motor car was debited to motor expenses account.		

3 **Errors of original entry** – this occurs where an original amount is incorrect and is then entered in double entry.

Example: Sales of £150 to T Higgins on 13 May 2010 have been entered as both a debit and a credit of £130. The accounts would appear thus:

Dr		T Higgins Account			Cr
2010			£		
May 13	Sales		130		

Dr		Sales Account			Cr
			2010		£
			May 13	Sales day book (part of total)	130

The error is found on 31 May 2010. The entries to correct it are now shown:

Dr		T Higgins Account			Cr
2010			£		
May 13	Sales		130		
May 31	Sales: error		20		

Dr		Sales Account			Cr
			2010		£
			May 13	Sales day book	130
			May 31	T Higgins: error corrected	20

To correct the error, the journal entries will be:

The Journal		Dr	Cr
2010		£	£
May 31	T Higgins	20	
	Sales		20
	Correction of error. Sales of £150 had been incorrectly entered as £130.		

4 **Errors of omission** – this is where transactions are not entered into the books at all.

Example: The purchase of goods from T Hope for £250 on 13 May 2010 had been completely omitted from the books. The error was found on 31 May 2010. The entries to correct it will be as follows:

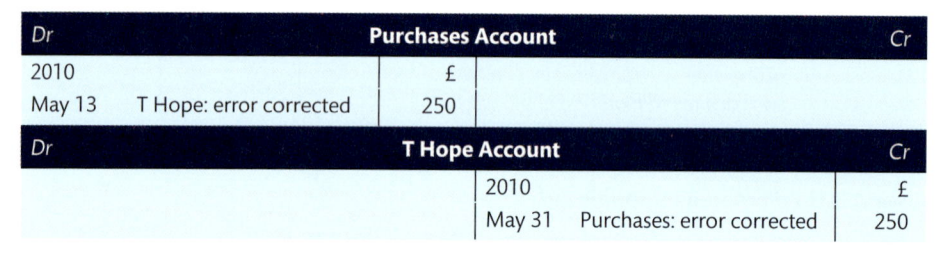

Dr	Purchases Account		Cr
2010		£	
May 13	T Hope: error corrected	250	

Dr	T Hope Account		Cr
		2010	£
		May 31 Purchases: error corrected	250

The journal entries to correct the error will be:

The Journal		Dr	Cr
2010		£	£
May 31	Purchases	250	
	T Hope		250
	Correction of error. Purchase omitted		

5 **Compensating errors** – These errors are where they cancel each other out.

Example: Let us take a case where incorrect totals had purchases of £7,900 and sales of £9,900. The purchases day book adds up to be £100 too much. In the same period, the sales day book also adds up to be £100 too much.

If these were the only errors in our books, the trial balance totals would equal each other. Both totals would be wrong – they would both be £100 too much – but they would be equal. In this case, the accounts would have appeared as follows:

Dr	Purchases Account		Cr
2010		£	
May 31	Purchases	7,900	

Dr	Sales Account		Cr
		2010	£
		May 31 Sales	9,900

When corrected, the accounts will appear as:

Dr			Purchases Account			Cr
2010		£	2010			£
May 31	Purchases	7,900	May 31	The Journal: Error corrected		100

Dr			Sales Account			Cr
2010		£	2010			£
May 31	The Journal: error corrected	100	May 31	Sales		9,900

Journal entries to correct these two errors will be thus:

The Journal			
		Dr	Cr
2010		£	£
May 31	Sales	100	
	Purchases		100
	Correction of compensating errors.		
	Totals of both purchases and sales day books incorrectly added up to £100 too much.		

6 Complete reversal of entries – this error is where the correct amounts are entered in the correct accounts, but each item is shown on the wrong side of each account.

Example: We pay a cheque for £200 on 28 May 2010 to D Charles. We enter it as follows in accounts with the letter (A). There has, therefore, been both a debit and a credit of £200.

Dr		Cash Book (A)			Cash	Bank	Cr
		Cash	Bank		£	£	
2010		£	£				
May 28	D Charles		200				

Dr		D Charles (A)		Cr
		2010		£
		May 28	Bank	200

This is incorrect. It should have been debit D Charles Account £200, credit Bank £200. Both items have been entered in the correct accounts, but each is on the wrong side of its account.

The way to correct this is more difficult to understand than with other errors. Let us look at how the items would have appeared if we had done it correctly in the first place. We will show the letter (B) behind the account names.

Dr		Cash Book (B)					Cr
		Cash	Bank		Cash	Bank	
		£	£	2010	£	£	
				May 28	D Charles	200	

Dr		D Charles (B)		Cr
2010		£		
May 28	Bank	200		

The error was discovered on May 31 and corrected as follows:

(a) First we have to cancel the error. This would mean entering these amounts:

Dr:	D Charles	£200	
Cr:	Bank		£200

(b) Then we have to enter up the transaction:

Dr:	D Charles	£200	
Cr:	Bank		£200

Altogether then, the entries to correct the error are twice the amounts first entered.

When corrected, the accounts appear as follows, marked (C).

Dr			Cash Book (C)					Cr
		Cash	Bank				Cash	Bank
2010		£	£	2010			£	£
May 8	D Charles		200	May 31	D Charles: error corrected			400

Dr			D Charles Account (C)			Cr
2010			£	2010		£
May 28	Bank: error corrected		400	May 28	Bank	200

You can see that accounts (C) give the same final answer as accounts (B).

				£	£
(B)	Dr:		D Charles	200	
	Cr:		Bank		200
(C)	Dr:		D Charles (£400 – £200)	200	
	Cr:		Bank (£400 – £200)		200

These would be shown as follows:

	The Journal			
			Dr	Cr
2010			£	£
May 31	D Charles		400	
	Bank			400
	Payment of £200 on 28 May 2010 to D Charles incorrectly credited to his account, and debited to bank. Error now corrected.			

14.4 Errors affecting trial balance agreement

We will now consider the various types of error that **do** affect the balancing of the trial balance:

- incorrect additions in any account
- making an entry on only one side of the accounts – for example, a debit but no credit, or a credit but no debit
- entering a different amount on the debit side from the amount on the credit side.

Suspense accounts and errors

If a trial balance does not balance it is important that errors are located and corrected as soon as possible. When they cannot be found, the trial balance totals should be made to agree with each other by inserting the amount of the difference between the two sides in a **suspense account**. In the following example there is a difference of £40.

Trial Balance as at 31 December 2009		
	Dr	Cr
	£	£
Totals after all the accounts have been listed	100,000	99,960
Suspense account		40
	100,000	100,000

To make the two totals the same, a figure of £40 for the suspense account has been shown on the credit side. A suspense account is opened and the £40 difference is also shown there on the credit side.

Dr	Suspense Account			Cr
		2009		£
		Dec 31	Difference per trial balance	40

Suspense account and the balance sheet

If the errors are not found before the financial statements are prepared, the suspense account balance will be included in the balance sheet. Where the balance is a credit balance, it should be included under current liabilities on the balance sheet. When the balance is a debit balance, it should be shown under current assets on the balance sheet. Large errors should always be found before the financial statements are drawn up.

Correction of errors – one error only

When errors are found, they must be corrected using double entry. Each correction must be described by an entry in the journal. Let us consider the following two examples:

Example 1: Assume that the error of £40 shown in the example above is found in the following year on 31 March 2010, the error being that the sales account was undercast (see section 14.5 below) by £40. The action taken to correct this is:

- Debit the suspense account to close it: £40.
- Credit the sales account to show item where it should have been: £40.

The double entry accounts and journal entry are shown below:

Dr		Suspense Account			Cr
2010		£	2009		£
Mar 31	Sales	40	Dec 31	Difference per trial balance	40

Dr		Sales Account			Cr
			2010		£
			Mar 31	Suspense	40

This can be shown in journal form as follows:

The Journal		Dr	Cr
2010		£	£
Mar 31	Suspense	40	
	Sales		40
	Correction of undercasting of sales by £40 in last year's accounts.		

Example 2: The trial balance on 31 December 2009 shows a difference of £168. It was a shortage on the debit side. A suspense account is opened and the difference of £168 is entered on the debit side.

On 31 May 2010 the error is found. We had made a payment of £168 to D Miguel to close his account. It was correctly entered in the cash book, but it was not entered in Miguel's account.

To correct the error, the account of D Miguel is debited with £168, as it should have been in 2009, and the suspense account is credited with £168 so that the account can be closed. The double entry accounts and journal entry are shown below:

Dr			D Miguel Account				Cr
2010			£	2010			£
May 31	Bank		168	Jan 1	Balance b/d		168

Dr			Suspense Account				Cr
2009			£	2010			£
Dec 31	Difference per trial balance		168	May 31	D Miguel		168

The Journal		Dr	Cr
2010		£	£
Mar 31	D Miguel	168	
	Suspense		168
	Correction of non-entry of payment last year in D Miguel's account.		

Correction of errors – more than one error

We can now look at an example where the suspense account difference has been caused by more than one error.

Example 3: A trial balance at 31 December 2009 shows a difference of £77, being a shortage on the debit side. A suspense account is opened, and the difference of £77 is entered on the debit side of the account.

On 28 February 2010 all the errors from the previous year were found:

a) A cheque of £150 paid to L Kent had been correctly entered in the cash book, but had not been entered in Kent's account.

b) The purchases account has been undercast by £20.

c) A cheque of £93 received from K Sand has been correctly entered in the cash book but has not been entered in Sand's account.

These three errors have resulted in a net error of £77, shown by a debit of £77 on the debit side of the suspense account. These are corrected by:

- making correcting entries in the accounts for (a), (b) and (c)
- recording the double entry for these items in the suspense account.

The double entry accounts and journal entry are shown below:

Dr		L Kent Account			Cr
2010			£		
Feb 28	Suspense (a)		150		

Dr		Purchases Account			Cr
2010			£		
Feb 28	Suspense (b)		20		

Dr		K Sand Account			Cr
		2010			£
		Feb 28	Suspense (c)		93

Dr		Suspense Account				Cr
2010		£	2010			£
Jan 1	Balance b/d	77	Feb 28	L Kent (a)		150
Feb 28	K Sand (c)	93	Feb 28	Purchases (b)		20
		170				170

The Journal

		Dr	Cr
2010		£	£
Feb 28	L Kent	150	
	Suspense		150
	Cheque paid omitted from Kent's account		
Feb 28	Purchases	20	
	Suspense		20
	Undercasting of purchases by £20 in last year's accounts		
Feb 28	Suspense	93	
	K Sand		93
	Cheque received omitted from Sand's account		

Only those errors that make the trial balance totals different from each other have to be corrected via the suspense account.

14.5 Casting

You will often notice the use of the expression **casting**, which means adding up. **Overcasting** means incorrectly adding up a column of figures to give an answer that is *greater* than it should be, whereas **undercasting** means incorrectly adding up a column of figures to give an answer that is *less* than it should be.

14.6 Recap on journal entries

Remember that when entering an unusual transaction that needs to go via the journal you need to think double entry, i.e. which account needs to be debited and which account should be credited. In the above examples we have shown the double entry accounts first, followed by the journal entry. This is to help the student to overcome the problem in recording journal entries. However, in practical circumstances the journal entry is always done first, followed by posting the transaction from the journal to the double entry accounts – see Exhibit 14.1.

Exhibit 14.1

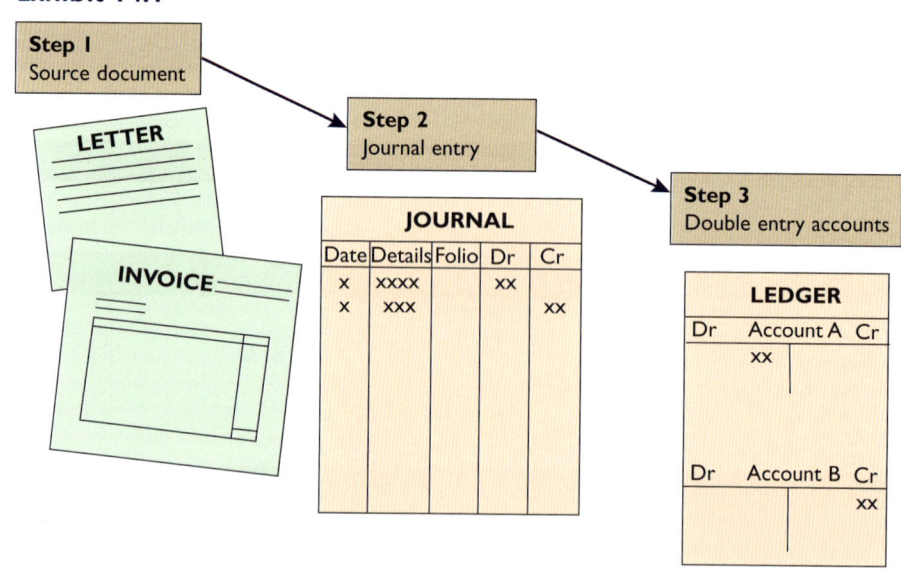

14.7 Examination guidance

When tackling examination questions involving journal entries you may find it useful to follow the following guideline:

- On your examination answer paper, write a heading entitled 'Workings'. Then, under that, show the double entry accounts.

- Now put a heading entitled 'Answer', and show the answer in the form of the journal, as shown in this chapter.

See Exhibit 14.2.

Exhibit 14.2

WORKINGS:

Name of Account		Name of Account
xxx		xxx

ANSWER:

The Journal

Date	Details	Folio	Dr £	Cr £
xxx	Name of Account 　　Name of Account Narrative		xxx	xxx

If you are already confident about dealing with these questions and you feel that you can manage them without showing your workings, then you may wish to leave out your workings from your answer.

If the question asks for 'journal entries' you must *not* fall into the trap of just showing the double entry accounts; you must show the journal entries as well, otherwise you may not be awarded any marks.

14.8 Advantages of using the journal

Recording transactions in the journal has the following advantages:

- There is less chance of further errors occurring by ensuring that the item is recorded properly and posted in the appropriate double entry accounts.
- Without such a record in the journal, fraudulent transactions could occur more easily.
- There is a permanent record of the transaction with reference to the prime source document.
- If a record of the transaction is kept it saves relying on a member of staff to remember all the details. Also, if the member of staff leaves then it becomes almost impossible at a later date to understand why a particular book-keeping entry was made in the accounting books.

Despite these advantages, many businesses do not use a journal.

End of Chapter Checklist

Summary

- The journal is an original book of entry and is used to record exceptional transactions that do not appear in the other books of original entry, i.e. purchase and sale of fixed assets, writing off bad debts, correction of errors and so on.
- When preparing a journal entry the date is entered first, followed by the name of the account to be debited and amount. This is followed by entering the name of the account to be credited, slightly indented, and the amount. Finally, a narrative, giving a brief description of the transaction, is written.
- There are two types of errors: those that affect the balancing of the trial balance and those that do not. Once identified, the errors should be corrected using the journal.
- Errors that can occur and yet the trial balance still agree are errors of commission, principle, original entry, omission, compensating and complete reversal of entries.
- If the totals in the trial balance do not agree it may be necessary to open a suspense account and enter the difference into the account until the error(s) can be located.
- In the unlikely event that the error(s) are not found when the balance sheet is prepared, it may be necessary to include the suspense account. If the suspense account shows a credit balance then it should be entered under the current liabilities, whereas a debit balance would be shown under current assets.
- Any errors found should be corrected using a journal and subsequently posted to the appropriate double entry accounts. If the error affects the suspense account then the posting should be made to that account.
- Overcasting is incorrectly adding up a column of figures to give an answer greater than the correct total, whereas undercasting means adding a column of figures up to less than it should be.
- There are many advantages to using a journal, including having a permanent record of the transaction and less risk of fraudulent transaction.
- Since many students have problems answering examination questions involving journal entries, it is recommended that they prepare a 'working section' to show the double entry aspect prior to preparing the journal entry which usually forms the 'Answer' to the question.

Questions

14.1 *Show the journal entries, narratives not are required, to record the following:*

2010	
Jan 1	Bought computer equipment on credit from Data Systems for £4,000 for use in the business
Jan 5	No entries had been made in the books for stock £120 taken by the proprietor for his own use
Jan 8	A debt of £220 owing to us by J Oddy is written off as a bad debt
Jan 15	Bought a motor vehicle from Smithy Garage paying by cheque, £15,500
Jan 29	J Street owes us £250. She is unable to pay her debt and we agree to take some filing cabinets valued at £250 from her to cancel the debt

Ignore VAT.

14.2X *Show the journal entries, narratives are not required, for April 2010 necessary to record the following items:*

a) Apr 1	Bought fixtures on credit from J Harper, £1,809
b) Apr 4	The proprietor takes £500 goods out of the business stock. No entries had been made in the books.
c) Apr 9	The proprietor had taken £100 cash from the business for his own use. No entries had been made in the books.
d) Apr 12	K Lamb owes us £500. He is unable to pay his debt. We agree to take some office equipment from him at the value and so cancel the debt.
e) Apr 18	Some of the fixtures bought from J Harper, £65 worth, are found to be unsuitable and are returned to him for full allowance
f) Apr 24	A debt owing to us by J Brown of £68 is written off as a bad debt
g) Apr 30	Office equipment bought on credit from Super Offices for £2,190

Ignore VAT.

End of Chapter Checklist

Questions

14.3 *Show the journal entries necessary to correct the following errors. Narratives are not required.*

a) A sale of goods £678 to J Harkness had been entered in J Harker's account.
b) The purchase of a machine on credit from L Pearson for £4,390 had been completely omitted from our books.
c) The purchase of a motor vehicle for £10,800 had been entered in error in the motor expenses account.
d) A sale of £221 to E Fletcher had been entered in the books – both debit and credit – as £212.
e) Commission received £257 had been entered in error in the sales account.

Ignore VAT.

14.4X *Show the journal entries needed to correct the following errors. Narratives are not required.*

a) Purchases £699 on credit from K Webb had been entered in H Weld's account.
b) A cheque of £189 paid for advertisements had been entered in the cash column of the cash book instead of in the bank column.
c) Sale of goods £443 on credit to B Maxim had been entered in error in B Gunn's account.
d) Purchase of goods on credit from K Innes £89 entered in two places in error as £99.
e) Cash paid to H Mersey £89 has been entered on the debit side of the cash book and the credit side of H Mersey's account.

14.5X On 30 September 2010, the totals of the trial balance drawn up for Indira's business did not agree. The difference was entered in a suspense account. An investigation of the difference revealed the following errors relating to the period for which the trial balance has been prepared.

- The sales day book had been overcast by £240
- No entries had been made for stock £750 taken by Indira for her own use
- Goods purchased for £1,250 from Pointer Brothers had been posted to their account at £1,520
- £85 discount allowed to Farmer & Co had been debited to their account
- A credit purchase from A Patel for £500 had been credited to the account of L Patel.

a) Set out the journal entries for the items that do **not** involve the suspense account. Narrations are required and must state the **type** of error involved.
b) Write up the suspense account, including the opening balance. Assume that the trial balance totals agree after the errors have been corrected.
c) Before discovery of the errors, which side of the trial balance was deficient (lighter) and by how much?
d) State why a trial balance which agrees may **not** provide a true check of accuracy. Use an example to support your answer.

IGCSE

Section B: The ledger

Chapter 15: Sales ledger and purchase ledger control accounts

Getting started

Edexcel specification
The ledger, 2.25, 2.26.

After you have studied this chapter you should be able to:

- understand the need for control accounts
- prepare a sales ledger control account from entries in the day books, cash book and ledger accounts
- prepare a purchase ledger control account from entries in the day books, cash book and ledger accounts
- appreciate the advantages of control accounts.

CONTROL ACCOUNT – an account which checks the arithmetical accuracy of a ledger.

15.1 The principle of control accounts

In Chapter 8 we saw how the books of account were divided into various books of original entry and ledgers. At the end of an accounting period the accounts are balanced off and a trial balance prepared to check the accuracy of the book-keeping entries. If a trial balance fails to balance this usually indicates that an error or errors may have been made and needs to be identified. As the business expands the accounting requirements increase which may lead to more errors occurring which are very difficult to find.

To help alleviate the problem of identifying errors more easily, what is required is a type of mini trial balance for the sales and purchase ledgers and this is met by a **control account**. The two main control accounts are as follows:

- **Sales ledger control account** – an account which summarises the customer accounts (debtors) in the Sales Ledger
- **Purchase ledger control account** – an account which summarises all the supplier accounts (creditors) in the Purchase Ledger.

Control accounts are often referred to as 'total accounts' since they contain the 'totals' of the various transactions that have taken place during the period. Therefore, if the total of the opening balances for each individual ledger account is known, together with information of the total additions and total deductions made into these accounts during a particular period, then the total amount outstanding at the end of that period can be calculated.

The total amount outstanding in the control account can then be checked against a list of the individual balances of the ledger accounts. Provided that no errors have occurred then the two total figures should agree. As mentioned above, control accounts act like a mini trial balance and if an error has occurred in the ledger it can be identified more easily if control accounts are maintained since a control account failing to balance would mean the error lies within that particular ledger.

Exhibit 15.1

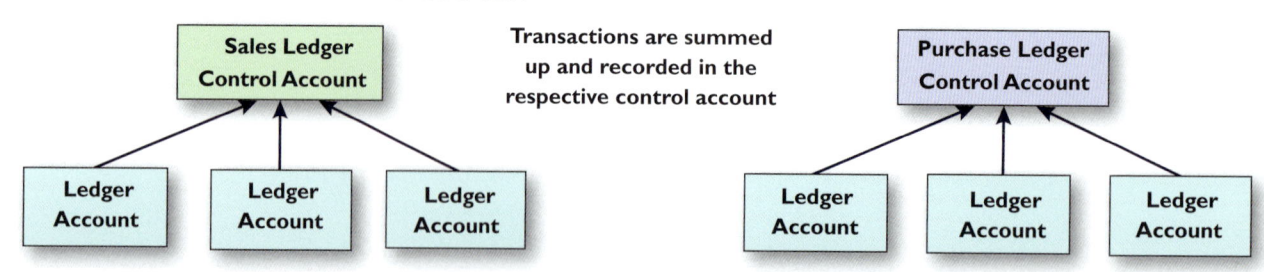

Transactions are summed up and recorded in the respective control account

15.2 Example of a sales ledger control account

Let us now look at the following sales ledger. Suppose there were only four accounts in the sales ledger for the month of May 2010 as shown below:

Sales Ledger

Dr			T Allen Account			Cr
2010		£	2010			£
May 1	Balance b/d	850	May 7	Bank		820
May 4	Sales	900	May 7	Discounts allowed		30
May 30	Sales	350	May 31	Balance c/d		1,250
		2,100				2,100
Jun 1	Balance b/d	1,250				

Dr			P May Account			Cr
2010		£	2010			£
May 1	Balance b/d	1,500	May 9	Sales returns		200
May 28	Sales	400	May 14	Bank		900
			May 14	Discounts allowed		20
			May 31	Balance c/d		780
		1,900				1,900
Jun 1	Balance b/d	780				

Dr			K White Account			Cr
2010		£	2010			£
May 1	Balance b/d	750	May 20	Sales returns		110
May 15	Sales	600	May 31	Balance c/d		1,240
		1,350				1,350
Jun 1	Balance b/d	1,240				

Dr			C Young Account			Cr
2010		£	2010			£
May 1	Balance b/d	450	May 28	Bad debts		450

A **control account**, in this case a **sales ledger control account**, would consist only of the totals of each of the items in the sales ledger. Let us therefore first list the totals for each type of item.

May 1 Balances b/d:	£850 + £1,500 + £750 + £450 = £3,550
Sales in May:	£900 + £350 + £400 + £600 = £2,250
Cheques received in May:	£820 + £900 = £1,720
Discounts allowed in May:	£30 + £20 = £50
Sales returns in May:	£200 + £110 = £310
Bad debts written off in May:	£450

Now, looking at the totals only, it is possible to draw up a sales ledger control account. You will notice that transactions in the control account are entered on the same side as they would be in the personal accounts:

TIP – entries in the Control Accounts go on the same side as they would in the personal accounts, i.e. debtors or creditors.

Dr			Sales Ledger Control Account			Cr
2010		£	2010			£
May 1	Balance b/d	3,550	May 31	Bank		1,720
May 31	Sales for the month	2,250	May 31	Discounts allowed		50
			May 31	Sales returns		310
			May 31	Bad debts		450
			May 31	Balance c/d (A)		?
		5,800				5,800
Jun 1	Balance b/d (B)	?				

From your studies of double entry you can see that the Balance c/d (A) is the figure needed to balance the account, i.e. the difference between the two sides, which is £5,800 − £2,530 = £3,270.

We can now look at the sales ledger to see if that is correct. The balances are £1,250 + £780 + £1,240 = £3,270. As this has now proved to be correct, the figure of £3,270 can be shown in the sales ledger control account as the balances carried down (A) and the balances brought down (B).

In the above straightforward example, there were only four ledger accounts. Suppose instead that there were 400 – or 4,000 or 40,000 – ledger accounts. In these cases, the information concerning the totals of each type of item cannot be obtained so easily.

Remember that the main purpose of a control account is to act as a check on the accuracy of the entries in the ledgers. The total of a list of all the balances extracted from the ledger should equal the balance on the control account. If not, a mistake, or even many mistakes, may have been made and will have to be found.

15.3 Information for control accounts

The following tables show where information needed to draw up control accounts is obtained.

	Sales Ledger Control	Source
A	Opening debtors	List of debtors' balances drawn up at the end of the previous period.
B	Credit sales	Total from sales day book.
C	Sales returns	Total of sales returns day book.
D	Cheques received	Cash book: Bank column on debit (received) side. List extracted or total of a special column for cheques which have been included in the cash book.
E	Cash received	Cash book: Cash column on debit (received) side. List extracted or total of a special column which has been included in the cash book.
F	Discounts allowed	Total of discounts allowed column in the cash book.
G	*Closing debtors	List of debtors' balances drawn up at the end of the period.

*NB: The final total of outstanding debtors at the end of the period is shown on the Balance Sheet under the heading Current Assets – this will be dealt with in Chapter 17.

Refer to Exhibit 15.2 for illustration of 'Sales ledger control account – source of data'.

	Purchase Ledger Control	Source
A	Opening creditors	List of creditors' balances drawn up at the end of the previous period..
B	Credit purchases	Total from purchases day book
C	Purchase returns	Total of purchase returns day book.
D	Cheques paid	Cash book: Bank column on credit (payments) side. List extracted or total of a special column which has been included in the cash book.
E	Cash paid	Cash book: Cash column on credit (payments) side. List extracted or total of a special column which has been included in the cash book.
F	Discounts received	Total of discounts received column in the cash book.
*G	Closing creditors	List of creditors' balances drawn up at the end of the period.

*NB: The final total of outstanding creditors at the end of the period is shown on the Balance Sheet under the heading Current Liabilities – this will be dealt with in Chapter 17.

Refer to Exhibit 15.3 for illustration of purchase ledger control account – source of data.

Exhibit 15.2

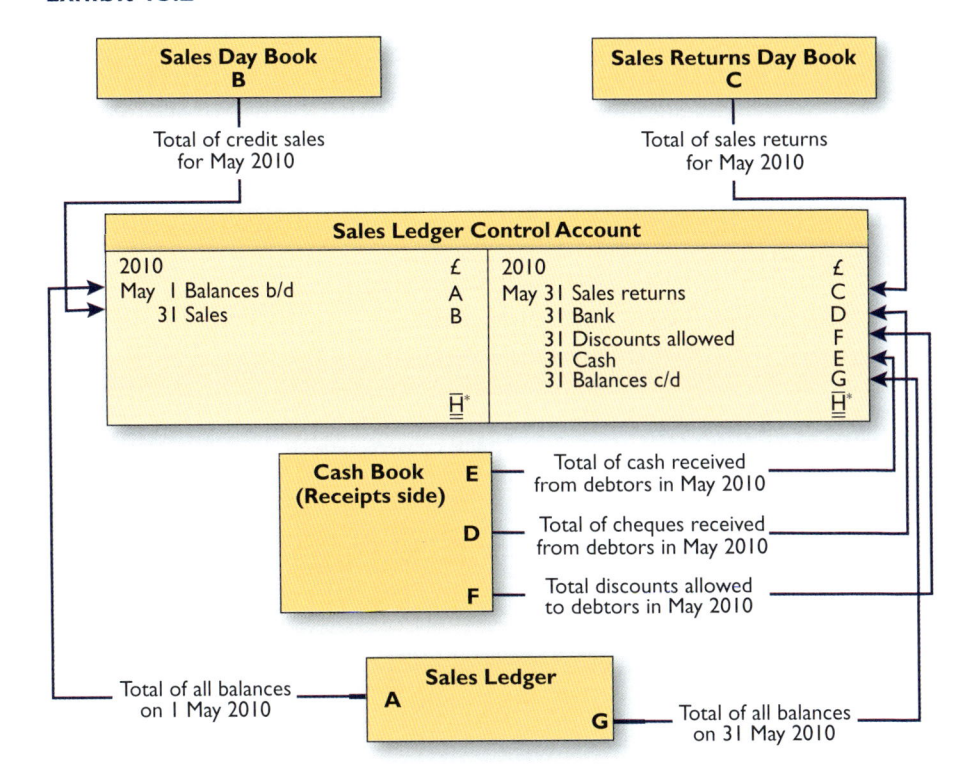

Sales Day Book B — Total of credit sales for May 2010

Sales Returns Day Book C — Total of sales returns for May 2010

Sales Ledger Control Account

2010		£	2010		£
May 1	Balances b/d	A	May 31	Sales returns	C
31	Sales	B	31	Bank	D
			31	Discounts allowed	F
			31	Cash	E
			31	Balances c/d	G
		H̄*			H̄*

Cash Book (Receipts side)
- E — Total of cash received from debtors in May 2010
- D — Total of cheques received from debtors in May 2010
- F — Total discounts allowed to debtors in May 2010

Sales Ledger
- A — Total of all balances on 1 May 2010
- G — Total of all balances on 31 May 2010

Control accounts are normally prepared in the same form as an account, with the totals of the debit entries in the ledger on the left-hand side of the control accounts, and the totals of the various credit entries in the ledger on the right-hand side.

Exhibit 15.2 shows how information is used to construct a sales ledger control account for the month of May 2010. The letters A, B, C, etc. from the above tables, relate to the items in the diagram.

Exhibit 15.3

Purchase Ledger Control Account

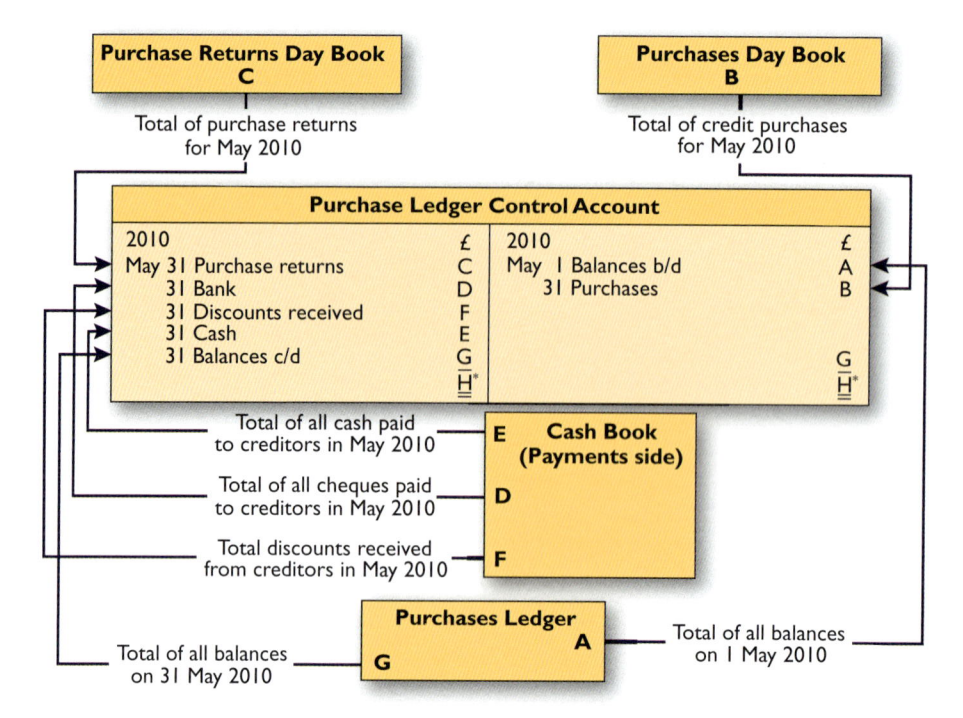

2010		£	2010		£
May 31	Purchase returns	C	May 1	Balances b/d	A
31	Bank	D	31	Purchases	B
31	Discounts received	F			
31	Cash	E			
31	Balances c/d	G			
		H*			G
					H*

Inputs:
- Purchase Returns Day Book (C) → Total of purchase returns for May 2010
- Purchases Day Book (B) → Total of credit purchases for May 2010
- Cash Book (Payments side): E = Total of all cash paid to creditors in May 2010; D = Total of all cheques paid to creditors in May 2010; F = Total discounts received from creditors in May 2010
- Purchases Ledger: G = Total of all balances on 31 May 2010; A = Total of all balances on 1 May 2010

Exhibit 15.3 now shows the construction of a **purchase ledger control account** for May 2010.

15.4 Further examples

Exhibit 15.4 shows an example of a sales ledger control account for a sales ledger in which all the entries are arithmetically correct.

Exhibit 15.4 – Sales ledger control account

Sales ledger	£
Debit balances on 1 July 2010	11,364
Total credit sales for the month	61,740
Cheques received from customers in the month	43,704
Cash received from customers in the month	7,416
Sales returns from customers during the month	1,776
Debit balances on 31 July as extracted from the sales ledger	20,208

Dr			Sales Ledger Control Account			Cr
2010		£	2010			£
July 1	Balance b/d	11,364	July 31	Bank		43,704
31	Sales	61,740	31	Cash		7,416
			31	Sales returns		1,776
			31	Balances c/d		20,208
		73,104				73,104

We have proved the ledger to be arithmetically correct because the totals of the control account equal each other. Were they not equal, it would prove that an error had occurred.

Exhibit 15.5 shows an example where an error is found to exist in a purchase ledger. The ledger will have to be checked in detail, the error found, and the control account corrected.

Exhibit 15.5 – Purchase ledger control account

Purchases ledger	£
Credit balances on 1 July 2010	11,670
Cheques paid to suppliers during the month	10,860
Purchase returns to suppliers in the month	285
Bought from suppliers in the month	14,808
Credit balances on 31 July as extracted from the purchase ledger	15,453

Dr		Purchase Ledger Control Account			Cr
2010			£	2010	£
July 31	Bank		10,860	July 1 Balances b/d	11,670
31	Purchases returns		285	31 Purchases	14,808
31	Balance c/d		15,453		
			26,598*		26,478*

*As can be seen from the totals at the bottom of the control account, there is a £120 (£26,598 − £26,478) error in the purchase ledger. We will have to check that ledger in detail to find the error.

Notice that a double line does not appear under the totals figures. The account will not be finalised and ruled off until the error is traced and corrected.

15.5 Other transfers

Bad debts – Transfers to bad debt accounts will have to be recorded in the sales ledger control account because they involve entries in the sales ledgers.

Contra account – Similarly, a contra account, whereby the same business is both a supplier and a customer and inter-indebtedness is 'set off', will also need entering in the control accounts. An example of this follows:

1 The business has sold A Hughes £600 goods on 1 May
2 Hughes has supplied the business with £880 goods on 12 May
3 The £600 owing by Hughes is set off against £880 owing to him on 30 May
4 This leaves £280 owing to Hughes on 31 May

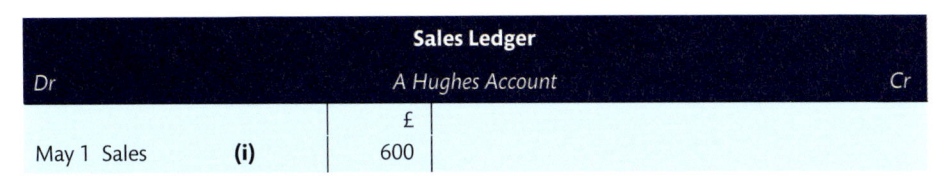

	Sales Ledger		
Dr	A Hughes Account		Cr
	£		
May 1 Sales (i)	600		

	Purchase Ledger		
Dr	A Hughes Account		Cr
			£
	May 12 Purchases (ii)		880

The set-off now takes place:

Sales Ledger
A Hughes Account

Dr			£				Cr £
May 1 Sales	(i)		600	May 30	Set-off: Purchases ledger	(iii)	600

Purchase Ledger
A Hughes Account

Dr			£				Cr £
May 30 Set-off: Sales ledger	(iii)		600	May 12 Purchases		(ii)	880
May 31 Balance c/d	(iv)		280				
			880				880
				Jun 1 Balance b/d		(iv)	280

> TIP – when dealing with contra items (i.e. set-offs) think of the set-off as cash received or paid; the entries go on the same side of the control accounts as these items.

The transfer of the £600 will appear on the **credit side** of the sales ledger control account and on the **debit side** of the purchase ledger control account.

Students often find it difficult to work out which side of each control account contra items (set-offs) are shown. Think of the 'set-off' as cash received or cash paid, the entries go on the same sides of the control accounts as these items. Thus, a contra item will appear on the credit side of the sales ledger control account (the same side as cash received from debtors) and will appear on the debit side of the purchases ledger control account (the same side as cash paid to creditors would appear). Remember this and you won't get it wrong.

15.6 Control accounts and computerised accounting systems

Control accounts are used by many businesses, especially those using manual accounting systems. For businesses using computerised accounting systems, the control accounts are an integral part of the accounting package and are prepared automatically. This is because computerised systems ensure that all double entry transactions are completed upon entry, thereby ensuring that the ledgers all balance. However, even these businesses with computerised accounting packages often prepare their own manual control accounts to ensure that the ledgers balance and to detect any errors.

15.7 Advantages of control accounts

There are several advantages a business can benefit from by using control accounts, as shown below:

- *Location of error* – By preparing control accounts any arithmetical errors that may have occurred are identified. Also, if a clerk has inadvertently omitted entering an invoice or payment in the personal accounts these too would be identified since the control account acts as a mini trial balance. However, it must be pointed out that there are other errors that may still be contained in the ledgers such as mispostings or compensating errors.

- *Prevention of fraud* – Normally the control accounts are under the supervision of a senior member of the accounting team or accounts manager. This makes fraud more difficult since any transaction entered into a ledger account must also be included in the control account. Since a different member of staff would be responsible for maintaining the ledgers from the member supervising the control account, it would be more difficult to carry out fraudulent transactions. Therefore, the supervisor or manager provides an internal check on the procedures.

- *Information for management* – For management purposes the balances on the control accounts can always be taken to equal debtors and creditors without waiting for an extraction of individual balances. Management control is thereby aided because the speed at which information is obtained is one of the prerequisites of efficient control.

End of Chapter Checklist

Summary

- Control accounts are 'total' accounts which contain the total of the various individual personal account balances which are held in subsidiary ledgers, such as the 'sales ledger' or 'purchase ledger' and information gathered from the various accounting books, including sales and purchases day books, sales returns and purchase returns day books and cash book.

- The two main control accounts are:
    1. Sales ledger control account
    2. Purchase ledger control account.

- Control accounts are usually prepared at the end of each month or period. By comparing the balance on the control account with the total outstanding balances in a subsidiary ledger, the arithmetical accuracy can be checked and errors easily located and corrected.

- Transfers between the sales and purchase ledgers are called 'contra entries' or sometimes 'set-offs'. Remember to enter these on the same side in the control account as you would normally enter cash either received or paid, i.e.
    1. purchase ledger control account is **debited**
    2. sales ledger control account is **credited**

- The advantages of using control accounts include:
    1. helping to locate errors
    2. prevention of fraud
    3. provides up-to-date information to management on the total debtors or creditors.

- Finally, remember that when making entries into the control accounts the entry goes on exactly the same side as it would do in the personal account.

Questions

15.1 You are required to prepare a sales ledger control account from the following:

2010		£
Oct 1	Sales ledger balances	12,340
	Total of entries for Oct:	
	Sales day book	124,790
	Sales returns day book	2,847
	Cheques and cash received from customers	116,225
	Discounts allowed	3,638
Oct 31	Sales ledger balances	14,420

15.2X You are required to prepare a sales ledger control account from the following information and ascertain the figure of closing debtors as at 28 February 2010.

2010		£
Feb 1	Sales ledger balances	33,950
	Totals for February:	
	Discounts allowed	4,497
	Cash and cheques received from debtors	332,920
	Sales day book	347,480
	Bad debts written off	977
	Sales returns day book	11,095
	Set-offs against balances in purchase ledger	1,400
	Cheques dishonoured	791

End of Chapter Checklist

Questions

15.3 Draw up a purchase ledger control account from the following information:

2010		£
July 1	Purchase ledger balances	19,450
	Totals for July:	
	Purchases day book	28,200
	Purchase returns day book	1,575
	Cash and cheques paid to creditors	26,150
	Discounts received	550
July 31	Purchase ledger balances	?

15.4X You are required to draw up a purchase ledger control account from the following information:

2010		£
Jan 1	Purchase ledger balances	35,010
	Totals for January:	
	Purchases day book	50,760
	Purchase returns day book	2,835
	Cash and cheques paid to creditors	45,070
	Discounts received	990
	Set-offs against balances in the sales ledger	2,000
Jan 31	Purchase ledger balances	?

15.5X At the end of December 2009 the sales ledger of Ravi Singh showed total debtors to be £78,540. Ravi believes this figure may be incorrect and obtains the following figures from his books for the period 1 January to 31 December 2009.

	£
Opening balance in the sales ledger at 1 January 2009	65,000
Credit sales	453,900
Returns inwards	6,430
Receipts from debtors	432,000
Discount allowed	7,540
Bad debts	650
Purchase ledger balance set-off	1,650
Customer's cheque returned by bank	750

a) Prepare the sales ledger control account for the period 1 January–31 December 2009, showing clearly the closing balance.
b) Explain the reason why Ravi believes there may have been errors in his sales ledger.
c) Explain, with reasons, where the closing balance of the sales ledger control account would appear in the final accounts of Ravi Singh.

IGCSE

Section C: Final accounts

Chapter 16: Trading account and profit and loss account of a sole trader

Getting started

Edexcel specification
The ledger, 2.9, 2.10
Trading account, profit and loss account, balance sheet of a sole trader, 3.1, 3.2, 3.4, 3.5, 3.6, 3.7, 3.11

After you have studied this chapter you should be able to:

- understand why profit is calculated and explain the purpose of the trading account and profit and loss account
- calculate the cost of goods sold, gross profit and net profit
- distinguish between gross profit and net profits
- understand that an adjustment needs to be made for the stock of unsold goods at the end of the trading period
- close off sales, purchases and relevant expense accounts at the end of the trading period by double entry; and transfer the balances to the trading account and profit and loss account
- prepare a trading account and profit and loss account from a trial balance
- transfer the net profit and drawings to the capital account at the end of the period
- appreciate that after preparing the trading account and profit and loss account all remaining balances in the books of account are required for preparation of the balance sheet.

TRADING ACCOUNT – an account in which the Gross Profit or Gross Loss is calculated.

16.1 Introduction to the trading and profit and loss account

The trading and profit and loss account is one of the most important financial statements and, as stated in Chapter 1, is a requirement for correct financial reporting. Its purpose is to show how much profit or loss has been made over a period of time. It is prepared at least once a year but could easily be made available for a shorter period if required, especially with the use of accounting software.

The main purpose of a trading and profit and loss account is for the owners to be able to see how profitably the business is operating. Chapter 1 details other groups who will be interested in the financial results of a business, such as banks should the business require a loan, and the tax authorities.

Uses of the trading and profit and loss account

One of the most important uses of the trading and profit and loss account is that of comparing the results obtained with the results expected. In a trading organisation, much attention is paid to how much profit is made before deducting expenses, i.e. the gross profit which appears in the first section of the trading and profit and loss account. In the next section of the account the net profit is shown and, again, this is equally important to the owners and other groups.

Gross profit: (calculated in the Trading Account)	This is the excess of sales over the **cost of goods sold** in the period.
Net profit: (calculated in the Profit and Loss Account)	This is what is left of the gross profit after all other expenses have been deducted.

It would be possible to have one account called a **trading account**, and another called a **profit and loss account**. Normally they are combined together to form one account called the **trading and profit and loss account**.

> PROFIT AND LOSS ACCOUNT – an account in which the Net Profit or Net Loss is calculated.

16.2 Preparation of a trading and profit and loss account

A trial balance needs to be drawn up before a trading and profit and loss account can be prepared. This contains nearly all the information needed. (Later on in this book, you will see that certain adjustments have to be made, but we will ignore these at this stage.) Set out in Exhibit 16.1 is the trial balance of D Bode made up to the end of his first year's trading. This information is needed to prepare his trading and profit and loss account for the year ended 31 December 2010. For now, we will assume that D Bode has no closing stock at 31 December 2010.

To calculate gross profit

Remember that:

> Sales − Cost of Goods Sold = Gross Profit

Exhibit 16.1

D Bode
Trial Balance as at 31 December 2010

	Dr £	Cr £
Sales		39,650
Purchases	27,150	
General expenses	2,550	
Fixtures and fittings	6,840	
Debtors	2,460	
Creditors		2,180
Capital		8,800
Drawings	7,750	
Bank	3,820	
Cash	60	
	50,630	50,630

We could, in fact, calculate this by simply using arithmetic. However, we must remember that we are using double entry methods. To enable you to see fully how the calculations are performed using double entry, we will show the balances for sales and purchases from Exhibit 16.1, and demonstrate how the entries are made to transfer these items into the calculations within the trading account.

The following steps should be carried out:

Step 1 Transfer the credit balance of the sales account to the credit of the trading account portion of the trading and profit and loss account.

> Debit: sales account
> Credit: trading account.

Step 2 Transfer the debit balance of the purchases account to the debit of the trading account.

> Debit: trading account
> Credit: purchases account.

Remember that, in this case, there is no stock of unsold goods. This means that purchases = **cost of goods sold**.

Step 3 If sales are greater than the cost of goods sold, the difference is gross profit. (If not, the answer would be a **gross loss**.) We will carry this gross profit figure from the trading account part down to the profit and loss part.

The double entry for gross profit is:

> Debit: trading account
> Credit: profit and loss account.

GROSS LOSS – this occurs when the cost of sales is greater than the sales.

The double entry transactions for the above transfers are shown in Exhibit 16.2.

Exhibit 16.2

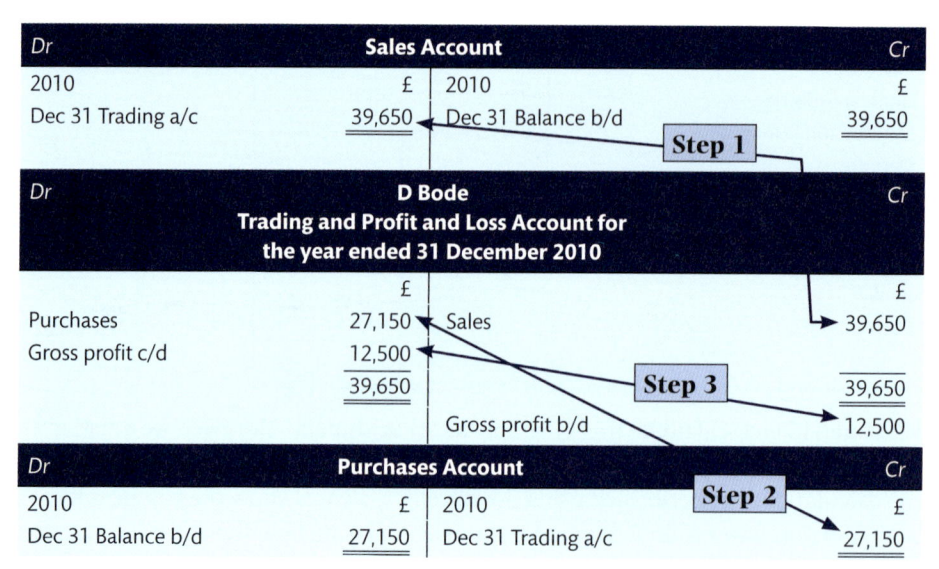

Dr	Sales Account			Cr
2010		£	2010	£
Dec 31 Trading a/c		39,650	Dec 31 Balance b/d	39,650

Step 1

Dr	D Bode Trading and Profit and Loss Account for the year ended 31 December 2010			Cr
		£		£
Purchases		27,150	Sales	39,650
Gross profit c/d		12,500		
		39,650		39,650
			Gross profit b/d	12,500

Step 3

Dr	Purchases Account			Cr
2010		£	2010	£
Dec 31 Balance b/d		27,150	Dec 31 Trading a/c	27,150

Step 2

Notice that, after the trading account has been completed, there are no balances remaining in the sales and purchases accounts. These accounts are now said to be 'closed off'.

To calculate net profit and record it

> Gross Profit − Expenses = Net Profit

To increase the capital account and record it

> Old Capital + Net Profit = New Capital

The double entries needed to transfer the expense accounts to the profit and loss account, and the net profit to the capital account, are as follows:

Step 1 — Transfer the debit balances on expenses accounts to the debit of the profit and loss account.

> Debit: profit and loss account
> Credit: expenses accounts.

Step 2 — Transfer the net profit, when found, to the capital account to show the increase in capital.

> Debit: profit and loss account
> Credit: capital account.

The results are shown in Exhibit 16.3.

Exhibit 16.3

D Bode
Trading and Profit and Loss Account for the Year ended 31 December 2010

Dr	£		Cr £
Purchases	27,150	Sales	39,650
Gross profit c/d	12,500		
	39,650		39,650
General expenses	2,550	Gross profit b/d	12,500
Net profit	9,950		
	12,500		12,500

General Expenses Account

Dr 2010	£	2010	Cr £
Dec 31 Balance b/d	2,550	Dec 31 Profit and loss a/c	2,550

Capital Account

Dr		2010	Cr £
		Dec 31 Balance b/d	8,800
		Dec 31 Net Profit	9,950
			18,750

TRADING AND PROFIT AND LOSS ACCOUNT – a combined account in which both gross and net profits (or losses) are calculated.

Note: See Section 16.3 for completion of this account.

16.3 Completion of capital account

You will see from the capital account shown above that it has been increased by net profit amounting to £9,950 so increasing the total capital to £18,750.

In the trial balance shown in Exhibit 16.1, the drawings amounted to £7,750. **Drawings** are withdrawals of capital and need to be transferred to the capital account as follows:

- **Debit**: capital account
- **Credit**: drawings account.

The completed capital and drawings accounts are as follows:

Dr		Drawings Account		Cr
2010	£	2010		£
Dec 31 Balance b/d	7,750	Dec 31 Capital		7,750

Dr		Capital Account		Cr
2010	£	2010		£
Dec 31 Drawings	7,750	Dec 31 Balance b/d		8,800
Dec 31 Balance c/d	11,000	Dec 31 Net profit		9,950
	18,750			18,750
		2011		
		Jan 1 Balance b/d		11,000

16.4 Stock of unsold goods at end of period

Usually some of the goods bought (purchases) may not have been sold by the end of the accounting period. We have already seen that gross profit is calculated as follows:

$$\text{Sales} - \text{Cost of Good Sold} = \text{Gross Profit}$$

However, purchases only equals cost of goods sold if there is no stock at the end of a period. We can calculate cost of goods sold as follows:

What we bought in this period:	Purchases
Less Goods bought but not sold in this period:	Closing Stock
	= Cost of Goods Sold

Remember, we are concerned here with the trading and profit and loss account of a business where there is no opening stock. In Chapter 18, Section 18.3 we will look at the later years of a business.

Now let us look at the preparation of a trading and profit and loss account for B Swift. His trial balance is shown as Exhibit 16.4 and was drawn up after his first year of trading:

Exhibit 16.4

B Swift
Trial Balance as at 31 December 2010

	Dr	Cr
	£	£
Sales		38,500
Purchases	29,000	
Rent	2,400	
Electricity	1,500	
General expenses	600	
Fixtures and fittings	5,000	
Debtors	6,800	
Creditors		9,100
Bank	15,100	
Cash	200	
Drawings	7,000	
Capital		20,000
	67,600	67,600

Note: On 31 December 2010, at the close of trading, B Swift had goods costing £3,000 that were unsold.

First, the cost of goods sold figure needs to be calculated:

	£
Purchases	29,000
Less Closing stock	3,000
Cost of goods sold	26,000

The gross profit will be:

	£
Sales	38,500
Less Cost of goods sold	26,000
Gross profit	12,500

GROSS PROFIT is sales less costs of goods sold.

The net profit will be:

	£	£
Gross profit		12,500
Less Expenses		
Rent	2,400	
Electricity	1,500	
General expenses	600	
		4,500
Net profit		8,000

NET PROFIT is gross profit plus other income less expenses.

The double entry for the above transactions is now shown in Exhibit 16.5.

Exhibit 16.5

Dr	Sales Account			Cr
2010		£	2010	£
Dec 31 Trading a/c		38,500	Dec 31 Balance b/d	38,500

Dr	Purchases Account			Cr
2010		£	2010	£
Dec 31 Balance b/d		29,000	Dec 31 Trading a/c	29,000

Dr	Rent Account			Cr
2010		£	2010	£
Dec 31 Balance b/d		2,400	Dec 31 Profit and loss a/c	2,400

Dr	Electricity Account			Cr
2010		£	2010	£
Dec 31 Balance b/d		1,500	Dec 31 Profit and loss a/c	1,500

Dr	General Expenses Account			Cr
2010		£	2010	£
Dec 31 Balance b/d		600	Dec 31 Profit and loss a/c	600

To record the stock we need to:

- **Debit**: stock account
- **Credit**: trading account.

This is shown below:

Dr	Stock Account		Cr
2010		£	
Dec 31 Trading a/c		3,000	

Dr	B Swift Trading and Profit and Loss Account for the year ended 31 December 2010			Cr
2010	£	2010		£
Purchases	29,000	Sales		38,500
Gross profit c/d	12,500	*Closing stock		3,000
	41,500			41,500
Rent	2,400	Gross profit b/d		12,500
Electricity	1,500			
General expenses	600			
Net profit	8,000			
	12,500			12,500

Note: The above Trading and Profit and Loss Account is shown using the horizontal method of presentation; in Section 16.6 we will use the vertical method of presentation.

In the above Trading and Profit and Loss Account of B Swift you will see that there is now a figure of £3,000 shown as the *closing stock figure. It was necessary to record this figure at the end of the financial year since the business had this asset of stock, i.e. closing stock. The records have now been brought up to date by showing the stock in our accounts.

16.5 The capital account

The capital account for B Swift can now be completed as follows:

Dr	Capital Account		Cr
2010	£	2010	£
Dec 31 Drawings	7,000	Jan 1 Cash	20,000
Dec 31 Balance c/d	21,000	Dec 31 Net profit from profit and loss a/c	8,000
	28,000		28,000
		2011	
		Jan 1 Balance b/d	21,000

Dr	Drawings Account		Cr
2010	£	2010	£
Dec 31 Balance b/d	7,000	Dec 31 Capital	7,000

16.6 The vertical layout for trading and profit and loss accounts

The trading and profit and loss account shown above is written in the horizontal format to demonstrate how the double entry system works. However, the trading and profit and loss account is more often shown in the vertical format, and it is this format that we will use in future in this book. The trading and profit and loss account of B Swift, in the vertical format, is shown below:

B Swift
Trading and Profit and Loss Account for the year ended 31 December 2010

	£	£
Sales		38,500
Less Cost of goods sold		
Purchases	29,000	
Less Closing stock	3,000	
		26,000
Gross profit		12,500
Less Expenses		
Rent	2,400	
Electricity	1,500	
General expenses	600	
		4,500
Net profit		8,000

You can see that the figures used are exactly the same using either the horizontal or vertical layout. The vertical layout is more widely used today since it is intended to make accounts easier to read and shows a more modern method of presentation.

16.7 The balances remaining in the books of account

Taking Exhibit 16.5, including the adjustment of closing stock valued at £3,000, we can now ascertain the balances still remaining in the books of account after the preparation of the trading and profit and loss accounts. The following accounts have been closed in this process:

Sales
Purchases } transferred to trading account

Rent
Electricity
General expenses } transferred to profit and loss account

Drawings } transferred to capital account

With the remaining balances we can draw up a trial balance which is shown in Exhibit 16.6.

Exhibit 16.6

B Swift
Trial Balance as at 31 December 2010
(after Trading and Profit and Loss Accounts completed)

	Dr	Cr
	£	£
Fixtures and fittings	5,000	
Debtors	6,800	
Creditors		9,100
Stock	3,000	
Bank	15,100	
Cash	200	
Capital		21,000
	30,100	30,100

The one account that was not in the original trial balance was the stock account. It was not brought into our books until the trading account was prepared. These balances will be used when we look at the preparation of the balance sheet in the next chapter. They are also carried forward to the next accounting period.

End of Chapter Checklist

Summary

- One of the main uses of the trading and profit and loss account is to provide information on the profit/losses made in the period and compare these figures with previous year's results.
- How to calculate the cost of goods sold, gross profit and net profit.
- How to close off the sales, purchases and relevant expense accounts at the end of a period and post the entries to the trading and profit and loss account.
- How to transfer the net profit and drawings to the capital account at the end of a period.
- How to treat stock of unsold goods at the end of a period.
- The preparation of the trading and profit and loss account from a trial balance using both the horizontal and vertical methods of presentation.
- Any balances still remaining in the books of account after preparation of the trading and profit and loss account represent assets, liabilities and capital. These balances are entered into the Balance Sheet (see the next chapter) and then carried forward to the next accounting period.

Questions

Note: All answers should show the vertical layout of the trading and profit and loss accounts.

16.1 From the following details of Lucy Chan, draw up her trading and profit and loss account using the vertical style for the year ended 31 December 2010, this being her first year of trading:

Year to 31 December 2010	£
Purchases	84,665
Sales	133,770
Rent	4,595
Wages and salaries	28,865
Printing and stationery	2,940
Electricity expenses	2,485
General expenses	1,295

Note: At 31 December 2010, the stock was valued (at cost) at £15,085.

16.2X From the following details of Charles Drew, draw up his trading and profit and loss account using the vertical style for his first year of trading for the year ended 31 December 2010.

Year to 31 December 2010	£
Sales	128,452
Purchases	96,547
Wages	11,229
Rent	5,330
Office expenses	1,620
Motor expenses	922
Electricity expenses	1,350

Note: Stock at 31 December 2010 amounted in value to £18,495.

End of Chapter Checklist

Questions

16.3 From the following trial balance of G Singh, extracted after one year's trading, prepare the trading and profit and loss account for the year ended 31 December 2010. A balance sheet is not required.

G Singh
Trial Balance as at 31 December 2010

	Dr £	Cr £
Sales		73,848
Purchases	58,516	
Wages	8,600	
Motor expenses	2,080	
Rates	2,680	
Insurance	444	
General expenses	420	
Buildings	20,000	
Motor vehicle	12,000	
Debtors	7,800	
Creditors		6,418
Cash at bank	6,616	
Cash in hand	160	
Drawings	8,950	
Capital		48,000
	128,266	128,266

Stock at 31 December 2010 was valued at £10,192.

(Retain your answer – it will be used later in Exercise 17.1.)

16.4X From the following trial balance of R Cairns after his first year's trading, you are required to draw up a trading and profit and loss account for the year ended 30 June 2010.

R Cairns
Trial Balance as at 30 June 2010

	Dr £	Cr £
Sales		99,082
Purchases	71,409	
Rates	2,000	
Printing and stationery	562	
Electricity	1,266	
Wages	9,492	
Insurance	605	
Premises	145,000	
Computer equipment	8,000	
Debtors	9,498	
Sundry expenses	1,518	
Creditors		3,618
Cash at bank	6,541	
Drawings	12,200	
Motor vehicle	16,500	
Motor expenses	3,109	
Capital		185,000
	287,700	287,700

Stock at 30 June 2010 was valued at £11,498.

(Retain your answer – it will be used later in Exercise 17.2X.)

16.5X A business has been trading for one year. Extract a trading and profit and loss account for the year ended 31 March 2010 for T Leung. The trial balance as at 31 March 2010 is as follows:

T Leung
Trial Balance as at 31 March 2010

	Dr £	Cr £
Rent and rates	6,708	
Insurance	1,312	
Electricity expenses	2,219	
Motor expenses	2,429	
Salaries and wages	26,855	
Sales		153,080
Purchases	133,171	
General expenses	3,466	
Motor van	15,050	
Creditors		13,975
Debtors	29,283	
Equipment	17,028	
Buildings	120,400	
Cash at bank	4,876	
Drawings	16,994	
Capital		212,736
	379,791	379,791

Stock at 31 March 2010 was £42,828.

(Keep your answer – it will be used later in Exercise 17.3)

Section C: Final accounts

Chapter 17: The Balance Sheet

Getting started

Edexcel specification
Trading account, profit and loss account, balance sheet of a sole trader. 3.8 to 3.12, 3.14, 3.15.

After you have studied this chapter you should be able to:

- define a balance sheet
- understand that a balance sheet is prepared from the remaining balances in the trial balance after preparation of the trading and profit and loss accounts
- explain why a balance sheet is not part of the double entry system
- explain the meaning of the terms fixed assets, current assets, current liability and long-term liability
- prepare a balance sheet using the vertical method of presentation
- understand the importance of the term net current assets/working capital
- know which items appear in the owner's capital account.

BALANCE SHEET – a statement showing the assets, capital and liabilities of a business at a specific date.

17.1 Definition and content of a balance sheet

A **balance sheet** is a financial statement setting out the book values of assets, liabilities and capital 'as at' a particular point in time. In simple terms, a balance sheet shows what a business 'owns' and what it 'owes' at a specific date.

Details of the assets, liabilities and capital have to be found in the records of the business and then written out as a balance sheet. These details are readily available since they consist of all the balances remaining in the records once the trading and profit and loss account for the period have been completed. All balances remaining have to be assets, liabilities or capital since the other balances should have been closed off when the trading and profit and loss account was completed.

17.2 Preparing a balance sheet

Let us look at Exhibit 17.1, the trial balance of B Swift (from Exhibit 16.6) as on 31 December 2010 after the trading and profit and loss account had been prepared.

Exhibit 17.1

B Swift
Trial Balance as at 31 December 2010
(after Trading and Profit and Loss Accounts completed)

	Dr £	Cr £
Fixtures and fittings	5,000	
Debtors	6,800	
Creditors		9,100
Stock	3,000	
Bank	15,100	
Cash	200	
Capital		21,000
	30,100	30,100

We can now draw up a balance sheet as at 31 December 2010, and this is shown in Exhibit 17.2. The layout is discussed further in Section 17.4.

Exhibit 17.2

B Swift
Balance Sheet as at 31 December 2010

	£	£	£
Fixed assets			
Fixtures and fittings	5,000	-------	5,000
Current assets			
Stock	3,000		
Debtors	6,800		
Cash at bank	15,100		
Cash in hand	200	25,100	
Less Current liabilities			
Creditors	9,100	9,100	
Net current assets (Working Capital)			16,000
Less Long-term liabilities			
Long-term loan			-------
Net assets			21,000
Financed by:			
Capital account			
Cash introduced			20,000
Add net profit for the year			8,000
			28,000
Less Drawings			7,000
			21,000

NET CURRENT ASSETS – the value of the current assets less that of current liabilities. Also known as WORKING CAPITAL

17.3 No double entry in balance sheets

It may seem strange to you to learn that balance sheets are *not* part of the double entry system. When accounts such as the cash account, rent account, sales account, trading and profit and loss account and so on are drawn up, entries are made on the debit and credit side of these accounts since they are part of the double entry system.

When preparing a balance sheet no entries are made in any of the various accounts. We do not actually transfer the 'Fixtures and fittings balance' or the 'Stock balance', or any of the other accounts, to the balance sheet. All that is necessary is to list the balances for assets, capital and liabilities to form a balance sheet. This means that none of these accounts have been closed off. *Nothing is entered in the accounts*.

When the next accounting period starts, these accounts contain balances which are brought forward as 'opening balances'. During the next accounting period, business transactions are then entered into these accounts as part of the normal double entry system.

Hint

- If you see the word 'account' you will know that it is part of the double entry system and it will include debit and credit entries, i.e. Buildings Account, Bank Account.

TIP –
- If you see the word 'account' then you will know it is part of the double entry system
- If the word 'account' cannot be used then it is not part of the double entry system.

- If the word 'account' cannot be used, it is not part of double entry system for example:

  Trial balance: A list of balances to see whether the records are correct.

  Balance sheet: A list of balances arranged according to whether they are assets, capital or liabilities.

17.4 Balance sheet layout

The balance sheet is one of the most important financial statements and as such it is important that the reader of this statement finds it easy to follow and understand. Over the years, various ways of presenting the financial information have evolved. The present format of the balance sheet is shown in Exhibit 17.2 above.

You will see that the balance sheet starts by listing all the assets which the business 'owns' as at the date of the balance sheet. The assets are split into two categories, fixed and current assets, and this is followed by details of the funds acquired to finance the business.

Click the icon on this page, there is a model layout of the financial statements of a sole trader, namely the Trading and Profit and Loss Account and Balance Sheet. You may find it useful to take a copy of these layouts and use them when undertaking exercises on the preparation of the financial statements.

Assets

Assets are shown under two headings, namely, fixed assets and current assets.

Fixed assets

Fixed assets are assets that:

- are expected to be of use to the business for a long time
- are to be used in the business, and
- were not bought only for the purposes of resale.

Examples are buildings, machinery, motor vehicles, fixtures and fittings. Fixed assets are listed first in the balance sheet, starting with those that the business will keep the longest, down to assets with the shortest life expectancy. For instance:

Fixed assets

1 Land and buildings
2 Fixtures and fittings
3 Machinery
4 Motor vehicles

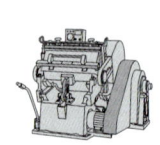

Examples of fixed assets

> FIXED ASSETS – assets bought which have a long life and are to be used in the business.

Current assets

Current assets are assets that are likely to change in the near future and usually within 12 months of the balance sheet date. They include stock of goods for resale at a profit, amounts owed by debtors, cash at bank and any cash in hand. These are listed starting with the asset that is least likely to be turned into cash, finishing with cash itself. The accepted order is listed as:

Current assets

1 Stock   2 Debtors   3 Cash at bank   4 Cash in hand

> **CURRENT ASSETS** – assets consisting of cash, goods for resale, or items having a shorter life.

Examples of current assets

Liabilities

There are two categories of liabilities, **current liabilities** and **long-term liabilities**.

> **LIABILITIES** – total of money owed for assets supplied to the business.

Current liabilities

Current liabilities are liabilities due for repayment in the short term, usually within one year. Examples are bank overdrafts, amounts due to creditors for the supply of goods for resale.

> **CURRENT LIABILITIES** – liabilities that are to be paid in the near future (i.e. within one year).

Current liabilities are deducted from the current assets, as shown in Exhibit 17.2, to give the **net current assets** or **working capital**. This figure is very important in accounting since it shows the amount of resources the business has in the form of readily available cash to meet everyday running expenses.

Long-term liabilities

Long-term liabilities are liabilities not due for repayment in the near future. Examples are bank loans, loans from others such as friends or relatives, and mortgages. Long-term liabilities are deducted from the total figure of assets plus the net current assets as illustrated in Exhibit 17.2.

> **LONG-TERM LIABILITIES** – liabilities that do not have to be paid in the near future (i.e. longer than one year).

Capital account

This is the proprietor's or partners' account with the business. It will start with the balance brought forward from the previous accounting period, to which is added any personal cash introduced into the business and the net profit made by the business in this accounting period. Deducted from the capital account will be amounts drawn from the business and any loss made by the business. The final balance on the capital account should equal the net assets or net liabilities figure – and hence the balance sheet balances. Exhibit 17.3 gives the standard format.

Exhibit 17.3

Capital Account

		£	£
Balance b/d			X
Add	Cash introduced		X
	Net profit for the period		X
			X
Less	Drawings	X	
	Net loss for the period	X	X
			X

It is important to note that the balance sheet shows the position of the business at one point in time: the balance sheet date, i.e. 'as at 31 December 2010'. It is like taking a snapshot of the business at one moment in time. On the other hand, the trading and profit and loss account shows the profit/loss of that business for a period of time (normally a year), i.e. 'for the year ended 31 December 2010'.

End of Chapter Checklist

Summary

- A balance sheet is a financial statement which lists the book values of assets, liabilities and capital 'as at' a specific date. It shows what a business 'owns' and 'owes' at a particular point in time.
- The balance sheet is prepared from the remaining balances in the trial balance after the trading and profit and loss account has been completed.
- The balance sheet is *not* part of the double entry system.
- Most balance sheets are set out using the vertical method of presentation which shows the assets divided into two categories, namely, fixed assets and current assets followed by current liabilities, long-term liabilities and capital.
- The term 'fixed assets' means assets of a more permanent nature such as land and building, equipment and cars that are owned by the business. These are listed in the balance sheet in descending order with the most permanent asset shown first.
- The term 'current assets' refers to assets that are likely to change within one year, for example, stock, debtors, cash at bank and cash in hand. These are listed in order of liquidity with the least liquid of the assets shown first, i.e. stock and the most liquid asset shown at the bottom, i.e. cash in hand.
- The term 'net current assets' or 'working capital' is an important figure in accounting since it represents the amount of resources readily available for paying everyday running expenses.
- The capital account contains money invested by the owner of the business, plus the net profit for the period, less amounts taken out by the owner in the form of 'drawings'. If there is no net profit then a net loss will have been incurred.

Questions

17.1 Complete exercise 16.3 by drawing up a balance sheet as at 31 December 2010 for G Singh.

17.2X Complete exercise 16.4x by drawing up a balance sheet as at 30 June 2010 for R Cairns.

17.3 Complete exercise 16.5x by drawing up a balance sheet as at 31 March 2010 for T Leung.

17.4X The following trial balance was taken from the books of Sarah Joshi at the end of her first year's trading. You are required to prepare a trading and profit and loss account for the year ended 31 May 2010 together with a balance sheet as at that date.

Trial balance of Sarah Joshi as at 31 May 2010	Dr £	Cr £
Capital		237,240
Sales		103,658
Rent	3,000	
General expenses	822	
Motor expenses	3,473	
Cash at bank	13,850	
Printing and stationery	605	
Wages and salaries	12,465	
Computer equipment	3,600	
Purchases	85,691	
Heating and lighting	1,319	
Buildings	180,000	
Debtors	11,398	
Drawings	8,640	
Creditors		4,343
Motor vehicle	19,800	
Insurance	578	
	345,241	345,241

The closing stock was valued at £14,998 as at 31 May 2010.

Section C: Final accounts

Chapter 18: Financial statements: other considerations

Getting started

Edexcel specification
Trading account, profit and loss account, balance sheet of a sole trader, 3.1, 3.2, 3.4, 3.6 to 3.10, 3.15
Adjustments, 4.2

After you have studied this chapter you should be able to:

- record sales returns and purchase returns in the trading and profit and loss account
- record carriage inwards on goods purchased as part of the cost of goods sold
- record carriage outwards as an expense in the profit and loss account
- adjust financial statements to record the opening and closing stocks of the period
- appreciate that the cost of putting goods into a saleable condition is charged to the trading account
- prepare a trading and profit and loss account if either a gross profit/net profit is made or a gross loss/net loss is incurred.

RETURNS IN THE TRADING ACCOUNT –
Deduct:
–Sales returns from Sales
–Purchase returns from Purchases.

18.1 Dealing with sales and purchase returns in the trading account

When businesses deal with the purchase and sale of goods it is inevitable that there are occasions when goods have to be returned by the purchaser to the supplier because they are damaged, faulty or perhaps not to the specification ordered. This was discussed fully in Chapter 3 where both sales and purchase returns were entered into the double entry system (see Section 3.4). In this chapter, we are going to take these returns into consideration when preparing the trading account and determining the gross profit.

In the trading account the sales returns and purchase returns are dealt with as follows:

- sales returns should be deducted from **sales**
- purchase returns should be deducted from **purchases**.

Suppose that in Exhibit 16.1 the trial balance of D Bode, rather than simply containing a sales account balance of £39,650 and a purchases account balance of £27,150, the balances showing stock movement had been:

D Bode
Trial Balance as at 31 December 2010 (extract)

	Dr	Cr
	£	£
Sales		40,000
Purchases	27,350	
Sales returns	350	
Purchase returns		200

If we compare the two trial balances, i.e. the one shown in Exhibit 16.1 and the one shown above, the gross profit amount will be exactly the same. Sales in the original example were £39,650, while in the above example the sales returns is deducted from sales as follows:

	£
Sales	40,000
Less Sales returns	350
Net sales	39,650

Purchases were originally shown as £27,150 but in the above example purchase returns will need to be deducted from purchases to ascertain the amount of goods retained by the business as shown below:

	£
Purchases	27,350
Less Purchase returns	200
Net purchases	27,150

The trading account using the figures from the above example will now appear as in Exhibit 18.1.

Exhibit 18.1

D Bode
Trading and Profit and Loss Account for the year ended 31 December 2010

	£	£
Sales		40,000
Less Sales returns		350
		39,650
Less Cost of goods sold		
Purchases	27,350	
Less Purchase returns	200	27,150
Gross profit		12,500

The gross profit in the above example is £12,500 which is exactly the same amount as shown in Exhibit 16.3. You will notice that the trading and profit and loss account prepared in Exhibit 16.3 was prepared using the horizontal method. The trading and profit and loss account shown above in Exhibit 18.1 has been presented using the vertical method of presentation which will be used on all further examples in this book.

Student hint:

Many students have difficulty deciding whether sales returns should be deducted from sales or purchases figures and vice versa. The same applies to the purchase returns figure. The following illustration shows that the returns are always deducted from the figure on the opposite side so forming an 'X' in the trial balance:

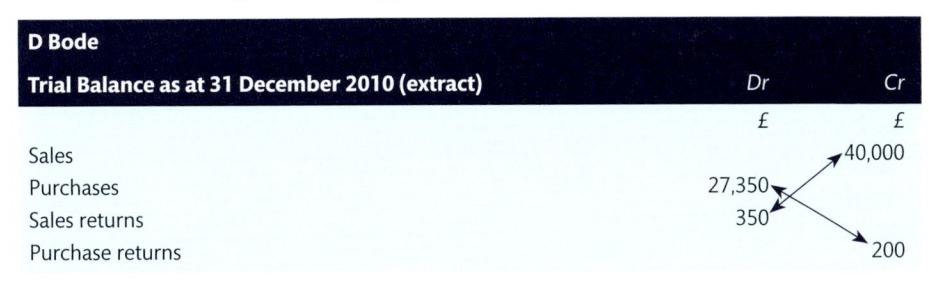

> TIP – Remember that returns are deducted from Sales and Purchases and form an 'X' in the Trial Balance.

D Bode
Trial Balance as at 31 December 2010 (extract)

	Dr	Cr
	£	£
Sales		40,000
Purchases	27,350	
Sales returns	350	
Purchase returns		200

18.2 Dealing with carriage in the trading account

When a business buys goods from a supplier the cost of delivering or transporting the goods also has to be paid. In accountancy terms, this cost of transport is often referred to as 'carriage'. Carriage charges for transporting goods purchased into a business is known as **carriage inwards**, whereas, carriage charges for the delivery of goods to a business's customers is known as **carriage outwards**.

Carriage inwards

When goods are purchased one supplier may include carriage within the purchase cost whilst another may charge separately for carriage. When this happens the carriage inwards charge is always added to the cost of purchases in the trading account.

> TIP: CARRIAGE INWARDS – cost of transport of goods into a business

CARRIAGE OUTWARDS – cost of transport of goods to the customers of the business.

Carriage outwards

Carriage outwards is the cost of delivering the goods to the business's customers. It is an expense and not part of the selling price of the goods. Carriage outwards is always charged as an expense in the profit and loss account.

Suppose that, in the illustration shown earlier of D Bode, the goods had been bought for the same total figure of £27,350 but, in fact, £27,200 was the figure for purchases and £150 for carriage inwards. Let us also assume that part of the general expenses figure of £2,550, in Exhibit 16.1 was, in fact, carriage outward amounting to £400. The trial balance would appear as shown in Exhibit 18.2.

Exhibit 18.2

D Bode
Trial Balance as at 31 December 2010 (extract)

	Dr £	Cr £
Sales		40,000
Purchases	27,200	
Sales returns	350	
Purchase returns		200
Carriage inwards	150	
Carriage outwards	400	
General expenses	2,150	

The trading and profit and loss account would then be shown in Exhibit 18.3.

Exhibit 18.3

D Bode
Trading and Profit and Loss Account for the year ended 31 December 2010

		£	£
Sales			40,000
Less Sales returns			350
			39,650
Less	Cost of goods sold		
	Purchases	27,200	
	Less Purchase returns	200	
		27,000	
Add	Carriage inwards	150	27,150
Gross profit			12,500
Less	Expenses:		
	General expenses	2,150	
	Carriage outwards	400	2,550
Net profit			9,950

It can be seen that the three versions of D Bode's trial balance have all been concerned with the same overall amount of goods bought and sold by the business, at the same overall prices. Therefore, in each case, the same gross profit of £12,500 is shown. The net profit of £9,950 also remains the same.

18.3 The second year of a business

Following on from Exhibit 17.2 in the previous chapter, we assume that B Swift carries on his business for another year. He then extracts a trial balance as on 31 December 2011 as shown in Exhibit 18.4. At that date the closing stock was valued at £5,500.

Exhibit 18.4

B Swift		
Trial Balance as at 31 December 2011	Dr	Cr
	£	£
Sales		67,000
Purchases	42,600	
Electricity	1,900	
Rent	2,400	
Wages	5,200	
General expenses	700	
Carriage outwards	1,100	
Buildings	20,000	
Fixtures and fittings	7,500	
Debtors	12,000	
Creditors		9,000
Bank	1,200	
Cash	400	
Loan from J Marsh		10,000
Drawings	9,000	
Capital		21,000
Stock (at 31 December 2010)	3,000	
	107,000	107,000

Adjustments needed for stock

So far, we have prepared the accounts for new businesses only. When a business starts it has no stock brought forward. B Swift started his new business on 1 January 2010 so his first year of trading ended on 31 December 2010, at which time he had a closing stock of £3,000. Therefore, when preparing his trading and profit and loss account for that year we are only concerned with the closing stock figure of £3,000. When we prepare the trading and profit and loss account for the second year of business we can see the difference.

In the trading and profit and loss account for the first year of trading, i.e. the year ended 31 December 2010, only one stock figure appears; that is the closing stock of £3,000. This figure of closing stock for the year ended 31 December 2010 becomes the opening stock for the second year of trading and will be entered into the trading account in Swift's second year of trading. Therefore, both opening and closing stock figures are shown in the trading and profit and loss account for the year ended 31 December 2011.

TIP – the closing stock of one year becomes the opening stock of the next year.

The stock figure shown in the trial balance given in Exhibit 18.4 is that brought forward from the previous year on 31 December 2010; it is, therefore, the opening stock. The closing stock at 31 December 2011 can only be found by stocktaking, assume that it amounts to £5,500.

The opening and closing stock account figures for Swift for the two years can now be summarised as follows:

Trading Account for period	Year to 31 December 2010	Year to 31 December 2011
Opening stock 1.1.2010	None	
Closing stock 31.12.2010	£3,000	
Opening stock 1.1.2011		£3,000
Closing stock 31.12.2011		£5,500

Double entry for stock

To enable you to understand the double entry aspect of stock, both the stock account and the trading account for B Swift for the year ended 31 December 2011 are shown below:

Dr		Stock Account			Cr
2010		£	2010		£
Dec 31 Trading a/c		3,000	Dec 31 Balance c/d		3,000
2011			2011		
Jan 1 Balance b/d		3,000	Dec 31 Trading a/c (Opening stock)		3,000
Dec 31 Trading a/c (Closing stock)		5,500	Dec 31 Balance c/d		5,500
		8,500			8,500

B Swift

Trading and Profit and Loss Account for the year ended 31 December 2011

	£		£
Opening stock	3,000	Sales	67,000
Purchases	42,600	Closing stock	5,500
Gross profit c/d	26,900		
	72,500		72,500

The stock at 31 December 2011 is £5,500 and had not been entered into the accounts previously. The entries above show how this has been recorded using double entry:

Debit: stock account £5,500

Credit: trading account £5,500.

Calculation of cost of goods sold

Let us now calculate the cost of goods sold for B Swift for the year ended 31 December 2011:

	£
Stock of goods at start of the year	3,000
Add Purchases	42,600
Total goods available for sale	45,600
Less What remains at the end of the year: (i.e. Closing stock)	5,500
Therefore the cost of goods that have been sold	40,100

Cost of goods sold = Opening stock + Purchases − Closing stock
                    └─── Stock available ───┘   └─ Unsold stock ─┘
                         for sale   at year end

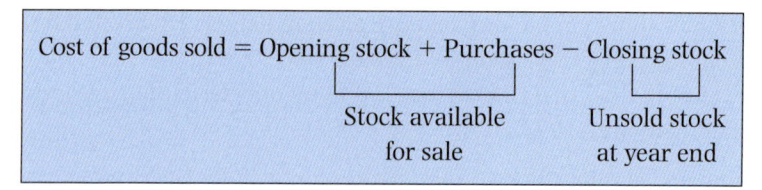

The gross profit can now be found by taking into consideration the effect the closing stock has on the gross profit. Remember that sales less cost of goods sold equals gross profit, therefore:

	£
Sales	67,000
Less Cost of goods sold (see above)	40,100
Gross profit	26,900

The trading and profit and loss account and balance sheet can now be drawn up as shown in Exhibits 18.5 and 18.6.

Exhibit 18.5

B Swift
Trading and Profit and Loss Account for the year ended 31 December 2011

	£	£
Sales		67,000
Less Cost of goods sold		
Opening stock	3,000	
Add Purchases	42,600	
	45,600	
Less Closing stock	5,500	
		40,100
Gross profit		26,900
Less Expenses		
Wages	5,200	
Carriage outwards	1,100	
Electricity	1,900	
Rent	2,400	
General expenses	700	
		11,300
Net profit		15,600

Exhibit 18.6

B Swift
Balance Sheet as at 31 December 2011

	£	£	£
Fixed assets			
Buildings	20,000	–	20,000
Fixtures and fittings	7,500	–	7,500
	27,500		27,500
Current assets			
Stock	5,500		
Debtors	12,000		
Cash at bank	1,200		
Cash in hand	400	19,100	
Less Current liabilities			
Creditors	9,000	9,000	
Net current assets (Working capital)			10,100
			37,600
Long-term liabilities			
Loan from J Marsh			10,000
Net assets			27,600
Financed by			
Capital account			
Balance at 1 January 2010			21,000
Add Net profit for the year			15,600
			36,600
Less Drawings			9,000
			27,600

18.4 Other expenses in the trading account

The costs of putting goods into a saleable condition should be charged in the trading account. In the case of a trader these are relatively few. An example might be a trader who sells clocks packed in boxes. If he bought the clocks from one source and the boxes from another source, both of these items would be charged in the trading account as purchases. In addition, if a person is paid wages to pack the clocks, then such wages would be charged in the trading account.

For goods imported from abroad it is usual to find that the costs of import duty, marine insurance and freight charges are also treated as part of the cost of goods sold and are, therefore, debited to the trading account.

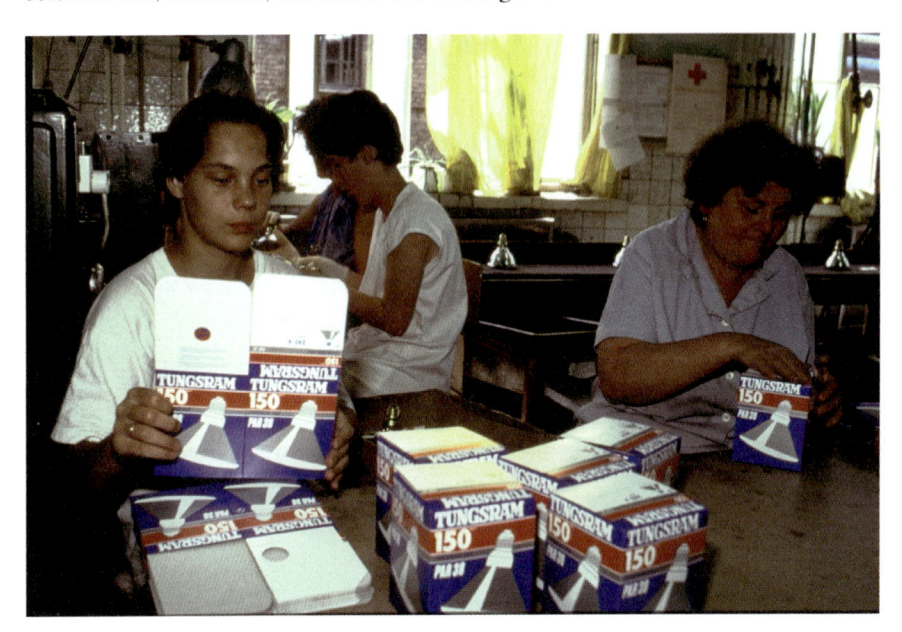

18.5 Losses incurred by a business

So far, we have looked at the situation in which both a gross profit and a net profit have been made by a business. This will not always be the case in every business. For all kinds of reasons, such as poor trading conditions, bad management, or unexpected increases in expenses, the business may trade at a loss for a given period.

We will look at two cases: A Barnes, who made a gross profit but a **net loss** for the year, and K Jackson, who made both a gross loss and a net loss. The details for the trading and profit and loss accounts for the year ended 31 December 2009 for Barnes and Jackson are as follows:

	A Barnes	K Jackson
	£	£
Opening stock 1 January 2009	3,500	9,200
Sales	21,000	33,000
Purchases	15,000	29,800
Closing stock 31 December 2009	2,200	4,800
Other expenses	6,300	3,900

The trading and profit and loss accounts for each business are shown in Exhibits 18.7 and 18.8.

Exhibit 18.7

A Barnes
Trading and Profit and Loss Account for the year ended 31 December 2009

	£	£
Sales		21,000
Less Cost of goods sold		
Opening stock	3,500	
Add Purchases	15,000	
	18,500	
Less Closing stock	2,200	16,300
Gross profit		4,700
Less Other expenses		6,300
Net loss		1,600

In the above example of A Barnes, a gross profit of £4,700 was made but since expenses of £6,300 were greater than that, the final result is a net loss of £1,600.

Exhibit 18.8

K Jackson
Trading and Profit and Loss Account for the year ended 31 December 2009

	£	£
Sales		33,000
Less Cost of goods sold		
Opening stock	9,200	
Add Purchases	29,800	
	39,000	
Less Closing stock	4,800	34,200
Gross loss		1,200
Add Other expenses		3,900
Net loss		5,100

In the above example of K Jackson, a gross loss of £1,200 occurred since the cost of goods sold amounted to £34,200 while sales were only £33,000. Added to this gross loss of £1,200 were the expenses of £3,900 for the period and a resultant net loss of £5,100.

Recording losses in the capital account

If a net loss occurs then it will be recorded in the owner's capital account as follows:

        Debit: capital account
        Credit: profit and loss account.

18.6 Financial statements

The term **financial statements** is often used to mean collectively the trading and profit and loss account and the balance sheet which are produced at the end of a trading period. They used to be referred to as **final accounts** but this term can be quite misleading since none of the financial statements are really 'accounts' in the book-keeping sense. Many people do, however, still refer to them as the 'final accounts' or just simply 'the accounts' of a business.

Note: On the CD you will find a model layout of the trading and profit and loss account and balance sheet of a sole trader, together with further step-by-step instructions in the preparation of the financial statements.

> FINANCIAL STATEMENTS consist of the Trading and Profit and Loss Account and the Balance Sheet. Previously referred to as 'Final Accounts'.

End of Chapter Checklist

Summary

- The sales returns should always be deducted from the sales and the purchase returns deducted from the purchases; both are shown in the trading account.
- Carriage inwards is the cost of transporting the goods purchased 'into' the business and, as such, is always *added* to the cost of purchases in the trading account, whilst carriage outwards is the cost of delivery and is charged to the profit and loss account.
- A stock account is updated to record the closing stock figure and to carry forward the balance from one period to the next, therefore the closing stock of one year becomes the closing stock of the next year.
- Cost of goods sold = opening stock + purchases − closing stock.
- The preparation of the trading and profit and loss account is shown including adjustments.
- The closing stock figure is entered in the current asset section in the balance sheet.
- Expenses needed to get goods into a saleable condition are charged in the trading account.
- A trading and profit and loss account is shown for when either a gross loss or net loss occurs.

Questions

18.1 The following details for the year ended 31 December 2010 are available. Prepare the trading account for that year for K Jepson.

		£
Carriage inwards		1,206
Sales		69,736
Purchases		47,536
Stocks of goods:	1 January 2010	12,463
	31 December 2010	13,480

18.2X The following details for the year ended 31 March 2010 are available. Prepare the trading account for that year for Jane Li.

		£
Stocks:	31 March 2009	29,686
	31 March 2010	33,307
Purchases		66,429
Carriage inwards		2,020
Sales		98,280

18.3 Prepare the trading and profit and loss account for the year ended 31 July 2010, in respect of T Mann, from the following details:

		£
Sales returns		1,029
Purchase returns		1,176
Purchases		65,100
Sales		110,859
Stocks of goods:	1 August 2009	11,949
	31 July 2010	8,883
Carriage inwards		3,570
Salaries and wages		10,521
Rent		3,066
Motor expenses		6,552
General expenses		882
Carriage outwards		1,659

End of Chapter Checklist

Questions

18.4X Prepare a trading and profit and loss account for the year ended 31 December 2010 for Emily Hart from the following information:

		£
Carriage outwards		931
Carriage inwards		400
Sales returns		2,850
Purchase returns		3,000
Wages		21,875
Rent and rates		2,800
General expenses		684
Sales		189,050
Purchases		122,683
Stocks of goods:	1 January 2010	34,732
	31 December 2010	32,984
Printing and stationery		525

18.5 From the following trial balance of S Shah, draw up a trading and profit and loss account for the year ended 30 June 2010, and balance sheet as at that date.

S Shah
Trial Balance as at 30 June 2010

	Dr	Cr
	£	£
Stock 1 July 2009	22,733	
Carriage outwards	1,920	
Carriage inwards	2,976	
Sales returns	1,968	
Purchase returns		3,091
Purchases	113,990	
Sales		178,560
Salaries and wages	37,075	
Rent and rates	2,918	
Insurance	749	
Motor expenses	4,250	
Telephone and internet	4,198	
Electricity	1,594	
General expenses	3,014	
Buildings	80,000	
Motor vehicles	17,280	
Computer equipment	3,360	
Debtors	37,402	
Creditors		32,618
Cash at bank	4,627	
Drawings	11,520	
Capital		137,305
	351,574	351,574

Stock at 30 June 2010 was £28,320.

18.6X The trial balance shown below was extracted from the books of J Collins on 31 March 2010. Prepare the trading and profit and loss account for the year ended 31 March 2010 and a balance sheet as at that date using the trial balance and the note regarding stock.

J Collins
Trial Balance as at 31 March 2010

	Dr	Cr
	£	£
Sales		74,400
Purchases	46,224	
Stock 1 April 2009	15,104	
Carriage outwards	1,304	
Carriage inwards	936	
Salaries and wages	11,788	
Printing and stationery	810	
Telephone	756	
Travel expenses	490	
Rent	1,824	
Rates	1,080	
Sundry expenses	2,808	
Computer equipment	9,600	
Fixtures and fittings	2,400	
Debtors	18,308	
Creditors		12,180
Cash at bank	15,504	
Cash in hand	480	
Drawings	8,540	
Capital		51,376
	137,956	137,956

Stock at 31 March 2010 was £19,992.

Section D: Adjustments

Chapter 19: The concept of depreciation of fixed assets

Getting started

Edexcel specification
Adjustments, 4.3.

After you have studied this chapter you should be able to:

- define depreciation
- explain why depreciation is charged
- calculate depreciation using the:
  1. straight line method
  2. reducing balance method (diminishing balance method)
  3. revaluation method.

DEPRECIATION is the part of the cost of the fixed asset consumed during its period of use by the business.

19.1 Depreciation of fixed assets

Fixed assets are those assets of material value that are purchased for use in the business, are not for resale and which have a long life. Whilst assets such as buildings, machinery, fixtures and fittings are used in the business for many years they do not last indefinitely, therefore, when they are disposed of, the difference between the cost price and the amount received on disposal is called **depreciation**.

Depreciation as an expense

Depreciation is part of the original cost of a fixed asset consumed during its period of use by the business. Since depreciation is an expense, it will have to be charged to the profit and loss account in the same way as expenses such as wages, rent, insurance etc. and will, therefore, reduce net profit. The amount charged each year for depreciation is based upon an estimate of how much economic use of the fixed asset has been used up in that accounting period.

For example, if a business purchased computer equipment costing £4,000 which was expected to last for four years, then each year a quarter of the overall usefulness would be consumed. The charge for depreciation would be a quarter of the cost of the computer equipment, i.e. £1,000. The net profit for the year would be reduced by £1,000 and the value of the equipment in the balance sheet would be reduced from £4,000 to £3,000.

19.2 Causes of depreciation

Fixed assets such as machinery, motor vehicles, plant and equipment etc. tend to fall in value (depreciate) for various reasons such as physical deterioration, economic factors, time and depletion. These are described more fully below:

Physical depreciation

1. **Wear and tear** – Fixed assets as described above eventually wear out, some lasting many years whilst others wear out more quickly.

2. **Erosion, rust, rot and decay** – Land may be eroded or wasted away by the action of wind, rain, sun or the other elements of nature. Similarly, the metals in motor vehicles or machinery will rust away. Wood will rot eventually. Decay is a process which will be present due to the elements of nature and a lack of proper attention.

Economic factors

Economic factors may be said to be the reasons for an asset being put out of use even though it is in good physical condition. The two main factors are usually obsolescence and inadequacy:

1. **Obsolescence** – This occurs when an asset becomes out of date due to advanced technology or a change in processes. For example, in the car industry much of the assembly work is now done by robots.
2. **Inadequacy** – This arises when an asset is no longer used because of the growth and change in the size of the business due to new regulations. The transport industry is now able to use much larger vehicles than previously, resulting in the business selling off their smaller vehicles.

Both obsolescence and inadequacy do not necessarily mean that the asset is destroyed. It is merely put out of use by the business, and another business will often buy it.

The time factor

There are some assets that have a legal life fixed in terms of years, for example, a lease. A business may decide to rent a property for ten years so takes out a lease and a legal agreement is drawn up between the parties. Each year, a proportion of the cost of the lease is depreciated until the lease expires and the value is nil. In such cases, the term **amortisation** may be used instead of the term depreciation.

Depletion

Some assets are of a 'wasting nature' such as the extraction of raw materials from mines or quarries, or oil from oil wells. Such natural resources are often sold in their raw state to other businesses for processing. To provide for the consumption of an asset of a wasting character is called provision for **depletion**.

> DEPLETION means the wasting away of an asset as it is used.

19.3 Provision for depreciation as an allocation of cost

Depreciation in total over the life of an asset can be calculated quite simply as cost less amount receivable when the asset is put out of use by the business. The amount received on disposal is often referred to as the **residual value** or **scrap value**. If an item is bought and sold for a lower amount within the same accounting period, then the difference in value is charged as depreciation in arriving at that period's net profit.

> RESIDUAL VALUE means the amount received on disposal of the asset, also referred to as 'scrap value'.

The difficulties start when the asset is used for more than one accounting period; an attempt has to be made to charge each period with the appropriate amount of depreciation.

Although depreciation provisions are now intended to allocate the cost of the fixed asset to each accounting period in which it is in use, it does not follow that there is any true and accurate method of performing even this task. All that can be said is that the cost should be allocated over the life of the asset in such a way as to charge it as equitably as possible to the periods in which the asset is used. The difficulties involved are considerable and include:

1. Apart from a few assets, such as a lease, how accurately can a business assess an asset's useful life? Even a lease may be put out of use if the premises leased have become inadequate due to the expansion of the business.

2. How is 'use' measured? A car owned by a business for two years may have been driven one year by a very careful driver and another year by a reckless driver. The standard of driving will affect the condition of the car and also the amount of cash receivable on its disposal. How should such a business apportion the car's depreciation costs?

3. There are other expenses beside depreciation, such as repairs and maintenance of the fixed asset. As both of these affect the rate and amount of depreciation, should they not also affect the depreciation provision calculations?

4. How can a business possibly know the amount receivable in a number of years' time when the asset is put out of use?

These are only some of the difficulties. Therefore, accounting has developed various methods of calculating depreciation as shown below.

19.4 Methods of calculating depreciation charges

The two main methods in use for calculating depreciation charges are the **straight line method** and the **reducing balance method**, often called the **diminishing balance method**. Most accountants think that, although other methods may be needed in certain cases, the straight line method is the one that is generally most suitable. Both methods are now described.

Straight line method

> STRAIGHT LINE METHOD – a depreciation calculation whereby depreciation remains at an equal amount each year.

This method involves the cost price of an asset, the estimated years of its use and the expected disposal value. The depreciation charge each year can be calculated thus:

$$\text{Depreciation charge per year} = \frac{\text{Cost Price} - \text{Disposal value}}{\text{Number of years of use}}$$

For example, if a car was purchased for £22,000 and the business decided to keep it for four years and then sell it for £2,000, the depreciation to be charged would be:

$$\frac{\text{Cost price} - \text{Disposal value}}{\text{Number of years of use}} = \frac{£22,000 - £2,000}{4} = £5,000 \text{ depreciation per year}$$

The depreciation charge of £5,000 would then be charged for four years.

If, after four years, the car had no disposal value, the charge for depreciation would have been:

$$\frac{\text{Cost price}}{\text{Number of years of use}} = \frac{£22,000}{4} = £5,500 \text{ depreciation each year for 4 years}$$

This method may sometimes be referred to as the 'fixed instalment method'.

Reducing balance method

Depreciation to be charged involves deciding on a percentage amount to be used each year. This percentage is then deducted from the cost price for the first year and in subsequent years from the reducing balances. This is illustrated in the following example:

Example: If a machine is bought for £10,000 and depreciation is to be charged at 20%, the calculations for the first three years would be as follows:

	£
Cost	10,000
First year: depreciation (20% of £10,000)	2,000
	8,000
Second year: depreciation (20% of £8,000)	1,600
	6,400
Third year: depreciation (20% of £6,400)	1,280
Net book value at the end of the third year	5,120

Note that **net book value** means the cost of a fixed asset with depreciation deducted. It is sometimes simply known as 'book value'.

Using this method means that much larger amounts are charged in the earlier years of use as compared with the latter years of use. It is often said that repairs and upkeep in the early years will not cost as much as when the asset becomes old. This means that:

In the early years		In the later years
A higher charge for depreciation		A lower charge for depreciation
+	will tend to be fairly equal to	+
A lower charge for repairs and upkeep		A higher charge for repairs and upkeep

A comparison of the two methods is shown below in the following example:

Worked example:

A joinery manufacturer has bought a machine for £16,000 with an expected life of four years and a disposal value of £1,000. The owner asks for a comparison of the depreciation to be charged using both methods, with a percentage of 50% to be used for the reducing balance method.

The depreciation for the straight line method is calculated as follows:

$$\text{Depreciation per year} = \frac{\text{Cost price} - \text{Disposal value}}{\text{Number of years of use}}$$

$$= \frac{£16,000 - £1,000}{4} = \frac{15,000}{4}$$

$$= £3,750$$

> **REDUCING BALANCE METHOD** is a depreciation calculation which is based on the net book value of the asset brought forward from the previous year. Therefore, the depreciation charge falls each year.

> **NET BOOK VALUE** – the cost of the asset less depreciation charges to date, also known as 'book value'.

A percentage figure of 50% will be used for the reducing balance method:

	Method 1 Straight Line		Method 2 Reducing Balance
	£		£
Cost	16,000		16,000
Depreciation: year 1	3,750	(50% of £16,000)	8,000
	12,250		8,000
Depreciation: year 2	3,750	(50% of £8,000)	4,000
	8,500		4,000
Depreciation: year 3	3,750	(50% of £4,000)	2,000
	4,750		2,000
Depreciation: year 4	3,750	(50% of £2,000)	1,000
Disposal value	1,000		1,000

It can be seen that depreciation charge remains the same each year using the straight line method in contrast to the reducing balance method. Here, a much higher charge occurs in the early years reducing to lower charges in later years.

Exhibit 19.1 Comparing depreciation charges for above worked example

Straight Line method

Reducing balance method

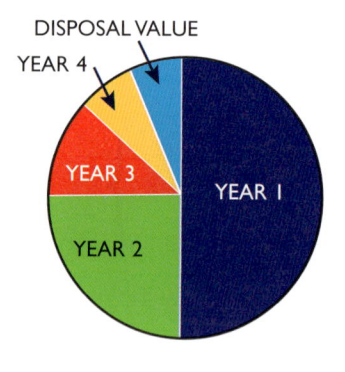

REVALUATION METHOD – used for calculating depreciation on large quantities of low-cost assets such as tools.

Revaluation method

Another method of depreciation, used mainly by self-employed people such as joiners, electricians, plumbers etc., is the revaluation method. These small businesses may have a number of low cost tools and equipment such as saws, drills, spanners and so on which are needed to enable them to carry out their jobs. It would be very difficult to use one of the previously discussed methods of depreciation for such low cost tools and equipment, therefore the revaluation method is used.

With this method, the tools and equipment etc. are valued at the beginning of the financial year and any further items purchased during the year for use in the business which are not for resale are added to the initial valuation. After using the tools etc. during the year, they are valued again at the end of the financial year. This figure is then deducted from the initial valuation, plus tools etc. purchased during the year, to find the depreciation to be charged to the profit and loss account. The following example shows the depreciation calculation for a joiner:

Example:

	£
Value of tools and equipment at start of period	2,500
Add Cost of items purchased during the period	500
	3,000
Less Value at close of the period	2,000
Depreciation for the year	1,000

19.5 Depreciation provisions and assets bought or sold

There are two main methods of calculating depreciation provisions for assets bought or sold during an accounting period.

1. Ignore the dates during the year that the assets were bought or sold and merely calculate a full period's depreciation on the assets in use at the end of the period. Therefore, assets sold during the accounting period will have no provision made for depreciation for that last period, irrespective of how many months they were in use. Conversely, assets bought during the period will have a full period of depreciation provision charged even though they may not have been owned throughout the whole period.

2. Provide for depreciation made on the basis of one month's ownership equals one month's depreciation. Fractions of months are usually ignored. This is obviously a more precise method than method 1.

The first method is the one normally used in practice. However, for examination purposes, where the dates on which the assets are bought and sold are shown, you should use method 2. If no such dates are given then, obviously, method 1 is the one to use. Often, the question will indicate which method to use so it is important to read the instructions carefully before attempting your answer.

End of Chapter Checklist

Summary

- Depreciation is charged on fixed assets in use during an accounting period.
- Fixed assets are defined as those assets of material value that are intended to be used in the business over a period of time and have not been bought with the intention of resale.
- Depreciation is an expense of the business and as such is charged to the profit and loss account.
- The main causes of depreciation are physical deterioration, economic factors, the time factor and depletion.
- The straight line method is where an equal amount of depreciation is charged each year.
- The reducing balance method is where a fixed percentage for depreciation is taken from the cost of the asset in the first year. In the second and later years, the same percentage is taken from the reduced balance (i.e. cost *less* depreciation already charged).
- With the revaluation method the assets are valued at the start of the period; additions are added to this figure from which the value of the assets at the end of the period is deducted. The difference is depreciation which is charged to the profit and loss account.

Questions

19.1 J Chen runs a small joinery business and purchases a new machine for £6,000. It has an estimated life of four years and a scrap value of £1,000. Chen is not sure whether to use the straight line or reducing (diminishing) method of depreciation for the purpose of calculating depreciation on the machine.

You are required to calculate the depreciation on the machine using both methods, showing clearly the balance remaining in the machine account at the end of the four years for each method. Assume that 40% per annum is to be used for the reducing (diminishing) balance method.

19.2 A machine costs £75,000 and will be kept for four years when it will be traded in at an estimated value of £30,720. Show the calculations of the figures for depreciation for each of the four years using the:

a) straight line method
b) reducing (diminishing) balance method, using a depreciation rate of 20%.

19.3X A motor vehicle costs £19,200 and will be kept for four years, and then sold for an estimated value of £1,200. Calculate the depreciation for each year using the:

a) reducing (diminishing) balance method, using a depreciation rate of 50%
b) straight line method.

19.4X Computer equipment costs £4,600. It will be kept for four years, and then sold at an estimated figure of £600. Show the calculations of the figures for depreciation (to the nearest pound) for each year using the:

a) straight line method
b) reducing (diminishing) balance method, using a depreciation rate of 25%.

19.5X A tractor cost £72,900 and has an estimated life of five years after which it will be traded in at an estimated value of £9,600. Show your calculations of the amount of depreciation each year using the:

a) reducing (diminishing) balance method at a rate of $33\frac{1}{3}$%
b) straight line method.

19.6 A dumper is bought for £18,000. It will last for three years and will then be sold back to the supplier for £3,000. Show the depreciation calculations for each year using the:

a) reducing (diminishing) balance method with a rate of 40%
b) straight line method.

End of Chapter Checklist

Questions

19.7X From the following information, which shows the depreciation for the first two years of use for two assets, you are required to answer the questions set out below.

	Machinery	Fixtures
	£	£
Cost Year 1	8,000	3,600
Year 1 Depreciation	1,600	900
	6,400	2,700
Year 2 Depreciation	1,600	675
	4,800	2,025

a) Which type of depreciation method is used for each asset?
b) What will be the book value of each of the assets after four years of use?
c) If, instead of the method used, the machinery had been depreciated by the alternative method but using the same percentage rate, what would have been the book value after four years? (Calculate your answer to the nearest £.)

Section D: Adjustments

Chapter 20: Double entry for depreciation and disposal of a fixed asset

Getting started

Edexcel specification
Adjustment, 4.4, 4.5, 4.6.

After you have studied this chapter you should be able to:

- incorporate depreciation calculations into the accounting records
- record the disposal of fixed assets and the adjustments needed to the provision for depreciation accounts.

RECORDING PURCHASE OF A FIXED ASSET –
1 DEBIT – Asset account
2 CREDIT – Bank account (if paid)

RECORDING DEPRECIATION CHARGES –
1 DEBIT – Profit and Loss account
2 CREDIT – Provision for depreciation account

20.1 Recording depreciation

When a business purchases fixed assets the cost price is recorded in the respective fixed asset account. Any depreciation subsequently charged on that asset is recorded separately in a **Provision for depreciation account** where the depreciation charge accumulates each year. The following example illustrates the purchase of machinery and the depreciation charge which is recorded using double entry principles:

Example: A business purchases machinery for use in their workshop for £2,000 on 1 January 2001. The company uses the reducing balance method of depreciation and a rate of 20% per annum, their year end is 31 December. The accounting records for the first three years are shown below:

1 The machinery is purchased on 1 January 2001 and paid for by cheque:

- **Debit** the machinery account £2,000
- **Credit** the bank account £2,000 (not shown in our example).

2 At the end of the year the asset is depreciated at 20% per annum using the reducing balance method. First of all, we need to calculate the amount of depreciation to be charged each year:

	£
Cost of machinery	2,000
First year: depreciation (20% of £2,000)	400
Reduced balance year 1	1,600
Second year: depreciation (20% of £1,600)	320
Reduced balance year 2	1,280
Third year: depreciation (20% of £1,280)	256
Net book value at end of third year	1,024

Note: Net book value = Cost price − Depreciation
= 2,000 − 976 = £1,024

3 To record the depreciation:

- **Debit** the 'profit and loss account' with the amount of depreciation each year
- **Credit** the 'provision for depreciation – machinery account' with the amount of the depreciation charged each year.

4 In the balance sheet the asset and total depreciation would be shown under the fixed asset section as follows:

- The asset, i.e. 'machinery', is always shown at **cost price**, i.e. £2,000.
- The total depreciation to date, i.e. £400 + £320 + £256 = £976, is shown as a deduction from the cost price of the machinery to arrive at the **net book value**, £2,000 − £976 = £1,024.

> **BALANCE SHEET ENTRIES –**
> 1 ASSET is always shown at cost price.
> 2 TOTAL DEPRECIATION TO DATE is shown as a deduction from the cost price to arrive at the NET BOOK VALUE.

Exhibit 20.1

Dr			Machinery Account			Cr
2001		£	2001			£
Jan 1	Cash	2,000	Dec 31	Balance c/d		2,000
2002			2002			
Jan 1	Balance b/d	2,000	Dec 31	Balance c/d		2,000
2003			2003			
Jan 1	Balance b/d	2,000	Dec 31	Balance c/d		2,000
2004						
Jan 1	Balance b/d	2,000				

Dr			Provision for Depreciation – Machinery Account			Cr
2001		£	2001			£
Dec 31	Balance c/d	400	Dec 31	Profit and loss a/c		400
2002			2002			
Dec 31	Balance c/d	720	Jan 1	Balance b/d		400
			Dec 31	Profit and loss a/c		320
		720				720
2003			2003			
Dec 31	Balance c/d	976	Jan 1	Balance b/d		720
			Dec 31	Profit and loss a/c		256
		976				976
			2004			
			Jan 1	Balance b/d		976

Profit and Loss Account (extracts) for the year ended 31 December			
			£
2001	Depreciation		400
2002	Depreciation		320
2003	Depreciation		256

The balance on the machinery account is shown on the balance sheet at the end of each year, less the balance on the provision for depreciation account as shown below:

Balance Sheet (extracts) as at 31 December			
	Cost	Total depreciation	Net book value
	£	£	£
2001			
Machinery	2,000	400	1,600
2002			
Machinery	2,000	720	1,280
2003			
Machinery	2,000	976	1,024

Let us look at another example of a business whose year end is 30 June. The business buys a motor car on 1 July 2001 for £8,000, another car is bought on 1 July 2002 for £11,000. Each car is expected to be in use for five years, and the disposal value of the first car is expected to be £500 and the second car £1,000. The method of depreciation to be used is the straight line method. First of all, the depreciation charge needs to be calculated, see below:

Depreciation per year – straight line method:

Motor Car No. 1 – Bought on 1 July 2001 at a cost price of £8,000.

$$\text{Depreciation charge per year} = \frac{\text{Cost price} - \text{Disposal value}}{\text{Number of years of use}}$$

$$= \frac{8,000 - 500}{5}$$

$$= £1,500 \text{ depreciation charge per year}$$

Motor Car No. 2 – Bought on 1 July 2002 at a cost price of £11,000.

$$\text{Depreciation charge per year} = \frac{\text{Cost price} - \text{Disposal value}}{\text{Number of years of use}}$$

$$= \frac{11,000 - 1,000}{5}$$

$$= £2,000 \text{ depreciation charge per year}$$

The book-keeping entries for the first two years are shown below:

Note: The entries in the cash book have not been shown in this example.

Exhibit 20.2

Dr		Motor Cars Account			Cr
2001		£	2002		£
Jul 1	Bank	8,000	Jun 30	Balance c/d	8,000
2002			2003		
Jul 1	Balance b/d	8,000	Jun 30	Balance c/d	19,000
Jul 1	Bank	11,000			
		19,000			19,000
2003					
Jul 1	Balance b/d	19,000			

Dr		Provision for Depreciation – Motor Cars Account			Cr
2002		£	2002		£
Jun 30	Balance c/d	1,500	Jun 30	Profit and loss a/c	1,500
			Jul 1	Balance b/d	1,500
2003			2003		
Jun 30	Balance c/d	5,000	Jun 30	Profit and loss a/c	3,500
		5,000			5,000
			Jul 1	Balance b/d	5,000

Profit and Loss Account (extracts) for the year ended 30 June

		£
2002	Depreciation	1,500
2003	Depreciation	3,500

Balance Sheet (extract) as at 30 June 2002

	Cost	Total depreciation	Net book value
	£	£	£
Motor cars	8,000	1,500	6,500

Balance Sheet (extract) as at 30 June 2003

	Cost	Total depreciation	Net book value
	£	£	£
Motor cars	19,000	5,000	14,000

20.2   The disposal of a fixed asset

Reason for accounting entries

Once an asset is sold it will need deleting from the accounts. This means that the cost of that asset needs to be taken out of the asset account. In addition, the depreciation of the asset that has been sold will have to be taken out of the depreciation provision. Finally, the profit or loss on sale, if any, will have to be calculated.

As we have already seen in the previous chapter, depreciation charges have to be estimated. When an asset is purchased initially the business will not know at that time exactly when the asset will be disposed of and for how much. Therefore, when the asset is eventually disposed of, the amount received is usually different from the original estimate.

Accounting entries needed

On the sale of a fixed asset, i.e. machinery, the following entries are required:

A Transfer the cost price of the asset sold to an assets disposal account (in this case, a machinery disposals account):

- **debit** machinery disposals account
- **credit** machinery account.

B Transfer the depreciation already charged to the assets disposal account:

- **debit** provision for depreciation – machinery account
- **credit** machinery disposals account.

C For the amount received on disposal:

- **debit** cash book
- **credit** machinery disposal account.

TIP – Learn the entries for disposal of an asset shown here.

D Transfer the difference (i.e. the amount to balance the machinery disposal account) to the profit and loss account.

  a) If the machinery disposals account shows a difference on the debit side of the account, it is a profit on sale:

   - **debit** machinery disposals account
   - **credit** profit and loss account.

  b) If the machinery disposals account shows a difference on the credit side of the account, it is a loss on sale:

   - **debit** profit and loss account
   - **credit** machinery disposals account.

These entries can be illustrated by looking at those needed if the machinery already shown in Exhibit 20.1 was sold. The records to 31 December 2003 show that the cost of the machine was £2,000 and a total of £976 has been written off as depreciation, leaving a net book value of (£2,000 − £976) = £1,024. If, therefore, the machine is sold on 2 January 2004 for *more than* £1,024, a profit on sale will be made; if, on the other hand, the machine is sold for *less than* £1,024, then a loss on disposal will be incurred.

Exhibit 20.3 shows the entries needed when the machine has been sold for £1,070 and a small profit on sale has been made. Exhibit 20.4 shows the entries where the machine has been sold for £950, thus incurring a loss on the sale. In both cases the sale is on 2 January 2004 and no depreciation is charged for the two days' ownership in 2004. The letters (A) to (D) in Exhibits 20.3 and 20.4 are references to the sequence of instructions shown above. **Note:** Cash book entries are not shown.

Exhibit 20.3

Dr				Machinery Account			Cr
2001			£	2004			£
Jan 1	Cash		2,000	Jan 2	Machinery disposals	(A)	2,000

Dr				Provision for Depreciation: Machinery Account			Cr
2004			£	2004			£
Jan 2	Machinery disposals	(B)	976	Jan 1	Balance b/d		976

Dr				Machinery Disposals Account			Cr
2004			£	2004			£
Jan 2	Machinery	(A)	2,000	Jan 2	Cash	(C)	1,070
Dec 31	Profit and loss a/c	(D)	46	2	Provision for depreciation	(B)	976
			2,046				2,046

Profit and Loss Account for the year ended 31 December 2004

			£
Gross Profit			xxx
Add Profit on sale of machinery		(D)	46

Exhibit 20.4

Dr		Machinery Account				Cr
2003			£	2004		£
Jan 1	Cash		2,000	Jan 2	Machinery disposals (A)	2,000

Dr		Provision for Depreciation: Machinery Account				Cr
2004			£	2004		£
Jan 2	Machinery disposals (B)		976	Jan 1	Balance b/d	976

Dr		Machinery Disposals Account				Cr
2004			£	2004		£
Jan 2	Machinery	(A)	2,000	Jan 2	Cash	(C) 950
				2	Provision for depreciation	(B) 976
				Dec 3	Profit and loss	(D) 74
			2,000			2,000

Profit and Loss Account for the year ended 31 December 2004		
		£
Gross Profit		xxx
Less Loss on sale of machinery	(D)	74

20.3 Depreciation provisions and the replacement of assets

Making a provision for depreciation does not mean that money is invested somewhere to finance the replacement of the asset when it is put out of use. It is simply a book-keeping entry, and the end result is that lower net profits are shown because the provisions have been charged to the profit and loss account.

It is not surprising to find that people who have not studied accounting misunderstand the situation. They often think that a provision is the same as money held in an account with which to replace the asset eventually.

On the other hand, lower net profits may also mean lower drawings by the owner(s) of the business. If this is the case, then there will be more money in the bank with which to replace the asset. However, there is no guarantee that lower profits mean lower drawings.

Note: A step-by-step guide dealing with depreciation in final accounts is available on CD attached at the back of this book.

End of Chapter Checklist

Summary

- Fixed assets are shown at cost price in the appropriate asset account; any depreciation charge is shown separately and accumulating in a 'Provision for depreciation account'.
- The depreciation charge for the period is then debited to the Profit and Loss Account.
- In the balance sheet the asset is shown at cost price, less the accumulated depreciation, so giving the 'Net book value' of the asset.
- On disposal of a fixed asset the book-keeping entries will involve a new account, i.e. 'asset disposal account'. It is then necessary to transfer the cost price of the asset, the accumulated depreciation and the cash received to this account when the asset is sold. The balancing figure in the asset disposal account may be either a profit or loss on disposal.
- A profit on disposal is added to the gross profit, whereas a loss on disposal is charged as an expense in the profit and loss account.
- Providing for depreciation does not mean that funds are invested elsewhere for financing the replacement of the asset.

Questions

20.1 A White, an exporter, bought a new car for his business on 1 January 2001 for £12,500. He decided to write off depreciation at the rate of 20%, using the reducing balance method.

Show the following for each of the financial years ended 31 December 2001, 2002 and 2003.

a) motor cars account
b) provision for depreciation account
c) extracts from the profit and loss accounts
d) extracts from the balance sheets.

20.2X H Slater, a jewellery manufacturer, purchased a new machine for £18,000 on 1 November 2001. Her business year end is 31 October, but she cannot decide which method of depreciation she should use in respect of the machine – the straight line method or the reducing (diminishing) balance method.

Required:

In order to assist her in making a decision, draw up the machinery account and the provision for depreciation account for the three years from 1 November 2001 using:

a) the straight line method   b) the reducing balance method.

Each account must indicate which method is being used, and each account should be balanced at the end of each of the three years. In both cases, the rate of depreciation is to be 10%, and calculations should be made to the nearest £.

c) Also show the extracts from the profit and loss accounts and balance sheets for each of the three years.

20.3 On 1 January 2001, the first day of his financial year, T Young bought computer equipment for £9,500. The equipment is to be depreciated by the straight line method at the rate of 20%, ignoring salvage value. On 1 January 2004 the equipment was sold for £4,250.

Show the following for the complete period of ownership.

a) The computer equipment account.
b) The provision for depreciation – computer equipment account.
c) The computer equipment disposal account.
d) The extracts from profit and loss accounts for four years.
e) The extracts from three years' balance sheets – 2001, 2002 and 2003.

20.4X Show the relevant disposal account for each of the following cases, including the transfers to the profit and loss account.

a) Motor vehicle: cost £12,000; depreciated £9,700 to date of sale; sold for £1,850.
b) Machinery: cost £27,900; depreciated £19,400 to date of sale; sold for £11,270.
c) Fixtures: cost £8,420; depreciated £7,135 to date of sale; sold for £50.
d) Buildings: cost £200,000; depreciated straight line 5% on cost for 11 years to date of sale; sold for £149,000.

End of Chapter Checklist

Questions

20.5 On 1 April 2004, Charles Simpson purchased new vehicles for his business at a cost of £35,000. He intends keeping the vehicles for four years and estimates that they will have a scrap value of £11,000 at that time.

Charles is aware of the need to depreciate the new vehicles but is unsure whether to write off the depreciation by the straight line or the diminishing (reducing) balance method.

a) Calculate depreciation for the years ended 31 March 2005 and 31 March 2006 using the straight line method.
b) Write up the provision for depreciation of vehicle account as it should appear for the years ended 31 March 2005 and 31 March 2006 under the reducing balance method, using a rate of 20% per annum.
c) State **two** reasons why vehicles depreciate.

IGCSE

20.6X The following details relate to the fixed assets of Rialto Traders for the year ended 30 April 2008:

(i)	**Fixed Assets at cost as at 1 May 2007**	
	Plant and Machinery	£500,000
	Motor Vehicles	£200,000
(ii)	**Provision for depreciation as at 1 May 2007**	
	Plant and Machinery	£200,000
	Motor Vehicles	£60,000
(iii)	**Depreciation policy**	
	Plant and Machinery – 10% per annum on straight line basis	
	Motor Vehicles – 25% per annum on reducing balance basis	

A full year's depreciation is charged in the year of purchase and no depreciation is charged in the year of disposal.

The following purchases and disposals of fixed assets took place during the year.

On 31 December 2007 plant and machinery which originally cost £200,000, with a written down value of £50,000, were sold at a loss of £10,000. The proceeds of the disposal were paid into the bank account. There were no purchases of plant and machinery during the year ended 30 April 2008.

On 1 February 2008 a new fleet of motor vehicles was purchased costing £100,000. This was paid by cheque. There were no disposals of motor vehicles during the year ended 30 April 2008.

a) Prepare the plant and machinery account, showing the balance carried down at the year end.
b) Prepare the motor vehicles account, showing the balance carried down at the year end.
c) Prepare the provision for depreciation (plant and machinery) account, showing the year end transfer and closing balance.
d) Prepare the disposal of machinery account, clearly identifying the profit or loss on disposal.
e) (i) State **two** accounting concepts which apply to the provision of depreciation of fixed assets.
   (ii) Evaluate the reasons why it is necessary to apply these concepts when preparing final accounts.

IGCSE

Section D: Adjustments

Chapter 21: Bad debts and provision for doubtful debts

Getting started

Edexcel specification
Adjustments, 4.10 to 4.13.

After you have studied this chapter you should be able to:

- understand how bad debts are written off and why provision for doubtful debts is made
- make accounting entries for recording a provision for doubtful debts
- make accounting entries for increasing or reducing the provision for doubtful debts
- make entries in the profit and loss account and balance sheet for bad debts and provision for doubtful debts
- make accounting entries for bad debts recovered.

BAD DEBTS – a debt owing to the business which is unlikely to be paid.

21.1 Bad debts

If a business finds that it is impossible to collect a debt, then that debt should be written off as a **bad debt**. This could happen if the debtor is suffering a loss in the business, or may even have gone bankrupt and is thus unable to pay the debt. A bad debt is, therefore, an expense on the business that is owed the money. An example of debts being written off as bad is shown below.

Exhibit 21.1

Martin Products Ltd sold goods costing £50 to Ken Leeming on 5 January 2010; unfortunately, Leeming experienced financial difficulties and was unable to pay his debt. Goods were also sold to T Young for £240 on 16 February 2010. Young paid £200 on account on 17 May 2010 but was unable to pay the outstanding £40.

When drawing up our final accounts to 31 December 2010, it was decided to write these off as bad debts. The accounting entries are shown in the table below.

Accounting entries	Explanation
Debit: Bad debts account	To transfer the amount of unpaid debt to the bad debts account
Credit: Debtor's account	To reduce the liability of the debtor who is unable to settle the debt
Debit: Profit and loss account	To record the amount of bad debts of the period concerned
Credit: Bad debts account	To transfer the amount of bad debts to profit and loss account

The accounts would appear as follows:

Dr			Ken Leeming Account			Cr
2010		£	2010			£
Jan 5	Sales	50	Dec 31	Bad debts		50

Dr			T Young Account			Cr
2010		£	2010			£
Feb 16	Sales	240	May 17	Cash		200
			Dec 31	Bad debts		40
		240				240

Dr			Bad Debts Account			Cr
2010		£	2010			£
Dec 31	Ken Leeming	50	Dec 31	Profit and loss a/c		90
Dec 31	T Young	40				
		90				90

Profit and Loss Account for the year ended 31 December 2010 (extract)

		£
Gross Profit		xxx
Less Expenses:		
Bad debts	90	90

21.2 Provision for doubtful debts

Let us look, as an example, at the accounts of K Clark, who started in business on 1 January 2007 and has just completed his first year of trading on 31 December 2007.

He has sold goods for £50,000 and they cost him £36,000, so his gross profit was (£50,000 − £36,000) = £14,000. However, included in the £50,000 sales was a credit sale to C Yates for £250. C Yates has died, leaving no money and he had not paid his account. The £250 debt is, therefore, a bad debt and should be charged in the profit and loss account as an expense.

Beside that debt, a credit sale of £550 on 1 December 2007 to L Hall is unlikely to get paid. Although Clark is not certain of this, he has been informed that Hall has not paid debts owing to other businesses. As Clark had given three months' credit to Hall, the debt is not repayable until 28 February 2008.

However, he has been requested by his bank to provide them with his financial statements for the year 2007. Unfortunately, Clark cannot wait until after 28 February 2008 to see whether the debt of £550 owing by Hall will be paid or not. If it is not paid then it will become a bad debt but in the meantime it is a **doubtful debt.**

What, therefore, can Clark do? When he presents his financial statements to the bank Clark wishes to achieve the following objectives:

(a) To charge as expenses in the profit and loss account for the year 2007 an amount representing sales of that year for which he will never be paid.

(b) To show in the balance sheet as correct a figure as possible for the true value of debtors at the balance sheet date.

PROVISION FOR DOUBTFUL DEBTS – an account showing the expected amounts of debtors who, at the balance sheet, may not be able to pay their outstanding accounts.

Clark can carry out (a) above by writing off Yates' debt of £250 and then charging it as an expense in his profit and loss account – see Exhibit 21.2 below.

For (b) he cannot yet write off Hall's debt of £550 as a bad debt because he is not certain about it being a bad debt. If he does nothing about it, then the debtors shown on the balance sheet will include a debt that probably has no value. The debtors on 31 December 2007, after deducting Yates' £250 bad debt, amount to £10,000. Exhibit 21.2 shows how the provision is charged to the trading and profit and loss account and the debtors' figure adjusted in the balance sheet.

> **BAD DEBTS WRITTEN OFF** – if a debt is unlikely to be paid it is written off and charged as an expense in the Profit and Loss Account.

Exhibit 21.2

K Clark
Trading and Profit and Loss Account for the year ended 31 December 2007

	£	£
Sales		50,000
Less Cost of goods sold:		36,000
Gross profit		14,000
Less Expenses:		
Other expenses	5,000	
Bad debts	250	
Provision for doubtful debts	550	5,800
Net profit		8,200

K Clark
Balance Sheet as at 31 December 2007 (extracts)

	£	£
Debtors	10,000	
Less Provision for doubtful debts	550	
		9,450

In the above exhibit **bad debts** and **provision for doubtful debts** have been shown as expenses in the year in which the sales were made and the debtors' figure in the Balance Sheet represents their true value.

The double entry for the above is explained in Section 21.4

21.3 Provision for doubtful debts: estimating provisions

The estimates of provision for doubtful debts can be made by:

- looking into each debt, and estimating which ones will be bad debts

- estimating, on the basis of experience, what percentage of the debts will result in bad debts, i.e. 5% of outstanding debtors' figure.

It is well known that the longer a debt is owing, the more likely it will become a bad debt, therefore, it is important for businesses to have an effective credit control system in place.

21.4 Accounting entries for provision for doubtful debts

The accounting entries required for the **provision for doubtful debts** are:

Year in which provision is *first* made:

- **Debit**: profit and loss account with the amount of provision (i.e. deduct it from gross profit as an expense)
- **Credit**: provision for doubtful debts account.

Exhibit 21.3

At 31 December 2007, the debtors' figure amounted to £10,000 after writing off £422 of definite bad debts. It is estimated that 2% of debtors (i.e. 2% × £10,000 = £200) will eventually prove to be bad debts, and it is decided to make a provision for these. The accounts will appear as follows:

Profit and Loss Account for the year ended 31 December 2007 (extracts)		
	£	£
Gross profit		xxx
Less Expenses:		
Bad debts	422	
Provision for doubtful debts	200	622

Dr	Provision for Doubtful Debts Account				Cr
2007		£	2007		£
Dec 31	Balance c/d	200	Dec 31	Profit and loss a/c	200
			2008		
			Jan 1	Balance b/d	200

In the balance sheet, the balance on the provision for doubtful debts will be deducted from the total of debtors, thus:

> TIP – *the **closing balance** of the provision for doubtful debts is deducted from the debtors in the balance sheet.

Balance Sheet (extracts) 31 December 2007		
Current assets	£	£
Debtors	10,000	
*Less Provision for doubtful debts	200	9,800

21.5 Increasing the provision

Using Exhibit 21.3 above, let us suppose that at the end of the following year, on 31 December 2008, the doubtful debts provision needed to be increased. This was because the debtors had risen to £12,000 with the provision remaining at 2%. Not included in the debtors' figure of £12,000 is £884 in respect of debts that had already been written off as bad debts during the year. A provision of £200 had been brought forward from the *previous* year, but we now want a total provision of £240 (i.e. 2% of £12,000). All that is needed is a provision for an extra £40.

The double entry will be:

- **Debit**: profit and loss account with the increase in the provision (i.e. deduct it as an expense from the gross profit)
- **Credit**: provision for doubtful debts account,

These entries are illustrated below in Exhibit 21.4:

TIP – the 'increase' in the provision is charged to the Profit and Loss Account.

Exhibit 21.4

Profit and Loss Account (extracts) for the year ended 31 December 2008

	£	£
Gross profit		xxx
Less Expenses:		
Bad debts	884	
Provision for doubtful debts	40	

Provision for Doubtful Debts Account

Dr		£				Cr £
2008				2008		
Dec 31	Balance c/d	240		Jan 1	Balance b/d	200
				Dec 31	Profit and loss a/c	40
		240				240
				2009		
				Jan 1	Balance b/d	240

Balance Sheet as at 31 December 2008 (extracts)

Current assets	£	£
Debtors	12,000	
Less Provision for doubtful debts	240	11,760

21.6 Reducing the provision

Outstanding debtors can reduce as well as increase and if a business finds that the amount outstanding has decreased it may decide to reduce the provision for doubtful debts. Reducing a provision is the opposite of increasing a provision.

In the provision for doubtful debts account a credit balance is shown, therefore, to reduce it, we would need a debit entry in the provision account. The credit would be in the profit and loss account. Again, using Exhibit 21.3 above, let us assume that on 31 December 2009 the debtors' figure had fallen to £10,500 but the provision remained at 2%, i.e. £210 (2% of £10,500). As the provision had previously been £240, it now needs a reduction of £30. Bad debts of £616 had already been written off during the year and are not included in the debtors' figure of £10,500.

The double entry is:

- **Debit**: provision for doubtful debts account
- **Credit**: profit and loss account (i.e. add it as a gain to the gross profit).

These entries are illustrated in Exhibit 21.5 below:

Exhibit 21.5

Balance Sheet as at 31 December 2009 (extracts)		
	£	£
Gross profit		xxx
Add Reduction in provision for doubtful debts		30
		xxx
Less Expenses:		
Bad debts	616	616

> TIP – the 'reduction' in the provision is credited in the Profit and Loss Account, i.e. added as a gain to the Gross Profit.

Dr		Provision for Doubtful Debts Account				Cr
2009			£	2009		£
Dec 31		Profit and loss a/c	30	Jan 1	Balance b/d	240
Dec 31		Balance c/d	210			
			240			240
				2010		
				Jan 1	Balance b/d	210

Balance Sheet as at 31 December 2009 (extracts)		
Current assets	£	£
Debtors		10,500
Less Provision for doubtful debts		210	10,290

The main points that you have to remember about provisions for doubtful debts are:

Year 1 – provision first made:

a) debit profit and loss account with full provision

b) show in balance sheet as a deduction from debtors.

Later years:

a) only the increase, or decrease, in the provision is shown in the profit and loss account, as follows:

- *to increase:* debit the profit and loss account, and credit the provision for doubtful debts account.
- *to decrease:* credit the profit and loss account, and debit the provision for doubtful debts account.

b) the balance sheet will show the amended figure of the provision as a deduction from debtors.

21.7 A worked example

Exhibit 21.6

A business started on 1 January 2007 and its financial year end is 31 December. A table of debtors, the bad debts written off and the estimated doubtful debts at the rate of 2% of debtors at the end of each year, as well as the double entry accounts and the extracts from the final accounts, is shown below:

Year to 31 December	Debtors at end of year (after bad debts written off)	Bad debts written off during year	Debts thought at end of year to be impossible to collect: 2% of debtors
	£	£	£
2007	6,000	423	120 (2% of £6,000)
2008	7,000	510	140 (2% of £7,000)
2009	7,750	604	155 (2% of £7,750)
2010	6,500	610	130 (2% of £6,500)

Dr		Provision for Doubtful Debts Account				Cr
2007			£	2007		£
Dec 31	Balance c/d		120	Dec 31	Profit and loss a/c	120
2008				2008		
Dec 31	Balance c/d		140	Jan 1	Balance b/d	120
				Dec 31	Profit and loss a/c	20
			140			140
2009				2009		
Dec 31	Balance c/d		155	Jan 1	Balance b/d	140
				Dec 31	Profit and loss a/c	15
			155			155
2010				2010		
Dec 31	Profit and loss a/c		25	Jan 1	Balance b/d	155
Dec 31	Balance c/d		130			
			155			155
				2011		
				Jan 1	Balance b/d	130

Dr		Bad Debts Account				Cr
2007			£	2007		£
Dec 31	Debtors		423	Dec 31	Profit and loss a/c	423
2008				2008		
Dec 31	Debtors		510	Dec 31	Profit and loss a/c	510
2009				2009		
Dec 31	Debtors		604	Dec 31	Profit and loss a/c	604
2010				2010		
Dec 31	Debtors		610	Dec 31	Profit and loss a/c	610

Profit and Loss Account(s) (extracts) for the year ended

		£	£
	Gross profit for 2007, 2008, 2009		xxx
2007	*Less* Expenses:		
	Bad debts	423	
	Provision for doubtful debts (increase)	120	543
2008	*Less* Expenses:		
	Bad debts	510	
	Provision for doubtful debts (increase)	20	530
2009	*Less* Expenses:		
	Bad debts	604	
	Provision for doubtful debts (increase)	15	619
2010	Gross profit for 2010		xxx
	Add Reduction in provision for doubtful debts		25
			xxx
	Less Bad debts		610
			xxx

Balance Sheet (extracts) as at 31 December

		£	£
2007	Debtors	6,000	
	Less Provision for doubtful debts	120	5,880
2008	Debtors	7,000	
	Less Provision for doubtful debts	140	6,860
2009	Debtors	7,750	
	Less Provision for doubtful debts	155	7,595
2010	Debtors	6,500	
	Less Provision for doubtful debts	130	6,370

21.8 Bad debts recovered

It is not uncommon for a *debt written off* in previous years to be *recovered* in later years. When this occurs, the book-keeping procedures are that you should reinstate the debt by making the following entries:

- **Debit**: debtor's account
- **Credit**: bad debts recovered account.

BAD DEBTS RECOVERED – a debt, previously written off, that is subsequently paid by the debtor.

The reason for reinstating the debt in the ledger account of the debtor is to have a detailed history of the account as a guide for granting credit in the future. By the time a debt is written off as bad, it will be recorded in the debtors' ledger account. Thus, when such a debt is recovered, it must also be shown in the debtors' ledger account.

When cash or a cheque is later received from the debtor in settlement of the account or part thereof, further book-keeping entries are necessary:

- **Debit**: cash/bank with the amount received
- **Credit**: debtor's account with the amount received.

At the end of the financial year, the credit balance on the bad debts recovered account will be transferred to either the bad debts account or direct to the credit side of the profit and loss account. The net effect of either of these entries is the same, since the bad debts account will be transferred to the profit and loss account at the end of the financial year. In other words, the net profit will be the same no matter which method is used.

Note: A step-by-step guide to dealing with bad debts and provision for doubtful debts in the financial statements is available on CD attached at the back of this book.

End of Chapter Checklist

Summary

- If a debt is unlikely to be paid then it is known as a bad debt and is usually written off by debiting the bad debts account and crediting the customer's account. The bad debt account is later credited and the profit and loss account debited, where it is charged as an expense against the gross profit.
- In case some of the outstanding debtors' fail to pay their account, a provision for doubtful debts is created which is charged to the profit and loss account and deducted from the debtors in the balance sheet.
- To increase the provision, debit the profit and loss account and credit the provision for doubtful debts account with the amount of the increase.
- To reduce the provision, debit the provision for doubtful debts account and credit the profit and loss account with the amount of the reduction.
- A debt that has previously been written off but is subsequently paid by the debtors is known as a bad debt recovered.

Questions

21.1 Hart & Partners started in business on 1 January 2009. During its first year of trading the following debts were found to be bad and the business decided to write them off as bad:

2009		
May 16	S Bayley	£550
July 31	J Carter	£223
November 9	T Roche	£467

On 31 December 2009, the schedule of remaining debtors, amounting in total to £26,000, is examined, and it is decided to make a provision for doubtful debts of 2%, i.e. £520. You are required to show:

a) the bad debts account and the provision for doubtful debts account
b) the charge to the profit and loss account
c) the relevant extracts from the balance sheet as at 31 December 2009.

21.2 A business started on 1 January 2007, and its financial year end is 31 December.

Date: 31 Dec	Total debtors	Profit and loss	Dr/Cr	Final figure for Balance Sheet
2007	7,000			
2008	8,000			
2009	6,000			
2010	7,000			

The table shows the figure for debtors appearing in a trader's books on 31 December of each year from 2007 to 2010. The provision for doubtful debts is to be 1% of debtors from 31 December 2007. Complete the table, indicating the amount to be debited or credited to the profit and loss accounts for the year ended on each 31 December, and the amount for the final figure of debtors to appear in the balance sheet on each date.

End of Chapter Checklist

Questions

21.3X A business started on 1 January 2007 and its financial year end is 31 December annually. The table shows the debtors, the bad debts written off and the estimated doubtful debts at the end of year.

Year to 31 December	Debtors at end of year (after bad debts written off)	Bad debts written off during the year	Debts thought at end of year to be unlikely to collect
2007	12,000	298	100
2008	15,000	386	130
2009	14,000	344	115
2010	18,000	477	150

Show the Bad Debts Account and Provision for Doubtful Debts Account, as well as the extracts from the profit and loss account for each year and the balance sheet extracts.

21.4X At the end of April, Steven is advised that one of his debtors, A. Carter, is unable to pay his outstanding amount of £500. Steven decides to write this off as a bad debt.

a) Prepare the journal entry for this transaction. Steven has experienced problems in the past year in collecting payments from credit customers. He has been advised by his accountant to introduce a provision for doubtful debts account at the end of the accounting period.

b) State the double entry required to create the provision for doubtful debts at the end of the accounting period.

c) Using the provision for doubtful debts as an example, evaluate the importance of the prudence concept to the preparation of the trading and profit and loss account and the balance sheet.

IGCSE

Section D: Adjustments

Chapter 22: Accruals, prepayments and other adjustments for financial statements

Getting started

Edexcel specification
Trading account, profit and loss account, balance sheet of a sole trader, 3.4, 3.7, 3.8, 3.9, 3.10, 3.11, 3.13. Adjustment, 4.7, 4.8, 4.9

After yotu have studied this chapter you should be able to:

- distinguish between amounts accrued and prepaid
- deal with accounts where accruals and prepayments arise
- adjust accounts with a stock carried forward, e.g. stationery
- show accruals, prepayments and revenue debtors in the balance sheet
- enter up the necessary accounts for goods taken for own use
- show the entries to record the revaluation of fixed assets
- distinguish between various kinds of capital
- enter discounts allowed and received in the financial statements
- prepare financial statements, incorporating the above mentioned adjustments, for a sole trader using the fully worked example and step-by-step guide.

22.1 Introduction

The trading and profit and loss accounts that have been prepared in the previous chapters have included sales for a specific period and shown *all* the expenses deducted appertaining to the period, resulting in either a net profit or net loss. So far, it has been assumed that the expenses incurred have belonged exactly to the specific period of the trading and profit and loss account.

While this generally applies to most expenses incurred by a business, there are occasions when some items of expenditure are paid in arrear and/or in advance. For example, a business may have some repair work carried out in one year but the invoice for the work may not be received until the following year. In order to show a correct figure of profit for the period, the amount of the repair bill should be accrued and charged against the profit for the period. Similarly, if an expense is paid in advance at the end of the period, an adjustment needs to be made to ensure that the profit for the period is correct. This is discussed more fully below:

Adjustments needed for expenses owing or paid in advance

Not all businesses pay their rent exactly on time and, indeed, some prefer to pay their rent in advance. The following examples illustrate the adjustments necessary if expenses are either owing or paid in advance at the end of a financial period. Two businesses each pay rent of £1,200 per year for their premises.

1. Business A pays £1,000 during the year and owes £200 rent at the end of the year:

   Rent expense used up during the year = £1,200

   Rent actually paid in the year = £1,000.

2. Business B pays £1,300 during the year, including £100 in advance for the following year:

   Rent expense used up during the year = £1,200

   Rent actually paid for in the year = £1,300.

A profit and loss account for the 12 months needs 12 months' rent as an expense, i.e. £1,200. This means that in the above two examples the double entry accounts will have to be adjusted.

In all the examples following in this chapter, the trading and profit and loss accounts are for the period ended 31 December 2008.

22.2 Accrued expenses (i.e. expenses owing)

> **ACCRUED EXPENSE** – an expense that has been incurred but not yet paid.

Assume that rent of £1,000 per year is payable at the end of every three months but is not always paid on time. Details are given in the table below:

Amount	Rent due	Rent paid
£250	31 March 2008	31 March 2008
£250	30 June 2008	2 July 2008
£250	30 September 2008	4 October 2008
£250	31 December 2008	5 January 2009

The rent account is now shown:

Dr		Rent Account			Cr
2008		£			
Mar 31	Cash	250			
Jul 2	Cash	250			
Oct 4	Cash	250			

The rent paid on 5 January 2009 will appear in the books for the year 2009 as part of the double entry book-keeping.

The expense for 2008 is obviously £1,000 since that is the year's rent and is the amount needed to be transferred to the profit and loss account at the end of the period. But if £1,000 was put on the credit side of the rent account (the debit being in the profit and loss account), the account would not balance. We would have £1,000 on the credit side of the account and only £750 on the debit side.

To make the account balance, the £250 rent owing for 2008 but paid in 2009 must be carried down to 2009 as a credit balance since it is a liability on 31 December 2008. Instead of rent owing, it could be called rent accrued (or just simply an **accrual**). The completed account can now be shown, thus:

Dr		Rent Account				Cr
2008		£	2008			£
Mar 31	Cash	250	Dec 31	Profit and loss		1,000
Jul 2	Cash	250				
Oct 4	Cash	250				
Dec 31	Accrued c/d	250				
		1,000				1,000
			2009			
			Jan 1	Accrued b/d		250

The balance c/d has been described as 'accrued c/d', rather than as a balance. This is to explain what the balance is for; it is for an **accrued expense**.

> **PREPAID EXPENSE** – is payment for an expense in advance.

22.3 Prepaid expenses

Insurance for a business is at the rate of £840 a year, starting from 1 January 2008. The business has agreed to pay this at the rate of £210 every three months. However, payments were not made at the correct times. The details are as follows:

Amount	Insurance due	Insurance paid
£210	31 March 2008	£210 – 28 February 2008
£210	30 June 2008	£420 – 31 August 2008
£210	30 September 2008	
£210	31 December 2008	£420 – 18 November 2008

The insurance account for the year ended 31 December 2008 will be shown in the books as:

Dr		Insurance Account		Cr
2008			£	
Feb 28	Bank		210	
Aug 31	Bank		420	
Nov 18	Bank		420	

The last payment shown of £420 is not just for 2008; it can be split as £210 for the three months to 31 December 2008 and £210 for the three months ended 31 March 2009. For a period of 12 months the cost of insurance is £840 and this is, therefore, the figure needing to be transferred to the profit and loss account.

If this figure of £840 is entered in the account then the amount needed to balance the account will be £210 and, at 31 December 2008, there is a benefit of a further £210 paid for but not used up – an asset that needs carrying forward as such to 2009, i.e. as a debit balance. It is a **prepaid expense**. The account can now be completed as follows:

Dr		Insurance Account				Cr
2008			£	2008		£
Feb 28	Bank		210	Dec 31	Profit and loss	840
Aug 31	Bank		420			
Nov 18	Bank		420	Dec 31	Prepaid c/d	210
			1,050			1,050
2009						
Jan 1	Prepaid b/d		210			

22.4 Adjustment for stock of stationery etc. carried forward

Prepayments can also occur when items other than purchases are bought for use in the business and are not fully used up in the period. For instance, packing materials and stationery items are normally not entirely used up over the period in which they are bought, there being a stock in hand at the end of the accounting period. This stock is, therefore, a form of prepayment and needs carrying down to the following period in which it will be used. This can be seen in the following example:

> Year ended 31 December 2008
> Stationery bought in the year £2,200
> Stationery in hand as at 31 December 2008 £400.

Looking at the example, it can be seen that in 2008 the stationery used up will have been (£2,200 − £400) = £1,800. There will be a stock of stationery valued £400 at 31 December 2008, to be carried forward to 2009 as an asset balance (debit balance) as follows:

Dr		Stationery Account				Cr
2008			£	2008		£
Dec 31	Bank		2,200	Dec 31	Profit and loss	1,800
				Dec 31	Stock c/d	400
			2,200			2,200
2009						
Jan 1	Stock b/d		400			

The stock of stationery is added to the other prepaid expenses in the balance sheet.

22.5 Revenue owing at the end of period

Sometimes there are other kinds of revenue, such as rent receivable, due that may not have been received by the end of the accounting period, therefore adjustments are needed as shown below:

Example: A business's warehouse is larger than needed, therefore they rent part of it to another business for £800 per annum. Details for the year ended 31 December are as shown in the table below.

Amount	Rent due	Rent received
£200	31 March 2008	4 April 2008
£200	30 June 2008	6 July 2008
£200	30 September 2008	9 October 2008
£200	31 December 2008	7 January 2009

REVENUE OWING – is other types of revenue (income) due to the business but has not been received at the end of the accounting period.

The account for 2008 will appear as follows:

Dr	Rent Receivable Account		Cr
	2008		£
	Apr 4	Bank	200
	Jul 6	Bank	200
	Oct 9	Bank	200

The rent received of £200 on 7 January 2009 will be entered in the books in 2009 (not shown).

Any **rent paid** by the business would be charged as a **debit** to the profit and loss account, therefore **rent received**, being the opposite, is transferred to the **credit** of the profit and loss account, since this is revenue/income.

The amount to be transferred for 2008 is that earned for the 12 months, i.e. £800. The rent received account is completed by carrying down the balance owing as a debit balance to 2009. The £200 owing is an asset on 31 December 2008. The rent receivable account can now be completed:

Dr		Rent Receivable Account			Cr
2008		£	2008		£
Dec 31	Profit and loss	800	Apr 4	Bank	200
			Jul 6	Bank	200
			Oct 9	Bank	200
			Dec 31	Accrued c/d	200
		800			800
2009					
Jan 1	Accrued b/d	200			

22.6 Expenses and revenue account balances and the balance sheet

In all the cases listed dealing with adjustments in the final accounts, there will still be a balance on each account after the preparation of the trading and profit and loss accounts. All such balances remaining should appear in the balance sheet. The only question left is where and how they should be shown.

The amounts owing for expenses are usually added together and shown as one figure and may be called 'expense creditors', 'expenses owing' or 'accrued expenses'. The items would appear in the balance sheet under current liabilities since they are expenses that have to be discharged in the near future.

The items prepaid are also added together and are called 'prepayments', 'prepaid expenses' or 'payments in advance'. They are shown in the balance sheet under current assets after the debtors. Amounts owing for rents receivable or other revenue owing are usually added to debtors.

The balance sheet in respect of the accounts so far seen in this chapter would appear as follows:

Balance Sheet as at 31 December 2008

	£	£	£
Current assets			
Stock		xxx	
Debtors		200	
Prepayments (210 + 400)		610	
Bank		xxx	
Cash		xxx	
		x,xxx	
Less Current liabilities			
Trade creditors	xxx		
Accrued expenses	250	xxx	
Net current assets			xxx

22.7 Goods for own use

Traders will often take items out of their business stocks for their own use, without paying for them. There is nothing wrong with this, but an entry should be made to record the event. This is done as follows:

- **Credit** the purchases account, to reduce cost of goods available for sale
- **Debit** the drawings account, to show that the proprietor has taken the goods for private use.

In the United Kingdom, an adjustment may be needed for value added tax. If goods supplied to a trader's customers have VAT added to their price, then any such goods taken for own use will need such an adjustment. This is because the VAT regulations state that VAT should be added to the cost of goods taken. The double entry for the VAT content would be:

- **Debit** the drawings account
- **Credit** VAT account.

Adjustments may also be needed for other private items. For instance, if a trader's private insurance had been incorrectly charged to the insurance account, then the correction would be:

- **Credit** the insurance account
- **Debit** the drawings account.

22.8 Revaluation of a fixed asset

Sometimes fixed assets are revalued at a higher price than when they were initially purchased, for example land and buildings. When a fixed asset is revalued,

> GOODS FOR OWN USE – goods taken out of the business by the owner(s) for their own use.

a reserve is created which is added to the owner's capital account – see example below:

Example: J Hine owns business premises that were originally purchased for £150,000 and appear in the financial statements at 1 January 2008 at their cost price. On 31 December 2008 the premises were revalued at £220,000 and it was decided to record the new valuation in the business's accounts. The balance in Hine's capital account at 31 December 2008 before the revaluation was £250,000.

Dr		**Premises Account**			Cr
2008			£		
Jan 1	Balance b/d		150,000		
Dec 31	Capital account		70,000		

Dr		**Capital Account**			Cr
		2008			£
		Jan 1	Balance b/d		250,000
		Dec 31	Premises account (revaluation)		70,000

In the above example, the premises account and J Hine's capital account have both increased by £70,000. This means that Hine's stake in his business is now £320,000. This transaction is referred to as a non-cash item in that no new cash has been introduced into the business. The increase in value has occurred as a result of the revaluation and has been entered in the records.

22.9 Distinctions between various kinds of capital

The capital account represents the claim of the proprietor against the assets of a business at a point in time. The word 'capital' is, however, often used in a specific sense. The main uses are listed below.

Capital invested

> CAPITAL INVESTED – the amount of money, or money's worth, brought into the business by the proprietor.

This means the actual amount of money, or money's worth, brought into a business by the proprietor from outside interests. The amount of **capital invested** is not affected by the amounts of profits made by the business or any losses incurred.

Capital employed

> CAPITAL EMPLOYED – amount of money 'employed' in the business.

The term **capital employed** has many meanings but, basically, it means the amount of money that is being used (or 'employed') in the business. If, therefore, all the assets were added up in value and the liabilities of the business deducted, the difference is the amount of money employed in the business (i.e. the net assets).

Another way of looking at the calculation of capital employed is to take the balance of the capital account and add this to any long-term loan. The result will be the same as the net assets, i.e. the capital employed.

Working capital (net current assets)

> WORKING CAPITAL – the difference between the Current Assets and Current Liabilities.

The difference between the current assets and current liabilities is often referred to as **working capital** or **'net current assets'**. This amount represents the money that is available to pay the running expenses of the business and, ideally, the current assets should exceed the current liabilities twice over, i.e. in the ratio 2:1. In simple terms it means that, for every £1 owed, the business should be able to raise £2.

22.10 Discounts allowed and discounts received in final accounts

In Chapter 11 we dealt with recording cash discounts in the cash book and ledgers and you will recall that such a discount could be either 'discounts allowed', which represents a reduction given to our customers for prompt payment of their account, or 'discounts received', when the reduction is given by a supplier to us when we pay their account within a specified period.

In the following exhibit of D Marston, let us assume that the discount allowed amounted to £310 and the discount received totalled £510. These items would appear in the trading and profit and loss account as follows:

Exhibit 22.1

Trading and Profit and Loss Account of D Marston for the year ended 31 December 2008		
	£	£
Gross profit		30,500
Less Expenses		
Discounts allowed	310	
Other expenses	10,000	10,310
		20,190
Add Income		
Discounts received		510
Net profit		20,700

22.11 Worked example of the financial statements for a sole trader

All the adjustments necessary before preparing the financial statements for a business have now been covered. These include adjustments for depreciation, from Chapter 20, writing off bad debts and the provision for doubtful debts from Chapter 21, and in this chapter we have dealt with accruals, prepayments, discounts allowed and received. You may also recall that Chapter 18 dealt with closing stock and sales returns and purchases returns and carriage inwards and outwards.

Exhibit 22.2 is a fully worked example that includes all the items mentioned above. There is also a step-by-step guide that deals with these rather tricky adjustments.

Exhibit 22.2

G Lea, a sole trader, extracted the following trial balance from his books for the year ended 31 March 2009.

G Lea
Trial Balance as at 31 March 2009

	Dr £	Cr £
Purchases and sales	224,000	419,700
Stock 1 April 2008	51,600	
Capital 1 April 2008		72,000
Bank overdraft		43,500
Cash	900	
Carriage inwards	4,600	
Discounts	14,400	9,300
Sales returns	8,100	
Purchase returns		5,700
Carriage outwards	21,600	
Rent and insurance	17,400	
Provision for doubtful debts		6,600
Office equipment	20,000	
Delivery vans	27,000	
Debtors and creditors	119,100	61,200
Drawings	28,800	
Bad debts written off	400	
Wages and salaries	89,000	
General office expenses	4,500	
Provision for depreciation		
Office equipment		8,000
Delivery vans		5,400
	631,400	631,400

Notes:

1. Stock 31 March 2009 was valued at £42,900.
2. Wages and salaries accrued £2,100 and office expenses owing £200 at 31 March 2009.
3. Rent prepaid 31 March 2009 was £1,800.
4. Increase the provision for doubtful debts to £8,100.
5. Provide for depreciation on the office equipment at 20% per annum using the straight line method.
6. Provide for depreciation on the delivery vans at 20% per annum using the reducing balance method.

You are required to prepare the trading and profit and loss account for the year ended 31 March 2009, together with a balance sheet as at that date.

G Lea
Trading and Profit and Loss Account for the year ended 31 March 2009

		£	£	£
Sales				419,700
Less Sales returns				8,100
				411,600
Less Cost of goods sold				
Opening stock			51,600	
Add Purchases		224,000		
Add Carriage inwards		4,600		
		228,600		
Less Purchase returns		5,700	222,900	
			274,500	
Less Closing stock			42,900	231,600
Gross Profit				180,000
Add Discounts received	(G)			9,300
				189,300
Less Expenses				
Wages and salaries (89,000 + 2,100)	(C)		91,100	
Discounts allowed	(F)		14,400	
Carriage outwards			21,600	
Rent and insurance (17,400 − 1,800)	(A)		15,600	
Bad debts written off	(N)		400	
General office expenses (4,500 + 200)	(D)		4,700	
Increase in provision for doubtful debts (8,100 − 6,600)	(L)		1,500	
Depreciation:				
Office equipment	(H)		4,000	
Delivery vans	(J)		4,320	157,620
Net Profit				31,680

G Lea
Balance Sheet as at 31 March 2009

Fixed Assets		Cost £	Total Depreciation £	Net Book Value £
Office equipment	(I)	20,000	12,000	8,000
Delivery vans	(K)	27,000	9,720	17,280
		47,000	21,720	25,280

Current Assets		£	£	£
Stock			42,900	
Debtors		119,100		
Less Provision for doubtful debts	(M)	8,100	111,000	
Prepaid expenses	(B)		1,800	
Cash in hand			900	156,600
Less Current Liabilities				
Creditors			61,200	
Bank overdraft			43,500	
Expenses owing (2,100 + 200)	(E)		2,300	107,000
Net Current Assets				49,600
				74,880

Financed by:		
Capital		72,000
Add Net Profit		31,680
		103,680
Less Drawings		28,800
		74,880

TIP – use these step-by-step guides when working on exercises involving adjustments to financial statements.

22.12 Step-by-step guide dealing with further adjustments to financial statements

Note: The letters (A) to (N) shown after each adjustment can be cross referenced to the Trading Profit and Loss Account and Balance Sheet of G Lea.

1 Prepayments (amounts paid in advance)
In the financial statements

a) If a trial balance is provided in a question then ensure that you *deduct* the amount of the prepayment from the appropriate expense account and put the resultant figure in the profit and loss account. Ensure that only the expenses incurred for that particular period are charged against the profits for that period. Refer to the worked example, note (3) rent prepaid £1,800. This amount should be deducted from the rent in the trial balance, i.e. £17,400 − £1,800 = £15,600. This figure should be entered as an expense in the profit and loss account (A).

b) In the balance sheet show the amount of the *prepayment* in the current assets section directly under the debtors, i.e. prepaid expenses £1,800 (B).

2 Accruals (amount owing)
In the financial statements

a) If a trial balance is provided in a question then *add* the amount of the accrual to the appropriate expense account and put this figure in the profit and loss account. Refer to the worked example, note (2) wages and salaries accrued £2,100 and office expenses owing £200. These figures should be added as follows:

Wages and salaries	£89,000 + £2,100 = £91,100
General office expenses	£4,500 + £200 = £4,700

The amounts to be charged as expenses to the profit and loss account are thus, wages and salaries £91,100 (C) and general office expenses £4,700 (D).

b) In the balance sheet show the amount of the *accrual* under the current liabilities section directly under the creditors, i.e. expenses owing £2,100 + £200 = £2,300 (E).

3 Discounts allowed and received
Discount allowed

Charge as an expense in the profit and loss account. Refer to the worked example where the discount allowed, £14,400, has been charged as an expense (F).

Discount received

Add as income in the profit and loss account directly underneath the gross profit figure. Again, refer to the worked example where there is discount received of £9,300 that has been added as income (G).

4 Depreciation
Straight line method (Refer to the worked example, note 5)

a)	Find the cost price of the office equipment	£20,000
b)	Using percentage given	20%
	calculate 20% of £20,000	= £4,000

then

c) Charge £4,000 as an expense in the profit and loss account (H).

d) In the balance sheet, deduct *total* depreciation £4,000 from this year plus depreciation deducted in previous years £8,000* = £12,000 from the cost price of the asset to give you the net book value of the asset £20,000 − £12,000 = £8,000. Enter each of these figures in the appropriate columns in the balance sheet (I). (*See trial balance credit side.)

Reducing balance method (Refer to the worked example, note 6)

a)	Find the cost price of the delivery vans	£27,000
b)	Find the total amount of depreciation to date (refer to trial balance credit side)	£5,400
c)	Find the difference (£27,000 − £5,400)	£21,600
d)	Using percentage given	20%
	calculate 20% of £21,600	= £4,320

then

e) Charge £4,320 as an expense in the profit and loss account (J).

f) In the balance sheet, deduct *total* depreciation £4,320 from this year plus depreciation deducted in previous years £5,400* = £9,720 from the cost price of the asset to give you the net book value of the asset £27,000 − £9,720 = £17,280. Enter these figures in the appropriate columns in the balance sheet (K). (*See trial balance credit side.)

5 Provision for doubtful debts

Creating a provision

a) If a provision is to be created for the first time, refer to the question for details of the amount to be set aside. Let us assume in our worked example that a provision had been created in 2008 amounting to £6,600.

b) The *provision for doubtful debts £6,600* would have been charged to the profit and loss account as an expense in 2008.

c) In the balance sheet, the *provision for doubtful debts £6,600* would have been deducted from the debtors. The debtors are to be found under the heading of current assets.

Increasing the provision

a) Refer to your question and ascertain the new provision. In our example the new provision is £8,100 for this year (see note 4).

b) Find last year's provision. Using our example the figure is £6,600 (this figure can be found in the trial balance, credit side).

c) Charge the difference between the new and old provision, £8,100 − £6,600 = £1,500 to the profit and loss account (L).

d) In the balance sheet, deduct the *new provision £8,100* from the debtors (M).

Reducing the provision

a) Refer to your question and ascertain the new provision. Using our worked example we will assume that in 2010 it was decided to reduce the provision to £5,000.

b) Find the old provision. Again, using our example this would be £8,100.

c) Take the difference between the old and the new provision, £8,100 − £5,000 = £3,100 then add this amount as income in the profit and loss account.

d) Deduct the *new provision for doubtful debts £5,000* from the debtors in the balance sheet.

6 Bad debts

Simply write them off as an expense in the profit and loss account. In our example you will see that bad debts written off are £400, this is shown as an expense in the profit and loss account (N).

Note: A model layout of the financial statements of a sole trader is available on CD attached to this at the back of this book.

End of Chapter Checklist

Summary

- Adjustments need to be made in the expense and revenue accounts to ensure that expenses incurred or revenue due for the period are included in that year's financial statements.
- Items owing are called 'accruals', items paid in advance are called 'prepayments'.
- Expenses owing (accruals) are shown in the balance sheet under the heading of current liabilities while expenses prepaid (prepayments) are shown under current assets after debtors. Amounts owing for rents receivable or other revenue due is usually added to the debtors.
- If the owner of a business takes goods for his or her own use without paying for them then an adjustment is made by crediting the purchases account and debiting the drawings account, plus an adjustment for VAT if appropriate.
- If a fixed asset is revalued, the increase in value is entered into the asset account and the owner's capital account credited, thus increasing their stake in the business.
- There are various forms of 'capital' used in a business: capital invested, capital employed and working capital.
- Discount allowed is charged to profit and loss account whereas discount received is added to the profit as income.
- A fully worked example of the financial statements for a sole trader, including all adjustments, is illustrated using the step-by-step guide.

Questions

22.1 *The first financial year's trading of C Homer ended on 31 December 2008. You are required to present ledger accounts showing the amount transferred to the profit and loss account in respect of the following items:*

a) Rent: paid in 2008 amounted to £1,600; owing at 31 December 2008, £400.

b) Insurance: paid in 2008 amounted to £900. Of the amount paid, £265 was in respect of insurance for 2009.

c) Motor expenses: paid in 2008, £7,215; owing at 31 December 2008, £166.

d) Rates: paid six months' rates on 1 January 2008, £750; on 1 July 2008 paid nine months' rates for the period 31 March 2009, £1,125.

e) K Whalley rented part of the buildings from C Homer for £400 per month from 1 January 2008. On 15 April 2008 he paid C Homer £2,000 and on 15 December 2008 he paid £4,400. Show these transactions in C Homer's accounts.

22.2 *The following accounts are from T Norton's books during his first year of trading to 31 December 2009.*

a) General expenses: paid in 2009, £615; still owing at 31 December 2009, £56.

b) Telephone: paid in 2009, £980; owing at 31 December 2009, £117.

c) Norton received commission from the sale of goods. In 2009 he received £3,056 and was owed a further £175 on 31 December 2009.

d) Carriage outwards: paid in 2009, £666; still owing at 31 December 2009, £122.

e) Insurance: paid 1 January 2009 for nine months' insurance, £1,080; paid 1 October 2009 the sum of £1,080 for insurance to 30 June 2010.

Show the ledger accounts balanced off at the end of the year, showing balances carried down and the amounts transferred to the final accounts for the year 2009.

22.3X *T Dale's financial year ended on 30 June 2009. Write up the ledger accounts, showing the transfer to the final accounts.*

a) Stationery: paid for the year to 30 June 2009, £855; stocks of stationery at 30 June 2008, £290; at 30 June 2009, £345.

b) General expenses: paid for the year to 30 June 2009, £590; owing at 30 June 2008, £64; owing at 30 June 2009, £90.

c) Rent and rates (combined account): paid in the year to 30 June 2009, £3,890; rent owing at 30 June 2008, £160; rent paid in advance at 30 June 2009, £250; rates owing at 30 June 2008, £205; rates owing at 30 June 2009, £360.

d) Motor expenses: paid in the year to 30 June 2009, £4,750; owing as at 30 June 2008, £180; owing as at 30 June 2009, £375.

e) Dale earned commission from the sales of goods. Received for the year to 30 June 2009, £850; owing at 30 June 2008, £80; owing at 30 June 2009, £145.

End of Chapter Checklist

Questions

22.4 The following balances were part of the trial balance of C Cainen on 31 December 2009:

	Dr	Cr
	£	£
Stock at 1 January 2009	2,050	
Sales		18,590
Purchases	11,170	
Rent	640	
Wages and salaries	2,140	
Insurance	590	
Bad debts	270	
Telephone	300	
General expenses	180	

On 31 December 2009 you ascertain that:

a) the rent for four months of 2010, £160, has been paid in 2009
b) £290 is owing for wages and salaries
c) insurance has been prepaid £190
d) a telephone bill of £110 is owed
e) stock is valued at £3,910.

Draw up Cainen's trading and profit and loss account for the year ended 31 December 2009.

22.5 The following were part of the trial balance of K Tyler on 31 December 2010:

	Dr	Cr
	£	£
Stock at 1 January 2010	8,620	
Sales		54,190
Purchases	30,560	
Sales returns	200	
Wages and salaries	4,960	
Motor expenses	2,120	
Rent and rates	1,200	
Discounts allowed	290	
Lighting expenses	580	
Computer running expenses	1,210	
General expenses	360	

Given the information that follows, you are to draw up a trading and profit and loss account for the year ended 31 December 2010.

a) stock on 31 December 2010 is £12,120
b) items prepaid: rates £160; computer running expenses £140
c) items owing: wages £510; lighting expenses £170
d) £700 is to be charged as depreciation of motor vehicles.

22.6X From the following trial balance of J Sears, a store owner, prepare a trading and profit and loss account for the year ended 31 December 2010 and a balance sheet as at that date, taking into consideration the adjustments shown below:

Trial Balance as at 31 December 2010

	Dr	Cr
	£	£
Sales		80,000
Purchases	70,000	
Sales returns	1,000	
Purchase returns		1,240
Stock at 1 January 2010	20,000	
Provision for doubtful debts		160
Wages and salaries	7,200	
Telephone	200	
Store fittings	8,000	
Motor van	6,000	
Debtors and creditors*	1,960	1,400
Bad debts	40	
Capital		35,800
Bank balance	600	
Drawings	3,600	
	118,600	118,600

Adjustments:

a) closing stock at 31 December 2010 is £24,000
b) accrued wages £450
c) telephone prepaid £20
d) provision for bad debts to be increased to 10% of debtors
e) depreciation on store fittings £800, and motor van £1,200.

Note: Sometimes, in examinations, two items will be shown on the same line. The examiner is testing to see whether the student knows which of the figures relate to the account titles. In the above exercise, item 'Debtors and creditors' is shown on the same line.

> TIP – in a Trial Balance debtors always go on the "Dr" side and creditors go on the "Cr" side

Section E: Incomplete records

Chapter 23: Incomplete records

23.1 Introduction

There are many types of businesses that are run by a person on their own, such as the shopkeeper, market stall holder, window cleaner, and so on. In such cases, it may be impractical for them to record their finances by the use of a full double entry system of book-keeping. In fact, many of them would be unable to write up double entry records and it is more likely that they would enter details of a transaction once only, thereby using a single entry system. Also, many would fail to record every transaction resulting in incomplete accounting records.

Getting started

Edexcel specification
Incomplete records. 5.1 to 5.9
Books of original entry, 1.9.

After you have studied this chapter you should be able to:

- *appreciate that many businesses use single entry for recording transactions*
- *ascertain the profit figure from incomplete records*
- *ascertain sales and purchases from incomplete records*
- *prepare financial statements from incomplete records.*

Since accounting is carried out to assist management in the successful running of a business, it is important to remember that the task should not be too onerous for the owner of the business. Many small businesses, like small retail shops, have all the information they require just by keeping a cash book and a record of their debtors and creditors, which in most cases is not recorded using double entry. Where a business uses a single entry system of recording their financial transactions, and indeed where not every transaction is recorded, this is known as incomplete records.

23.2 Preparing final accounts from incomplete records

When a business has not kept full accounting records it is still necessary to prepare the financial statements at the end of the business's financial year. The method used to prepare the accounts in these circumstances is to compare the capital at the **beginning** and **end** of the accounting period.

The only way that capital can be increased is by the owner putting in additional funds or by making profits. Consider a business where capital at the end of 2009 is £20,000. During 2010 there had been no drawings or extra cash brought in by the owner. At the end of 2010 the capital was £30,000. The profits of the business for the year can be found as follows:

	This year's capital		Last year's capital	
Net profit =	£30,000	−	£20,000	= £10,000

If the drawings had been £7,000, the profits must have been £17,000, calculated thus:

Last year's capital + Profits − Drawings = This year's capital

£20,000 + ? − £7,000 = £30,000

We can see that £17,000 profits was the figure needed to complete the formula, filling in the missing figure by normal arithmetical deduction:

£20,000 + £17,000 − £7,000 = £30,000

If, during the second year of trading, the owner had decided to contribute additional capital then the calculation would be as follows:

Last year's capital + capital introduced + profits − drawings = Closing capital

Exhibit 23.1 shows the calculation of profit where insufficient information is available to draft a trading and profit and loss account, only information of assets and liabilities being known.

Exhibit 23.1

H Taylor has not kept proper book-keeping records, but he has kept notes in diary form of the transactions of his business. He is able to give you details of his assets and liabilities as at 31 December 2008 and at 31 December 2009 as follows:

			£
At 31 December 2008 Assets:	Motor van	10,000
	Fixtures	7,000
	Stock	8,500
	Debtors	9,500
	Bank	11,100
	Cash	100
Liabilities:	Creditors	8,000
	Loan from J Ogden	6,000
At 31 December 2009 Assets:	Motor van (after depreciation)	8,000
	Fixtures (after depreciation)	6,300
	Stock	9,900
	Debtors	11,240
	Bank	11,700
	Cash	200
Liabilities:	Creditors	8,700
	Loan from J Ogden	4,000
Drawings were £9,000		

STATEMENT OF AFFAIRS – a statement drawn up to ascertain the owner's capital at a given date. This is deduced by deducting liabilities from the assets to find the capital.

First of all, a **statement of affairs** is drawn up as at 31 December 2008. This is the name given to what would have been called a balance sheet if it had been drawn up from a set of records. The capital is the difference between the assets and liabilities.

H Taylor
Statement of Affairs as at 31 December 2008

	£	£
Fixed assets		
Motor van		10,000
Fixtures		7,000
		17,000
Current assets		
Stock	8,500	
Debtors	9,500	
Bank	11,100	
Cash	100	
	29,200	
Less Current liabilities		
Creditors	8,000	
Net current assets		21,200
		38,200
Less Long-term liability		
Loan from J Ogden		6,000
		32,200
Financed by		
Capital (difference)		32,200

A statement of affairs is now drafted at the end of 2009. The formula of opening capital + profit − drawings = closing capital is then used to deduce the figure of profit.

H Taylor
Statement of Affairs as at 31 December 2009

	£	£
Fixed assets		
Motor van		8,000
Fixtures		6,300
		14,300
Current assets		
Stock	9,900	
Debtors	11,240	
Bank	11,700	
Cash	200	
	33,040	
Less Current liabilities		
Creditors	8,700	
Net current assets		24,340
		38,640
Less Long-term liability		
Loan from J Ogden		4,000
		34,640
Financed by		
Capital balance at 1.1.2009		32,200
Add Net profit	(C)	?
	(B)	?
Less Drawings		9,000
	(A)	?

Deduction of net profit Opening capital + net profit − drawings = closing capital. Find the missing figures (A), (B) and (C) by deduction:

(A) is the figure needed to make the statement of affairs totals equal, i.e. £34,640;

(B) is therefore £34,640 + £9,000 = £43,640;

(C) is therefore £43,640 − £32,200 = £11,440.

To check:

		£
Capital		32,200
Add Net profit	(C)	11,440
	(B)	43,640
Less Drawings		9,000
	(A)	34,640

Obviously, this method of calculating profit is very unsatisfactory as it is much more informative when a trading and profit and loss account can be drawn up. Therefore, whenever possible, the 'comparison of capital' method of ascertaining profit should be avoided and financial statements drawn up from the available book-keeping records.

23.3 Step-by-step guide to incomplete records

TIP – follow the step-by-step guide when tackling an exercise on incomplete records.

In preparing financial statements from incomplete records a formal approach should be followed.

Using the following 'Step-by-step guide', together with the example of M Cole, the various stages necessary to prepare the financial statements will be demonstrated.

Exhibit 23.2

M Cole requires his financial statements to be drawn up for the year ended 31 December 2009 but has not kept full accounting records. He has, however, been able to provide the following information:

a) The sales are mostly on a credit basis. No record of sales has been made, but £100,000 has been received, £95,000 by cheque and £5,000 by cash, from persons to whom goods have been sold.

b) Amount paid by cheque to suppliers during the year = £72,000.

c) Expenses paid during the year: by cheque, rent £2,000, general expenses £1,800; by cash, rent £500.

d) M Cole took £100 cash per week (for 52 weeks) as drawings.

e) Other information is available:

	At 31.12.2008	At 31.12.2009
	£	£
Debtors	11,000	13,200
Creditors for goods	4,000	6,500
Rent owing	–	500
Bank balance	11,300	30,500
Cash balance	800	100
Stock	15,900	17,000

f) The only fixed asset consists of fixtures that were valued at 31 December 2008 at £8,000. These are to be depreciated at 10% per annum.

Step-by-step guide

Step 1

First, draw up a statement of affairs, taking into account all the opening figures, on the closing day of the last accounting period. This is shown below:

M Cole
Statement of Affairs as at 31 December 2008

	£	£
Fixed Assets		
Fixtures		8,000
Current Assets		
Stock	15,900	
Debtors	11,000	
Bank	11,300	
Cash	800	
	39,000	
Less Current Liabilities		
Creditors	4,000	
Net current assets		35,000
		43,000
Financed by		
Capital (difference)		43,000
		43,000

Step 2

Next, a cash and bank summary, showing the totals of each separate item plus opening and closing balances, is drawn up. Thus:

Dr	Cash	Bank		Cash	Bank	Cr
	£	£		£	£	
Balances 31.12.2008	800	11,300	Suppliers		72,000	
Receipts from debtors	5,000	95,000	Rent	500	2,000	
			General Expenses		1,800	
			Drawings	5,200		
			Balances 31.12.2009	100	30,500	
	5,800	106,300		5,800	106,300	

TIP – when preparing the cash and bank summary, remember to include the opening and closing balances of cash and bank if given in the question.

Step 3

Calculate the figures for **purchases** and **sales** to be shown in the trading account. Remember that the figures needed are the same as those which would have been found if double entry records had been kept.

Purchases

In double entry, purchases means goods that have been bought in the period, irrespective of whether or not they have been paid for during the period. The figure of payments to suppliers must therefore be adjusted to find the figure for purchases. In our example, the purchases are ascertained as follows:

	£
Paid during the year	72,000
Less Payments made for goods which were purchased in a previous year (creditors 31.12.2008)	4,000
	68,000
Add Purchases made in this year but payment has not yet been made (creditors 31.12.2009)	6,500
Goods bought in this year, i.e. **purchases**	74,500

The same answer could have been obtained if the information had been shown in the form of a total creditors account, the figure for purchases being the amount required to make the account totals agree*.

Dr	Total Creditors' Account			*Cr*
	£			£
Cash paid to suppliers	72,000	Balances b/f		4,000
Balances c/d	6,500	*Purchases (missing figure)		74,500
	78,500			78,500

Discounts received and purchase returns

Discounts received – the total discount received by a business when paying its creditors would also have to be entered in the total creditors' account on the debit side. The balancing figure of purchases would, therefore, be affected.

Purchase returns – the total of purchase returns for the period would also need to be included on the debit side of the total creditors' account and again affect the balancing figure of purchases.

These items are covered fully in Chapter 15.

Sales

The sales figure will only equal receipts where all the sales are for cash. Therefore, the receipts figures need adjusting to find sales. This can be done as follows:

	£
Amount received during the year:	
Bank	95,000
Cash	5,000
	100,000
Less Receipts for goods sold in a previous year	
(debtors 31.12.2008)	11,000
	89,000
Add Sales made this year but payment not yet received	
(debtors 31.12.2009)	13,200
Goods sold this year, i.e. **sales**	102,200

The same answer could have been obtained if the information had been shown in a total debtors' account, the figure for sales being the amount required to make the account totals agree*.

Dr	Total Debtors' Account			Cr
	£			£
Balances b/f	11,000	Receipts: Cash		5,000
		Cheque		95,000
*Sales (missing figure)	102,200	Balances c/d		13,200
	113,200			113,200

Bad debts, discount allowed and sales returns

Bad debts – if during the year a debt has been written off as bad then this figure would be included in the total debtors' account on the credit side and would affect the balancing figure of sales.

Discounts allowed – the total of any discounts allowed to a business's customers (debtors) would also need to be included in the total debtors' account. The total discount allowed would be entered on the credit side and would, therefore, again affect the balancing figure of sales.

Sales returns – if there are any sales returns then the total for the period should also be entered on the credit side in the total debtors' account.

All the above items are dealt with fully in Chapter 15.

Step 4 Expenses

Where there are no accruals or prepayments, either at the beginning or end of the accounting period, then expenses paid will equal the expenses used up during the period. These figures will be charged to the trading and profit and loss account.

In contrast, where such prepayments or accruals exist, then an expense account should be drawn up for that particular item. When all known items have been entered, the missing figure will be the expenses (i.e. *rent) to be charged for the accounting period.

In our example, only the rent account needs to be drawn up:

Dr	Rent Account		Cr
	£		£
Cheques	2,000	*Rent (missing figure)	3,000
Cash	500		
Accrued c/d	500		
	3,000		3,000

Alternatively, the rent for the year can be found using the following calculation:

Accrual – Rent	
	£
Paid: Bank	2,000
Cash	500
	2,500
Add: Owing 31.12.09	500
Rent for the year	3,000

Chapter 23: Incomplete records

TIP – when preparing the Balance Sheet at the end of the period, remember to include the closing cash and bank balances from the 'cash and bank summary'.

Step 5

Check to see if any depreciation needs to be charged to the profit and loss account. In our example of M Cole, (f), it states that the fixtures are valued at £8,000 and should be depreciated at 10% per annum. Therefore, depreciation charge for the year is 10% of £8,000 = £800; this amount should be charged to the profit and loss account. In the balance sheet, remember to deduct the depreciation from the fixtures, i.e. £8,000 − £800 = £7,200, to give you the net book value of the asset.

Now prepare the financial statements using all the information given in the details and the figures you have calculated.

M Cole
Trading and Profit and Loss Account for the year ended 31 December 2009

	£	£
Sales (Step 3)		102,200
Less Cost of goods sold		
Stock at 1.1.2009	15,900	
Add Purchases (Step 3)	74,500	
	90,400	
Less Stock at 31.12.2009	17,000	73,400
Gross profit		28,800
Less Expenses		
Rent (Step 4)	3,000	
General expenses	1,800	
Depreciation: Fixtures	800	5,600
Net profit		23,200

Balance Sheet as at 31 December 2009

	£	£	£
Fixed Assets			
Fixtures at 1.1.2009		8,000	
Less Depreciation (Step 5)		800	7,200
Current Assets			
Stock		17,000	
Debtors		13,200	
Bank (Step 2)		30,500	
Cash (Step 2)		100	
		60,800	
Less Current Liabilities			
Creditors	6,500		
Rent owing	500	7,000	
Net current assets			53,800
			61,000
Financed by			
Capital (Step 1)			
Balance 1.1.2009 (per opening statement of affairs)			43,000
Add Net profit			23,200
			66,200
Less Drawings			5,200
			61,000

23.4 Incomplete records and missing figures

In practice, part of the information relating to cash receipts or payments is often missing. If the missing information is in respect of one type of payment, then it is normal to assume that the missing figure is the amount required to make both totals agree in the cash column of the cash and bank summary. This does not happen with bank items since another copy of the bank statement can always be obtained from the bank.

Exhibit 23.3 shows an example when the drawings figure is unknown.

Exhibit 23.3

The following information on cash and bank receipts and payments is available:

	Cash £	Bank £
Cash paid into the bank during the year	5,500	
Receipts from debtors	7,250	800
Paid to suppliers	320	4,930
Drawings during the year	?	–
Expenses paid	150	900
Balances at 1.1.2009	35	1,200
Balances at 31.12.2009	50	1,670

Dr		Cash £	Bank £			Cash £	Bank Cr £
Balances 1.1.2009		35	1,200	Bankings	C	5,500	
Received from debtors		7,250	800	Suppliers		320	4,930
Bankings	C		5,500	Expenses		150	900
				*Drawings		?	
				Balances 31.12.2009		50	1,670
		7,285	7,500			7,285	7,500

The amount needed to make the two sides of the cash columns agree is £1,265. Therefore, this is taken as the figure of *drawings.

Exhibit 23.4 is an example of where the receipts from debtors have not been recorded.

Exhibit 23.4

Information of cash and bank transactions is available as follows:

	Cash £	Bank £
Receipts from debtors	?	6,080
Cash withdrawn from the bank for business use (this is the amount which is used besides cash receipts from debtors to pay drawings and expenses)		920
Paid to suppliers		5,800
Expenses paid	640	230
Drawings	1,180	315
Balances at 1.1.2009	40	1,560
Balances at 31.12.2009	70	375

Dr	Cash	Bank		Cash	Bank Cr
	£	£		£	£
Balances 1.1.2009	40	1,560	Suppliers		5,800
Received from debtors	*?	6,080	Expenses	640	230
Withdrawn from Bank C	920		Withdrawn from Bank C		920
			Drawings	1,180	315
			Balances 31.12.2009	70	375
	1,890	7,640		1,890	7,640

Receipts from *debtors is, therefore, the amount needed to make each side of the cash column agree, namely £930.

It must be emphasised that balancing figures are acceptable only when all the other figures have been verified. Should, for instance, a cash expense be omitted when cash received from debtors is being calculated, then this would result in an understatement not only of expenses but also ultimately of sales.

23.5 Where there are two missing pieces of information

If both cash drawings and cash receipts from debtors were not known, it would not be possible to deduce both of these figures. The only course available would be to estimate whichever figure was more capable of being accurately assessed, use this as a known figure, and deduce the other figure. However, this is a most unsatisfactory position as both of the figures are no more than pure estimates, the accuracy of one relying entirely upon the accuracy of the other.

23.6 Cash transactions for sales and purchases

Where there are cash sales as well as sales on credit terms, then the cash sales must be added to sales on credit to give the total sales for the year. This total figure of sales will be the one shown in the trading account.

Similarly, purchases for cash will need adding to credit purchases to give the figure of total purchases for the trading account.

End of Chapter Checklist

Summary

- Where no proper accounts are kept, possibly the only way to ascertain the amount of profit is to compare the capital account at the beginning and end of an accounting period. Provided no additional funds have been invested in the business or drawings taken out, then the difference must be either profit or loss.
- A statement of affairs is often prepared to ascertain the capital of the proprietor. This statement shows the value of the assets and liabilities at a specific date and by using the accounting equation the capital can be found.
- Using the step-by-step method, the financial statements can be prepared from records not kept by the double entry system of book-keeping.
- Where there are missing figures it is possible to deduce the figure by careful analysis of data available and process of elimination.
- The disadvantage of single entry/incomplete records is that insufficient financial information is available to the owner(s) of the business.

Questions

23.1 The following figures have been extracted from the records of K Rogers, who does not keep a full record of his transactions on the double entry system:

		£
1 November 2008	Debtors	2,760
1 November 2008	Creditors	1,080
1 November 2008	Stock	2,010
31 October 2009	Debtors	3,090
31 October 2009	Creditors	1,320
31 October 2009	Stock	2,160

All goods were sold on credit and all purchases were made on credit. During the year ended 31 October 2009, cash received from debtors amounted to £14,610, whereas cash paid to creditors amounted to £9,390.

Required:

(a) Calculate the amount of sales and purchases for the year ended 31 October 2009.

(b) Draw up the trading account for the year ended 31 October 2009.

23.2X The following figures for a business are available:

		£
1 June 2008	Stock	11,590
1 June 2008	Creditors	3,410
1 June 2008	Debtors	5,670
31 May 2009	Stock	13,425
31 May 2009	Creditors	4,126
31 May 2009	Debtors	6,108
Year to 31 May 2009:		
Received from debtors		45,112
Paid to creditors		29,375

All goods were bought or sold on credit.

Required:

Draw up the trading account for the year 31 May 2009, deducing any figures that might be needed.

23.3 On 1 July 2008, D Lewinski commenced business with £60,000 in his bank account. After trading for a full year, he ascertained that his position on 30 June 2009 was as follows:

	£		£
Plant	36,000	Fixtures	3,600
Creditors	7,200	Bank balance	6,000
Debtors	9,300	Stock-in-trade	13,500
Cash in hand	1,350	Drawings	16,000

End of Chapter Checklist

Questions

You are required to:

(a) calculate D Lewinski's capital at 30 June 2009
(b) prepare D Lewinski's balance sheet at 30 June 2009 (assuming a profit of £18,550), set out in such a manner as to show clearly the totals normally shown in a balance sheet.

23.4 J Marcano is a dealer who has not kept proper books of account. At 31 August 2008 her state of affairs was as follows:

	£
Cash	115
Bank balance	2,209
Fixtures	3,500
Stock	16,740
Debtors	11,890
Creditors	9,952
Motor van (at valuation)	3,500

During the year to 31 August 2009, her drawings amounted to £7,560. Winnings from the lottery of £12,800 were put into the business. Extra fixtures were bought for £2,000.

At 31 August 2009 Marcano's assets and liabilities were: cash £84; bank overdraft, £165; stock, £24,891; creditors for goods £6,002; creditors for expenses £236; fixtures to be depreciated by £300; motor van to be valued at £2,800; debtors, £15,821; prepaid expenses, £72.

You are required to draw up a statement showing the profit or loss made by Marcano for the year ended 31 August 2009.

23.5X A Hanson is a sole trader who, although keeping very good records, does not operate a full double entry system. The following figures have been taken from his records:

	31 March 2008	31 March 2009
	£	£
Cash at bank	1,460	1,740
Office furniture	600	500
Stock	2,320	2,620
Cash in hand	60	80

1 Debtors on 31 March 2008 amounted to £2,980 and sales for the year ended 31 March 2009 to £11,520. During the year ended 31 March 2009, cash received from debtors amounted to £10,820.
2 Creditors on 31 March 2008 amounted to £1,880 and purchases for the year ended 31 March 2009 to £8,120. During the year ended 31 March 2009, cash paid to creditors amounted to £7,780.
3 During the year to 31 March 2009 no bad debts were incurred. Also during the same period, there were neither discounts allowed nor discounts received.

Required (with all calculations shown):

a) Calculate debtors and creditors as at 31 March 2009.
b) Calculate Hanson's capital as at 31 March 2008 and 31 March 2009.
c) Calculate his net profit for the year ended 31 March 2009, allowing for the fact that during the year Hanson's drawings amounted to £2,540.

23.6X Faisa Kharaja is the owner of a retail business selling electrical goods. She has never found the time to keep proper books. The following information is available for the year ended 30 November 2006.

	1 December 2005	30 November 2006
	£	£
Trade creditors	12,900	13,456
Trade debtors	450	578
Cash at bank and in hand	5,456	44,350
Rent prepaid	350	490
Shop assistant's wages due	470	240

The summarised receipts and payments for the year ended 30 November 2006 are shown below:

Receipts: bank loan at 7% per year taken on 1 December 2005 £10,000; debtors £7,500; cash takings £200,552.

Payments: fixtures £2,000; creditors £125,400; rent £8,900; business rates £3,560; shop assistant's wages £15,000; administrative expenses £5,698; loan interest £600.

Faisa took £1,500 for personal use each month, direct from cash takings.

Required:

a) For the year ended 30 November 2006, Faisa asks you to:
   (i) prepare the trade debtors account and the calculation of her total sales
   (ii) prepare the rent account, showing the year end transfer
   (iii) prepare the loan interest account, showing the year end transfer.
b) Using the figures taken from Faisa's business, evaluate the importance of the accruals concept to the preparation of the profit and loss account and balance sheet.

IGCSE

Section F: Non-profit organisations

Chapter 24: Accounting for non-profit making organisations

24.1 Non-profit making organisations

The organisations we have covered so far have all been profit making businesses. However, there are other organisations whose objective is not to make a profit but instead provide facilities for their members to pursue a hobby, sporting activity or provide voluntary services. These clubs and associations do not have to prepare a trading and profit and loss account since they are not formed to carry on trading and make profits. Instead, the financial statements prepared by them are either 'receipts and payments accounts' or 'income and expenditure accounts'.

24.2 Receipts and payments account

Receipts and payments accounts are usually prepared by the treasurer of the club or association. This account is a summary of the cash book for the period and if the organisation has no assets (other than cash) and no liabilities, a summary of the cash book tells the members all they need to know about the financial activities during a period. An example of a receipts and payments account is shown below:

Getting started

Edexcel specification
Non-profit making organisations 6.1 to 6.10.

After you have studied this chapter you should be able to:

- appreciate that non-profit making organisations such as clubs, charities, associations and societies prepare different financial statements from profit making organisations
- prepare a receipts and payments account
- prepare income and expenditure accounts and balance sheet for non-profit making organisations
- calculate the value of subscriptions for a period and make entries into the ledger accounts including the treatment of lifetime subscriptions
- calculate profits and losses from special activities and incorporate them into the financial statements
- appreciate that various forms of income may need special treatment
- be aware of treasurer's responsibilities.

RECEIPTS AND PAYMENTS ACCOUNT – a summary of the cash book of a non-profit making organisation.

Mossley Sports Club			
Receipts and Payments Account for the year ended 31 December 2010			
Receipts	£	*Payments*	£
Bank balance 1.1.2010	590	Rent of sports facilities	2,340
Subscriptions received for 2010	2,900	Equipment	346
Donations	60	Committee expenses	180
Raffle profit	110	Postage, stationery etc.	74
		Bank balance 31.12.2010	720
	3,660		3,660

> **INCOME AND EXPENDITURE ACCOUNT** – an account for a non-profit making organisation to find the surplus or deficit made during a period.

24.3 Income and expenditure accounts

When assets are owned, and/or there are liabilities, the receipts and payments account is not a good way of drawing up financial statements. Other than the cash received and paid out, it shows only the cash balances; the other assets and liabilities are not shown at all. Therefore, what is needed is:

- a balance sheet, and
- an account showing whether the association's capital has increased.

The second of these two requirements is provided via an **income and expenditure account.** Such an account follows the same rules as trading and profit and loss accounts, the only differences being the terms used.

A comparison of terms used now follows:

Profit making organisation	Non-profit organisation
1 Trading and profit and loss account	1 Income and expenditure account
2 Net profit	2 Surplus of income over expenditure
3 Net loss	3 Excess of expenditure over income

24.4 Profit or loss for a special purpose

Sometimes there are reasons why a **non-profit making organisation** would want a profit and loss account. This is where something is done to make a profit. The profit is not to be kept, but used to pay for the main purpose of the organisation.

For instance, a football club may have discos or dances that people pay to attend. Any profit from these events helps to pay football expenses. For these discos and dances, a trading and profit and loss account would be drawn up. Any profit (or loss) would be transferred to the income and expenditure account.

> **ACCUMULATED FUND** – a form of capital account for non-profit making organisations.

24.5 Accumulated fund

A sole trader or a partnership would have capital accounts. A non-profit making organisation would instead have an **accumulated fund**. It is in effect the same as a capital account since it is the difference between assets and liabilities.

For a sole trader or partnership:

$$\textbf{Capital} = \textbf{Assets} - \textbf{Liabilities}$$

In a non-profit-making organisation:

Accumulated Fund = Assets − Liabilities

24.6 Drawing up income and expenditure accounts

We can now look at the preparation of an income and expenditure account and a balance sheet of a club. This is drawn up on the basis of a trial balance.

Long Lane Football Club
Trial Balance as at 31 December 2009

	Dr	Cr
	£	£
Sports equipment	8,500	
Club premises	29,600	
Subscriptions received		6,490
Staff wages	4,750	
Furniture and fittings	5,260	
Rates and insurance	1,910	
General expenses	605	
Accumulated fund 1 January 2009		42,016
Donations received		360
Telephone and postage	448	
Bank	2,040	
Bar purchases	9,572	
Creditors for bar supplies		1,040
Bar sales		14,825
Bar stocks 1 January 2009	2,046	
	64,731	64,731

The following information is also available:

(i) Bar stocks at 31 December 2009 amount in value to £2,362.

(ii) Provide for depreciation: sports equipment £1,700; furniture and fittings £1,315.

The club's trading account for its bar is as follows:

Long Lane Football Club Bar
Trading Account for the year ended 31 December 2009

	£	£
Sales		14,825
Less Cost of goods sold		
Opening stock	2,046	
Purchases	9,572	
	11,618	
Closing stock	2,362	
		9,256
Gross profit		5,569

TIP – sometimes questions include profit making activities such as a Club Bar. If this is the case, then a Trading Account must be prepared prior to preparation of the Income and Expenditure Account.

The result of the club bar operation is calculated separately. The gross profit/loss will then be incorporated into the club's income and expenditure account for calculation of the overall result, as shown below:

Income and Expenditure Account for the year ended 31 December 2009

	£	£
Income		
Gross profit from bar		5,569
Subscriptions		6,490
Donations received		360
		12,419
Less Expenditure		
Staff wages	4,750	
Rates and insurance	1,910	
Telephone and postage	448	
General expenses	605	
Depreciation: Furniture	1,315	
Sports equipment	1,700	
		10,728
Surplus of income over expenditure		1,691

TIP – the 'surplus of income over expenditure' figure shown here is included in the Balance Sheet under Accumulated fund.

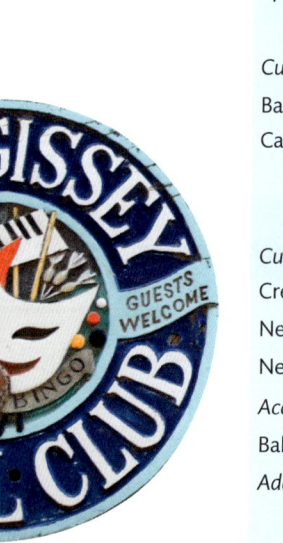

Balance Sheet at 31 December 2009

	£	£	£
Fixed assets	Cost	Depreciation	Net book value
Club premises	29,600	—	29,600
Furniture and fittings	5,260	1,315	3,945
Sports equipment	8,500	1,700	6,800
	43,360	3,015	40,345
Current assets			
Bar stocks		2,362	
Cash at bank		2,040	
		4,402	
Current liabilities			
Creditors for bar supplies		1,040	
Net current assets			3,362
Net assets			43,707
Accumulated fund			
Balance at 1 January 2009			42,016
Add Surplus of income over expenditure			1,691
			43,707

24.7 Subscriptions

No subscriptions owing

Where there are no subscriptions owing, or paid in advance, at the beginning and the end of a financial year, then the amount shown on the credit side of the subscriptions account can be transferred to the credit side of the income and expenditure account, as follows:

Dr	Subscriptions Account				Cr
2009		£	2009		£
Dec 31	Income & expenditure a/c	3,598	Dec 31	Bank (total received)	3,598

Income and Expenditure Account for the year ended 31 December 2009 (extract)

	£
Income:	
Subscriptions	3,598

> SUBSCRIPTIONS – amounts paid by members of a club or society, usually on an annual basis, to enable them to participate in the activities of the organisation.

Subscriptions owing

On the other hand, there may be subscriptions owing at both the start and the end of the financial year. In a case where £325 was owing at the start of the year, a total of £5,668 was received during the year, and £554 was owing at the end of the year, then this would appear as follows:

Dr	Subscriptions Account				Cr
2009		£	2009		£
Jan 1	Owing b/d	325	Dec 31	Bank (total received)	5,668
Dec 31	Income & expenditure a/c (difference)	5,897	Dec 31	Balance c/d	554
		6,222			6,222

Income and Expenditure Account for the year ended 31 December 2009 (extract)

	£
Income:	
Subscriptions	5,897

In the balance sheet, the subscription owing at the end of December 2009 would be shown under the heading of 'Current assets' as a debtor, as shown below:

Balance Sheet as at 31 December 2009 (extract)

Current assets	£
Stock	x,xxx
Debtors (xxx + 554)	xxx

Subscriptions owing and paid in advance

In the third case, at the start of the year there are both subscriptions owing from the previous year and also subscriptions paid in advance. In addition, there are also subscriptions paid in the current year for the next year (in advance) and subscriptions unpaid (owing) at the end of the current year. The example below concerns an amateur theatre organisation.

An amateur theatre organisation charges its members an annual subscription of £20 per member. It accrues for subscriptions owing at the end of each year and also adjusts for subscriptions received in advance. The following applies:

(A) On 1 January 2009, 18 members owed £360 for the year 2008.

(B) In December 2008, 4 members paid £80 for the year 2009.

(C) During the year 2009, the organisation received cash subscriptions of £7,420 as follows:

For 2008	£ 360
For 2009	£ 6,920
For 2010	£ 140
	£ 7,420

(D) At the close of 31 December 2009, 11 members had not paid their 2009 subscriptions.

These facts are translated into the accounts as set out below:

Dr				Subscriptions Account			Cr
2009			£	2009			£
Jan 1	Owing b/d	(A)	360	Jan 1	Prepaid b/d	(B)	80
Dec 31	Income and expenditure a/c		*7,220	Dec 31	Bank	(C)	7,420
Dec 31	Prepaid c/d	(C)	140	Dec 31	Owing c/d	(D)	220
			7,720				7,720
2010				2010			
Jan 1	Owing b/d	(D)	220	Jan 1	Prepaid b/d	(C)	140

* The difference between the two sides of the account.

Income and Expenditure Account for the year ended 31 December 2009 (extract)	
Income:	£
Subscriptions	7,220

In this last case in the balance sheet as at 31 December 2009, the amounts owing for subscriptions (D), £220, will be shown under current assets as a debtor. The subscriptions (C) paid in advance for 2010 will appear as an item under current liabilities as subscriptions received in advance, £140, as shown below:

Balance Sheet as at 31 December 2009 (extract)	
Current Assets	
Stock	xxx
Debtors (xxx + 220)	xxx
Current Liabilities	
Subscriptions in advance	140

Note: Treasurers of clubs and societies are very much aware that if subscriptions are outstanding for a long time it is unlikely that they will ever be paid – the member may have lost interest or moved on to another organisation. Consequently, many clubs and indeed charities do not include unpaid subscriptions as an asset in the balance sheet.

24.8 Donations

Small **donations** received are usually shown as income in the year that they are received. If, however, the donation is a considerable sum, for example a legacy of, say, £10,000 from a deceased member, then it would be added to the accumulated fund and shown in the balance sheet.

> DONATIONS – a monetary gift donated to the club or society.

24.9 Entrance fees

New members often have to pay an entrance fee in the year that they join, in addition to the membership fee for that year. Entrance fees are normally included as income in the year that they are received.

24.10 Life membership

In some clubs and societies members can pay a one-off amount for **life membership.** This membership will last for their lifetime. In this case, all of the money received from life membership should not be credited to the income and expenditure account of the year in which it is received.

> LIFE MEMBERSHIP – where members pay one amount for membership to last them their lifetime.

In a club where members joined at age 20 and would probably be members for 40 years, then one-fortieth ($2\frac{1}{2}\%$) of the life membership fee should be credited in the income and expenditure account each year. The balance not transferred to the income and expenditure account would appear in the balance sheet as a long-term liability. This is because it is the liability of the club to allow the members to use the club for the rest of their lives without paying any more for membership.

On the other hand, a club especially for people over the age of 60 would transfer a much bigger share of the life membership fee paid to the income and expenditure account. This is because the number of years of future use of the club will be far less because people are already old when they join. It may be, in those circumstances, that 10% of the life membership fee per year would be transferred to the credit of the income and expenditure account.

24.11 Treasurers' responsibilities

Treasurers of clubs or societies have a responsibility for maintaining proper accounting records in the same way as an accountant has when looking after the financial affairs of a business. It is important to ensure that any monies paid out by the treasurer have been properly authorised, especially when purchasing an item of capital expenditure (such as new sound equipment for a dramatic society). In such cases, the authorisation for purchase will more than likely have been approved at a committee meeting and noted in the minutes of the meeting. For smaller items of expenditure such as postages, telephone calls, etc., the club or society's rules will provide the treasurer with the authority to make payments against receipted bills.

It is also important for the treasurer to keep all invoices, receipted accounts and any other documents as evidence against payments. Treasurers should also provide receipts for any monies received. All documents should be filed and available at the year end for the club's auditor to carry out an audit and for preparation of the club's year end financial statements.

End of Chapter Checklist

Summary

- The main objective of non-profit making organisations is to provide members with facilities to pursue a leisure activity and not to trade and make profits.
- The financial statements prepared for non-profit making organisations may be either a 'receipts and payments account', which is like a cash book summary, or an 'income and expenditure account'. This is similar to a trading and profit and loss account except the terminology is different. A profit is referred to as a 'surplus of income over expenditure' and a loss as 'excess expenditure over income'.
- The 'accumulated fund' is basically the same as a capital account.
- Occasionally, activities are held to generate profits for the benefit of the club and its members.
- Members' subscriptions may involve subscriptions owing and/or paid in advance.
- Donations should be treated as income in the year in which they are received unless they are of a substantial amount when they may be added to the accumulated fund.
- Entrance fees are usually treated as income in the year in which the member joins.
- Life membership subscriptions should be spread over the anticipated length of membership.
- Club treasurers carry an important role and, as such, are responsible for maintaining the organisation's accounting records and looking after their financial affairs.

Questions

24.1 Distinguish between the following:

a) Receipts and payments account and income and expenditure account.
b) The capital of a business and the accumulated fund.
c) The profit in a business and a surplus of income over expenditure.

24.2 The following are the details of the Horton Hockey Club for its year to 30 June 2009:

Payments:	£
Teams' travel expenses	1,598
Groundsman's wages	3,891
Postage and stationery	392
Rent of pitches and clubhouse	4,800
General expenses	419
Cost of prizes for raffles	624
Receipts:	
Subscriptions	8,570
Donations	1,500
Receipts from raffles	3,816
Cash and bank balances:	£
1 July 2008	2,715
30 June 2009	4,877

You also find out that members owe £160 subscriptions on 30 June 2009. On that date, the club owed £400 for rent and £75 for wages.

You are required to draw up:

a) a receipts and payments account for the year ended 30 June 2009.
b) an income and expenditure account for the year ended 30 June 2009.

24.3X The financial details of the Superball Football Club for the year to 31 May 2009 are:

Payments:	£
Hire of transport	3,710
Ground maintenance costs	1,156
Groundsman's wages	5,214
Committee expenses	906
Costs of disco	1,112
Rent of ground	2,450
General expenses	814
Receipts:	
Members' subscriptions	8,124
Prize money for winning cup	1,000
Receipts from disco	3,149
Collections at matches	5,090
Cash and bank balances:	£
1 June 2008	905
31 May 2009	2,906

End of Chapter Checklist

Questions

Members' subscriptions owing on 31 May 2008 amount to £160 and on 31 May 2009 to £94. On 31 May 2009 the rent had been prepaid £200, and owing were transport hire £90 and committee expenses £170.

You are required to draw up:

   a) a receipts and payments account for the year ended 31 May 2009.
   b) an income and expenditure account for the year ended 31 May 2009.

24.4 *The following receipts and payments account for the year ending 31 May 2008 was prepared by the treasurer of the Down Town Sports and Social Club.*

Receipts	£	Payments	£
Balance at bank 1 June 2007	286	Purchases of new equipment	166
Subscriptions	135	Bar stocks purchased	397
Net proceeds of jumble sale	91	Hire of rooms	64
Net proceeds of dance	122	Wages of part-time staff	198
Sale of equipment	80	Balance at bank 31 May 2008	352
Bar takings	463		
	1,177		1,177

Notes:

(i) On 1 June 2007, the club's equipment was valued at £340. Included in this total, valued at £92, was the equipment sold during the year for £80.

(ii) Bar stocks were valued as follows: 31 May 2007, £88; 31 May 2008, £101. There were no creditors for bar supplies on either of these dates.

(iii) Allow £30 for depreciation of equipment during the year ending 31 May 2008. This is additional to the loss on equipment sold during the year.

(iv) No subscriptions were outstanding at 31 May 2007, but on 31 May 2008 subscriptions due but unpaid amounted to £14.

Required (with calculations shown):

   a) Calculate the accumulated fund of the club as at 1 June 2007.
   b) Draw up the income and expenditure account of the club for the year ending 31 May 2008.

24.5X *The treasurer of the Sevenoaks College Drama Society has produced the following statements for the society's committee, covering the financial year ended 31 December 2010.*

Sevenoaks College Drama Society Statement of Affairs As at 1 January 2010

	£	£
Assets		
Scenery (Net Book Value)	7,500	
Stock of refreshments	100	
Subscriptions due	50	
Bank balance	3,000	
		10,650
Liabilities		
Costume hire fee outstanding		650
		10,000

Sevenoaks College Drama Society Receipts and Payments Accounts For Period 1 January 2010 – 31 December 2010

Receipts	£	Payments	£
Bank balanced 1 January 2010	3,000	Hire of costumes	1,500
Subscriptions: 2009	50	Rent of theatre	750
2010	1,600	Administrative expenses	440
2011	90	Purchase of refreshments	845
Ticket sales	4,000	Purchase of new scenery	7,000
Refreshment sales	1,200		
Bank balance 31 December 2010	595		
	10,535		10,535

The following additional information is available on 31 December 2010 and is to be taken into account.

- The closing stock of refreshments is valued at £165.
- Scenery has been valued at £12,500.
- There are no subscriptions outstanding for 2010.

   a) Prepare the trading and profit and loss account for the society to show the profit or loss on the sale of refreshments for the year ended 31 December 2010.
   b) Prepare the income and expenditure account for the society, showing clearly the surplus or deficit for 2010.
   c) Prepare the balance sheet for the society as at 31 December 2010.

IGCSE

End of Chapter Checklist

Questions

24.6X a) Define each of the following terms:

Accumulated Fund

Surplus

b) Where should the items below appear in the balance sheet of a sports club?

Subscriptions in arrears

Rent of cricket pitch accrued

c) (i) What is the purpose of a receipts and payments account?

(ii) In which section of the balance sheet would the debit balance of the receipts and payments account be shown?

(iii) Name **one** item that would appear in the receipts and payments account but **not** in the income and expenditure account.

(iv) Name **one** item that would appear in the income and expenditure account but **not** in the receipts and payments account.

d) A sports club has received a donation of £10,000 from a local business. Explain, giving reasons, how the club should account for this donation.

IGCSE

Section G: Manufacturing accounts

Chapter 25: Manufacturing accounts

25.1 Manufacturing accounts

So far, the book has dealt with businesses solely involved in trading. However, companies with manufacturing activities need to prepare a **manufacturing account** to ascertain the cost of producing goods. This account, which is normally for internal management purposes, will show the production cost and this figure will be transferred to the trading account.

Cost records are essential if an accurate assessment of the production cost is to be achieved. Regular reviews of the production cost by management are vital on, say, a monthly basis. Action can then be taken if, for example, increases in material costs have occurred or production targets are not being met.

25.2 Direct and indirect costs

Direct costs are those that can be directly identified with specific products or individual contracts and need to be calculated first. A manufacturing company builds up the production costs in stages, starting with the direct costs followed by the indirect costs.

- Direct materials – raw materials required for the manufacture of a product.
- Direct labour – wages of the machine operator who makes the product.
- Direct expenses – expenses that can be identified to each unit of production, for example, the hire of a special machine, or the payment of a royalty for the use of a patent or copyright.

The total of all the **direct costs** is known as the **prime cost** – see Exhibit 25.1 below.

Indirect costs are those that occur in the factory or other places where production is being carried out but cannot be easily traced to the items being manufactured. Examples include:

- rent of premises and business rates
- insurance of premises
- depreciation of equipment
- factory heating and lighting
- wages of supervisors.

Indirect costs are also referred to as indirect manufacturing costs, production overheads or **factory overhead cost**s (see Exhibit 25.1).

Getting started

Edexcel specification
Manufacturing accounts 7.1, 7.2, 7.3, 7.4.

After you have studied this chapter you should be able to:

- understand that a company producing goods records the cost in a manufacturing account
- understand that regular review of the production cost can aid management
- calculate the prime cost and production cost of goods manufactured
- define direct costs and indirect costs
- prepare a manufacturing account
- calculate the production cost per unit.

MANUFACTURING ACCOUNT – prepared to ascertain the cost of producing goods.

DIRECT COSTS can be directly traced to the item being manufactured.

PRIME COST is direct material + direct labour + direct expenses.

INDIRECT COSTS are factory costs but not easily traced to items being made.

FACTORY OVERHEAD COSTS are another name for indirect manufacturing costs or production overheads.

Exhibit 25.1 Total cost calculation

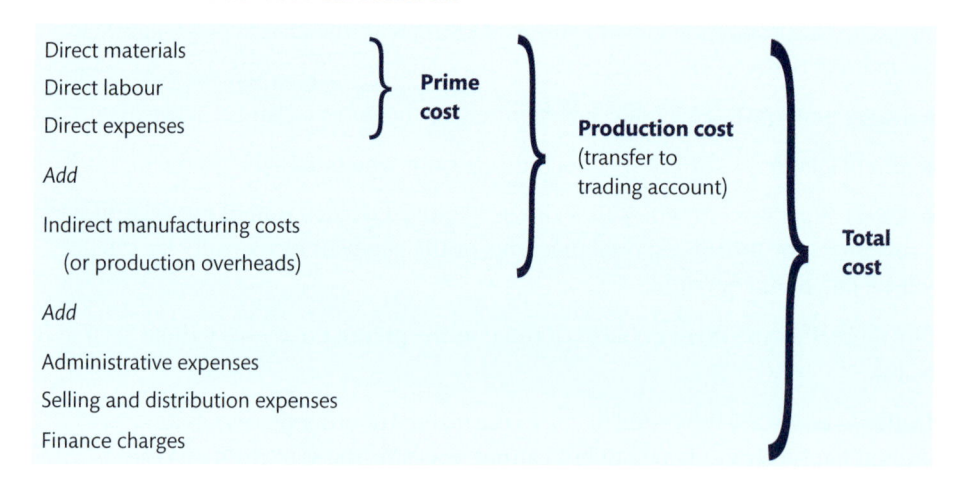

Direct materials		
Direct labour	} Prime cost	
Direct expenses		} Production cost (transfer to trading account)
Add		
Indirect manufacturing costs		
(or production overheads)		} Total cost
Add		
Administrative expenses		
Selling and distribution expenses		
Finance charges		

25.3 Format of financial statements

As previously mentioned, if a company manufactures its own products then it would prepare a manufacturing account prior to the trading and profit and loss accounts. The financial statements would be as follows:

- Manufacturing Account
- Trading Account
- Profit and Loss Account
- Balance Sheet.

Manufacturing account section

This is charged with the production cost of goods completed during the accounting period. It consists of:

- **Direct material** – this is found as follows:
  1. opening stock of raw materials
  2. **add** the cost of purchases of raw materials plus carriage inwards charges
  3. **less** closing stock of raw materials
  4. this gives **the cost of raw material consumed.**

To this figure **add** the following:

- **Direct labour**
- **Direct expenses**
- This now gives the figure of **prime cost.**

Now add:

- **Indirect manufacturing costs** such as wages of supervisor, factory rent, depreciation of equipment, etc.
- **Add** opening work in progress and **deduct** closing work in progress
- This now gives **production cost of goods completed.**

When completed, the manufacturing account shows the total production costs relating to the goods manufactured and available for sale during the accounting period. This figure is then transferred to the trading account section of the trading and profit and loss accounts.

Note: Many students are so used to deducting expenses such as wages, rent, depreciation, etc. in profit and loss accounts that they can easily fall into the trap of *deducting* these instead of *adding* them in the manufacturing account. Remember, we are building up the cost of manufacture so all costs are **added.**

> TIP – Manufacturing account: remember to *add* expenses, i.e. wages, rent, etc.

Trading account section

This account includes:

- production cost brought down from the manufacturing account
- opening and closing stocks of finished goods
- sales.

When completed, this account will disclose the gross profit. This figure will then be carried down to the profit and loss account section of the final accounts.

The Manufacturing Account and the Trading Account can be shown in the form of a diagram.

Manufacturing Account	
	£
Production costs for the period:	
Direct materials	xxx
Direct labour	xxx
Direct expenses	xxx
Prime cost	xxx
Indirect manufacturing costs (or production overheads)	xxx
*****Production cost of goods completed c/d to trading account**	xxx

Trading Account		
	£	£
Sales		xxx
Less **Production cost of goods sold:**		
Opening stock of finished goods (A)	xxx	
Add *****Production costs of goods completed b/d**	xxx	
	xxx	
Less Closing stock of finished goods (B)	xxx	xxx
Gross profit		xxx

> TIP – the 'Production Costs' of goods manufactured is transferred to the Trading Account.

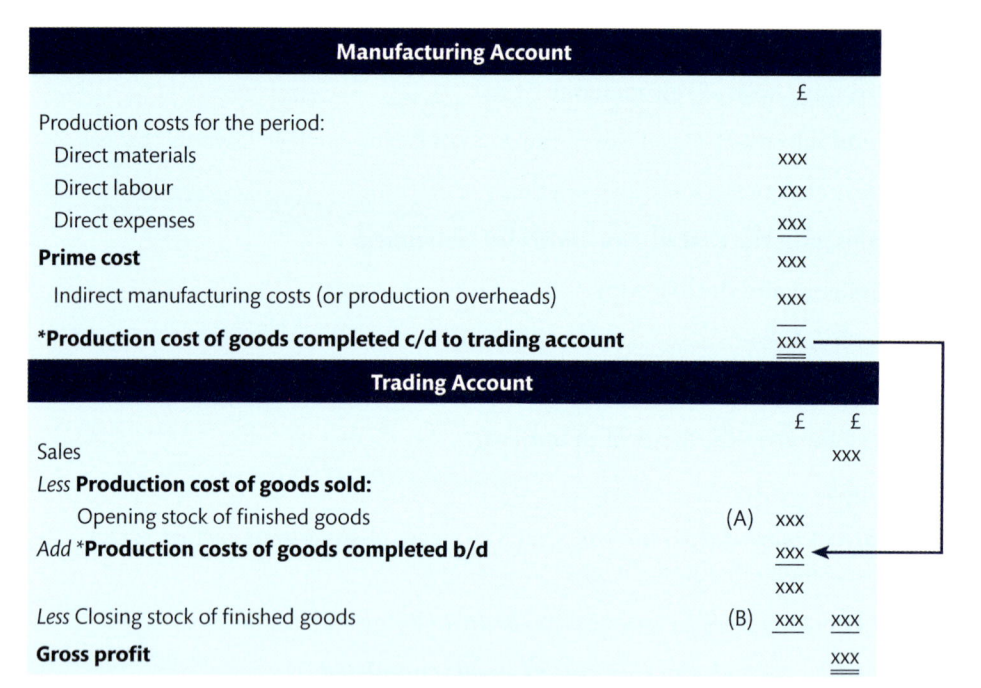

(A) is production costs of goods unsold in previous period.

(B) is production costs of goods unsold at end of the current period.

Profit and loss account section

This section includes:

- gross profit brought down from the trading account
- all administration expenses – e.g. managers' salaries, legal and accountancy fees, secretarial salaries and expenses etc.
- all selling and distribution expenses – e.g. sales staff salaries and commission, carriage outwards, advertising etc.
- all finance charges – loan interest charged on loan, bank charges, discounts allowed etc.

Since some of the charges usually found in the profit and loss account will have already been included in the manufacturing account, only the remainder need charging to the profit and loss account.

When complete, the profit and loss account will show the net profit.

Balance sheet

The balance sheet of a manufacturing company is virtually the same as balance sheets prepared for other organisations with one exception. In the *Current assets* section all three closing stocks must be included, i.e.:

- stock of raw materials
- stock of work-in-progress
- stock of finished goods.

> BALANCE SHEET – be sure to include all three closing stocks:
> - stock of raw materials
> - stock of work-in-progress
> - stock of finished goods.

25.4 Work in progress

The production cost to be carried down to the trading account is the 'production cost of goods completed during the period'. If items have not been completed, they cannot be sold. Therefore, they should not appear in the trading account. For instance, from the following information, we can calculate the transfer to the trading account:

> WORK IN PROGRESS are items not completed at the end of a period.

	£
Total production costs expended during the year	60,000
Production costs last year on goods not completed last year, but completed in this year (work in progress)	3,600
Production costs this year on goods which were not completed by the year end (work in progress)	5,280
The calculation is:	£
Total production costs expended this year	60,000
Add Costs from last year, in respect of goods completed in this year (work in progress)	3,600
	63,600
Less Costs in this year, for goods to be completed next year (work in progress)	5,280
Production costs expended on goods completed this year	58,320

25.5 A worked example for a manufacturing account

From the following list of balances as at 31 December 2009 for a lawnmower manufacturer, the steps to determine the prime cost, production cost of goods completed and the cost per unit based on 2,100 units being produced are shown in Exhibit 25.2.

Exhibit 25.2

	£
1 January 2009, Stock of raw materials	7,200
31 December 2009, Stock of raw materials	9,450
1 January 2009, Work in progress	3,150
31 December 2009, Work in progress	3,780
Year to 31 December 2009	
Wages: Direct	35,640
Indirect	22,950
Purchase of raw materials	78,300
Fuel and power	8,910
Direct expenses	1,260
Lubricants	2,700
Carriage inwards on raw materials	1,800
Rent of factory	6,400
Depreciation of factory plant and machinery	3,780
Internal transport expenses	11,620
Insurance of factory buildings and plant	11,350
General factory expenses	2,970

Manufacturing Account for the year ended 31 December 2009

	£	£
Stock of raw materials 1.1.2009		7,200
Add Purchases		78,300
Carriage inwards		1,800
		87,300
Less Stock of raw materials 31.12.2009		9,450
Cost of raw materials consumed		77,850
Direct wages		35,640
Direct expenses		1,260
Prime cost		114,750
Add Indirect Manufacturing Cost		
Fuel and power	8,910	
Indirect wages	22,950	
Lubricants	2,700	
Rent	6,400	
Depreciation of plant	3,780	
Internal transport expenses	11,620	
Insurance	11,350	
General factory expenses	2,970	70,680
		185,430
Add Work in progress 1.1.2009		3,150
		188,580
Less Work in progress 31.12.2009		3,780
Production cost of goods completed c/d		184,800

Unit cost of production

Once the total cost of production is calculated the production cost per unit can easily be ascertained. In the above example, 2,100 units were produced at the cost of £184,800 (see Manufacturing Account). The cost per unit is as follows:

$$\text{Cost per unit} = \frac{\text{Cost of production}}{\text{No. of units produced}} = \frac{£184,80}{2,100 \text{ units}} = £88 \text{ per unit}$$

Trading account

The trading account is concerned with finished goods. If, in Exhibit 25.2, there had been £31,500 stock of finished goods at 1 January 2009 and £39,600 at 31 December 2009, and the sales of finished goods amounted to £275,000, then the trading account would appear thus:

Trading Account for the year 31 December 2009

	£	£
Sales		275,000
Less Cost of goods sold		
Stock of finished goods 1.1.2009	31,500	
Add Production cost of goods completed b/d	184,800	
	216,300	
Less Stock of finished goods 31.12.2009	39,600	176,700
Gross profit c/d		98,300

The profit and loss account is then constructed in the normal way. In the Balance Sheet all three closing stock figures would appear under the 'Current Assets' section as follows:

Balance Sheet as at 31 December 2009 (extract)

	£
Current Assets	
Stock:	
Raw materials	9,450
Work in progress	3,780
Finished goods	39,600

25.6 Apportionment of expenses

Quite often, expenses will have to be divided between:

- Indirect manufacturing costs: to be charged in the manufacturing account section
- Administration expenses:
- Selling and distribution expenses: to be charged in the profit and loss account section
- Financial charges:

An instance of this could be the rent expense. If the rent is paid separately for each part of the organisation, then it is easy to charge the rent to each sort of expense. However, only one figure of rent might be paid, without any indication as to how much is for the factory part, how much is for the selling and distribution part, and that for the administration buildings.

How the rent expense will be apportioned in the latter case will depend on circumstances, but will use the most equitable way. A range of methods may be used, including ones based upon:

- floor area
- property valuations of each part of the buildings and land.

25.7 Fixed and variable costs

Fixed costs are costs that, in the short term, remain the same irrespective of the level of business activity. Examples of a fixed cost would be rent, business rates, insurance, etc., and such costs would have to be paid if the company produced 100 units or 1,000 units.

Variable costs vary depending on the level of production. For example, raw materials used in manufacture would vary depending upon the level of goods produced; the more goods produced, the greater the cost of raw materials. If fewer goods were produced, the costs of raw materials would be reduced.

Note: Students often find the preparation of manufacturing accounts difficult to grasp and may find it useful to remember the following areas in which they could easily make a mistake:

1 Remember to add any item appearing under the heading of 'Indirect Manufacturing Costs', i.e. rent, wages, depreciation, power and lighting, etc.

2 In the trading account 'Cost of goods sold' section, ensure you use the **Production cost** of goods completed, i.e. (from Exhibit 25.2 £184,800), and *not* the **purchases** figure.

3 In the balance sheet, under 'Current assets', be sure to include all ***three closing stocks*** if applicable to your question, i.e.:

   (i) stock of raw materials

   (ii) stock of work in progress

   (iii) stock of finished goods.

FIXED COSTS remain the same, in short term, irrespective of level of business activity.

VARIABLE COSTS vary depending on levels of business activity.

End of Chapter Checklist

Summary

- When a company manufactures its own products the production cost can be found by preparing a manufacturing account.
- Direct costs are those costs that can be traced to the specific item being manufactured.
- Indirect costs, also known as 'indirect manufacturing costs', are those costs relating to the manufacture of an item that cannot be easily allocated, for example, a supervisor's wages.
- The total of direct materials, labour and expenses gives the prime cost. To this figure is added any indirect manufacturing costs, plus the opening stock of work in progress, less closing stock of work in progress, to give the production cost of goods completed.
- Where a business manufactures its own goods the financial statements consist of: a manufacturing account, which gives the production cost of goods completed; the trading and the profit and loss account, which shows the gross and net profits respectively; and the balance sheet.
- It is important to adjust the manufacturing account for any work in progress at the start and end of the accounting period.
- Fixed costs remain the same whatever the level of productive activity, whereas variable costs, such as raw materials, varies according to the number of units produced.
- The areas likely to cause errors when preparing financial statements for manufacturing organisations are:
  - Manufacturing account – under the heading 'Indirect expenses' remember to *add* the expenses, i.e. rent, power and lighting, depreciation, etc.
  - Trading account – when calculating the 'Cost of goods sold' ensure you use the 'Production cost of goods manufactured', not purchases!
  - Balance sheet – include all *three* closing stock under the heading of 'Current assets', i.e. raw materials, work in progress and finished goods.

Questions

25.1 From the following information, prepare the manufacturing and trading account of E Smith for the year ended 31 March 2009.

	£
Stocks at 1 April 2008:	
Finished goods	6,724
Raw materials	2,400
Work in progress	955
Carriage on purchases (raw materials)	321
Sales	69,830
Purchases of raw materials	21,340
Manufacturing wages	13,280
Factory power	6,220
Other manufacturing expenses	1,430
Factory rent and rates	2,300
Stocks at 31 March 2009	
Raw materials	2,620
Work in progress	870
Finished goods	7,230

25.2X From the following details, you are to draw up a manufacturing, trading and profit and loss account of P Lucas for the year ended 30 September 2009.

	30.9.2008	30.9.2009
	£	£
Stocks of raw materials, at cost	8,460	10,970
Work in progress	3,070	2,460
Finished goods stock	12,380	14,570
For the year:		£
Raw materials purchased		38,720
Manufacturing wages		20,970
Factory expenses		12,650
Depreciation:		
Plant and machinery		7,560
Delivery vans		3,040
Office equipment		807
Factory power		6,120
Advertising		5,080
Office and administration expenses		25,910
Sales representatives' salaries and expenses		26,420
Delivery van expenses		5,890
Sales		174,610
Carriage inwards		2,720

End of Chapter Checklist

Questions

25.3X Joey Peterson is a manufacturer of musical instruments. The following balances were extracted from the business records at the end of the financial year, 30 June 2010.

	£
Stock at 1 July 2009	
Raw materials	81,600
Work in progress	125,300
Finished goods	115,440
Stocks at 30 June 2010	
Raw materials	94,500
Work in progress	154,300
Finished goods	85,440
Insurance	66,900
General expenses	43,200
Factory rent and rates	96,000
Selling and distribution expenses	29,700
Direct factory power	40,000
Purchase of raw materials	314,000
Direct factory wages	450,000
Indirect factory wages	98,600
Administration staff salaries	136,800
Sales of finished goods	2,000,000

The following additional information is available at 30 June 2010 and is to be taken into account:

- Direct factory wages £8,900 are accrued
- Insurance £6,900 is prepaid
- Factory plant and machinery is to be depreciated by £50,000
- Expenditure on insurance and general expenses is to be allocated on the following basis: Factory one-third, Administration two-thirds.

a) Prepare a manufacturing account for the year ended 30 June 2010 showing clearly:
  - Cost of raw materials consumed
  - Prime cost
  - Cost of production.

b) Prepare a Trading Account for the year ended 30 June 2010 showing clearly:
  - Cost of goods sold
  - Gross Profit.

IGCSE

25.4X Ahmed Patel is a manufacturer of high performance motor car engines. His manufacturing account for 2008–2009 is shown below:

Ahmed Patel
Manufacturing Account
For the Year Ended 30 September 2009

	£000	£000	£000
Opening stock of raw materials	120		
Purchases of raw materials	540		
	660		
Closing stock of raw materials	100		
		560	
Manufacturing wages		720	
			1,280
Factory rent and insurance		180	
Depreciation of machinery		220	
Factory light and heat		80	
Factory supervisor wages		260	
		740	
			2,020
Work in progress			
Opening stock		60	
Closing stock		?	
			(20)
			2,000

(a) For the year ended 30 September 2009 identify
  (i) cost of raw materials consumed
  (ii) prime cost
  (iii) total factory overheads
  (iv) value of the closing stock of work in progress.

The following additional information is available on 30 September 2009 and is to be taken into account.

- During the year 1,000 engines were manufactured
- Three-quarters of production was sold
- The firm's pricing policy is to mark up factory cost of production by 50%.

(b) For the year ended 30 September 2009 calculate:
  (i) the selling price of **one** engine
  (ii) the total gross profit
  (iii) the value of the closing stock of finished goods based on factory cost of production.

IGCSE

Section H: Partnerships

Chapter 26: Partnership accounts

26.1 The need for partnerships

So far, we have considered mainly businesses owned by only one person. Businesses that set up to make a profit can often have more than one owner and there are various reasons for multiple ownership. There are two types of multiple ownership: **partnerships** and limited companies. This chapter deals only with partnerships; in the following chapter we will look at limited companies.

Advantages of partnerships

Partnerships are easier to set up than limited companies and have much lower set-up costs. The advantages of partnerships include:

- More capital can be raised, i.e. with additional partners.
- Additional partners bring in a variety of skills and expertise that benefit the partnership.
- The experience or ability required to manage the business cannot always be provided by one person working alone.
- The responsibility of management could be shared by additional partners.
- A partnership of family members can bring a stronger desire to succeed within a dependable environment.
- Partnerships are ideal organisations for professional practices such as medicine, law and accounting.
- Profits from partnership are taxed as the personal income of the partnership.

Disadvantages of partnerships

The disadvantages include:

- The partners have unlimited liability (except a **limited partner**, see Section 26.3) and may be responsible for the debts of other partners.
- A partnership is dissolved on the death of a partner.
- It is difficult to liquidate or transfer partnerships.
- A partnership may have difficulty in raising sufficient capital for large-scale operations. Increased unlimited liability could also be a deterrent to expanding the business.

Getting started

Edexcel specification
Partnership
8.1 to 8.11.

After you have studied this chapter you should be able to:

- understand exactly what a partnership is and the rules relating to the number of partners
- distinguish between limited and unlimited partners
- describe the main features of a partnership deed or agreement
- understand the position if no partnership deed or agreement exists
- draw up the capital and current accounts for the partnership
- prepare the financial statements of a partnership.

PARTNERSHIP – a group of a minimum of two people and a maximum of 20 people who, together, are in business with a view to making a profit.

26.2 Nature of a partnership

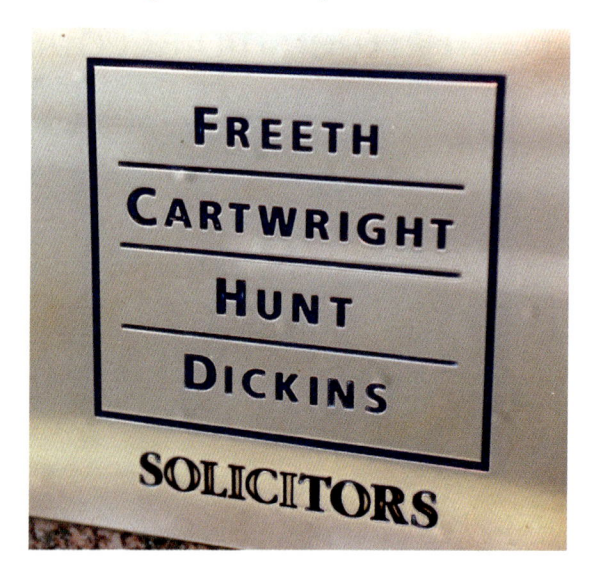

A partnership has the following characteristics:

1 It is formed to make profits.
2 It must obey the law as given in the Partnership Act 1890. If there is a limited partner, as described in Section 26.3, they must comply with the Limited Partnerships Act of 1907.
3 Normally, there can be a minimum of two and a maximum of 20 partners. Exceptions are banks, where there cannot be more than 10 partners; also, there is no maximum limit for firms of accountants, solicitors, stock exchange members or other professional bodies receiving the approval of the relevant government body for this purpose.
4 Each partner (except for limited partners, described below) must pay his or her share of any debts that the partnership is unable to pay; they are personally liable. If necessary, partners could be forced to sell their private possessions to pay their share of any debts. This can be said to be 'unlimited' liability.

LIMITED PARTNER – a partner whose liability is limited to the capital invested in the firm.

26.3 Limited partners

A partnership may be unlimited, as previously discussed, or limited. In a **limited partnership** there must be at least one partner who is not limited. All limited partnerships must be registered with the Registrar of Companies. Limited partners are not liable for the debts as in Section 26.2 (4) above. The following characteristics are found in limited partnerships:

1 Their liability for the debts of the partnership is limited to the capital they have invested in the partnership. They can lose that capital, but they cannot be asked for any more money to pay the debts unless they break the regulations relating to the involvement in the partnership (2 and 3 below).
2 The partners are not allowed to take out or receive back any part of their contribution to the partnership during its lifetime.

3 They are not allowed to take part in the management of the partnership business.
4 All the partners cannot be limited partners as mentioned above; there must be at least one partner with unlimited liability.

26.4 Partnership deed or agreement

Partnership deeds or agreements in writing are not necessary for partnerships, however, it is advisable to have a written **partnership deed or agreement** drawn up by a solicitor or accountant to prevent problems between partners occurring. The written agreement can contain as much, or as little, as the partners want since there are no requirements in law as to what they must contain. The usual accounting contents are as follows:

1 The capital to be contributed by each partner.
2 The ratio in which profits (or losses) are to be shared.
3 The rate of interest, if any, to be paid on capital before the profits are shared.
4 The rate of interest, if any, to be charged on partners' drawings.
5 Salaries to be paid to partners.
6 Performance-related payments to partners.
7 *Arrangement for the admission of a new partner.
8 *Procedures to be carried out when a partner retires or dies.

*The latter two points are outside the scope of the syllabus and will be dealt with later on in your studies.

PARTNERSHIP DEED OR AGREEMENT – the contractual relationship, either written or verbal, between partners, which covers details such as how profit/losses should be shared and responsibilities of the partners.

1 Capital contributions

Partners need not contribute equal amounts of capital. What matters is how much capital each partner *agrees* to contribute.

2 Profit (or loss) sharing ratios

Although partners can in fact agree to share profits/losses in any ratio that they desire, it is often thought by students that profits should be shared in the same ratio as that in which capital is contributed. For example, suppose the capitals were Allen £20,000 and Beet £10,000; many people would share the profits in the ratio of two-thirds to one-third, even though the work to be done by each partner is similar. A look at the division of the first few years' profits on such a basis would be:

PROFIT SHARING – profits/losses do not have to be shared in the same ratio as capital contributed.

Years	1	2	3	4	5	Total
	£	£	£	£	£	£
Net profits	18,000	24,000	30,000	30,000	36,000	
Shared:						
Allen $\frac{2}{3}$	12,000	16,000	20,000	20,000	24,000	92,000
Beet $\frac{1}{3}$	6,000	8,000	10,000	10,000	12,000	46,000

It can be seen from the above table that Allen would receive £92,000, or £46,000 more than Beet. To treat each partner fairly, the difference between the two shares of profit when the duties of the partners are the same should be adequate to compensate Allen for putting extra capital into the business. Some might feel that £46,000 extra profits is far more than adequate for this purpose.

Consider, too, the position of capital ratio sharing of profits when one partner has put in £99,000 and the other £1,000 as capital. In this case, one partner would get 99/100ths of the profits, while the other would get only 1/100th!

To overcome the difficulty of compensating for the investment of extra capital, the concept of interest on capital was devised.

3 Interest on capital

> INTEREST ON CAPITAL – an agreed rate of interest credited to a partner to compensate for unequal capital contributions.

If the work to be done by each partner is of equal value but the capital contributed is unequal, it is reasonable to grant **interest on the partners' capital**. This interest is treated as a deduction prior to the calculation of profits and its distribution according to the profit-sharing ratio. The rate of interest is a matter of agreement between the partners, but it should equal the return that they would have received if they had invested the capital elsewhere.

Taking Allen and Beet's business again, but sharing the profits equally after charging 5% per annum interest on capital, the division of profits would become:

Years	1	2	3	4	5	Total
	£	£	£	£	£	£
Net profits	18,000	24,000	30,000	30,000	36,000	
Interest on capital						
Allen	1,000	1,000	1,000	1,000	1,000	
Beet	500	500	500	500	500	
Remainder shared:						
Allen $\frac{1}{2}$	8,250	11,250	14,250	14,250	17,250	65,250
Beet $\frac{1}{2}$	8,250	11,250	14,250	14,250	17,250	65,250

Summary	Allen	Beet
	£	£
Interest on capital	5,000	2,500
Balance of profits	65,250	65,250
	70,250	67,750

Here, Allen has received £2,500 more than Beet which the partners consider appropriate for his having invested a larger amount over five years.

4 Interest on drawings

> INTEREST ON DRAWINGS – interest debited to partners to discourage them from excessive drawings.

It is clearly in the best interests of the business that cash is withdrawn from the business by the partners in accordance with the two basic principles of: (a) as little as possible, and (b) as late as possible. The more cash that is left in the business, the more expansion can be financed, the greater the economies of having ample cash to take advantage of bargains and of not missing cash discounts.

To deter the partners from taking out cash unnecessarily, the concept can be used of charging the partners **interest on each withdrawal**, calculated from the date of withdrawal to the end of the financial year. The amount charged to them helps to swell the profits divisible between the partners. The rate of interest should be sufficient to achieve this without being too harsh.

Suppose that Allen and Beet have decided to charge interest on drawings at 5% per annum, and that their year end is 31 December. The following drawings are made:

Allen

Drawings		Interest		£
1 January	£1,000	5% of £1,000 for 1 year	=	50
1 March	£2,400	5% of £2,400 for 10 months	=	100
1 May	£1,200	5% of £1,200 for 8 months	=	40
1 July	£2,400	5% of £2,400 for 6 months	=	60
1 October	£ 800	5% of £800 for 3 months	=	10
		Interest charged to Allen	=	260

Beet

Drawings		Interest		£
1 January	£ 600	5% of £600 for 1 year	=	30
1 August	£4,800	5% of £4,800 for 5 months	=	100
1 December	£2,400	5% of £2,400 for 1 month	=	10
		Interest charged to Beet	=	140

The interest charged to each partner would vary depending on when and how much money was taken out as drawings.

5 Salaries to partners

One partner may have more responsibility or tasks than others. As a reward for this, and rather than change the profit and loss sharing ratio, that partner may have a **partnership salary**, which is deducted before sharing the balance of profits.

> PARTNERSHIP SALARIES – agreed amounts payable to partners in respect of duties undertaken by them.

6 Performance-related payments to partners

Partners may agree that commission or performance-related bonuses should be payable to some or all the partners in a way that is linked to their individual performance. As with salaries, these would be deducted before sharing the balance of profits.

26.5 An example of the distribution of profits

Taylor and Clarke have been in partnership for one year, sharing profits and losses in the ratio of Taylor three-fifths and Clarke two-fifths. They are entitled to 5% per annum interest on capital, Taylor having put in £20,000 and Clarke £60,000. Clarke is to have a salary of £20,000. They charge interest on drawings, Taylor being charged £500 and Clarke £1,000. The net profit, before any distributions to the partners, amounts to £50,000 for the year ended 31 December 2009. The results are shown in Exhibit 26.1 shown below:

Exhibit 26.1

	£	£	£
Net profit			50,000
Add Charged for interest on drawings:			
Taylor		500	
Clarke		1,000	
			1,500
			51,500
Less Salary: Clarke		20,000	
Interest on capital (@ 5%)			
Taylor	1,000		
Clarke	3,000		
		4,000	
			24,000
			27,500
Balance of profits shared:			
Taylor (three-fifths)		16,500	
Clarke (two-fifths)		11,000	27,500
			27,500

The £50,000 net profits have therefore been shared as follows:

	Taylor	Clarke
	£	£
Balance of profits	16,500	11,000
Interest on capital	1,000	3,000
Salary	–	20,000
	17,500	34,000
Less Interest on drawings	500	1,000
	17,000	33,000
	£50,000	

26.6 The financial statements

If the sales, stock and expenses of a partnership were exactly the same as that of a sole trader, then the trading and profit and loss account would be identical with that as prepared for the sole trader. However, a partnership would have an extra section shown under the profit and loss account. This section is called the profit and loss **appropriation account**, and it is in this account that the distribution of profits is shown. The heading to the trading and profit and loss account does not include the words 'appropriation account'. It is purely an accounting custom not to include it in the heading.

The trading and profit and loss account of Taylor and Clarke from the details given would appear as shown in Exhibit 26.2.

Exhibit 26.2

Taylor and Clarke
Trading and Profit and Loss Account for the year ended 31 December 2009

(Trading Account – same as for sole trader) (Profit and Loss Account – same as for sole trader)
Profit and loss appropriation account

	£	£	£
Net profit			50,000
Interest on drawings:			
Taylor		500	
Clarke		1,000	1,500
			51,500
Less:			
Interest on capital:			
Taylor	1,000		
Clarke	3,000	4,000	
Salary		20,000	24,000
			27,500
Balance of profits shared:			
Taylor (three-fifths)		16,500	
Clarke (two-fifths)		11,000	27,500
			27,500

26.7 Fixed capital accounts plus current accounts

With **fixed capital accounts**, the capital account for each partner remains year by year at the figure of capital put into the business by the partners. The profits, interest on capital, and the salaries to which the partner may be entitled are then credited to a separate current account for the partner, and the drawings and the interest on drawings are debited to it. The balance of the current account at the end of each financial year will then represent the amount of undrawn (or withdrawn) profits. A credit balance will be undrawn profits, while a debit balance will be drawings in excess of the profits to which the partner is entitled.

Using the financial information from Sections 26.5 and 26.6 for Taylor and Clarke, their capital and current accounts, assuming drawings of £12,000 for Taylor and £20,000 for Clarke, would appear as follows:

Taylor
Capital Account

Dr					Cr
		2009			£
		Jan 1	Bank		20,000

Clarke
Capital Account

Dr					Cr
		2009			£
		Jan 1	Bank		60,000

Taylor
Current Account

Dr			£				Cr
2009				2009			£
Dec 31	Cash: Drawings		12,000	Dec 31	Profit and loss appropriation account:		
Dec 31	Profit and loss appropriation account:				Interest on capital		1,000
	Interest on drawings		500		Share of profits		16,500
Dec 31	Balance c/d		5,000				
			17,500				17,500
				2010			
				Jan 1	Balance b/d		5,000

Clarke
Current Account

Dr			£				Cr
2009				2009			£
Dec 31	Cash: Drawings		20,000	Dec 31	Profit and loss appropriation account:		
Dec 31	Profit and loss appropriation account:				Interest on capital		3,000
	Interest on drawings		1,000		Share of profits		11,000
Dec 31	Balance c/d		13,000		Salary		20,000
			34,000	2010			34,000
				Jan 1	Balance b/d		13,000

Notice that the salary of Clarke was not paid to him but was merely credited to his account. If in fact it was paid in addition to his drawings, the £20,000 cash paid would have been debited to the current account, changing the £13,000 credit balance into a £7,000 debit balance.

26.8 Where no partnership agreement exists

Where no formal partnership agreement exists – either express or implied – Section 24 of the Partnership Act 1890 governs the situation. The accounting content of this section states:

- Profits and losses are to be shared equally.
- There is to be no interest allowed on capital.
- No interest is to be charged on drawings.
- Salaries are not allowed.
- If a partner puts a sum of money into a business in excess of the capital he or she has agreed to subscribe, that partner is entitled to interest at the rate of 5% per annum on such an advance.

This section applies where there is no agreement. There may be an agreement, not by a partnership deed but in a letter, or it may be implied by conduct – for instance, when a partner signs a balance sheet that shows profits shared in some ratio other than equally. Where a dispute arises as to whether agreement exists or not, and this cannot be resolved by the partners, only the courts will be competent to decide.

> WHERE NO PARTNERSHIP DEED EXISTS – the accounting section of the Partnership Act 1890 applies.

26.9 The balance sheet

The capital side of the balance sheet will appear as follows for our example. Note that figures in brackets, e.g. '(20,000)', is an accounting convention indicating a negative amount.

Balance Sheet as at 31 December 2009

	£ Taylor	£ Clarke	£ Total
Capital accounts			
Balance	20,000	60,000	80,000
Current accounts			
Interest on capital	1,000	3,000	
Share of profits	16,500	11,000	
Salary	–	20,000	
	17,500	34,000	
Less Drawings	(12,000)	(20,000)	
Interest on drawings	(500)	(1,000)	
	5,000	13,000	18,000

If one of the current accounts had finished in debit – for instance, if the current account of Taylor had finished up as £5,000 debit – the figure of £5,000 would appear in brackets and the balances would appear net in the totals column:

	Taylor	Clarke	
	£	£	£
Closing balance	(5,000)	13,000	8,000

If the net figure – for example, the £8,000 just shown – turned out to be a debit figure, then this would be deducted from the total of the capital accounts.

26.10 A fully worked exercise

We can now look at a fully worked exercise covering nearly all the main points shown in this chapter.

Kidd and Mellor are in partnership. They share profits in the ratio: Kidd three-fifths to Mellor two-fifths. The following trial balance was extracted as at 31 March 2010:

Trial balance as at 31 March 2010

	Dr £	Cr £
Equipment at cost	26,000	
Motor vehicles at cost	36,800	
Provision for depreciation at 31.3.2009:		
Equipment		7,800
Motor vehicles		14,720
Stock at 31 March 2009	99,880	
Debtors and creditors	83,840	65,100
Cash at bank	2,460	
Cash in hand	560	
Sales		361,480
Purchases	256,520	
Salaries	45,668	
Office expenses	1,480	
Motor expenses	2,252	
Heating and lighting	2,000	
Current accounts at 31.3.2009:		
Kidd		5,516
Mellor		4,844
Capital accounts:		
Kidd		86,000
Mellor		50,000
Drawings:		
Kidd	16,000	
Mellor	22,000	
	595,460	595,460

A set of final accounts for the year ended 31 March 2010 for the partnership are to be drawn up taking into consideration the following notes:

   a) Stock at 31 March 2010 was valued at £109,360.

   b) Office expenses owing £440.

   c) Provision for depreciation: motor vehicles 20% of cost, equipment 10% of cost.

   d) Charge interest on capital at 6%.

   e) Charge interest on drawings: Kidd £628, Mellor £892.

   f) Charge £15,000 for salary for Mellor.

The financial statements are now shown below in Exhibit 26.3

Exhibit 26.3

Kidd and Mellor
Trading and Profit and Loss Account for the year ended 31 March 2010

	£	£	£
Sales			361,480
Less Cost of sales:			
Opening stock		99,880	
Add Purchases		256,520	
		356,400	
Less Closing stock		109,360	247,040
Gross profit			114,440
Less Expenses:			
Salaries*		45,668	
Heating and lighting		2,000	
Office expenses (1,480 + 440)		1,920	
Motor expenses		2,252	
Depreciation: Motor vehicles	7,360		
Equipment	2,600	9,960	61,800
Net profit			52,640
Add Interest on drawings: Kidd		628	
Mellor		892	1,520
			54,160
Less Interest on capital: Kidd		5,160	
Mellor		3,000	8,160
			46,000
Less Salary: Mellor			15,000
			31,000
Balance of profits shared: Kidd ($\frac{3}{5}$ths)		18,600	
Mellor ($\frac{2}{5}$ths)		12,400	31,000
			31,000

The gross profit is calculated in this section.

The net profit is found here.

This section shows the distribution of the profits between the partners.

*Does not include partner's salary.

Kidd and Mellor
Balance Sheet as at 31 March 2010

	Cost £	Depreciation £	NBV £
Fixed assets			
Equipment	26,000	10,400	15,600
Motor vehicles	36,800	22,080	14,720
	62,800	32,480	30,320
Current assets			
Stock	109,360		
Debtors	83,840		
Bank	2,460		
Cash	560	196,220	
Less Current liabilities			
Creditors	65,100		
Expenses owing	440	65,540	
Net Current assets			130,680
			161,000

	Kidd	Mellor	Total
Capital accounts			
Balance	86,000	50,000	136,000
Current accounts			
Balances as at 1.4.2009	5,516	4,844	
Add Interest on capital	5,160	3,000	
Add Salary	—	15,000	
Add Share of profits	18,600	12,400	
	29,276	35,244	
Less Drawings	(16,000)	(22,000)	
Less Interest on drawings	(628)	(892)	
Balances as at 31.3.2010	12,648	12,352	25,000
			161,000

The amount of capital invested by the partners.

The partners' current accounts show the balances at the end of the year.

End of Chapter Checklist

Summary

- Partnerships are formed with two or more partners carrying on in business with a view to making a profit.
- There are two types of partnership, an unlimited and a limited partnership.
- Where there is a limited partnership there must be at least one unlimited partner within the partnership. Limited partnerships should be registered with the Registrar of Companies and comply with the Limited Partnership Act 1907.
- Limited partners cannot withdraw any of the capital they invested in the partnership, nor may they take part in the management of the partnership.
- It is advisable for all partnerships to draw up a Partnership Deed or Agreement detailing the accounting requirements of the partnership (Section 26.4).
- If there is no partnership agreement then the provisions of the Partnership Act 1890 will apply (Section 26.8).
- The partners' capital and current accounts are illustrated.
- The financial statements of a partnership are: trading and profit and loss account that has an additional section called the 'appropriation account' and balance sheet. The balance sheet will show the capital and current accounts of all the partners.

Questions

26.1 *Stead and Jackson are partners in a retail business in which they share profits and losses equally. The balance on the partners' capital and current accounts at the year end 31 December 2010 were as follows:*

	Capital Account	Current Account
	£	£
Stead	24,000	2,300 Cr
Jackson	16,000	3,500 Cr

During the year, Stead had drawings amounting to £15,000 and Jackson £19,000. Jackson was to receive a partnership salary of £5,000 for extra duties undertaken. The net profit of the partnership, before taking any of the above into account, was £45,000.

You are required to:

a) Draw up the appropriation account for the partnership for the year ended 31 December 2010.
b) Show the partners' capital and current accounts.

26.2X *Wain, Brown and Cairns own a garage, and the partners share profits and losses in the ratio of Wain 50%, Brown 30% and Cairns 20%. Their financial year end is 31 March 2010 and the following details were extracted from their books on that date:*

	Wain	Brown	Cairns
	£	£	£
Capital account balances	30,000	50,000	70,000
Current account balances	2,400 Cr	3,100 Cr	5,700 Cr
Partnership salaries	10,000	8,000	–
Drawings	12,000	15,050	14,980

The net profit for the year ended 31 March 2010 amounted to £60,000 before taking any of the above into account.

You are required to:

a) Prepare an appropriation account for the year ended 31 March 2010.
b) Draw up the partners' capital and current accounts in columnar form for the year ended 31 March 2010.

End of Chapter Checklist

Questions

26.3 Simpson and Young are in partnership, sharing profits and losses in the ratio 3:2. At the close of business on 30 June 2010 the following trial balance was extracted from their books:

	Dr	Cr
	£	£
Buildings	28,000	
Motor vans (cost £16,000)	11,000	
Office equipment (cost £8,400)	5,600	
Stock 1 July 2009	18,000	
Purchases	184,980	
Sales		254,520
Wages and salaries	32,700	
Rent, rates and insurance	3,550	
Electricity	980	
Stationery and printing	420	
Motor expenses	3,480	
General office expenses	1,700	
Debtors and creditors	28,000	15,200
Capital accounts: Simpson		50,000
Young		20,000
Drawings: Simpson	10,000	
Young	5,000	
Current accounts: Simpson		640
Young		300
Cash at bank	7,250	
	340,660	340,660

Notes:

1. Interest is to be allowed on capital accounts at the rate of 10% per annum, and no interest is to be charged on drawings.
2. Rates prepaid at 30 June 2010 amount to £250.
3. Wages due at 30 June 2010 are £500.
4. Provision for depreciation is as follows: motor van at 20% per annum on cost; office equipment at 10% using the reducing balance method.
5. Stock 30 June 2010 was valued at £19,000.

Required:

Prepare the trading and profit and loss appropriation account for the year ended 30 June 2010, and a balance sheet as at that date.

26.4X Michael and Morgan are partners in a retail business. Their partnership deed states that:

(i) Michael is to receive a salary of £30,000 per annum.
(ii) Remaining profits or losses are to be shared:
Michael ($\frac{2}{5}$ ths)
Morgan ($\frac{3}{5}$ ths)

On 30 September 2009, after the trading account had been prepared, the following balances were extracted from the partnership's books.

		£
Capital Account:	Michael	50,000
	Morgan	40,000
Current Account:	Michael (debit)	1,500 (debit)
	Morgan (credit)	2,000 (credit)
Drawings:	Michael	9,650
	Morgan	8,200
Shop Fittings		76,000
Provision for Depreciation: Shop Fittings		28,000
Gross Profit		385,000
Administration Expenses		6,790
Advertising		7,375
Discount Received		15,000
Rent and Rates		12,000
Wages and Salaries		135,000

The following additional information is available at 30 September 2009.

- Staff salaries of £5,000 were outstanding.
- Depreciation on shop fittings to be charged at the rate of 25% per annum using the reducing balance method
- On 1 January 2009 a payment of £6,000 was made for rates for the year ending 31 December 2009.
- No entry has been made in the books for advertising charges of £125 which Michael had paid from his private funds.

Required:

a) Prepare the profit and loss account (including appropriation section) for the year ended 30 September 2009.
b) Prepare the current account of Michael as it would appear in the ledger.
c) Prepare a balance sheet extract for the partnership as at 30 September 2009, showing the partners' capital and current accounts.

IGCSE

Section I: Limited companies

Chapter 27: Limited company accounts

27.1 Features of a limited company

In the previous chapter we considered partnerships which were owned and run by more than one person. Another type of business organisation is a **limited company**. If a business wishes to expand it will inevitably require additional capital; forming a limited company makes it possible to raise the required funds and also provides additional features that are attractive to the owner(s) as follows:

- **Limited liability** – the capital of a limited company is divided into **shares**. Shares can be of any nominal amount, for example, 10p, 25p, £1, £5, £10 per share. To become a member of a limited company, or a **shareholder**, a person must buy one or more of the shares.

- A shareholder can only lose the amount they have invested in the company which comprises of money paid for shares or the balance due on shares, their personal assets are safe. This is known as **limited liability** and the company is known as a **limited company**.

- **Separate legal entity** – one of the most important features of a limited company is its status in law as a **separate legal entity**. This means that the company is treated separately from the shareholders who own the company. Thus, a company may sue someone in its own name and likewise be sued in the company name.

- **Raising capital** – one of the main reasons for forming a limited company is to raise large amounts of capital to finance the business. The way in which companies raise capital is by issuing shares to prospective investors. In smaller private companies, shares are issued to family and business colleagues who then become shareholders (i.e. members) of the company. Large public limited companies issue their shares to the general public, hence the name 'public' limited companies.

27.2 Private and public companies

There are two classes of company: the **public limited company** (abbreviated PLC) and the **private limited company** (abbreviated Ltd). In the UK, private limited companies far outnumber public limited companies. A public company must have a minimum of two **directors**.

A private limited company is usually, but not always, a smaller business, and may be formed by one or more people and have at least one director who may be the only shareholder. It is defined by the 2006 Companies Act as a company that is not a public company. The main differences between a private company and a public company are that a private company:

- can have an authorised share capital of less than £50,000, and from October 2009 need have no authorised share capital at all

- cannot offer its shares for subscription to the public at large, whereas public companies can.

Getting started

Edexcel specification
Limited companies
9.1 to 9.5

After you have studied this chapter you should be able to:

- distinguish between a private and public limited company
- appreciate the legal status of a limited company
- distinguish between the different types of share capital
- distinguish between ordinary and preference shares and debentures
- understand and prepare the financial statements of limited companies
- appreciate the concept of reserves and distinguish between revenue and capital reserves.

LIMITED LIABILITY – the liability of shareholders in a company is limited to any amount they have agreed to invest.

Public limited companies are required to have a Company Secretary but this is no longer the case for private limited companies since the implementation of the Companies Act 2006. However, a private limited company may decide to have a company secretary, and in this case it is up to the company to specify the Company Secretary's duties and responsibilities.

Limited companies are governed by the various Companies Acts 1985, 1989 and, more recently, the Companies Act 2006 which requires that all companies produce financial statements.

27.3 Share capital

The **share capital** is the capital of a company which is divided into shares which are then bought and owned by the shareholders. There are two main types of share capital, namely, **authorised share capital** and **issued share capital**, it is important to distinguish between the two:

1 **Authorised share capital** – is the maximum share capital that a company is allowed to issue, also called the 'nominal capital'.

Note: In the new Companies Act 2006, a company will no longer be required to have authorised share capital and only the issued/allotted share capital will be included in the financial statements. However, since many of the examining bodies may still be using existing syllabuses when setting examination papers, it was felt necessary to include the definition of authorised share capital.

2 **Issued share capital** – is the amount of share capital that the company has actually issued.

If all of the authorised share capital has been issued then items (1) and (2) above are the same. The authorised share capital can be shown as a note to the balance sheet for information, whereas the issued capital is included in the *Financed by* section.

27.4 Shares and dividends

The share capital may be divided into two main types of share:

1 **Ordinary shares** – these shares are by far the most popular way that companies use to raise capital. Ordinary shareholders will receive a variable share of the profits in the form of a **dividend** based on the number of shares that each shareholder owns. If a company makes a loss, no dividend would be likely to be paid, hence the shares are more risky than preference shares – see below.

As owners of an ordinary share, shareholders can attend the **annual general meeting** and other company meetings and vote on agenda items. As stated earlier, if a company fails, shareholders could lose all their investment since other creditors have first call on any assets left in the company.

2 **Preference shares** – shareholders buy these shares knowing that they will get an agreed percentage rate of dividend. They will be paid this agreed amount before dividends are paid to ordinary shareholders. Preference shareholders can attend company meetings but have no voting rights.

AUTHORISED SHARE CAPITAL – the total amount of share capital or number of shares which a company can issue at any given time.

ISSUED SHARE CAPITAL – the amount of share capital the company has actually issued.

ORDINARY SHARES – shares entitled to dividends after the preference shareholders have been paid their dividends.

PREFERENCE SHARES – shares that are entitled to an agreed rate of dividend before the ordinary shareholders receive anything.

Dividends payable – a successful company is very likely to pay a dividend based on its net profit. It is, however, unlikely that all this profit will be available for distribution since the company may decide to retain a proportion in the form of **revenue reserves**.

Exhibit 27.1 shows how dividends are distributed between ordinary and preference shareholders.

Exhibit 27.1

Dee Dee Transport has issued 30,000 5% preference shares of £1 each and 300,000 ordinary shares of £1 each, which have all been taken up. The profit available for dividends over the past four years has been:

Year 1 – £12,000

Year 2 – £19,500

Year 3 – £24,000

Year 4 – £34,500

The profit would have been distributed as follows:

Year	1	2	3	4
	£	£	£	£
Profits available for dividends	12,000	19,500	24,000	34,500
Preference shares	1,500	1,500	1,500	1,500
Balance for Ordinary shares	(3.5%) 10,500	(6%) 18,000	(7.5%) 22,500	(11%) 33,000

In the above example, the preference share dividend remains constant at 5%, whereas the ordinary share dividend depends upon the success or otherwise of the company's performance. In the above case, the company has achieved a yearly growth in profits.

27.5 Debentures

DEBENTURES – loan to a company.

A **debenture** is a loan which is taken out by a limited company. A company may borrow money from a bank, or from other sources, and when this occurs a debenture certificate is issued by the lender. The features of a debenture include:

- A fixed rate of interest is paid by the company to the investor annually (the **debenture interest**).
- The interest must be paid irrespective of whether the company makes a profit.
- Debentures are often secured on the fixed assets of the business, thereby making it a safer investment for the investor.
- If the company gets into financial difficulties the debenture holders are one of the first claimants to be paid.

27.6 The financial statements of a limited company

Trading and profit and loss accounts

The trading and profit and loss account for limited companies are prepared in the same way as they would be for sole traders and partnerships. While there is no difference to the trading account, the profit and loss account does contain *two* additional types of expense:

1 **Directors' remuneration** – directors are appointed by the shareholders and are employees of the company. As such, they are entitled to receive what is termed **directors' remuneration**, in other words, pay in return for their services to the company. Such remuneration is charged to the profit and loss account.

2 **Debenture interest** – this is interest that has to be paid each year to the debenture holder for lending the company money. As mentioned in Section 27.5, the interest is usually at a fixed rate and has to be paid even if the company makes a loss.

Appropriation account

This section of the accounts shows how the net profits are to be apportioned, i.e. how the profits are to be taxed and the balance distributed. Items for distribution include:

- dividends declared
- transfer to and from reserves
- amounts of goodwill written off*
- amounts of **preliminary expenses** written off – these are all the costs incurred when a company is formed.*

*Note that taxation, goodwill written off and preliminary expenses are outside the scope of this book.

Exhibit 27.2 shows the distribution of the company's profit for the first three years of trading as a new business.

Exhibit 27.2

Delta Ltd has a share capital of 200,000 ordinary shares of £1 each and 100,000 – 5% preference shares of £1 each.

- The net profits for the first three years of business, ending on 31 December, are as follows:

  2008 = £35,936

  2009 = £40,728

  2010 = £47,500

- Transfers to reserves are made as follows:

  2008 = Nil

  2009 = General reserve £20,000

  2010 = Fixed asset replacement reserve £25,000

- Dividends were declared for each year on the preference shares and on the ordinary shares at:

  2008 = 6%

  2009 = 8%

  2010 = 10%

The appropriation section of the trading and profit and loss account for Delta Ltd for the three years would be as follows:

Delta Ltd
Profit and Loss Appropriation Accounts (1) For the year ended 31 December 2008

	£	£
Net profit for the year		35,936
Less Appropriations:		
Dividends:		
Preference dividend 5% (5% × £100,000)	5,000	
Ordinary dividend 6% (6% × £200,000)	12,000	(17,000)
Retained profits carried forward to next year		18,936

(2) For the year ended 31 December 2009

	£	£
Net profit for the year		40,728
Add Retained profits brought forward from last year		18,936
		59,664
Less Appropriations:		
Transfer to general reserve	20,000	
Dividends:		
Preference dividend 5% (5% × £100,000)	5,000	
Ordinary dividend 8% (8% × £200,000)	16,000	(41,000)
Retained profits carried forward to next year		18,664

(3) For the year ended 31 December 2010

	£	£
Net profit for the year		47,500
Add Retained profits brought forward from last year		18,664
		66,164
Less Appropriations:		
Transfer to fixed assets replacement reserve	25,000	
Dividends:		
Preference dividend 5% (5% × £100,000)	5,000	
Ordinary dividend 10% (10% × £200,000)	20,000	(50,000)
Retained profits carried forward to next year		16,164

Balance sheet

In Exhibit 27.3 is a worked example of the financial statements of a limited company which includes the Balance Sheet.

27.7 Reserves in the balance sheet

There are two types of reserves in a company, revenue reserves and capital reserves:

Revenue reserves are reserves that are transferred from the trading activities of the company, i.e. the net profit, and set aside for future use by the company. They often appear under the heading of *General reserve*. Another revenue reserve is retained profit, i.e. the balance of profit remaining after distribution of dividends and transfers to reserve accounts. This figure is shown at the bottom of the appropriation account as **Retained profit** *carried forward to next year* and is subsequently included in the balance sheet where it is shown as *Profit and loss account*.

REVENUE RESERVES – the transfer of apportional profits to accounts for use in future years.

> **CAPITAL RESERVE** – reserves which cannot be used for the payment of dividends.

Capital reserves, unlike revenue reserves, cannot be used for payment of dividends; the most common capital reserves is the *share premium account*:

The **share premium** account arises when shares are issued at a premium, i.e. above their par or nominal value. For example, a company may wish to expand its business and require additional funds. The nominal value of its ordinary shares is £1 but the valuation of each share is calculated to be £3. The extra funds acquired in this case, £2 per share, will be put into the share premium account while the remainder will be part of the ordinary share capital.

Note: It is thought by many that reserves represent money available whenever the company needs extra funding but this is not the case. Both revenue and capital reserves are not cash funds, they are reserves which are represented by the net assets owned by the company. The assets belong to the company which is owned by the shareholders.

27.8 A fully worked example of the financial statements

An example of a limited company's financial statements is now shown in Exhibit 27.3:

Exhibit 27.3

This worked example includes ordinary and preference shares, debentures and share premium account.

The following trial balance was extracted from the books of Dobson Ltd as at 31 December 2010:

Dobson Ltd
Trial Balance as at 31 December 2010

	Dr £	Cr £
8% Preference share capital		35,000
Ordinary share capital		125,000
10% Debentures (repayable 2015)		20,000
Share premium		21,000
Profit and loss account b/forward at 1 January 2010		13,874
Equipment at cost	122,500	
Motor vehicles at cost	99,750	
Provision for depreciation: Equipment		29,400
Provision for depreciation: Motor vehicles		36,225
Stock 1 January 2010	136,132	
Sales		418,250
Purchases	232,225	
Sales returns	4,025	
General expenses	1,240	
Salaries and wages	46,260	
Directors' remuneration	18,750	
Rent, rates and insurance	18,095	
Motor expenses	4,361	
Debenture interest	1,000	
Bank	12,751	
Cash	630	
Debtors	94,115	
Creditors		93,085
	791,834	791,834

The following adjustments are needed:

a) Stock at 31.12.10 was £122,000.

b) Accrue rent £2,000.

c) Accrue debenture interest £1,000.

d) Depreciate the equipment at 10% on cost and motor vehicles at 20% on cost.

e) Transfer to general reserve £5,000.

f) It is proposed to pay the 8% preference dividend and a 10% dividend on the ordinary shares.

g) Authorised share capital is £35,000 in preference shares and £200,000 in £1 ordinary shares.

Dobson Ltd
Trading and Profit and Loss for the year ended 31 December 2010

		£	£
Sales			418,250
Less Sales returns			4,025
			414,225
Less Cost of goods sold:			
Opening stock		136,132	
Add Purchases		232,225	
		368,357	
Less Closing stock		122,000	246,357
Gross profit			167,868
Less Expenses:			
Salaries and wages		46,260	
Rent, rates and insurance (18,095 + 2,000)		20,095	
Motor expenses		4,361	
General expenses		1,240	
Directors' remuneration	(A)	18,750	
Debenture interest (1,000 + 1,000)	(B)	2,000	
Depreciation:			
Equipment (10% × 122,500)		12,250	
Motor vehicles (20% × 99,750)		19,950	124,906
Net profit			42,962
Add Retained profits brought forward from last year			13,874
			56,836
Less Appropriations			
Transfer to general reserve		5,000	
Preference share dividend (8% × 35,000)		2,800	
Ordinary share dividend (10% × 125,000)	(C)	12,500	20,300
Retained profits carried forward to next year			36,536

Notes:

(A) Directors' remuneration is shown as an expense in the profit and loss account.

(B) Debenture interest is an expense to be shown in the profit and loss account.

(C) The final dividend of 10% is based on the issued ordinary share capital and not on the authorised ordinary share capital.

Dobson Ltd
Balance Sheet as at 31 December 2010

		£ Cost	£ Aggregate Depreciation	£ Net Book Value
Fixed assets	(A)			
Equipment		122,500	41,650	80,850
Motor Vehicles		99,750	56,175	43,575
		222,250	97,825	124,425
Current assets				
Stock		122,000		
Debtors		94,115		
Bank		12,751		
Cash		630	229,496	
Creditors: Amounts falling due within one year				
Creditors (93,085 + 2,000)		95,085		
Dividends payable: Preference shares		2,800		
: Ordinary shares		12,500		
Debenture interest due		1,000	111,385	
Net current assets				118,111
				242,536
Creditors: Amounts falling due after more than one year				
10% Debentures				20,000
				222,536
Capital and reserves				
Called-up share capital				160,000
Capital reserve				
Share premium	(B)			21,000
Revenue reserves	(C)			
General reserve				5,000
Profit and loss account				36,536
				222,536

Notes:

(A) Notes to be given in an appendix as to cost, acquisitions and sales in the year and depreciation.

(B) The share premium account is a capital reserve, refer to Section 27.7.

(C) 'Reserves' consist either of those undistributed profits remaining in the appropriation account, or those transferred to a reserve account appropriately titled (e.g. general reserve, refer to Section 27.7).

Workings:

Equipment cost £122,500 less depreciation to date £41,650 (£29,400 + £12,250) gives a net book value of £80,850. Motor vehicles cost £99,750 less depreciation to date £56,175 (£36,225 + £19,950) gives a net book value of £43,575.

27.9 Shareholders' funds

This is the amount of share capital and reserves 'owned' by the shareholders. In Exhibit 27.3 shown above the **shareholders' funds** of Dobson Ltd would be:

	£
Called-up capital	160,000
Share premium account	21,000
General reserve	5,000
Profit and loss account	36,536
Shareholders' funds	222,536

End of Chapter Checklist

Summary

- There are many features which make forming a limited company attractive to investors, including limited liability, whereby a shareholder may lose the amount invested in the company but their personal assets are safe.
- Limited companies are a separate legal entity to the shareholders and as such can sue and be sued in their own name.
- A public company is one that can issue its shares publicly and there is no maximum number of shareholders. It must also have an issued share capital of at least £50,000. A private company must issue its shares privately.
- Authorised share capital is the maximum amount of share capital or number of shares the company would be allowed to issue. Note that in the Companies Act 2006, from October 2009 there will no longer be a requirement to have an authorised share capital.
- Issued share capital is the amount of share capital actually issued to shareholders.
- There are two main types of shares: (1) preference shares – here, the shareholders get an agreed percentage rate of dividend before the ordinary shareholders receive anything; (2) ordinary shares – the shareholders are entitled to a dividend after the preference shareholders have been paid their dividends. The amount they receive fluctuates depending on the profits available.
- A debenture is a loan to the company upon which a fixed rate of interest is paid annually. The interest must be paid even if the company makes a loss. Debentures are often secured on the assets of the business.
- The financial statements for a limited company consist of a trading and profit and loss account, which includes an appropriation section and a balance sheet.
- Both debenture interest and directors' remuneration must be charged to the profit and loss account.
- Any undistributed profits are carried forward to the next accounting period and must also be shown in the balance sheet. (**Note:** These can sometimes be referred to as 'retained profits' and 'profit and loss account balance'.)
- Reserve accounts contain appropriated profits that have been transferred for use in future years, such as a general reserve. They are classed as revenue reserves and may be distributed to shareholders as dividend.
- Share premium is another class of reserve that arises when shares are issued above the face or nominal value. The extra amount received above the nominal value is credited to the share premium account. This account is classed as a capital reserve which means it cannot be distributed to shareholders as dividend.

End of Chapter Checklist

Questions

27.1 C Blake Ltd has an authorised share capital of 90,000 ordinary shares of £1 each and 10,000 10% preference shares of £1 each. The company's trial balance, extracted after one year of trading, was as follows on 31 December 2009:

	£
Net profit for the year to 31 December 2009	11,340
Debentures	30,000
Issued ordinary share capital, fully paid	60,000
Issued preference share capital, fully paid	10,000
Creditors	3,550
Debtors	4,120
Cash	2,160
Stock	8,800
Provision for doubtful debts	350
Provision for depreciation: Equipment	4,500
Equipment at cost	45,000
Buildings at cost	50,000
Bank (use the balancing figure)	?

The directors decide to transfer £1,500 to the general reserve and to `recommend a dividend of $12\frac{1}{2}$% on the ordinary shares. The preference dividend was not paid until after January 2010.

You are required to:

  a) draw up the appropriation account for the year ended 31 December 2009
  b) draft a balance sheet as at 31 December 2009.

27.2X On 30 September 2009, Reynolds Ltd had an authorised capital of £250,000, divided into 200,000 ordinary shares of £1 each and 50,000 7% preference shares of £1 each. All the preference shares were issued and fully paid, while 150,000 of the ordinary shares were issued and fully paid. The company also had a balance on the general reserve account of £45,000 and a balance brought forward on the profit and loss account of £30,000.

During the year ended 30 September 2010, the company made a net profit of £70,000, out of which a transfer of £8,000 was made to the general reserve account. The directors had paid an interim dividend of 6p per share on the ordinary share capital and now propose to pay the preference dividend and a final dividend of 14p per share on the ordinary share capital.

From the information given above, you are required to prepare for Reynolds Ltd:

  a) a profit and loss appropriation account for the year ended 30 September 2010
  b) the capital and reserves section of the balance sheet as at 30 September 2010.

27.3 The trial balance extracted from the books of Chang Ltd at 31 December 2010 was as follows:

	£	£
Share capital		100,000
Unappropriated profits brought forward from last year		34,280
Freehold premises at cost	65,000	
Machinery at cost	55,000	
Provision for depreciation on machinery account as at 31 December 2009		15,800
Purchases	201,698	
Sales		316,810
General expenses	32,168	
Wages and salaries	54,207	
Rent	4,300	
Lighting expenses	1,549	
Bad debts	748	
Provision for doubtful debts as at 31 December 2009		861
Debtors	21,784	
Creditors		17,493
Stock in trade as at 31 December 2009	25,689	
Bank balance	23,101	
	485,244	485,244

You are given the following additional information:

  a) The authorised and issued share capital is divided into 100,000 shares of £1 each.
  b) Stock in trade as at 31 December 2010 was £29,142.
  c) Wages and salaries due at 31 December 2010 amounted to £581.
  d) Rent paid in advance at 31 December 2010 amounted to £300.
  e) A dividend of £10,000 is proposed for 2010.
  f) The provision for doubtful debts is to be increased to £938.
  g) A depreciation charge is to be made on machinery at the rate of 10% per annum at cost.

Required:

Draw up a trading and profit and loss account for the year ended 31 December 2010 and a balance sheet at that date.

End of Chapter Checklist

Questions

27.4X The following trial balance has been extracted from the books of Wayland Limited after the production of the profit and loss account for the year ended 31 December 2010.

Account	Debit (£000)	Credit (£000)
Ordinary shares of £1 each		750
6% Preference shares of £1 each		250
5% Debentures (2014)		250
Land and buildings (cost)	1,500	
Fixtures and fittings (cost)	50	
Fixtures and fittings (accumulated depreciation)		10
Motor vehicles (cost)	85	
Motor vehicles (accumulated depreciation)		15
Closing stock	165	
Interim ordinary dividend – paid	20	
Share premium		100
General reserve		50
Net profit for the year		250
Profit and loss account balance – 1 January 2010		195
Bank	107	
Debtors and creditors	103	135
Value added tax		25
	2,030	2,030

The following additional information is available on 31 December 2010 and is to be taken into account.

- £25,000 is to be transferred to the general reserve.
- The preference dividend is to be provided for.
- A final dividend of 8% should be provided for.

Required:

a) Prepare the profit and loss appropriation account for Wayland Limited for the year ended 31 December 2010.

b) Prepare the balance sheet for Wayland Limited as at 31 December 2010, showing fixed assets, current assets, current liabilities, working capital and shareholders' funds.

IGCSE

Section J: Analysis accounts

Chapter 28: Analysis and interpretation of financial statements

Getting started

Edexcel specification
Analysis and interpretation of accounts, 10.1, 10.2.

After you have studied this chapter you should be able to:

- appreciate the importance of analysing financial statements for the benefit of interested parties
- distinguish between profitability and liquidity
- calculate and analyse ratios
- understand the term 'capital employed'
- calculate and understand the importance of working capital.

28.1 Interpretation of accounts

The whole purpose of recording and classifying financial information about a business, and communicating this to the owners and managers in the form of the financial statements, is to assess the performance of the business. The information contained in the financial statements can be used to evaluate various aspects of the company by the use of accounting ratios. For the ratios to be a reliable guide to performance, two criteria need to be applied:

1. The financial statements used for calculating the current ratios must be *up to date*.

2. Each ratio must be *compared* with the same ratio from the previous year's accounts or with those from a competitor's accounts.

The concept of comparison is crucial, since this identifies trends in the business and allows action to be taken.

The analysis of a business using accounting ratios is widely practised by both internal and external parties and the main ones are listed in Exhibit 28.1.

Exhibit 28.1

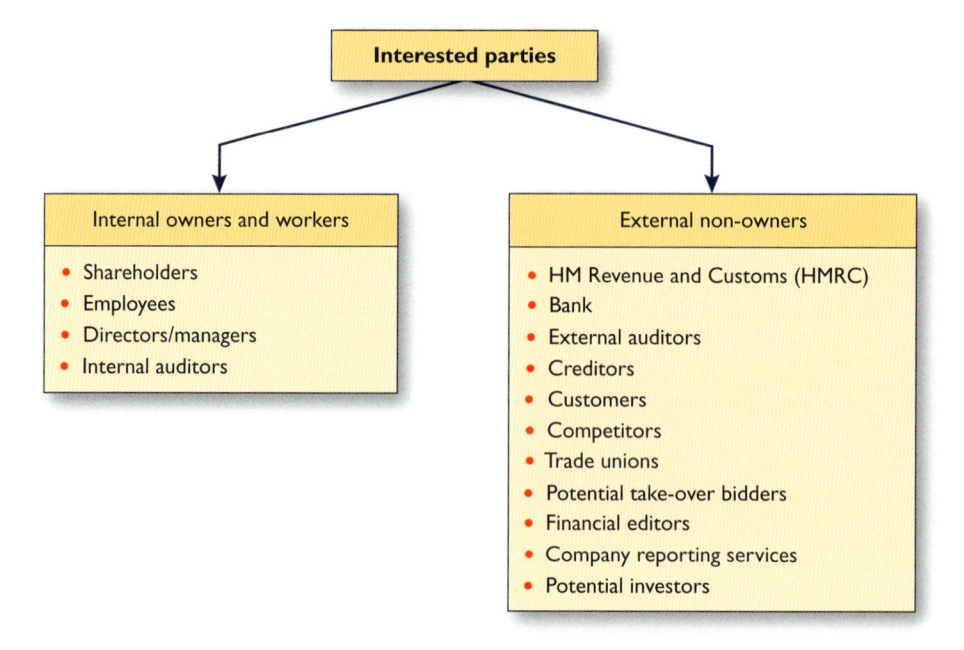

Interested parties

Internal owners and workers
- Shareholders
- Employees
- Directors/managers
- Internal auditors

External non-owners
- HM Revenue and Customs (HMRC)
- Bank
- External auditors
- Creditors
- Customers
- Competitors
- Trade unions
- Potential take-over bidders
- Financial editors
- Company reporting services
- Potential investors

28.2 Profitability and liquidity

There are two basic but essential factors in the operation of a business, the first is to maintain, and if possible, increase profit. The ability to make profit is known as **profitability**.

The second essential factor is for the business to have sufficient funds at all times so that it can pay its debts as they become due. The level of funds available to pay creditors is known as **liquidity**.

The importance of both these factors cannot be too highly stressed. A business which operates with a good profits record and sound liquidity will become well regarded by both customers and suppliers.

If a business is consistently unable to generate profits it will fail. Even when a business makes a profit but has weak liquidity it would demonstrate a failure to control its cash flow. Late or slow payments to creditors could lead to suppliers not wishing to deal with the company. Once a business gains a poor financial reputation it could affect its trading performance, which would further weaken it and cause it to fail.

> PROFITABILITY – the effective operation of a business to make ongoing profits to ensure its long-term viability.

> LIQUIDITY means the ability of a business to pay its debts as they fall due and meet unexpected expenses within a reasonable settlement period.

28.3 Profitability ratios

The **profitability ratios** measure the success or otherwise of a business's trading activities in respect of profit during an accounting period. The main ratios used to examine profitability are:

1. Gross profit margin/sales
2. Gross profit mark-up/cost of sales
3. Net profit margin/sales
4. Expenses (or overheads)/sales
5. Return on capital employed (ROCE)
6. Rate of stock turnover

1 Gross profit margin/sales

The basic formula is:

$$\frac{\text{Gross profit}}{\text{Sales}} \times 100 = \text{Gross profit as percentage of sales (Gross profit margin)}$$

> TIP – it is useful to learn the following formula.

This is the amount of gross profit for every £100 of sales and is known as the gross profit margin. If the answer turns out to be 15% this would mean that for every £100 of sales, £15 gross profit is made before any expenses are paid. This ratio is used as a test of the profitability of the sales. Even if sales are increased it may not mean that the gross profit will increase. This is illustrated in the trading accounts shown in Exhibit 28.2.

Exhibit 28.2

D Clive
Trading Accounts for the years ended 31 December 2009 and 2010

	2009 £	2009 £	2010 £	2010 £
Sales		70,000		80,000
Less Cost of goods sold				
Opening stock	5,000		9,000	
Add Purchases	60,000		72,000	
	65,000		81,000	
Less Closing stock	9,000	56,000	11,000	70,000
Gross profit		14,000		10,000

In the year 2009 the gross profit as a percentage of sales was:

$$\frac{14{,}000}{70{,}000} \times 100 = 20\%$$

In the year 2010 it became:

$$\frac{10{,}000}{80{,}000} \times 100 = 12.5\%$$

Although sales had increased from £70,000 to £80,000, the gross profit had fallen from £14,000 to £10,000, a decrease of 7.5% (20% − 12.5%). There can be many reasons for such a fall in the gross profit percentage.

- Perhaps the goods being sold have cost more, but the selling price of the goods has not risen to the same extent.
- Perhaps, in order to increase sales, reductions have been made to the selling price of goods.
- There could be a difference in how much has been sold of each sort of goods, called the sales mix, between this year and last, with different kinds of goods carrying different rates of gross profit per £100 of sales.
- There may have been a greater wastage or theft of goods.

These are only some of the possible reasons for the decrease. The point of calculating the ratio is to find out why and how such a change has taken place.

2 Gross profit mark-up/cost of sales

The basic formula is:

$$\frac{\text{Gross profit}}{\text{Cost of sales}} \times 100 = \text{Gross profit as a percentage of cost of sales (Gross profit mark-up)}$$

This ratio shows the percentage of profit to the cost of sales, in other words, the amount the trader has marked up its products. For example, if a trader buys a product for £1 and decides to mark it up by 20% (20% of £1 = 20p) then the selling price becomes £1.20.

Using the figures in Exhibit 28.2, the gross profit as a percentage of cost of sales would be as follows:

In the year 2009 the gross profit as a percentage of cost of sales:

$$\frac{14,000}{56,000} \times 100 = 25\%$$

In the year 2010 it became:

$$\frac{10,000}{70,000} \times 100 = 14.29\%$$

3 Net profit margin/sales

Here, the formula is:

$$\frac{\text{Net profit}}{\text{Sales}} \times 100 = \text{Net profit as percentage of sales}$$

This calculation will show how much net profit has been made for every £100 of sales. It brings the expenses (or overheads) into the calculation, as opposed to the gross profit percentage, which ignores expenses. Changes in the ratio will be due either to:

- the gross profit ratio changing, and/or
- the expenses per £100 of sales changing.

When changes are due to expenses, they will be examined to see if anything can be done in future to minimise the expenses and ensure that a reasonable net profit is made.

4 Expenses (or overheads) to sales

This ratio is calculated as follows:

$$\frac{\text{Expenses}}{\text{Sales}}$$

Normally, this is referred to as a percentage and is calculated as follows:

$$\text{Expenses as a percentage of sales} = \frac{\text{Expenses}}{\text{sales}} \times 100 = x\%$$

It is useful to compare the expenses/sales percentage with the previous results. If an increase was evident, this would indicate an increase in the expenses of the business and would require further investigation by management. If the result remained stable or in fact had reduced, this would indicate that expenses incurred in running the business had been carefully monitored.

5 Return on capital employed ratio (ROCE)

This ratio is calculated as follows:

$$\frac{\text{Net profit}}{\text{Capital employed}}$$

Normally, this is referred to as a percentage and is calculated as follows:

$$\text{Return of capital employed} = \frac{\text{Net profit}}{\text{Capital employed}} \times 100 = x\%$$

It shows (as a percentage) the net profit made for each £100 of capital employed, the higher the ratio the more profitable the business. This is the most important ratio of all.

There has never been an agreed definition of the term 'capital employed'. Very often it has been taken to mean the average capital. For this, the opening capital for the period is added to the closing capital and then the total is divided by two. In an examination, use the method stated by the examiner. If you are given only the closing capital, use the closing capital figure.

In the following example, two businesses of sole traders (A) and (B) have made the same profits, but the capital employed in each case is different. From the balance sheets that follow, the return on capital employed is calculated using the average of the capital account as capital employed.

Balance Sheets	(A)	(B)
	£	£
Fixed Assets + Current Assets − Current Liabilities	100,000	160,000
Capital Accounts:		
Opening balance	80,000	140,000
Add Net profits	36,000	36,000
	116,000	176,000
Less Drawings	16,000	16,000
	100,000	160,000

Return on capital employed is calculated thus for the two businesses:

(A) $\dfrac{£36,000}{(£80,000 + £100,000) \div 2} \times 100\% = 40\%$

(B) $\dfrac{£36,000}{(£140,000 + £160,000) \div 2} \times 100\% = 24\%$

The ratio illustrates that what is important is not simply how much profit has been made but how well the capital has been employed. Business (A) has made far better use of its capital, achieving a return of £40 net profit for every £100 invested, whereas (B) has received a net profit of only £24 per £100.

In this case, only the accounts of sole traders have been dealt with, so that a straightforward example could be used. In Section 28.5, other meanings of the term 'capital employed' will be considered, when dealing with:

- sole traders who have received loans to help finance their businesses
- partnerships
- limited companies.

6 Rate of stock turnover

Every business should operate both to keep its stock to as low a figure as possible without losing profitability, and to sell its goods as quickly as possible. The stock turnover ratio measures how well the business is managing to do these things. Any increase in stocks or slowdown in sales will show a lower ratio.

The ratio is calculated as follows:

$$\frac{\text{Cost of goods sold}}{\text{Average stock}} = \text{Stock turnover ratio}$$

If only the opening and closing stocks are known the average stock is found by adding these two figures and dividing them by two (i.e. averaging them). The higher this ratio, the more profitable the business. For example, if £5 gross profit was made on a particular product and the stock turnover is 6 times a year then the business would make a gross profit of £5 × 6 = £30. If, however, the stock turnover ratio increased to 9, then gross profit would be £5 × 9 = £45.

28.4 Liquidity ratios

A business that has satisfactory liquidity (see Section 28.2) will have sufficient funds, normally referred to as 'working capital', to pay creditors at the required time. The ability to pay creditors on time is vital to ensure that good business relationships are maintained. The ratios used to examine liquidity, i.e. the **liquidity ratios**, are:

1 Current ratio (working capital ratio)
2 Acid test ratio (quick ratio)
3 Debtors : sales ratio (debtors' collection period)
4 Creditors : purchases ratio (creditors' payment period).

Each of the liquidity ratios stated can be compared period by period to see whether that particular aspect of liquidity is getting better or worse. In the case of the current ratio, it was often thought in the past that the ideal ratio should be around 2:1 and that, ideally, the acid test ratio should be in the region of 1:1 to 1.5:1. However, in recent years it has become recognised that such a fixed figure cannot possibly apply to every business, as the types and circumstances of businesses vary so widely.

1 Current ratio (or working capital ratio)

The current ratio measures current assets against current liabilities. It will compare assets that will be turned into cash within the next 12 months with any liabilities that will have to be paid within the same period. The current ratio is thus stated as:

$$\frac{\text{Current assets}}{\text{Current liabilities}}$$

If, therefore, the current assets are £125,000 and the current liabilities are £50,000, the current ratio will be:

$$\frac{£125,000}{£50,000} = 2.5:1, \text{ or } 2.5 \text{ times}$$

If the ratio increases by a large amount, the business may have more current assets than it needs. If the ratio falls by a large amount, then perhaps too little is being kept as current assets.

2 Acid test ratio (or quick ratio)

To determine a further aspect of liquidity, the **acid test ratio** takes into account only those current assets that are cash or can be changed very quickly into cash. This will normally mean Cash + Bank + Debtors. You can see that this means exactly the same as current assets less stock. The acid test ratio may, therefore, be stated as:

$$\frac{\text{Current assets less stock}}{\text{Current liabilities}}$$

For instance, if the total of current assets is £40,000 and stock is £10,000, and the total of current liabilities is £20,000, then the ratio will be:

$$\frac{£40,000 - £10,000}{£20,000} = 1.5:1, \text{ or } 1.5 \text{ times}$$

This ratio shows whether there are enough liquid assets to be able to pay current liabilities quickly. It is dangerous if this ratio is allowed to fall to a very low figure. If suppliers and others cannot be paid on time, supplies to the business may be reduced or even stopped completely. Eventually, the business may not have enough stock to be able to sell properly. In that case, it may have to cease business.

3 Debtors to sales ratio (debtors' collection period)

This ratio assesses how long it takes for debtors to pay what they owe. The calculation is made as follows:

$$\frac{\text{Debtors}}{\text{Sales for the year}} \times 12 = \text{Number of months that debtors (on average) take to pay up}$$

For example:

	(C)	(D)
Sales for the year	£240,000	£180,000
Debtors as per balance sheet	£60,000	£30,000

In business (C), debtors take three months on average to pay their accounts, calculated from:

$$\frac{£60,000}{£240,000} \times 12 = 3 \text{ months}$$

In business (D), debtors take two months on average to pay their accounts, given from:

$$\frac{£30,000}{£180,000} \times 12 = 2 \text{ months}$$

If the ratio is required to be shown in days instead of months, the formula should be multiplied by 365 instead of 12. The higher the ratio, the worse a business is at getting its debtors to pay on time. The lower the ratio, the better it is at managing its debtors.

Businesses should make certain that debtors pay their accounts on time. There are two main reasons for this. First, the longer a debt is owed, the more likely it will become a bad debt. Second, any payment of money can be used in the business as soon as it is received, and so this increases profitability; it can help reduce expenses. For example, it would reduce a bank overdraft and therefore reduce the bank overdraft interest.

4 Creditors to purchases ratio (creditors' payment period)

This ratio shows how long it takes a business (on average) to pay its suppliers. The calculation is made as follows:

$$\frac{\text{Creditors}}{\text{Purchases for the year}} \times 12 = \text{Number of months it takes (on average) to pay up suppliers}$$

For example:

	(E)	(F)
Purchases for the year	£120,000	£90,000
Creditors as per balance sheet	£40,000	£22,500

Business (E) therefore takes four months' credit on average from its suppliers, i.e.

$$\frac{£40,000}{£120,000} \times 12 = 4 \text{ months}$$

Business (F) takes on average three months to pay its suppliers, i.e.

$$\frac{£22,500}{£90,000} \times 12 = 3 \text{ months}$$

Taking longer to pay suppliers could be a good thing or a bad thing, depending upon circumstances. If so long is taken to pay that possible discounts are lost, or that suppliers refuse to supply again, then it would be undesirable. On the other hand, paying before it is necessary simply takes money out of the business early without gaining any benefit.

28.5 Definition of capital employed in various circumstances

In Section 28.3 (5), it was pointed out that there is not one single agreed definition of the term 'capital employed'. In answering an exam question in this area, you must follow the examiner's instructions, if any are given; otherwise, state what basis you have used.

> There are several meanings of 'CAPITAL EMPLOYED'.

Sole proprietorships

'Capital employed' could mean any of the following:

- closing balance on capital account at the end of a financial period
- average of opening and closing balances on the capital account for the accounting period
- capital balances plus any long-term loans.

Partnerships

'Capital employed' could mean any of the following:

- closing balance on the fluctuating capital accounts at the end of a financial period
- average of opening and closing balances on the fluctuating capital accounts for an accounting period
- total of fixed capital accounts plus total of partners' current accounts at the end of a financial period
- average of opening and closing balances on the partners' capital and current accounts for an accounting period
- any of the above, plus long-term loans to the partnership.

Limited companies

Given the following details, different figures for capital employed may be used.

	£
a) Ordinary share capital	100,000
b) Preference share capital	40,000
c) Total of different types of reserves including balance in profit and loss account	35,000
d) Debentures	60,000

- To calculate return on ordinary shareholders' funds, it would be
 (a) £100,000 + (c) £35,000 = £135,000.

- To calculate return on total shareholders' fund, it would be
 (a) £100,000 + (b) £40,000 + (c) £35,000 = £175,000.

- To calculate return on total capital employed, i.e. including borrowed funds, it would be (a) £100,000 + (b) £40,000 + (c) £35,000 + (d) £60,000 = £235,000.

Any question involving return of capital employed for limited companies should be read very carefully indeed. Use the method suggested by the examiner. If no indication is given, use that of *(a) + (c)* above, but you must state what method you have used.

28.6 Definition of working capital

Working capital is the amount by which current assets exceed current liabilities. It is also known as 'net current assets' (see Chapter 17).

It is vital for businesses to have sufficient working capital to enable them to have funds available to pay everyday running expenses. Working capital tends to circulate through a business, as shown in the diagram in Exhibit 28.3. As it flows, profits are made as stock is sold to debtors; the quicker it is sold, the quicker the business makes profits.

Exhibit 28.3

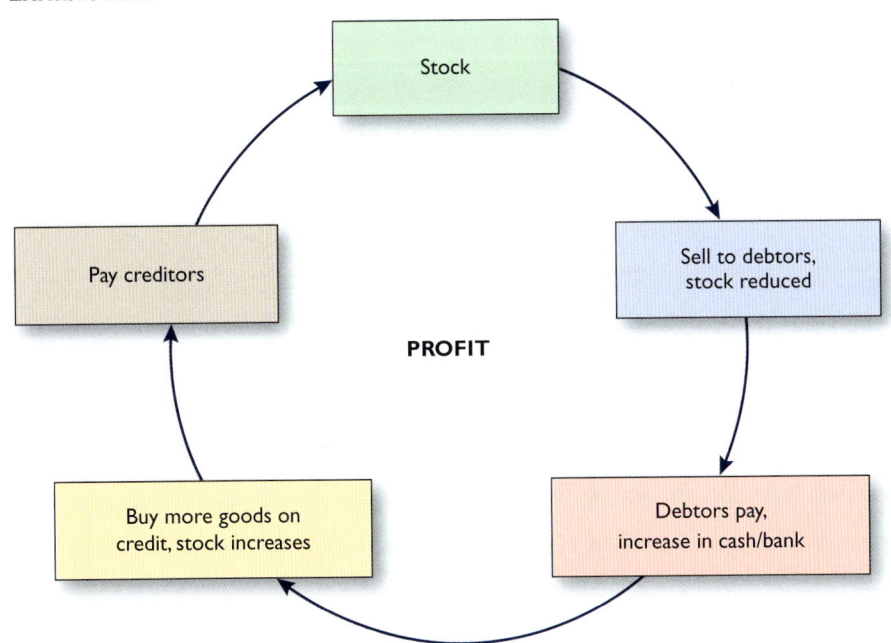

28.7 A fully worked example of calculating ratios

A fully worked example of calculating ratios and interpreting accounts is shown in Exhibit 28.4. Check all the calculations yourself and see whether your conclusions about the changes in the ratios agree with the author's.

Exhibit 28.4

The following are the final accounts for two similar types of retail stores:

Trading and Profit and Loss Accounts

	J £	J £	K £	K £
Sales		80,000		120,000
Less Cost of goods sold:				
Opening stock	25,000		22,500	
Add Purchases	50,000		91,000	
	75,000		113,500	
Less Closing stock	15,000	60,000	17,500	96,000
Gross profit		20,000		24,000
Less Depreciation	1,000		3,000	
Other expenses	9,000	10,000	6,000	9,000
Net profit		10,000		15,000

Balance Sheets

	J £	J £	K £	K £
Fixed Assets				
Equipment at cost	10,000		20,000	
Less Depreciation to date	8,000	2,000	6,000	14,000
Current Assets				
Stock	15,000		17,500	
Debtors	25,000		20,000	
Bank	5,000		2,500	
	45,000		40,000	
Less Current Liabilities				
Creditors	5,000		10,000	
Net current assets		40,000		30,000
		42,000		44,000
Financed by:				
Capital				
Balance at start of year		38,000		36,000
Add Net profit		10,000		15,000
		48,000		51,000
Less Drawings		6,000		7,000
		42,000		44,000

The following ratios will now be calculated correct to one decimal place:

a) Gross profit margin as a percentage of sales

b) Net profit margin as a percentage of sales

c) Expenses as a percentage of sales

d) Stock turnover ratio

e) Rate of return of net profit on capital employed (use the average of the capital account for this purpose)

f) Current ratio

g) Acid test ratio (quick ratio)

h) Debtors : Sales ratio

i) Creditors : Purchases ratio

		J	K
a)	Gross profit as a % of sales	$\dfrac{£20,000}{£80,000} \times 100\% = 25\%$	$\dfrac{£24,000}{£120,000} \times 100\% = 20\%$
b)	Net profit as a % of sales	$\dfrac{£10,000}{£80,000} \times 100\% = 12.5\%$	$\dfrac{£15,000}{£120,000} \times 100\% = 12.5\%$
c)	Expenses as a % of sales	$\dfrac{£10,000}{£80,000} \times 100\% = 12.5\%$	$\dfrac{£9,000}{£120,000} \times 100\% = 7.5\%$
d)	Stockturn	$\dfrac{£60,000}{(£25,000 + £15,000) \div 2} = 3$ times	$\dfrac{£96,000}{(£22,500 + £17,500) \div 2} = 4.8$ times
e)	Rate of return on capital employed	$\dfrac{£10,000}{(£38,000 + £42,000) \div 2} \times 100\% = 25\%$	$\dfrac{£15,000}{(£36,000 + £44,000) \div 2} \times 100\% = 37.5\%$
f)	Current ratio	$\dfrac{£45,000}{£5,000} = 9:1$	$\dfrac{£40,000}{£10,000} = 4:1$
g)	Acid test ratio	$\dfrac{£45,000 - £15,000}{£5,000} = 6:1$	$\dfrac{£40,000 - £17,500}{£10,000} = 2.25:1$
h)	Debtors : Sales ratio	$\dfrac{£25,000}{£80,000} \times 12 = 3.75$ months	$\dfrac{£20,000}{£120,000} \times 12 = 2$ months
i)	Creditors : Purchases ratio	$\dfrac{£5,000}{£50,000} \times 12 = 1.2$ months	$\dfrac{£10,000}{£91,000} \times 12 = 1.3$ months

Having calculated the ratios, we will now briefly analyse our findings.

Note: It is not sufficient to say that the ratios differ, but also try to give reasons why they differ relevant to the particular business.

Business K is more profitable, both in terms of actual net profits (£15,000 compared with £10,000), but also in terms of capital employed. K has managed to achieve a return of £37.50 for every £100 invested, i.e. 37.5%, whereas J return was lower at 25%. The reasons for the difference could be down to the following:

- Possibly, K managed to sell far more merchandise because of lower prices, i.e. it took only 20% margin as compared with J's 25% margin.
- Maybe K made more efficient use of mechanised means in the business. Note that it has more equipment, and perhaps as a consequence it kept other expenses down to £6,000 as compared with J's £9,000.
- K did not have as much stock lying idle. K turned over stock 4.8 times in the year, as compared with 3 times for J.
- J's current ratio of 9:1 was far greater than normally needed. K kept it down to 4:1. J therefore had too much money lying idle.
- The acid test ratio for J was higher than necessary and followed a similar trend to that shown by the current ratio.
- One reason for the better current and acid test ratios for K was that debts were collected on a two months' average.
- J also paid creditors more quickly than K – but only slightly faster.

When all these factors are considered, it is clear that business K is being run much more efficiently and, consequently, more profitably.

End of Chapter Checklist

Summary

- Financial statements are analysed and interpreted for internal and external parties. It is important to remember that a ratio on its own is of no use at all. It must be compared with previous years' results or the results of a competitor to be meaningful.
- Profitability and liquidity are equally important factors when running a business.
- The use of the profitability ratios ensure owners of a business keep a careful check on figures such as cost of goods, sales, expenses, gross and net profits.
- Liquidity ratios measure the ability of a business to pay its debts as they fall due and ensure smooth cash flow.
- Working capital is found by deducting current liabilities from current assets. It is vital for businesses to have sufficient working capital to ensure they can pay their debts as they fall due.
- There are various methods of calculating capital employed depending upon the type of business, i.e. sole trader, partnership or limited company.

Note: You will find a summary of the formulae and a worksheet that you can photocopy and use to answer questions on ratio analysis on the CD attached at the back of this book.

Questions

28.1 The following accounts are of two companies that each sell sports goods:

Trading and Profit and Loss Accounts

	M Ltd £	M Ltd £	N Ltd £	N Ltd £
Sales		360,000		250,000
Less Cost of goods sold:				
Opening stock	120,000		60,000	
Add Purchases	268,000		191,500	
	388,000		251,500	
Less Closing stock	100,000	288,000	64,000	187,500
Gross profit		72,000		62,500
Less Expenses:				
Wages	8,000		11,300	
Directors' remuneration	12,000		13,000	
Other expenses	8,800	28,800	3,200	27,500
Net profit		43,200		35,000
Add Retained profits from last year		16,800		2,000
		60,000*		37,000*
Less Appropriations:				
General reserve	8,000		2,000	
Dividends	40,000	48,000	30,000	32,000
Retained profits carried to next year		12,000		5,000

Balance Sheets

	M Ltd £	M Ltd £	N Ltd £	N Ltd £
Fixed Assets:				
Fixtures at cost	200,000		180,000	
Less Depreciation to date	50,000	150,000	70,000	110,000
Motor vans at cost	80,000		120,000	
Less Depreciation to date	30,000	50,000	40,000	80,000
		200,000		190,000
Current Assets:				
Stock	100,000		64,000	
Debtors	60,000		62,500	
Bank	40,000		3,500	
	200,000		130,000	
Less Current Liabilities				
Creditors	50,000		65,000	
Net current assets		150,000		65,000
		350,000		255,000
Financed by:				
Issued share capital		300,000		200,000
General reserve		38,000		50,000
Profit and loss		12,000		5,000
		350,000		255,000

End of Chapter Checklist

Questions

Required:

a) Calculate the following ratios to one decimal place:
   (i) current ratio
   (ii) acid test ratio
   (iii) stockturn
   (iv) debtors : sales ratio
   (v) creditors : purchases ratio
   (vi) gross profit as a percentage of sales
   (vii) net profit as a percentage of sales
   (viii) rate of return on shareholders' funds.
b) Compare the results of the two companies, giving possible reasons for the different results.

28.2 *Cruise Furnishings and Holmes Suppliers are two rival businesses. The following information has been extracted from their recent sets of accounts:*

Results for Year Ended 31 August 2009	Cruise Furnishings £000	Holmes Supplies £000
Turnover	1,800	2,400
Cost of Sales	1,200	1,800
Average Stock	120	150
Gross Profit	600	600
Net Profit	150	160

Balances at 31 August 2009	Cruise Furnishings £000	Holmes Supplies £000
Fixed Assets	2,136	2,910
Current Assets	210	180
Stock (included in Current Assets)	111	120
Current Liabilities	66	60
Long Term Liabilities	30	2,070
Owner's Capital	2,250	960

a) Calculate the following for both businesses to two decimal places:
   (i) The gross profit margin
   (ii) The net profit margin
   (iii) Current ratio.
b) Calculate the rate of stock turnover for Cruise Furnishings.

The owner of Holmes Supplies believes the performance of her business is superior to that of her rival, Cruise Furnishings.

c) Using figures and including both profitability and liquidity, evaluate the owner's belief.

IGCSE

28.3X *The following figures were extracted from the books of Haydesh Kordi at the end of the previous two years' trading.*

	Year ended 28 February 2009	Year ended 29 February 2010
	£	£
Sales	35,000	52,000
Opening Stock	2,900	4,000
Purchases	14,500	19,500
Closing Stock	4,000	7,000
Gross Profit	21,600	35,500
Business Expenses	5,600	9,500
Net Profit	16,000	26,000

a) Stating clearly the formula used, calculate the net profit margin for **each** of the two years. (Round to **two** decimal places.)
b) Stating clearly the formula used, calculate the mark up for **each** of the two years. (Round to **two** decimal places.)
c) Stating clearly the formula used, calculate the rate of stock turnover in times for **each** of the two years.
d) Using the figures calculated in the above sections, evaluate the profitability of the business over the last two years.

IGCSE

Section J: Analysis of accounts

Chapter 29: Computers and accounting systems

Getting started

Edexcel specification
Books of original entry, 1.22.

After you have studied this chapter you should be able to:

- appreciate the uses of computer technology in recording financial information
- appreciate the different types of financial accounting packages available
- understand the functions and benefits of computer accounting software
- appreciate the benefits of having online facilities within a computer system
- realise the importance of backing up data when using a computerised accounting package
- understand the importance of security when using an accounting package and the benefits of using a password
- describe the advantages and disadvantages of using a computerised accounting system.

TIP – accurate input of data ensures reliable output.

29.1 Introduction

Today there is widespread use of computers to operate accounting systems. Sophisticated technology is now available at a reasonable cost. Large to medium-sized concerns have used specially written packages for a number of years, but smaller enterprises were initially discouraged from setting up their own systems by the cost of such packages. However, small businesses can now afford to use a computerised system using off-the-shelf packages such as Sage or QuickBooks. These packages carry out the same double entry functions of data processing and recording financial information as manual systems and also offer other features such as management information.

The rapid development of the internet means that accounting information and transactions can be carried out online. Consequently, businesses that do not have computer facilities could easily get left behind and miss out on the opportunities that internet access provides.

29.2 Functions of computerised accounting packages

A **computerised accounting package** offers all the functions that a manual system provides but in addition it provides useful reports and management information. Since the system is integrated, basic data is entered, processed and automatically posted to supplier and customer accounts and the general (nominal) ledger updated. At the same time, stock records are updated and, in some instances, automatic re-ordering systems are in place. The main functions of a computerised accounting package are listed below.

Sales

Preparation and printing of sales invoices, credit notes and month end statements. Data from the above documents is entered, processed and recorded:

- in the customer accounts in the sales ledger
- by automatic update of the stock records.

Purchases

Data from the purchase invoice and credit notes is entered, processed and recorded:

- in the supplier accounts in the purchase ledger
- by automatic update of the stock records
- via a print-out of remittance advices.

Bank account

- Recording data such as customer receipts, supplier payments, other payments and receipts.
- Many banks offer online banking facilities which have the added advantage of the organisation's bank account being completely up to date.
- All receipts and payments are linked to the personal accounts of the debtors and creditors and the system provides for such transactions to automatically update these accounts.

General (nominal) ledger

Automatic updating of the general (nominal) ledger.

Wages/salaries

Organisations have the option of using a combined computerised accounting and wages/salary package; alternatively, they may use a separate 'payroll package'. Such packages perform all the necessary payroll functions.

Stock control

As mentioned above, under sales and purchases these functions are linked to the stock records. This means that stock records are automatically updated after each sales invoice and purchase invoice is entered into the system so providing an accurate figure of stock held at any particular point in time.

At the end of the financial year when an organisation undertakes stocktaking, the use of a computerised system enables up-to-date stock lists to be made available. These lists are used in the physical stocktake and enable variances to be identified and amended.

The functions are summarised in Exhibit 29.1.

Exhibit 29.1

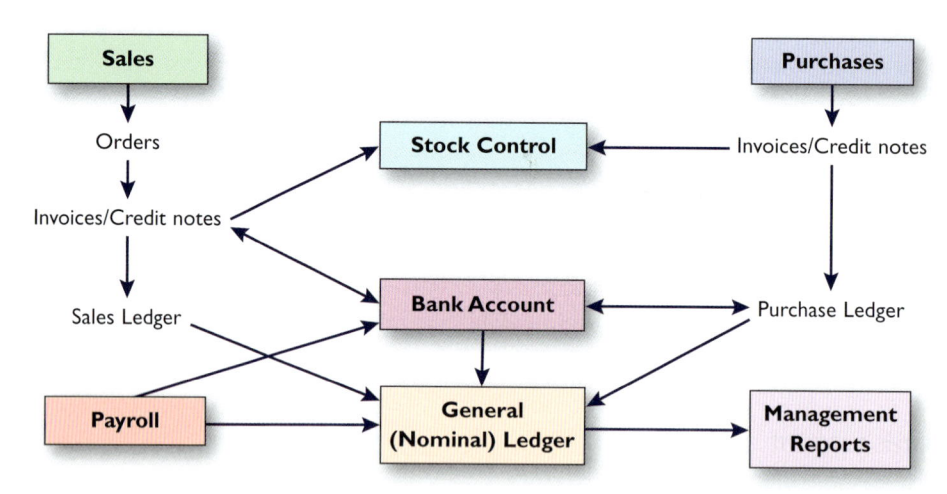

[Diagram showing flow between: Sales → Orders → Invoices/Credit notes → Sales Ledger; Sales → Stock Control ← Purchases; Purchases → Invoices/Credit notes → Purchase Ledger; Bank Account connected to Stock Control, Sales Ledger, Purchase Ledger, and General (Nominal) Ledger; Payroll → General (Nominal) Ledger → Management Reports]

> MANAGEMENT REPORTS – management can receive reports regularly to monitor the performance of the business.

Management reports

One of the main features of a computerised accounting system is the facility to provide the owners of the business and/or management with useful financial data and reports. At the end of each month or specific accounting period, certain 'month end/year end' functions are carried out to provide the following information:

- day books for customers and suppliers
- general (nominal) ledger and bank account transactions
- activity reports on all ledger transactions
- an audit trail
- analysis reports for aged debtors and creditors
- financial statements including the trial balance, trading and profit and loss accounts and balance sheet
- ratio analysis.

Other useful functions

Spreadsheets The use of spreadsheets is another facility that a computer has to offer. Spreadsheets can be used to provide financial budgets or cash-flow budgets, a fixed asset register, calculation of loan interest payments, plus many other uses.

Internet access As mentioned above, internet access can provide such things as online banking, payment of suppliers and other payments such as wages/salaries. An organisation having its own website can advertise its products and services and offer online ordering systems. In addition, the internet is a useful source of information and data that an organisation may from time to time need to access.

29.3 Data back-up

It is important that data held on the computer is regularly saved. The regularity has to be determined by the business relative to the type of operation. It could mean every few minutes, after a specified computer task, or, after a longer time scale, say, every hour.

It is also vital to back up data held on the system. Back-up can be achieved by copying data onto a floppy disc, a CD, or by transferring it to another computer, either on the premises or at a remote location. A recent development for storing information is USB pen drives, or memory sticks, which are small but robust solid state devices and are easily carried in a pocket or briefcase.

Some large organisations may deem it essential to keep their CDs, floppy discs, etc. containing stored information off-site in a secure location. This is particularly the case where the loss of such data could have catastrophic implications for the business.

> DATA – data must be regularly backed up based on the needs of the business.

29.4 Security

All organisations regard their financial information as sensitive and, as such, it should remain confidential, except where legislation demands certain information be made available to external bodies.

Staff working on computerised accounting systems will be allocated passwords which will restrict access to their area of work. Passwords should be changed regularly to help prevent the possibility of non-authorised persons accessing the system.

When a system uses internet connections there is the constant threat of fraudulent access and corruption. Most computer systems have packages to resist viruses and attack by hacking. These have to be constantly reviewed and updated.

29.5 Computerised accounting systems

The following advantages and disadvantages of using accounting packages are detailed below.

Advantages

- Data is inputted and processed very rapidly, far faster than in a manual system.
- Greater accuracy since data is only input once and transactions carried out automatically whereas, with a manual system, data may have to be entered twice or more.
- Documents such as invoices, credit notes, statements, remittance advices can be produced automatically.
- Constant updating of the accounting records gives the accurate state of customers' accounts enabling remedial action to be taken as necessary.
- Management information can quickly be made available in report form, i.e. aged debtors' and creditors' analysis reports.

- A system connected to the internet can make financial transactions electronically.
- More efficient use of resources, for example, less accounting staff.

Disadvantages

- The cost of installation can be considerable, together with the ongoing costs of maintenance and updating.
- The introduction of the system will affect most other areas of the business, leading to considerable disruption. Staff may also be resentful of any new system.
- Staff will need to be trained to use the system and training costs have to be considered.
- System downtime can be very disruptive.
- Data back-up is essential at regular intervals.
- Fraudulent access can seriously affect the business operation and its profitability.
- Security measures are vital, for example, passwords for staff and protection against viruses and hacking.
- Health risks associated with the operation of computer keyboards and screens, which include eyestrain, back problems due to poor posture, and muscular fatigue in the arm and wrist from keyboard use. Regular rest intervals away from work stations are essential.

End of Chapter Checklist

Summary

- Computers are widely used in organisations for operating accounting systems.
- Most computerised accounting packages are integrated systems linking together the sales ledger, purchase ledger, general (nominal) ledger and the bank account.
- The computerised accounting package also produces various documents such as invoices, credit notes, statements and remittance advices.
- Other features include providing financial information for the owners of the business and/or management and the use of the internet for online facilities, and spreadsheets for such things as preparing budgets, etc.
- It is essential that users of computerised accounting packages regularly back up data using one of the various methods available.
- Security within any system is paramount for any organisation and every effort must be made to ensure that data is safe and secure.
- Organisations must consider the benefits of operating a computer accounting package such as the speed at which data is entered, accuracy, cost effectiveness and the information output, such as management reports.
- The disadvantages include the cost of installing equipment, buying software and providing training, together with security concerns. There may also be some resentment from staff and lack of motivation.

Questions

29.1 A flag manufacturer's business has recently received a large increase in orders from overseas to meet the requirements of major sporting events. This demand for flags has had a considerable effect on the present manual accounting system. The Finance Director has decided that he would like to introduce a fully integrated computer accounting system. He intends to put his case forward at the next Directors' Meeting and asks you to prepare some notes on his behalf.

Required:
Prepare notes for the Finance Director to present at the meeting, including the main advantages to be gained by making the change. You must also anticipate the arguments that may be used by a board member objecting to the proposed change.

29.2 The security of data is a very important consideration when using a computerised accounting package. Explain the measures that a medium-sized company could initiate to provide protection for the company against the security of its financial data and records.

29.3X You work in the accounts department of an advertising agency where a new member of staff has recently joined the accounts team. You have been asked to help her settle in the department and provide training on the computerised accounting system. One of the areas that you feel is very important is security and backing up data.

Required:
Draft a memo to the trainee outlining the importance of security of financial data and the agency's procedures for backing up data.

29.4X
a) Outline the benefits that are available to a small business when it has internet facilities.

b) If the firm decided to obtain the services of a web designer to develop a website, what benefits would this provide to the business?

c) If the website was developed, what do you think would be the disadvantages to offering such a service?

End of Chapter Checklist

Questions

29.5X A local garage, which carries out servicing and repairs mainly to cars and small commercial vehicles, is run by the owner with two other employees. The book-keeping and accounting is carried out on a part-time basis by an employee who works one day per week. She uses a manual accounting system to deal with customer invoices and payments, paying suppliers for goods received, banking monies received, petty cash and paying wages.

The owner is considering a computerised accounting system but is unsure as to the benefits to be gained from a large initial investment.

Required:
Put forward the benefits that might be gained, but also consider the adverse aspects of such an investment.

29.6 One business use of computerised accounting software is in stock control. Explain **one other** business use of computerised accounting software.

IGCSE

Glossary

Glossary of accounting terms

The chapter number where the term first appears is shown at the end of each definition.

Account The place in a ledger where all the transactions relating to a particular asset, liability or capital, expenses or revenue item are recorded. Accounts are part of the double entry book-keeping system. They are sometimes referred to as 'T accounts' or ledger accounts. (2)

Accounting A skill or practice of maintaining accounts and preparing reports to aid the financial control and management of a business. (1)

Accounting concepts The rules which lay down the way in which the activities of a business are recorded. (1)

Accounting equation If a business starts trading it will require resources, expressed as: resources supplied by the owner = resources in the business or capital = assets − liabilities. (1)

Accrual An expense that has been incurred but not yet paid. (22)

Accrual concept Where net profit is the difference between revenues and expenses. (1)

Accrued expense An expense that has been incurred and the benefit received but that has not been paid for at the end of the accounting period. Also referred to as an accrual. (22)

Accumulated fund A form of capital account for a non-profit-making organisation. (24)

Acid test ratio A ratio comparing current assets less stock with current liabilities. Also known as the 'quick ratio'. (28)

Amortisation A term used instead of depreciation when assets are used up simply because of the time factor. (19)

Analytical day books Book of original entry in which sales and/or purchase invoices are entered. The book has various analysis columns, which are totalled at the end of the month and posted to the general ledger and control accounts. (8)

Appropriation account An addition to the Profit and Loss Account of partnerships. The appropriation account shows how profit earned is divided in accordance with the partnership deed or agreement. (26)

Assets Resources owned by the business. (1)

Auditors Independent professionals who undertake audits for organisations and prepare financial statements

Authorised share capital The total amount of share capital or number of shares which a company can have in issue at any given time. (27)

Bad debt A debt owing to a business which is unlikely to be paid. (14)

Balance sheet A statement showing the assets, capital and liabilities of a business at specific a date. (1)

Balancing the account Finding and entering the difference between the two sides of an account. (4)

Bank giro credit (BGC) Method used by businesses to pay creditors, wages and/or salaries. A bank giro credit list and slips containing information about each person or organisation to be paid and the amount payable are sent to the bank, together with one cheque to cover all the payments. The bank then automatically transfers the funds from the business's account to the account of each of the respective people or organisations. (13)

Bank overdraft What results when we have paid more out of our bank account than we have paid into it. (11)

Bank reconciliation statement A calculation comparing the cash book balance with the bank statement balance. (13)

Bank statement Copy of a customer's account sent to them by their bank (13)

Bankers' Automated Clearing Service (BACS) Computerised payment transfer system that is a very popular way of paying creditors, wages and salaries. (13)

Book-keeping The recording of accounting data in the books of account or using a computerised accounting package. (1)

Books of original entry Books where the first entry of a transaction is made. (8)

Budgets The usual term for financial plans. (1)

Business entity concept Concerning only transactions that affect the business, and ignoring the owner's private transactions. (1)

Capital The total of resources supplied to a business by its owner. (1)

Capital employed This term has many meanings, but basically it means the amount of money that is being used up (or 'employed') in the business. It is the balance of the capital account plus any long-term loan or, alternatively, the total net assets of the business. (28)

Capital expenditure When a business spends money to buy or add value to a fixed asset. (7)

Capital invested The amount of money, or money's worth, brought into a business by its proprietor from outside. **(22)**

Capital reserve Reserves which cannot be used for the payment of dividends. The two most common types of capital reserve are the Share Premium Account and Revaluation Reserve Account. **(27)**

Carriage inwards Cost of transport of goods into a business. **(18)**

Carriage outwards Cost of transport of goods to the customers of a business. **(18)**

Carriage paid The cost of transport that has been included in the cost of the goods. **(18)**

Cash book Book of original entry for cash and bank receipts and payments. **(8)**

Cash discount An allowance given for quick payment of an account owing. **(11)**

Cash float The sum held as petty cash. **(12)**

Casting Adding up figures. **(14)**

Club accounts Accounts prepared for non-profit-making organisations such as the local tennis club. **(24)**

Coding of invoices A process used, particularly in computerised accounting, to code the invoice to the supplier or purchaser, and also to the relevant account in the general ledger. **(9)**

Compensating error Where two errors of equal amounts but on opposite sides of the accounts, cancel out each other. **(14)**

Complete reversal of entries Where the correct amounts are entered in the correct accounts but each item is shown on the wrong side of each account. **(4)**

Computerised accounting packages A software accounting package which involves the inputting of financial data. The data is recorded in both the individual account and ledgers in one transaction. The package also provides additional financial management reports and information. **(29)**

Consistency concept Adhering to the same method of recording and processing transactions. **(1)**

Contra A contra is where both the debit and credit entries are shown in the cash book. **(11)**

Control account An account which checks the arithmetical accuracy of a ledger. **(15)**

Cost of goods sold This is calculated as follows: Opening stock plus purchases during the period less the value of the stock at the end of the period (closing stock). **(16)**

Credit The right-hand side of the accounts in double entry. **(2)**

Credit control The measures and procedures a business undertakes to ensure that its customers pay their accounts when they fall due. This includes evaluating the credit worthiness of customers before allowing them credit. **(8)**

Credit note A document sent to a customer showing the allowance given by supplier in respect of unsatisfactory or unsuitable goods. **(6)**

Creditor A person to whom money is owed for goods or services supplied. **(4)**

Creditors : purchases ratio A ratio assessing how long it takes a business to pay its creditors. Also known as 'creditors' payment period'. **(28)**

Current assets Assets consisting of cash, goods for resale, or items having a shorter life. **(17)**

Current liabilities Liabilities to be paid for in the near future. **(17)**

Current ratio A ratio comparing current assets with current liabilities. Also known as the 'working capital' ratio. **(27)**

Debenture Loan to a company. **(27)**

Debenture interest An agreed percentage of interest paid to a debenture holder for lending a company money. **(27)**

Debit The left-hand side of the accounts in double entry. **(2)**

Debtor A person who owes money to the business for goods or services supplied. **(4)**

Debtors : Sales ratio A ratio assessing how long it takes debtors to pay a business. Also known as 'debtors' collection period'. **(28)**

Depletion The wasting away of an asset as it is used up. **(19)**

Depreciation The part of the cost of the fixed asset consumed during its period of use by a business. **(19)**

Diminishing balance method Refer to reducing balance method. **(19)**

Direct costs Costs which can be traced to the item being manufactured. **(25)**

Direct debit Where the business gives permission for an organisation to collect amounts owing to them direct from its bank account. **(13)**

Directors Officials appointed by shareholders to manage the company for them. **(27)**

Directors' remuneration Directors are legally employees of the company and any pay they receive is called directors' remuneration. **(27)**

Discounts allowed A reduction given to customers who pay their accounts within the time allowed. **(11)**

Discounts received   A reduction given to us by a supplier when we pay their account before the time allowed has elapsed. **(11)**

Dishonoured cheque   A cheque that the bank refuses to honour (pay). **(13)**

Dividends   The amount given to shareholders as their share of the profits of the company. **(27)**

Donation   A monetary gift donated to the club or society, monies received should be shown as income in the year that they are received. **(24)**

Double entry book-keeping   A system where each transaction is entered twice, once on the debit side and once on the credit side. **(2)**

Doubtful debt   A debt which may not be paid in the time requested. **(21)**

Drawings   Cash or goods taken out of a business by the owner for private use. **(16)**

Equity   Another name for the capital of the owner. Also described as 'net worth'. **(1)**

Error of commission   Where a correct amount is entered, but in the wrong person's account. **(4)**

Errors, complete reversal of entries   See 'complete reversal of entries'. **(4)**

Error of omission   Where a transaction is completely omitted from the books. **(4)**

Error of original entry   Where an item is entered, but both debit and credit entries are of the same incorrect amount. **(4)**

Error of principle   Where an item is entered in the wrong type of account, for example, a fixed asset entered in an expense account. **(4)**

Error of transposition   Where figures are transposed incorrectly. **(4)**

Exempted businesses   Businesses that do not have to add VAT to the price of goods and services supplied by them, and that cannot obtain a refund of VAT paid on goods and services purchased by them. **(5)**

Exempt supplies   Supplies which are outside the scope of VAT and, therefore, VAT cannot be charged. **(5)**

Expenses   Costs of operating the business. **(3)**

Expenses : Sales ratio   A ratio which indicates whether costs are rising against sales or whether sales are falling against expenses. **(28)**

Factory overhead costs   Refer to: Indirect manufacturing costs. **(25)**

Final accounts   At the end of the accounting period or year a business usually prepares its final accounts, which includes the trading and profit and loss account and balance sheet. **(18)**

Financial statements   Formal documents produced by an organisation to show the financial status of the business at a particular time. These include the trading and profit and loss account and the balance sheet. **(1)**

Fixed assets   Assets bought which have a long life and are to be used in the business. **(17)**

Fixed costs   Costs that remain the same (in the short term) irrespective of levels of production or business activity. **(25)**

Flat rate scheme   This scheme allows businesses to calculate VAT as a percentage of annual sales. **(5)**

Folio columns   Columns used for entering reference numbers. **(11)**

General ledger   All accounts other than those for customers and suppliers also called the nominal ledger. **(8)**

Going concern concept   The assumption that a business is to continue for the foreseeable future. **(1)**

Goodwill   The extra amount paid for an existing business above the value of its other assets. **(27)**

Gross loss   When the 'cost of goods sold' exceeds 'sales', then the business has incurred a gross loss. **(18)**

Gross profit   Found by deducting cost of goods sold from sales. **(16)**

Gross profit as a percentage of sales (Gross profit margin)   A ratio which states gross profit as a percentage of sales; can indicate how effectively a business has controlled their cost of goods. **(28)**

Gross profit to cost of sales (Gross profit mark-up)   The percentage of gross profit to the cost of sales. **(28)**

Impersonal accounts   All accounts other than debtors' and creditors' accounts. **(8)**

Imprest system   A system used for controlling expenditure of small cash items which are recorded in the petty cash book. A cash 'float' of a fixed amount is provided initially to the person responsible for operating the petty cash system. Any cash paid out during a particular period, i.e. a week, is reimbursed to the petty cashier so restoring the 'float' to its original sum. **(12)**

Inadequacy   When an asset is no longer used because of changes within an organisation due to growth, competition or product range changes. **(19)**

Income and expenditure account   An account for a non-profit-making organisation to find the surplus or deficit made during a period. **(24)**

Incomplete records   Where only some transactions are recorded in the books of account, the missing information has to be obtained by other means. **(23)**

Indirect manufacturing costs Costs which occur in a factory or other production facility but cannot be easily traced to the items being manufactured. (25)

Input VAT The VAT charged to a business on its purchases and expenses (inputs). (5)

Inputs The value of goods and services purchased by a business. (5)

Interest on capital An agreed rate of interest that is credited to a partner to compensate for unequal capital contributions. (26)

Interest on drawings An amount, at an agreed rate of interest, that is based on the drawings taken out and is debited to the partners. (26)

Invoice A document prepared by the seller and sent to the purchaser whenever a business buys goods or services on credit. It gives details of the supplier and the customer, the goods purchased and their price. (6)

Issued share capital The amount of the authorised share capital of a company that has been issued to shareholders. (27)

Journal A book of account used to record rare or exceptional transactions that should not appear in the other books of original entry in use. (8)

Ledger A book of account in which all double entry transactions are recorded. (8)

Liabilities Total of money owed for assets supplied to the business. (1)

Life membership Where members pay one amount for membership to last them their lifetime. (24)

Limited company An organisation owned by its shareholders, whose liability is limited to their share capital. (1)

Limited liability The liability of shareholders, in a company, is limited to any amount they have agreed to invest. (27)

Limited partner A partner whose liability is limited to the capital invested in the firm. (26)

Limited partnership A form of partnership in which limited partners' liabilities are limited to their investment and in which general partners with unlimited liability operate the business. (26)

Liquidity The ability of a business to pay its debts as they fall due and to meet unexpected expenses within a reasonable settlement period. (28)

Liquidity ratios Ratios that attempt to indicate the ability of a business to meet its debts as they become due and include current ratio and acid test ratio. (28)

Loan capital Money owing by a company for debentures and for loans from banks and other sources that are not repayable in the near future. (27)

Loan interest The extra amount levied by the lender of funds to recompense them for making the loan. (7)

Long-term liabilities Liabilities not having to be paid for in the near future. (17)

Loss Result of selling goods for less than they have cost the business. (18)

Manufacturing account An account in which production cost is calculated. (25)

Margin Profit shown as a percentage or fraction of the selling price. (28)

Mark-up Profit shown as a percentage or fraction of the cost price. (28)

Matching concept Another term for the accrual concept. (1)

Materiality concept This concept applies when the value of an item is relatively small and does not warrant separate recording. (1)

Money measurement concept Accounting is only concerned with the money measurement of things and where most people will agree to the monetary value of a transaction. (1)

Narrative A description and explanation of the transaction recorded in the journal. (14)

Net book value The cost of a fixed asset less depreciation charges to date, also known as 'book value'. (19)

Net current assets The value of current assets less that of current liabilities. Also known as 'working capital'. (17)

Net loss This occurs when total expenses exceed the gross profit. (18)

Net profit Gross profit less expenses. (16)

Net profit as a percentage of sales A ratio that states net profit as a percentage of sales and brings expenses into the calculation. (28)

Net worth See 'equity'. (1)

Nominal accounts Accounts in which expenses, revenue and capital are recorded. (8)

Nominal ledger Ledger for impersonal accounts (also called general ledger). (8)

Non-profit-making organisations Clubs, associations and societies operated to provide a service or activity for members since their main purpose is not trading or profit making. (24)

Non-trading organisations These include clubs, associations and other non-profit-making organisations that are normally run for the benefit of their members to engage in a particular activity. (1)

Obsolescence Becoming out of date. (19)

Ordinary shares Shares entitled to dividends after the preference shareholders have been paid their dividends. (27)

Output VAT The VAT charged by a business on its supplies (outputs). **(5)**

Outputs The value of goods and services sold to a business. **(5)**

Overcasting Incorrectly adding up a column of figures to give an answer which exceeds the correct total. **(14)**

Partly exempt businesses These will sell some goods that are exempt from VAT and some goods that are either standard-rated or zero-rated. They may reclaim part of the input VAT paid by them. **(5)**

Partnership A group of a minimum of two people and a maximum of twenty, who together are in business, with a view to making profit. **(1)**

Partnership agreement/deed The contractual relationship, either written or verbal, between partners, which usually covers details such as how profits or losses should be shared and the relevant responsibilities of the partners. **(26)**

Partnership salaries Agreed amounts payable to partners in respect of duties undertaken by them. **(26)**

Personal accounts Accounts for both creditors and debtors. **(8)**

Petty cash book A cash book used for making small (petty) payments. Payments are usually analysed and the totals of each column later posted to the various accounts in the general ledger. The source document used for entry into the petty cash book is a petty cash voucher. **(8)**

Petty cash voucher A form used by anyone requesting payment for a small item of expenditure incurred on behalf of the business. The form gives details of the expense and should be signed and duly authorised. **(12)**

Posting The act of using one book as a means of entering the transactions to another account. **(11)**

Preference shares Shares that are entitled to an agreed rate of dividend before the ordinary shareholders receive anything. **(27)**

Preliminary expenses All the costs that are incurred when a company is formed. **(27)**

Prepaid expense An expense – usually a service – that has been paid for in one accounting period, the benefit of which will not be received until a subsequent period. It is a payment for an expense that has been paid for in advance. **(22)**

Prepayment Also referred to as 'prepaid expense'. **(22)** (See above)

Prime cost Direct materials plus labour plus direct expenses. **(25)**

Private ledger Ledger for capital and drawings accounts. **(8)**

Private limited company A legal entity with at least two shareholders, where the liability of the shareholders is limited to the amount of their investment. The public cannot subscribe for its shares. **(1)**

Production cost Prime cost plus indirect manufacturing costs. **(25)**

Profit The result when goods are sold for more than they cost. (If they are sold for less than they cost, then a *loss* is incurred.) **(16)**

Profit and loss account Account in which net profit or net loss is calculated. **(16)**

Profitability The effective operation of a business to make ongoing profits to ensure its long-term viability. **(28)**

Profitability ratios Ratios that attempt to indicate the trend in a business's ability to make profit. These include gross profit and net profit to sales and return on capital employed. **(28)**

Provision for doubtful debts An account showing the expected amounts of debtors, who at the balance sheet date, may not be able to pay their outstanding accounts. **(21)**

Provision for depreciation account An account where depreciation is accumulated for balance sheet purposes. In the balance sheet the cost price of the asset is shown, less the depreciation to date, to give the net book value. **(20)**

Prudence concept Ensuring that profit is not shown as being too high, or assets shown at too high a value in the balance sheet. **(1)**

Public limited company A legal entity with many shareholders since the public can subscribe for its shares. Shareholder liability is limited to the amount of their investment. **(1)**

Purchase invoice A document received by purchaser showing details of goods bought and their prices. **(6)**

Purchase order This is a document prepared by the purchaser and it contains details of the goods or services required by the purchaser. **(6)**

Purchases Goods bought by the business for the purpose of selling them again. **(3)**

Purchases day book Book of original entry for credit purchases. **(8)**

Purchases journal Another name for the purchases day book. **(8)**

Purchases ledger A ledger for suppliers' personal accounts. **(8)**

Purchase ledger control account An account containing the total of the various individual personal ledger account balances. By comparing the balance on the control account with the outstanding balances in a subsidiary ledger the arithmetical accuracy can be checked and errors rectified. **(15)**

Purchase returns   Goods returned by the business to its suppliers. See also returns outwards. **(3)**

Purchase returns day book   Book of original entry for goods returned to suppliers. **(8)**

Quick ratio   Same as the acid test ratio. **(28)**

Real accounts   Accounts in which possessions of the business are recorded e.g. property, stock etc.**(8)**

Receipt   A form acknowledging receipt of money for goods or services rendered. **(12)**

Receipts and payments account   A summary of the cash book of a non-profit-making organisation. **(24)**

Reduced rate VAT   A rate of VAT that applies to certain goods and services such as domestic fuel, etc. **(5)**

Reducing balance method   Depreciation calculation which is based on the net book value of the asset brought forward from the previous year. Therefore, the depreciation charge falls each year. **(19)**

Remittance advice   A document which accompanies payments by cheque or via BACS and gives details of the payment. **(6)**

Reserve accounts   The transfer of apportioned profits to accounts for use in future years. **(27)**

Residual value   The amount received on disposal of an asset, also referred to as 'scrap value'. **(19)**

Retained profits   Profits earned in a year but not paid out in dividends. **(27)**

Return on capital employed (ROCE)   A ratio that shows the net profit made for each £100 of capital employed. **(28)**

Returns inwards   Goods returned to the business by its customers. **(3)**

Returns inwards day book   Book of original entry for goods returned by customers. **(8)**

Returns outwards   Goods returned by the business to its suppliers. **(3)**

Returns outwards day book   Book of original entry for goods returned to suppliers. **(8)**

Revaluation method of depreciation   Used for calculating depreciation on quantities of low-cost fixed assets such as tools. **(19)**

Revenues   The sales/services of a business plus money coming into it from other sources i.e. rent received. **(1)**

Revenue expenditure   Expenses needed for the day-to-day running of the business. **(7)**

Revenue reserve   Reserves of a company which are available for distribution as a dividend. **(27)**

Sales   Goods sold by the business. **(3)**

Sales day book   Book of original entry for credit sales. **(8)**

Sales invoice   A document showing the details of goods sold and the prices of those goods. **(8)**

Sales journal   Another name for sales day book. **(8)**

Sales ledger   A ledger for customers' personal accounts. **(8)**

Sales ledger control account   See 'purchases ledger control account'. **(15)**

Sales returns   Goods returned to the business by its customers. **(3)**

Sales returns day book   Book of original entry for goods returned by customers. **(8)**

Separate legal entity   A feature of a limited company. **(27)**

Shareholder   An owner of shares in a company. **(27)**

Shares   The division of the capital of a limited company into parts. **(27)**

Share capital   The capital of a company divided into shares owned by its shareholders. **(27)**

Shareholders' funds   The amount of share capital and reserves 'owned' by the shareholders. **(27)**

Share premium   The excess in price of an issued share over its nominal value. **(27)**

Single entry   Where transactions are only recorded once in the books of account. **(23)**

Sole trader   A business owned by one person only. **(1)**

Source documents   Where original information is found (e.g. sales and purchases invoices and credit notes). **(8)**

Spreadsheets   A computer program which consists of rows and columns. The program carries out calculations and is a useful facility when preparing financial budgets such as cash flow forecasts. **(29)**

Standard-rated businesses   These businesses add VAT to the value of the sales invoice and can also claim back VAT paid on purchases. **(5)**

Standing order   Instructions given by a business to a bank to pay specified amounts at a given dates.**(13)**

Statement of account   This is normally sent to purchasers at the end of each month and it states the amount owing to the supplier at the end of that particular month. **(6)**

Statement of affairs   A statement drawn up to ascertain the owners capital at a given date. This is deduced by deducting the liabilities from the assets to find the capital. **(23)**

Stock   Unsold goods. **(3)**

Stock turnover (or stockturn) ratio   A ratio comparing the cost of goods sold to the average stock. It shows the number of times stock is sold in an accounting period. **(28)**

Straight line method Depreciation calculation which remains at an equal amount each year. **(19)**

Subscriptions Amounts paid by members of a club or society, usually on an annual basis, to enable them to participate in the activities of the organisation. **(24)**

Suspense account Account in which you can enter the amount equal to the difference in trial balance while the error(s) are located. **(14)**

T accounts Accounts presented in the shape of a letter 'T'. **(2)**

Total cost Production cost plus administration, selling and distribution expenses. **(25)**

Trade discount A reduction given to a customer when calculating the selling prices of goods. **(8)**

Trading account Account in which gross profit is calculated. **(1)**

Trading and profit and loss account Combined account in which both gross and net profits are calculated. **(1)**

Transaction Where data is entered into the books of account. **(2)**

Trial balance A list of all the balances in the books at a particular point in time. The balances are shown in debit and credit columns. These columns should balance provided no errors have occurred. **(4)**

Undercasting Incorrectly adding up a column of figures to give an answer which is less than the correct total. **(14)**

Unpresented cheque A cheque which has been sent but has not yet gone through the receivers bank account. **(13)**

Value Added Tax (VAT) A tax charged on the supply of most goods and services. The tax is borne by the final consumer of the goods or services, not by the business selling them to the consumer. VAT is administered by HMRC. **(5)**

Variable cost Costs that vary depending on levels of production or business activity. **(25)**

Work in progress Items not completed at the end of a period. **(25)**

Working capital The amount by which the current assets exceed the current liabilities. Also known as 'net current assets'. **(17)**

Working capital ratio Same as the current ratio. **(28)**

Zero-rated businesses Businesses that do not have to add VAT to goods and services supplied to others by them, but they can receive a refund of VAT paid on goods and services purchased by them. **(5)**

Zero-rated supplies Goods or services where VAT is charged at the rate of 0%. **(5)**

Index

A

accounting books diagram 63
accounting equation 6–8
accruals/accrual concept 5, 205
accrued expenses 195, 198
accumulated funds 222–3
acid test ratio 272, 277
adjustments 168–208
agreements, partnerships 243–6
aims of business 1
amortisation 169
    see also depreciation
analysis of accounts 266–86
annual general meetings 256
appropriation accounts 247, 258–9
assets 7, 9
    asset accounts 34
    balance sheets 154–5
    depreciation 173
    double entry 13–14
    net current 153, 155, 200
    see also fixed assets
auditors 9
authorised share capital 256

B

BACS (Bankers' Automated Clearing Service) 112
bad debts 184–93
    accounts 190
    adjustments 206
    control accounts 137
    doubtful debts 184–93
    incomplete records 215
    journals 118–19
    recovery 191
    worked example 190–1
    writing off 118–19, 184, 186, 206
balance sheets 152–7
    assets 154–5
    bad debts 186, 187–9, 191
    capital accounts 155–6
    capital employed 270
    contents 152
    cost of goods sold 163
    depreciation 177, 179
    double entry 153–4
    expenses 198–9
    incomplete records 215
    layout 154–6
    liabilities 155
    limited companies 259–60, 262
    manufacturing accounts 234, 237
    non-profit making organisations 223–6
    partnerships 249, 252
    preparation 152–3
    ratio example 276
    revenue adjustments 198–9
    sole traders 204
    suspense accounts 125
balancing accounts 32–42
    three-column accounts 34–5
    trial balances 37, 38–9
    worked examples 35–7
    see also bank reconciliation statements
bank accounts/statements 86–7, 281
bank giro credit (BGC) 108
bank overdrafts 94–5, 110–11
bank reconciliation statements 81, 106–15
    balance differences 107–9
    bank overdrafts 110–11

cash books 106–7, 109–10
direct debits 112
dishonoured cheques 111–12
standing orders 112
ticking matched items 106
Bankers' Automated Clearing Service (BACS) 112
BGC (bank giro credit) 108
book-keeping 9, 77–9
books of original entry 1–50, 62
budgets 3, 9
business entity concept 5

C
capital 6–7, 9
  double entry 13–14
  invested 200
  partnerships 243–4
  working 153, 155, 200–1, 275
  see also capital...
capital accounts 35, 145–8, 155–6, 247–8
capital employed 200, 269–70, 274–5
capital expenditure 57–61
capital-raising 255
capital reserves 260
carriage 159–60
cash
  accounts 86–7
  discounts 47, 89–94
  sales 64–7
  transactions 11–21, 29, 218
  see also petty cash
cash books 62, 86–97
  BACS payments 112
  bank overdrafts 94–5
  bank reconciliation statements 106–7, 109–10
  cash discounts 89–94

cash paid into bank 87–8
control accounts 135–6
drawing up 86
entry errors 123–4
folio columns 88–9
petty cash 62, 100–3
VAT columns 95
casting 128
cheques 107–8, 111–12
classification of accounts 64
coding of invoices 74
commission, errors of 119–20
compensating errors 122–3
computerised systems 138, 280–6
concepts of accounting 3–5
consistency concept 4
contra accounts 137–8
control accounts 132–41
  advantages 139
  bad debts 137
  computerised systems 138
  contra accounts 137–8
  examples 133–4, 136–7
  information sources 134–6
  purchase ledgers 132–41
  sales ledgers 132–41
cost of goods sold 142–4, 146, 162–3
cost price 177
costs 169–70, 231–3, 237–8
credit
  balance 34, 38, 48
  control 68
  notes 51, 53–4, 77–80
  purchases 72
  sales 64–7, 72–3
  transactions 22–31

credit side of account
   cash discounts 92
   contra accounts 138
   credit notes 78–80
   credit purchases 72
   credit sales 65
   depreciation 176
   double entry 12–13, 29
creditors 32, 103
   accounts 35
   ledgers 63
   payment period 273
creditors to purchases ratio 273, 277
current accounts 247–8
current assets 155
current liabilities 155
current ratio 271–2, 277

D

data back-up 283
debentures 257–8
debit balance 33–4, 38
debit side of account
   cash discounts 92
   contra accounts 138
   credit notes 78–80
   credit purchases 72
   credit sales 65
   depreciation 176
   double entry 12–13, 29
   VAT 48
debtors 32, 35, 63, 272
debtors to sales ratio 272–3, 277
debts *see* bad debts
deeds of partnership 243–6
definition of accounting 9

depletion 169
depreciation 176–83
   assets bought/sold 173
   calculating charges 170–3
   causes 168–9
   as cost allocation 169–70
   double entry 176–83
   as expense 168
   fixed assets 168–83
   incomplete records 215
   records 176–9
   reducing balance method 171–2, 205–6
   replacement of assets 181
   revaluation method 172–3
   straight line method 170, 178–9, 205
diminishing balance method, depreciation 170
direct costs 231–4
direct debits 112
directors 255, 258, 261
discounts
   allowed/received 201, 205, 214–15
   cash 47, 89–94
   final accounts 201
   incomplete records 214–15
   trade 67
dishonoured cheques 111–12
dividends 256–7
documentation 51–6
donations 227
double entry 11–31
   balance sheets 153–4
   cash transactions 11–21, 29
   credit transactions 22–31
   depreciation 176–83
   expenses 26–7
   history 11

IN and OUT approach 14
purchases 23, 25, 29
returns 25–6
rules 13–14
sales 24, 26, 29
T accounts 15
use of word 'account' 153–4
worked examples 15–19, 27–8
doubtful debts 184–93
accounting entries 187
provision for 185–91, 206
worked example 190–1
drawings 145–6, 148, 217, 244–5

E
entrance fees 227
equity 8–9
see also capital
errors 119–27
balance sheets 125
balancing accounts 38–9
of commission 119–20
compensating 122–3
control accounts 139
journals 119–27
more than one 126–7
of omission 122
one error only 125–6
of original entry 121–2
of principle 120–1
POR COW mnemonic 38
reversal of entries 123–4
suspense accounts 125–7
trial balances 119–27, 38–9
expenditure 57–61, 222–6
expense accounts 34–5

expenses
accrued 195, 198
adjustments 194–6
balance sheets 198–9
depreciation 168
double entry 26–7
incomplete records 215
manufacturing accounts 237–8
owing 194
prepaid 194, 196
trading accounts 164
expenses/sales ratio 269, 276–7

F
factory overhead costs 231
final accounts 165, 201, 209–12
financial control 2–3
financial statements 3, 9, 158–67
adjustments 194–208
analysis/interpretation 266–79
capital employed 274–5
final accounts 165
limited companies 257–62
liquidity 267, 271–3
manufacturing accounts 232–4
partnerships 247
profitability 267–71
sole traders 201–4
working capital 275
fixed assets
balance sheets 154
depreciation 168–83
disposal 179–81
double entry 176–83
purchase/sale 117–18
revaluation 199–200

fixed capital accounts 247–8
fixed costs 238
float for petty cash 98–9
folio columns 88–9
fraud prevention 139

G

general ledgers 63, 66–7
    cash discounts 91–2, 94
    computerised systems 281
    invoices 73–4
    journal entries 117–19
    petty cash 103
    returns 78–80
going concern concept 4
goods *see* stock
gross loss 144, 165
gross profit 59, 142–4, 146–7
gross profit margin/sales ratio 267–8, 276–7
gross profit mark-up/cost of sales ratio 268–9

H

HM Revenue and Customs (HMRC) 43–50

I

impersonal accounts 64
imprest petty cash system 98–105
income and expenditure accounts 222–6
incomplete records 209–20
    final accounts 209–12
    missing figures 217–18
    statements of affairs 210–11, 213
    step-by-step guide 212–16
indirect costs 231–4
information 134–6, 139
input VAT 43
interest 59, 244–5, 257–8

international standards 6
internet access 282
interpretation of accounts 266–86
investment capital 200
invoices 46, 51–3, 65–8, 71–4
issued share capital 256

J

journals 62, 116–31
    advantages 129
    bad debts 118–19
    casting 128
    error correction 119–27
    examination guidance 128–9
    fixed assets 117–18
    writing up entries 116–19, 128

L

ledgers 51–141, 63
    see also general ledgers; purchase ledgers; sales ledgers
legal frameworks 5–6
liabilities 7, 9, 14, 155, 255
life memberships 227
limited companies 8, 255–65
    capital employed 274–5
    debentures 257–8
    dividends 256–7
    features 255
    financial statements 257–62
    private 8, 255–6
    public 8, 255–6
    reserves in balance sheet 259–60
    shareholders' funds 262
    shares/share capital 256–7
    worked example 260–2
limited liability 255

limited partners 242–3
liquidity ratios 267, 271–3, 275–7
loan interest 59
long-term liabilities 155
loss 144, 164–5
    see also profit and loss accounts

M
management information 139
management reports 282
manufacturing accounts 231–40
    direct/indirect costs 231–4
    expenses apportionment 237–8
    financial statements 232–4
    fixed/variable costs 238
    unit cost of production 237
    work in progress 235
    worked example 235–7
matching concept 5
materiality concept 5
missing information 217–18
money measurement concept 5

N
narrative of journal 116
need for accounting 3
net book value 171, 177
net current assets 153, 155, 200
net loss 164–5
net profit
    capital/revenue expenditure 59
    incomplete records 212
    ROCE 269–70
    trading/profit/loss accounts 142, 144, 147
net profit margin/sales ratio 269, 276–7
net worth 8
    see also capital

nominal accounts 64
nominal capital 256
nominal ledgers 63, 281
    see also general ledgers
non-profit making organisations 221–30
    accumulated funds 222–3
    donations 227
    entrance fees 227
    income and expenditure accounts 222–6
    life memberships 227
    profit and loss accounts 222
    receipts and payments accounts 221–2
    subscriptions 225–6
    treasurers 227
non-trading organisations 9

O
omission, errors of 122
ordinary shares 256–7
original entry
    books 1–50, 62
    errors of 121–2
output VAT 43
overdrafts 94–5, 110–11
overheads 231, 269
owner's equity 9

P
partnerships 8, 241–54
    advantages/disadvantages 241
    agreements 243–6, 249
    balance sheets 249, 252
    capital contributions 243
    capital employed 274
    current accounts 247–8
    financial statements 247
    fixed capital accounts 247–8

interest 244–5
  limited partners 242–3
  nature of 242
  no formal agreement 249
  performance-related payments 246
  profit sharing 243–4, 246
  salaries 245–6
  worked examples 246, 250–2
performance-related payments 246
personal accounts 64
petty cash 98–105
  books 62, 100–3
  creditor payments 103
  floats 98–9
  imprest system 98–105
  receipts 100–1
  vouchers 98, 100–1
  worked example 99–103
POR COW errors mnemonic 38
posting 63
preference shares 256–7
prepayments 194, 196–8, 204
prime cost 231–2, 233, 236
principle, errors of 120–1
principles of accounting 1–10
private ledgers 63
private limited companies 8, 255–6
production cost 232–4
profit 8, 259
  see also gross profit...; net profit...; profit...
profit and loss accounts
  appropriation accounts 247, 258–9
  bad/doubtful debts 185, 187, 191
  depreciation 177, 179, 180–1
  limited companies 258–9

  manufacturing accounts 234
  non-profit making organisations 222
  see also trading and profit and loss accounts
profit sharing 243–4, 246
profitability ratios 267–71, 275–7
provision for depreciation account 176
provision for doubtful debts 185–91, 206
prudence concept 4
public limited companies 8, 255–6
purchase invoices 68, 71–4
purchase ledgers 63, 71–6
  cash discounts 91, 93–4
  control accounts 132–41
  journal entries 117–18
  returns 79–81
purchase orders 51–2
purchase returns 25, 158–9
purchase returns day books 62, 77–85, 136
purchases
  accounts 122–3, 127, 144, 147
  computerised systems 281
  creditors to purchases ratio 273, 277
  double entry 23, 25, 29
  incomplete records 213–14, 218
  see also purchase...
purchases day books 62, 71–6, 136

Q

quick ratio 272, 277

R

rate of stock turnover 271
ratios
  liquidity 267, 271–3, 275–7
  profitability 267–71, 275–7

real accounts 64
receipts 59, 221–2
reconciliation 80–2, 106–15
records 176–9
   see also incomplete records
reducing balance method, depreciation 171–2, 205–6
remittance advice 51, 55
rent paid/received 198
reserves 257, 259–60
residual value 169
retained profit 259
return on capital employed (ROCE) 269–70, 276–7
returns
   double entry 25–6
   inwards day book 77
   outwards day book 79
   purchase returns 25, 62, 77–85, 136, 158–9
   reconciling ledgers/statements 80–2
   sales returns 26, 62, 77–85, 158–9
   separate accounts 80
   trading accounts 158–9
revaluation methods
   depreciation 172–3
   fixed assets 199–200
revenue
   accrual concept 5
   balance sheets 198–9
   expenditure 57–61
   owing at period end 197–8
   reserves 257, 259
reversal of entries error 123–4
ROCE (return on capital employed) 269–70, 276–7

S

salaries 245–6, 281
sales
   accounts 121–3, 125, 144, 147
   computerised accounting 281
   double entry 24, 26, 29
   incomplete records 214–15, 218
   invoices 46, 65, 67–8, 71
   liquidity ratios 272–3, 277
   profitability ratios 267–9
   see also sales...
sales day books 62–70, 135
sales ledgers 62–70, 74
   cash discounts 91, 93
   control accounts 132–41
   journal entries 118–19
   returns 78
sales returns 26, 158–9
sales returns day books 62, 77–85, 135
scrap value 169
security 283
separate legal entities 255
share premium accounts 260
shareholders 255, 262
shares/share capital 256–7
single entry accounting 209
sole traders 8
   adjustments 201–4
   capital employed 270, 274
   financial statements 201–4
   ROCE 270
   trading/profit/loss accounts 142–51, 203
source documents 62
spreadsheets 282

standards 5–6
standing orders 112
statements
   of account 51, 54, 80–2
   of affairs 210–11, 213
   see also financial statements
stationery 197
stock
   computerised control 281–2
   cost of goods sold 142–4, 146, 162–3
   double entry 23–4, 162
   for own use 199
   prepayments 197
   purchase 23
   sales 24
   second year of business 160–3
   trading accounts 146–8, 160–3
   turnover ratio 271, 276–7
   unsold goods 146–8
straight line method, depreciation 170, 178–9, 205
subscriptions 225–6
supplier statements 80–2
suspense accounts 125–7

T

T accounts 15
taxation, VAT 43–50
three-column accounts 34–5
total accounts 132
total cost 232
trade discounts 67
trading accounts 142–67, 223, 233–4, 237
trading and profit and loss accounts 142–51
   bad/doubtful debts 186
   capital accounts 145–6, 148
   discounts 201
   incomplete records 215
   limited companies 257–8, 261
   losses 165
   partnerships 247, 251
   preparation 143–5
   ratio usage 276
   returns 159
   sole traders 142–51, 203
   stock 146–8, 162–3
   trial balances 143, 146, 149
   vertical layout 148–9
treasurers of clubs 227
trial balances
   books of original entry 37, 38–9
   carriage 160
   errors 38–9, 119–27
   income and expenditure accounts 223
   limited companies 260
   partnerships 250
   POR COW mnemonic 38
   returns 158–9
   second year of business 161
   sole traders 202
   trading/profit/loss accounts 143, 146, 149
   when not balancing 39

U

unpresented cheques 107–8

V

Value Added Tax (VAT) 19, 43–50
- accounts 47–8
- business categories 44–5
- calculations 45–6
- cash books 95
- cash discounts 47
- credit sales 65–6, 72–3
- how system works 45
- input/output 43
- the ledger 62–76
- payment 43–4
- petty cash book 101–2
- rates 44
- records 45
- worked examples 45, 47–8

variable costs 238
VAT *see* Value Added Tax
vouchers, petty cash 98, 100–1

W

wages 281
work in progress 235
working capital 153–5, 200–1, 275
working capital ratio 271–2